THE LEGALITY OF BAILOUTS AND BUY NATIONALS

This book examines the international regulation of crisis bailouts and buy national policies from a competition perspective. It undertakes this research with specific reference to the crisis years 2008–2012. The book includes a comparative analysis of the regulation of public procurement and subsidies aid at both multilateral and regional levels, identifying the strengths and weakness in the WTO legal framework and selected regional trade agreements (RTAs). Ultimately, the aim of this work is to provide options for improving the consistency of these laws and the regulation of these markets. This is of immediate relevance for good economic governance, as well as for managing future systemic financial crises in the interests of citizens: as tax payers and consumers.

Volume 17 in the series Hart Studies in Competition Law

Hart Studies in Competition Law

The Private Enforcement of Competition Law in Ireland
David McFadden

Cross-Border EU Competition Law Actions
Edited by Mihail Danov, Florian Becker and Paul Beaumont

Competition Laws, Globalization and Legal Pluralism: China's Experience
Qianlan Wu

Joint Ventures and EU Competition Law
Luis Silva Morais

Sanctions in EU Competition Law: Principles and Practice
Michael Frese

Fairness in Antitrust: Protecting the Strong from the Weak
Adi Ayal

European Merger Remedies: Law and Policy
Dorte Hoeg

Media Ownership and Control: Law, Economics and Policy in an Indian and International Context
Suzanne Rab and Alison Sprague

The Interface between Competition and the Internal Market: Market Separation under Article 102 TFEU
Vasiliki Brisimi

Anti-Cartel Enforcement in a Contemporary Age: Leniency Religion
Edited by Caron Beaton-Wells and Christopher Tran

Public Procurement and the EU Competition Rules
Albert Sánchez Graells

The Concept of Abuse in EU Competition Law: Law and Economic Approaches
Pınar Akman

The Competitive Effects of Minority Shareholdings: Legal and Economic Issues
Panagiotis Fotis and Nikolaos Zevgolis

The More Economic Approach to EU Antitrust Law
Anne C Witt

Private Power, Online Information Flows and EU Law
Angela Daly

The Role of Competitors in the Enforcement of State Aid Law
Fernando Pastor-Merchante

The Legality of Bailouts and Buy Nationals

International Trade Law in a Crisis

Kamala Dawar

• HART •
PUBLISHING
OXFORD AND PORTLAND, OREGON
2017

Hart Publishing
An imprint of Bloomsbury Publishing Plc

Hart Publishing Ltd
Kemp House
Chawley Park
Cumnor Hill
Oxford OX2 9PH
UK

Bloomsbury Publishing Plc
50 Bedford Square
London
WC1B 3DP
UK

www.hartpub.co.uk
www.bloomsbury.com

Published in North America (US and Canada) by
Hart Publishing
c/o International Specialized Book Services
920 NE 58th Avenue, Suite 300
Portland, OR 97213-3786
USA

www.isbs.com

HART PUBLISHING, the Hart/Stag logo, BLOOMSBURY and the Diana logo are trademarks of Bloomsbury Publishing Plc

First published 2017

British Library Cataloguing-in-Publication Data
A catalogue record for this book is available from the British Library.

ISBN: HB: 978-1-50990-824-0
ePDF: 978-1-50990-821-9
ePub: 978-1-50990-822-6

Library of Congress Cataloging-in-Publication Data

Names: Dawar, Kamala, author.

Title: The legality of bailouts and buy nationals : international trade law in a crisis / Kamala Dawar.

Description: Oxford ; Portland, Oregon : Hart Publishing, an imprint of Bloomsbury Publishing Plc, 2017. | Series: Hart studies in competition law ; volume 17 | Includes bibliographical references and index.

Identifiers: LCCN 2017021990 (print) | LCCN 2017022554 (ebook) | ISBN 9781509908226 (Epub) | ISBN 9781509908240 (hbk. : alk. paper)

Subjects: LCSH: Foreign trade regulation. | Bailouts (Government policy) | Export subsidies—Law and legislation. | Buy national policy.

Classification: LCC K3943 (ebook) | LCC K3943 .D39 2017 (print) | DDC 343.08/7—dc23

LC record available at https://lccn.loc.gov/2017021990

Typeset by Compuscript Ltd, Shannon
Printed and bound in Great Britain by Lightning Source UK Ltd

To find out more about our authors and books visit www.hartpublishing.co.uk. Here you will find extracts, author information, details of forthcoming events and the option to sign up for our newsletters

FOREWORD

Governments often implement measures that directly affect specific firms or industries. By doing so they may distort the functioning of the relevant markets, especially if the aim is to tilt the 'playing field' in a way that discriminates against foreign providers of goods or services. In this excellent book Kamala Dawar critically assesses the extant international disciplines that constrain the behavior of governments in two specific areas of policy: public procurement of goods and services, and subsidisation of specific industries or economic activities. In the case of both procurement and subsidy policy, the stylized fact that motivates the analysis is that governments do discriminate—preferences are often given to domestic firms in allocating procurement contracts, and subsidies are often restricted to domestic companies.

The book analyses applicable international disciplines in these two areas of government policy, focusing on the WTO, the EU and regional trade agreements, and does so in comparison to competition law disciplines pertaining to the behavior of firms. The value added of the volume is to investigate through a series of case studies the extent to which countries abided by applicable disciplines in the global financial crisis that erupted in 2008 and its aftermath. The crisis resulted in a collapse of demand with severe adverse consequences for profitability, turnover and employment/wages in many countries, and thus led to intense pressure on governments to support economic activity. This episode allows for an assessment of compliance with international legal norms of subsidy and procurement of measures taken to support banks and manufacturing activities in the US, the EU (with a focus on Ireland and the UK) and Brazil. It concludes that there are significant gaps in the prevailing international disciplines as much of what was done was 'legal' even though it arguably distorted competition and that application of extant rules was weakened as a result of a reliance on bilateral or transactional enforcement as opposed to collective enforcement of the rules of the game. The bottom line is that multilateral or regional disciplines had little impact in constraining the anti-competitive instincts of governments during and after the 2008 crisis.

A number of excellent arguments and contributions are made in this book, including as regards the potential reach of the GATT's most-favored-nation provision to encompass subsidy policies and the extent to which disciplines contained in the WTO's Agreement on Subsidies and Countervailing Measures may apply to public procurement. The analysis clearly identifies areas where governments need to strengthen the international legal framework so as to reduce the potential negative cross-border spillovers of national procurement and subsidy measures, and makes a compelling case for greater transparency and monitoring by the WTO Secretariat of both subsidies and procurement practices of WTO members.

One can only hope that governments will be willing to adopt the proposals made in this volume. Whether they do or not, the analysis undertaken in this book is of great salience to scholars and practitioners working in the area of international trade, competition and procurement law as well as students with an interest in international economic law and international relations.

Bernard Hoekman,
Robert Schuman Institute for Advanced Studies,
European University Institute

ACKNOWLEDGEMENTS

This book is the result of my doctoral thesis, which would not have been possible without the rigor of Joost Pauwelyn and the heroism of Albert Sanchez Graells—my supervisors—and the financial backing of the European Commission's Marie Skłodowska-Curie Research Fellowship. Among the many I thank for supporting me throughout this research and its development under Hart Publishing, I am particularly indebted to Stiftung Atelier Robert and—of course—Fredie, Bella and Bertie Beckmans.

Sussex 2017

CONTENTS

LIST OF ABBREVIATIONS

ARRA	The American Recovery and Reinvestment Act of 2009
ASCM	Agreement on Subsidies and Countervailing Measures
BAA	Buy America Act
CoJ	Court of Justice
CVM	Countervailing Measures
CU	Customs Union
DSB	Dispute Settlement Body
DSU	Dispute Settlement Understanding
EC	European Communities (ceased 2009)
ECA	European Court of Auditors
ECB	European Central Bank
EFTA	European Free Trade Association
EU	European Union
FTA	Free Trade Agreement
GATS	General Agreement on Trade in Services
GATT	General Agreement on Tariffs and Trade
GNP	Gross National Product
GPA	Government Procurement Agreement
GSP	Generalised System of Preferences
HS	Harmonised Commodity Description and Coding System
ICJ	International Court of Justice
ILO	International Labour Organization
IMF	International Monetary Fund
ITC	International Trade Centre
ITO	International Trade Organization
LDC	Less Developed Countries
MERCOSUR	Southern Common Market
MFN	Most-Favoured-Nation

MS	Member State
NAFTA	North American Free Trade Agreement
NT	National Treatment
OECD	Organisation for Economic Cooperation and Development
RTA	Regional Trade Agreement
S&D	Special and Differential Treatment (for developing countries)
SDR	Special Drawing Rights (IMF)
SELA	Latin American Economic System
SPS	Sanitary and Phytosanitary Measures
TBT	Technical Barriers to Trade
TEC	Treaty Establishing the European Community
TFEU	Treaty on the Functioning of the European Union
TPRB	Trade Policy Review Body
TPRM	Trade Policy Review Mechanism
TRIMs	Trade-related Investment Measures
TRIPS	Trade-related Aspects of Intellectual Property Rights
UK	United Kingdom
UN	United Nations
UNCTAD	UN Conference on Trade and Development
US	United States
VER	Voluntary Export Restraint
VRA	Voluntary Restraint Agreement
WCO	World Customs Organization
WIPO	World Intellectual Property Organization
WTO	World Trade Organization

TABLE OF CASES

GATT/WTO Disputes (alphabetical)

EU Cases

US Cases (alphabetical)

ICJ Cases (alphabetical)

1

Introduction

> Modern international law was not born to celebrate sovereignty but to attack it, and the intellectual development of the discipline has been about recurrent attempts to articulate always anew, and thus to strengthen the power of a cosmopolitan and gapless legal system over the sovereign egoism of the state.[1]

I. Overview

This book assesses the legality, under international and regional trade law, of the bailout and buy-national crisis measures that were implemented during the great recession of 2008–12. The unique feature of this banking crisis and consequent collapse of aggregate demand in Europe and North America was that it was systemic—unleashing a global recession. The turmoil surfaced in 2007 when major financial institutions began to incur heavy losses as a result of their exposure to the market for subprime mortgages. The subsequent uncertainty that emerged over the extent of these losses put a cap on lending and credit flows. Significantly, this cap was not only to businesses and consumers but also to banks. When investment bank Lehman Brothers failed in September 2008, equity values plummeted, along with the value of the housing market. Both firms and consumers reduced spending dramatically, resulting in a sharp fall in aggregate demand.

Lehman Brothers' collapse had global repercussions—contracting world trade and output sharply, triggering a global economic slowdown. The Chair of the Federal Reserve announced that the pressure placed on financial firms was the worst in history: out of the thirteen most important financial institutions in the United States, twelve were at risk of failure for a week or two.[2] Following Lehman Brothers' collapse, the crisis ripped through the global economy and in just one day it tore $700 billion off the value of investment portfolios, including retirement plans and government pension funds. This was to rise to $11 trillion before the

[1] M Koskenniemi, 'International Law as Therapy: Reading the Health of Nations' (2005) 16 *European Journal of International Law* 339.

[2] The Chair of the Federal Reserve announced that the pressure placed on financial firms was the worst in history: out of the thirteen most important financial institutions in the United States, twelve were at risk of failure within a period of a week or two (ibid, 345).

end of 2011.[3] The case of Lehman illustrated sharply that one major bank going down threatened others—not just by panic effects but by the potentially cascading effects of balance-sheet contagion.[4]

Having let Lehman Brothers fail, the US government did not then push the financial industry to find its own solution,[5] rather it used public money to rescue the ailing banking and manufacturing sectors. The Unites States was not alone. Various governments introduced explicit 'crisis' measures to reverse the recession through bank bailouts and stimulating employment and spending. By 2009, the WTO Trade Policy Review Body (TPRB) report had recorded policy slippages towards more trade restriction on the part of many countries,[6] including seventeen of the G20 countries.[7] These crisis measures were directed at borders through increased tariffs and export restraints, and behind borders through domestic subsidies, as well as through trade remedies such as anti-dumping and countervailing duties. In all countries, the political decisions to rescue the banks were met with fierce criticism, some of which focused on the close relationship between the financial industry and government which produced biased decision-making.[8]

An overview of the stimulus packages implemented in the six countries chosen for this research indicates[9] that, by 2009, the United States had implemented a $787 billion stimulus package under the American Recovery and Reinvestment Act (ARRA) comprising of a wide variety of tax incentives and procurement projects aimed at vigorous job creation and a swift revival of the economy. In the European Union, the €256 billion European Economic Recovery Plan (EERP) was approved in December 2008 to fund internal EU cross-border projects, including investments in clean energy and upgrading telecommunications infrastructure. At the Member State level, in addition to implementing bespoke domestic crisis measures, governments were requested to spend 1.5 per cent of GDP to boost consumer demand and tasked to invest in energy-efficient equipment and environmentally clean energy to create jobs and save energy.[10] Likewise, in Brazil a

[3] Financial Crisis Inquiry Commission, 'The Financial Crisis Inquiry Report: Final Report of the National Commission on the Causes of the Financial and Economic Crisis in the United States' (New York, Public Affairs, 2011) 339.

[4] J Vickers, 'The Financial Crisis and Competition Policy: Some Economics' [2008] *GCP* 7 (www.ucl.ac.uk/laws/jevons/docs/Vickers_Dec_08.pdf).

[5] See C Woll, *The Power of Inaction: Bank Bailouts in Comparison* (Ithaca, NY, Cornell University Press, 2014).

[6] WTO WT/TPR/OV/12, 18 November 2009.

[7] The increase in protectionist measures was documented by institutions including the IMF and the World Bank and notably the GlobalTradeAlert.org.

[8] B Ritholtz, *Bailout Nation: How Green and Easy Money Corrupted Wall Street and Shook the World Economy* (Hoboken, NJ, John Wiley, 2010); V Reinhart, 'A Year of Living Dangerously: The Management of the Financial Crisis in 2008' (2011) 25 *Journal of Economic Perspectives* 71; L Seabrooke and E Tsingou. 'Revolving Doors and Linked Ecologies in the World Economy: Policy Locations and the Practice of International Financial Reform', CSGR Working Paper no 260 (June 2009).

[9] See Appendix 1.

[10] WTO TPR, April 2009.

stimulus plan was implemented, which included supporting the car industry by extending $1.7 billion in credits for carmakers and a temporary reduction of the industrial products tax on car sales. The Provisional Programme for Investment Support created an additional credit line of $4 billion for sub-federal state governments to finance the production of capital goods destined for exports.[11] In India, the total fiscal stimulus administered was set at 6 per cent of GDP. The Indian government sought to increase liquidity with the banks, infusing about $29 billion[12] into the domestic money market to alleviate the pressures brought on by deterioration in the global financial environment.[13]

This book examines the legality of the crisis *bailouts* and *buy-national* measures implemented by these governments during the 2008–12 period. Part I of this book therefore identifies and characterises the legal frameworks that these governments have agreed upon to promote competition and non-discrimination—with the aim of preventing tit-for-tat retaliation and subsidy wars from undermining the benefits of international competition and economic liberalisation. This research follows a specific competition approach that is set out in this introductory chapter, and promoted throughout the book. It uses this competition perspective to identify the gaps and weaknesses of first the international and then the regional legal frameworks that have been set up to constrain governments' protectionist instincts towards distorting the competitive process by discriminating in favour of domestic interests. In an economic crisis the incentive and opportunity for vested interests to seek such favours from the political system are greater than usual, as are the incentives to form cartels to fix prices and rig bids.

Having established both the applicable rules that have been negotiated at both the international and regional level, Part II of this book examines how these agreed rules operated to constrain governments' protectionist instincts, under their most significant stress test since their negotiation: the 2008–12 great recession. These three chapters examine, as case studies, the legality of the crisis measures taken by six countries, including the United States, Brazil, India and three EU Member States. Four of these six countries are also signatory parties to the WTO Government Procurement Agreement (GPA)—the EU, representing the UK, Ireland and Germany, and the United States. India has been an observer since 2012. Finally, all of these six countries have also become signatories to regional trade agreements, with diverse competition and procurement laws and policies. After identifying the various bailout and buy-national measures that these governments implemented during the 2008–12 crisis, the book assesses their legality under the commitments that have been negotiated by the governments in both the WTO and in their Regional Trade Agreements (RTAs).

11 This offered an interest rate of 4.5%. WTO WT/TPR/OV/12, 18 November 2009.

12 Rs 2,00,000 crore is valued at $29,372,888,824 @ 68.09 Indian rupees to $1 dollar (http://convert.syzygy.in/what-is-200000-crores-in-millions-and-billions, accessed (9 January 2017).

13 S Mukherjee, 'India's Response to Financial Crisis', available at: www.economicsdiscussion.net/india/financial-crisis/indias-response-to-financial-crisis/11093.

The conclusions of this assessment of the 2008–12 crisis measures' compliance with these rules are then taken into Part III. The final chapters of this book discuss the enforcement of international trade rules from a competition perspective and with specific reference to a crisis. Chapter 7 looks at the enforcement of these rules during the crisis period, while Chapter 8 discusses when and why governments chose to obey international trade law. It submits that legal and political systems will inevitably face passing exigencies where the most positive way forward involves flexible application of the law. Nevertheless, such flexibility should be coordinated and cooperative to avoid undermining the objectives of the rules themselves. This book therefore concludes with some suggestions for improving the existing legal frameworks to better regulate crisis bailouts and buy-nationals from a competition perspective. This endeavour is undertaken in the belief that enhancing competition, particularly during a systemic crisis, is for the sustainable benefit of markets and citizens—as taxpayers and consumers.

II. Promoting Competition

> Antitrust laws … are the Magna Carta of free enterprise. They are as important to the preservation of economic freedom and our free enterprise system as the Bill of Rights is to the protection of our fundamental freedoms.[14]

The importance of competition or anti-trust[15] has been acknowledged for centuries.[16] As long ago as the eighteenth century Adam Smith famously argued that economic prosperity in England was primarily due to the laws and institutions that, in addition to protecting individual freedom, also defended property rights, contract law and legal security. Moreover, any market failures caused by abuse of dominance or collusion, for example, needed to be removed by law.[17] Nowadays, it is a basic proposition in industrial organisation that competition tends in most circumstances to generate lower prices and/or higher quality for a given price. That is, with contestable markets—or free entry and an absence of collusion—prices will be driven to marginal costs, moreover costs themselves will be minimised, as firms compete for survival. The dynamic of competition also serves as an important driver of

[14] *United States v Topco Assoc Inc*, 405 US 596, 610 (1972).

[15] This book uses the term competition and anti-trust interchangeably but for the sake of consistency employs the term competition.

[16] See E-U Petersmann's historical study of the constitutional and economic principles supporting competition policy from Plato to the WTO: 'International Competition Policies: Constitutional Functions of WTO "Linking Principles" for Trade and Competition' (1999–2000) 34 *New England Law Review* 145.

[17] A Smith, *An Inquiry into the Nature and Causes of the Wealth of Nations* (London, W Strahan & T Cadell, 1776).

innovation, as firms learn from one another to continuously improve their products, as well as their marketing, production and managerial techniques.[18]

This book uses the term 'competition policy' to refer to those *non-regulatory* government measures having an impact on the conditions of competition in markets,[19] both open markets and for public procurement purposes. Competition policy extends far beyond the enforcement of competition law. It rather comprises an entire set of measures and instruments used by governments to regulate or determine the conditions of competition and the contestability of markets.[20] It includes subsidies that distort competition, and in so doing it provides a workable yardstick with which to determine whether subsidies should be objectionable.[21] That is, in keeping with mainstream opinion, the present research explicitly positions competition law—regulating private markets—and government procurement law—regulating public markets—as two components or siblings located under the same conceptual umbrella of competition policy.

Whether or not there is a crisis, government interventions in the form of bailouts or buy-nationals are designed to provide an economic advantage to domestic firms. In principle, therefore, they may be covered by competition policy and laws in the form of subsidy control and government procurement law. These types of financial assistance can be distinguished from regulations.[22] In other words, although from the view point of an economist anything the government does that alters the producers' costs or revenues in a favourable direction could be regarded as a subsidy,[23] there is a crucial conceptual and legal difference: while a regulation is an expression of a general policy choice, a crisis subsidy in the form or a bailout or buy-national is antonym to norm.

A. Competition Policy and Allocative Efficiency

There is broad agreement on what competition policy is, along with its overall benefits for an economy. Nevertheless, beneath this general consensus domestic competition policies continue to vary widely. This can be partly attributed to the different legal traditions and customs in each jurisdiction. However, different governments do not have the same conception of what constitutes anti-competitive behaviour; governments treat the same types of practices differently. What is considered to be an anti-competitive or restrictive practice not only varies in different

[18] DW Carlton and JM Perloff, *Modern Industrial Organization* (Reading, MA, Addison-Wesley, 2004).

[19] International Competition Network, 'Report on Interface between Competition Policy and other Public Policies', prepared by the Turkish Competition Authority, presented at the 9th ICN Annual Conference, Istanbul, Turkey.

[20] B Hoekman, 'Economic Development, Competition Policy and the WTO', World Bank and CEPR (8 April 2003) 5.

[21] L Rubini, *The Definition of Subsidy and State Aid* (Oxford, Oxford University Press, 2009) 382.

[22] ibid, 91.

[23] R Hudec, in ibid, 92.

jurisdictions but also within countries. This is reflected in the number of different objectives competition policy may be used to pursue.

A frequently cited objective of competition policy is to maximise economic welfare through the achievement of *allocative efficiency*. This can be attained by ensuring that the competitive process is not distorted or impeded by restrictive practices. Anti-competitive behaviour has a detrimental effect on allocative efficiency and therefore levels of social welfare.[24] One essential aspect of the notion of welfare under allocative efficiency is that it deliberately sidesteps the issue of income distribution between consumers and producers. This is because the distribution of income is addressed through the use of other legal measures.[25]

Thus, although governments commonly pursue domestic social goals aimed at redistributing opportunities and income, for example, competition laws are not the most effective tools for achieving such a goal. Using competition policy would detract from achieving allocative efficiency and consequently diminishes total welfare. There may also be other less trade-distorting measures available to achieve the policy objective, for instance taxation laws, social security schemes, education, health and R&D. The rationale for avoiding issues of income distribution is twofold: first, if the intervention works, it produces a beggar-thy-neighbour effect that can lead to retaliation and spiral into a lose–lose trade war. Second, domestic policy interventions are prone to rent seeking, further reducing the likelihood of success.[26]

The GATT/WTO legal framework for regulating trade is based on the allocative model. The WTO Appellate Body has noted that to address a discrimination challenge under Article III GATT[27] a panel must examine 'whether a measure modifies the *conditions of competition* in the relevant market to the detriment of imported products'.[28] Moreover, any exceptions to the principle of non-discrimination, provided for under GATT Article XX General Exceptions, require an assessment of its contribution to the objective pursued and also an assessment of reasonably available alternative measures that may be less trade restrictive.[29]

This research also works from within the allocative efficiency paradigm. It submits that competition law should not be used as a first-best option to pursue secondary or redistribution objectives. Cost–benefit analyses are invaluable because the use of competition policy to promote secondary policies potentially

[24] W Kolasky and A Dick, 'The Merger Guidelines and the Integration of Efficiencies into Antitrust Review of Horizontal Mergers', paper presented at the 20th Anniversary of the 1982 Merger Guidelines, The Contribution of the Merger Guidelines to the Evolution of Antitrust Doctrine (2002) 49.

[25] M Motta, *Competition Policy, Theory and Practice* (Cambridge, Cambridge University Press, 2004) 18.

[26] PR Krugman, 'Is Free Trade Passé?' (1987) 1 *Journal of Economic Perspectives* 141.

[27] Art III GATT stipulates that internal taxation and regulation should not be applied to imported or domestic products so as to afford protection to domestic production.

[28] 'Appellate Body Report, Korea—Measures Affecting Imports of Fresh, Chilled and Frozen Beef', ¶137.

[29] A similar requirement is also included under the Sanitary and Phytosanitary Agreement (SPS) Art 5.6 and the Technical Barriers to Trade Agreement Art 2.2.

drains total welfare when other less trade-distorting measures are available to achieve the same goal.[30] Overall there will typically be less economic growth to redistribute through other more efficient tools. While one section of society may experience increased welfare through positive discrimination, this will be at the cost of others because the overall level of welfare in society will be less than optimal. An empirical basis is a prerequisite to inform policy-makers as defenders of the public interest of the 'optimal regime' of efficiency and equity. Quantitative analysis is necessary to estimate any possible side effects of a policy instrument. A simple 'rule of thumb' is to assign a single policy instrument to each target, for single policy instruments have been shown to have the least adverse effects for other policy goals.[31]

However, few governments make policy according to the principle of allocative efficiency or adhere to this rule of thumb. Moreover, governments do always act in the national interest, especially when influenced by sectional interest group pressures. As Paul Krugman noted in his defence of free trade as a rule of thumb in a world whose politics are as imperfect as its markets:

> Nobody who has followed US trade policy in sugar or lumber can be very sanguine about the ability of the government to be objective in applying a policy based on the Brander–Spencer model.[32]

In other words, in practice governments vary enormously in the emphasis that is placed on maximising total welfare. Domestic competition policies typically include 'fairness considerations' or public interest overrides,[33] in addition to those more misguided interventions undertaken as the result of the winners having more knowledge and influence than the losers.[34]

B. Competition Law

In contrast with the umbrella definition of competition policy provided above, the term 'competition law' refers specifically to the set of legal instruments created and maintained by governments to regulate unnecessary anti-competitive market distortions in the *open* market. Domestic frameworks regulating competition differ, operating as they do under different legal systems as well as different

[30] See SJ Evenett, 'Would Enforcing Competition Law Compromise Industry Policy Objectives?' (Oxford University Working Paper, 2005).

[31] See J Tinbergen, *On the Theory of Economic Policy* (Amsterdam, North-Holland, 1952).

[32] Krugman (n 26) 142 discussing the work of James Brander and Barbara Spencer which suggested that government policies such as export subsidies and import restrictions can, under certain circumstances, deter foreign firms from competing for lucrative markets.

[33] R Richardson, 'On the Objectives of Competition Law' (1998), cited in B Hoekman and P Holmes, 'Competition Policy, Developing Countries, and the World Trade Organization' [1999] *The World Economy* 875–93.

[34] Krugman (n 26) 142.

economic and political pressures. Competition laws can directly shape the strategic and tactical choices of governments and businesses as well as national economic interests. These laws can be applied on the basis of the effects of conduct, as well as on a territorial basis; consequently, several domestic laws may be applicable to the same conduct. The territorial principle was applied in the early *US–Banana* case, involving acts to induce monopolisation committed outside the United States.[35] This principle was subsequently applied, albeit more flexibly, until the landmark *Alcoa* case. The Court of Appeal for the Second Circuit held that: '[A]ny State may impose liabilities, even upon persons not within its allegiance, for conduct outside its borders that has consequences within its borders.'[36] This approach—known as the *effects doctrine*—has since dictated court practice, although with more restraint.[37] In the European Union, the effects doctrine is less controversially known as the *implementation test*.[38]

In addition to regulating firm behaviour, competition frameworks also address the anti-competitive behaviour of governments when providing anti-competitive subsidies or State aid.[39] This book is concerned with this latter category of competition rules: those provisions that condition a government's ability to provide subsidies to bailout a failing bank or firm.[40] These measures are addressed not to firms but to government bodies. These competition rules and regulations seek to limit the freedom of governments to grant financial advantages to certain sectors of their economy, irrespective of the technique that may be used, including tax or social security rebates.[41]

Unsurprisingly, subsidy or State aid control is a highly sensitive issue at both the regional and multilateral level due to its interference with national sovereignty and flexibility in policy-making. While the impact of these international rules is not that of a direct regime of governance taking over from the state, the impact is rather placed on the governance functions of the state. For as a result of these rules, there is a power shift or a 'subtle reversal of the internal order of values' due

[35] *American Banana Co v United Fruit Co*, 213 US 347 (1909). Here, the US Supreme Court categorically denied it had jurisdiction due to the territorial principle.

[36] *US v Aluminium Company of America et al*, 148 F 2d 416 (1944).

[37] *Timberlane Lumber Co v Bank of America National Trust & Savings Association*; later followed in *Uranium Antitrust Litig*, 617 F 2d 1248 (7th Cir 1980); *Munnington Mills Inc v Congoleum Corp*, 596 F 2d 1287 (3rd Cir 1979).

[38] The ECJ held during a case involving alleged price fixing activities among EU and non-EU wood pulp producers located throughout the world that the concerted practice complained of had been implemented in the EU and consequently EU competition law could be applied extraterritorially. Joined Cases 89, 104, 114, 116, 117 and 125–129/85, 27 September 1988, *Woodpulp* [1988] ECR 5193.

[39] This book uses the term subsidy and State aid interchangeably.

[40] The term 'subsidy' is defined both imprecisely as a government transfer of money to a private-sector firm or entity as well as the broader category of a favourable provision by a government of a good, service or other advantage to a private company. See AO Sykes, 'The Economics of WTO Rules on Subsidies and Countervailing Measures', The Chicago University John M Olin Law & Economics Working Paper no 186 (2003).

[41] C-D Ehlermann, 'State Aid Control in the EU: Success or Failure?' (1994) 18 *Fordham International Law Journal* 1218.

to changes in the law of justification, burdens of proof and legal presumptions.[42] Consequently, and as this research indicates, despite the general economic consensus that competition—whether in public or open markets—is beneficial, governments remain unwilling to commit themselves wholeheartedly to any such international or, for the most part, even regional control of these measures.

III. Government Procurement Law and Policy

Government or public procurement can be defined as the formal process through which official government agencies obtain the necessary goods and services, including construction, to undertake governmental activities that are not with a view to commercial sale or resale.[43] Since public spending increased significantly throughout the twentieth century[44] a vast range of government or public entities are routinely expected to procure the vast array of goods and services necessary for providing citizens with services as diverse as education, security, public health, utilities, infrastructure and renewable energy facilities. OECD data from cross-national studies suggest that government procurement typically constitutes in the range of 10–15 per cent of total economic activity,[45] and in many developing countries it is more.[46]

A domestic government procurement law is typically comprised of a series of detailed rules on tendering procedures and technical specifications, along with deadlines for the preparation, submission and receipt of tenders. It will also include guidelines on the evaluation of tenders and award of contracts, rules on post-contract information and publication, and a domestic bid challenge system or dispute resolution mechanism to support compliance. As with domestic competition policies, there are also contending objectives or 'desiderata' operating in a procurement system.[47] Again, these competing policy objectives range from aims as diverse as promoting allocative efficiency, customer satisfaction and integrity; to distributing wealth, avoiding risk and promoting uniformity.

[42] JHH Weiler, *The Geology of International Law—Governance, Democracy and Legitimacy* (Max-Planck-Institut für ausländisches öffentliches Recht und Völkerrecht, 2004) 559.

[43] Government procurement generally covers two main types of public expenditure: consumption expenditure and expenditure on capital formation, ie investment expenditure. OECD, *The Size of Government Procurement Markets* (Paris, OECD, 2002) annex II.

[44] See eg V Tanzi and L Schuknecht, *Public Spending in the 20th Century: A Global Perspective* (Cambridge, Cambridge University Press, 2000).

[45] See OECD, *The Size of Government Procurement Markets* (Paris, OECD, 2001).

[46] For example, China's government procurement market totalled approximately $88 billion in 2008, more than triple the amount in 2003. The EU's procurement market was worth over €1,500 billion, over 16 per cent of total EU GDP in 2004, and grew to over €2,150 billion in 2008. See: EC DG Internal Market Government Procurement Indicators (2008).

[47] S Schooner, 'Desiderata: Objectives for a System of Government Contract Law' (2002) 11 *Public Procurement Law Review.* 2.

Some advocate the use of procurement as a tool for advancing social values. This approach contends that a state should pursue certain social ends through procurement contract specifications, even when it is prohibited from pursuing the same ends through regulation.[48] Others opine that in a democracy the state should be bound by the same policy objectives whether it acts as a regulator or consumer.[49] Consequently, to 'hide' policy objectives in the tender specifications to avoid legal constraints at best is non-transparent and discriminatory, and at worst a scatter-gun approach without evidence or mandate to support such a departure from the principle of competition and value for money.

Ultimately, a degree of policy trade-off seems inevitable as there is little compatibility among some of the various objectives that government procurement can potentially serve. Value for money, for example, is unlikely to be obtained at the same time as the redistribution of wealth through preferential procurement policies or 'offsets'.[50] Requiring the best price for the best quality available could mean choosing a large foreign supplier over a small local firm or disadvantaged community. Equally, the experience and expertise required to identify the best value available in, for instance, a complex communications technology market will necessarily detract from short-term efficiency because the tendering process will require additional time and resources. It may involve training in a process as diverse as market research, tender design and contract negotiation.

Similar trade-offs emerge with due process and access to redress. A challenged tender will often hold up the completion of the contract. Nevertheless, the right to challenge a bid is one of the most effective monitoring and self-policing mechanisms a procurement system can have. Open competition could compromise welfare and efficiency if the required tender process takes several months to complete when the contract is an urgent requirement of society, such as building health facilities or emergency road repairs. And while costly, transparency in government procurement is necessary to ensure that procurement decisions are based only on considerations regarded as 'legitimate' within the system and encourages participation by suppliers.[51] Yet in the private sector, transparency is rarely considered let alone valued because it often proves antithetical to accepted commercial practices. In sum, the move towards faster and more commercial behaviour by procuring

[48] C McCrudden, *Buying Social Justice: Equality, Government Procurement, and Legal Change* (Oxford and New York, Oxford University Press, 2007).

[49] See JL Dunoff, 'Linking International Markets and Global Justice' (2009) 107 *Michigan Law Review* 1039.

[50] The WTO GPA defines offsets as 'measures used to improve local development or improve the balance-of-payments accounts by means of domestic content, licensing of technology, investment requirements, counter-trade or similar requirements'.

[51] S Arrowsmith, 'Towards a Multilateral Agreement on Transparency in Government Procurement' (1998) 47 *International and Comparative Law Quarterly* 793.

entities is not easy precisely because of the need for greater transparency and public accountability from the state as representative of citizens,[52] as well as compliance with applicable international trade laws.

IV. Integrating Competition and Government Procurement Laws

Traditionally, government procurement laws have been perceived as largely focused on eliminating public restrictions on the circulation of goods and services associated with protectionist measures by other governments. Competition law, on the other hand, is perceived as largely focused on private restraints of competition that damage consumers and contestable markets. Under this 'classical' perspective, very limited interaction between competition and government procurement law is envisaged. Both bodies of economic regulation seem to have different objectives, and, consequently, seem to offer weak reasons for their joint study or for the development of consistent rules and remedies.[53]

Indeed, most of the available literature undertakes separate assessments of competition policy and laws[54] and government procurement policy and laws.[55] There is also a body of theory that positions these laws within broader national and public policies, interests, strategies and priorities.[56] This research suggests that competition policy is, by design, both selective and episodic. The vast majority of markets, including some that are in fact not very competitive, escape through the net, and only a few markets come to be the subject of investigation.[57]

[52] S Schooner, 'Commercial Purchasing: The Chasm between the United States Government's Evolving Policy and Practice' in S Arrowsmith and M Trybus (eds), *Public Procurement: The Continuing Revolution* (London, Kluwer Law International, 2002) ch 8.

[53] A Sánchez Graells, 'Public Procurement and State Aid: Reopening the Debate?' (2012) 21 *Public Procurement Law Review* 205.

[54] Hoekman, and Holmes (n 33). See also SJ Evenett, 'What Is the Relationship between Competition Law and Policy and Economic Development?' (University of Oxford, 2005); and European Commission, 'Competition Policy in the New Trade Order: Strengthening International Cooperation and Rules', Report of the Group of Experts (July 1995) ('Van Miert Report'); P Cook, 'Competition and its Regulation: Key Issues', Centre on Regulation and Competition Working Paper Series no 2 (University of Manchester, October 2001).

[55] Arrowsmith and Trybus (n 52); S Arrowsmith and R Anderson (eds), *The WTO Regime on Government Procurement: Recent Developments and Challenges Ahead* (Cambridge, Cambridge University Press, 2011); S Schooner and C Yukins, 'Public Procurement: Focus on People, Value for Money and Systemic Integrity, Not Protectionism', GWU Law School Public Law Research Paper no 460. 2009.

[56] PE Areeda and H Hovenkamp, *Antitrust Law: An Analysis of Antitrust Principles and their Application* (New York, Aspen, 2011) 125.

[57] In the UK, it was estimated in 2002 that well under 5% of all mergers end up at the Competition Commission, an average of one to two market inquiries a year. This is in a country that hosts literally hundreds of markets which might, in principle, be investigated. See PA Geroski, 'Is Competition Policy Worth It?', Chairman, UK Competition Commission (September 2004).

Clearly, competition rules are not the sole expressions of relevant public policies and can never be isolated completely from other public policy choices relevant to democratic societies.[58] Non-efficiency considerations attached to both competition and procurement rules include: consumer welfare;[59] protection of national champions;[60] justice;[61] fairness;[62] promotion of entrepreneurial liberty and opportunity;[63] self-regulation by collective or professional bodies;[64] prevention of unethical business conduct;[65] environmental protection and green innovation;[66] inflation control;[67] intellectual property;[68] and national security.[69] These differences in domestic policies create a disparity in competitive conditions. And it is this disparity that ultimately affects the ease or difficulty of access into the national markets of other trading nations.

One underlying premise of this book is that the prevailing approach of separating the study of competition and procurement regimes overlooks important aspects of these rules as composing parts of the same system. If competition law fails to guarantee undistorted conditions of competition, government agencies will be unable to procure goods or services most efficiently. Similarly, when government procurement rules are not sufficiently pro-competitive, they can generate the very same market failures that competition law seeks to prevent.

[58] H Schweitzer, 'Competition Law and Public Policy—Reconsidering an Uneasy Relationship: The Example of Art 81', Working Paper, European University Institute (2007) 13; T Calvani, What Is the Objective of Antitrust?' in T Calvani and J Siegfried (eds), *Economic Analysis and Antitrust Law*, 2nd edn (Boston, MA, Little, Brown & Co, 1988) 7.

[59] See eg: J Vickers, 'Economics for Consumer Policy' (2004) 125 *Proceedings of the British Academy* 289; T Muris, 'The Interface of Competition and Consumer Protection', paper presented at the Fordham Corporate Law Institute's 29th Annual Conference on International Antitrust Law and Policy, New York (31 October 2002); K Dawar, 'Establishing Consumers as Equivalent Players in Competition Policy' in P Cook (ed), *Competitive Advantage and Competition Policy in Developing Countries* (Cheltenham, Edward Elgar, 2005).

[60] See SJ Evenett, 'Would Enforcing Competition Law Compromise Industry Policy Objectives?' (University of Oxford, 2005).

[61] McCrudden (n 48) 2007.

[62] See LS Liu, 'In Fairness We Trust?—Why Fostering Competition Law and Policy Ain't Easy in Asia' (2004) available at SSRN: https://ssrn.com/abstract=610822; LB Schwartz, '"Justice" and Other Non-economic Goals of Antitrust' (1979) 127 *University of Pennsylvania Law Review* 1076; Areeda and Hovenkamp (n 56).

[63] See R Pitofsky 'The Political Content of Antitrust' (1979) 127 *University of Pennsylvania Law Review*; AA Foer, 'American Idealism: Level Playing Fields' (1996) 96 *Business and Social Review* 27; W Adams and J Brock, 'Antitrust and Efficiency: A Comment' (1987) 62 *New York Law Review* 1116.

[64] CC Havighurst, 'A Comment—The Antitrust Challenge to Professionalism' (1981) 41 *Maryland Law Review* 30.

[65] R Lande, 'Wealth Transfers as the Original and Primary of Antitrust: The Efficiency Interpretation Challenged' (1982) 34 *Hastings Law Journal* 65, 115.

[66] See eg OECD, *Competition Policy and Environment* (Paris, OECD, 1996); and JH Adler, 'Conservation through Collusion: Antitrust Barriers to Cooperative Fishery Management' (2002), available at SSRN: https://ssrn.com/abstract=305921.

[67] Motta (n 25) 24.

[68] See RD Anderson and H Wager, 'Human Rights, Development, and the WTO: The Cases of Intellectual Property and Competition Policy' (2006) 9 *Journal of International Economic Law* 707.

[69] See eg the US disputes: *FTC v Imo Indus, Inc*, 1992-2 Trade Cas (CCH), 69, 943 (DDC 1989); *FTC v Alliant Techsystems, Inc*, 808 F Supp 9 (DDC 1992).

Yet an overview of the literature identifies few integrated studies in the international regulation of public restraints of competition in both open and government procurement markets. This lacuna is also apparent in analyses of the legal nature of these particular rules; particularly supported by empirical research into their levels of compliance and enforcement. The research undertaken here therefore seeks a holistic understanding of how the competition and public procurement rules operate together. It is premised on the belief that at the most general level, competition and procurement laws are both derived from the fundamental principle that in the long term, competitive markets produce benefits to the economy and to society as a whole.[70] Both sets of rules aim to regulate the competitive conditions of markets and are prima facie subject to same sovereign domestic decision-making pressures.

The influence of competition's economic principles is most obvious in the area of bid rigging and collusion amongst tenderers for public contracts.[71] This concentrates on the economic impact of procurement on competition, including the so-called *buyer power*.[72] Such work stresses the importance of preventing procurement processes being affected by egregious practices such as collusion, bid rigging, fraud and corruption.[73] It encompasses three main areas: first, the application of competition rules to prevent collusive tendering; second, the role of such policy in addressing regulatory and other barriers to competition, through 'competition advocacy' activities; and third, the application of other aspects of competition law including the treatment of mergers and joint ventures. The main thrust of this work is that competition policy is an essential complement to international liberalisation via mechanisms including government procurement agreements.[74]

The complexity of competition effects from procurement results in the public sector both promoting and restricting competition. Governments can do this through procurement policy, either by helping firms to overcome barriers to entry or by adopting procurement practices that restrict participation or discriminates against particular firms.[75] Their interdependent nature is also apparent in the impact of government procurement activities in the prospective analysis conducted in merger control cases, or on the impact of subsidies in public markets. These

[70] C Munro, 'Competition Law and Government Procurement: Two Sides of the Same Coin?' (2006) 6 *Public Procurement Law Review* 352.

[71] SE Weishaar, *Cartels, Competition and Public Procurement* (Cheltenham, Edward Elgar, 2013).

[72] The Bundeskartellamt, 'Buyer Power in Competition Law—Status and Perspectives', www.bundeskartellamt.de/wEnglisch/Vergaberecht_e/vergaberecht_eW3DnavidW2643.php.

[73] 'Public Procurement: The Role of Competition Authorities in Promoting Competition', OECD, DAF/COMP 2007:34.

[74] RD Anderson and WE Kovacic, 'Competition Policy and International Trade Liberalization: Essential Complements to Ensure Good Performance in Public Procurement Markets' [2009] *Public Procurement Law Review* no 2, 67.

[75] See eg J-J Laffont and J Tirole, *A Theory of Incentives in Procurement and Regulation* (London, MIT Press, 1994). They contend that procurement is a special case of regulation in which the roles of principal (regulator or designer of contract mechanisms) and buyer are combined; UK Office of Fair Trading, *Assessing the Impact of Public Sector Procurement on Competition. Vol 2—Case Studies* (OFT742b) (September 2004).

issues determine the competitiveness of markets where the public buyer sources goods, works and services, and can constrain the ability of the public buyer to obtain allocative efficiency and value for money.

There is, therefore, a direct relationship between the extent of competition in procurement markets and the costs of the goods and services that are procured. This is evinced by the resources private companies spend on ensuring competition for cost-effective public procurement in business-to-business commercial transactions, as well as in ensuring procurement departments make effective use of competition to reduce the cost and increase the quality of inputs.[76] Nevertheless, the effects and distortions that government procurement regulation and practice can generate in the market and the welfare losses that restrictive government procurement can provoke have been overshadowed by competition policy and law enforcement. Research into government procurement from the standpoint of industrial organisation has received limited attention because its analysis belongs with the relatively secondary field of microeconomics dedicated to the study of monopsony and buyer power.[77]

A. The Application of Competition Law to Public Procurement

A part of the reason for the lack of competition perspective in public procurement markets is the uncertainty surrounding the application of the competition rules to public-sector bodies. Within the EU, legal uncertainty can be traced to unpredictable case law, most notably the radical departure from prevailing interpretations during the case *FENIN v Commission*.[78] Here it was held that it is 'the act of placing goods or services on a given market which characterises the concept of economic activity and not purchasing activity as such'.[79] The earlier CAT *Bettercare* II decision concluded otherwise: rather, that the ability to generate the effects that the competition rules seek to prevent is a necessary but not a sufficient condition for an activity to be that of an undertaking.[80]

Policies to develop local renewable energy markets through the use of feed-in tariff programmes have presented a new opportunity to consider a more integrated approach,[81] with a view to filling gaps in the multilateral rulebook, particularly

[76] RD Anderson, WE Kovacic and AC Müller, in S Arrowsmith and R Anderson (eds), *The WTO Regime on Government Procurement: Challenge and Reform* (Cambridge, Cambridge University Press, 2012).

[77] See A Sánchez Graells, *Public Procurement and the EU Competition Rules* (Oxford, Hart Publishing, 2011).

[78] Munro (n 70) 352.

[79] Case C-205/03 P, *Fenin v Commission*, Judgment of the Court (Grand Chamber) 11 July 2006, ¶24.

[80] Case 1006/2/1/01, *BetterCare Group Limited v Director General of Fair Trading*.

[81] See eg L Rubini, 'Ain't Wastin' Time No More. Subsidies for Renewable Energy, the SCM Agreement, Policy Space and Law Reform' (2012) 15 *Journal of International Economic Law* 525; M Wilkes, 'Feed-in Tariffs for Renewable Energy and WTO Subsidy Rules: An Initial Legal Review', ICSTD Issue Paper no 4 (2011).

as regards local content requirements.[82] For as this book explicates, emerging disputes regarding the legality of horizontal policies in public procurement in both the WTO and EU have fuelled the growing awareness that the boundaries between public and private markets are blurred, and moreover, the legal uncertainty surrounding the application of the trade and competition rules to public-sector bodies should be addressed.[83]

In short, the 'public side' of the procurement phenomenon and, most notably, the impact of the market behaviour or the power of the public buyer on competition dynamics has remained substantially unexplored and are largely overlooked in current competition policy and law enforcement.[84] Limitations within current rules and case law prevent further tackling of publicly generated restrictions and distortions of market competition. The effects of government procurement on competition, and competition laws on government procurement merit further scrutiny from both an economic and legal perspective. Otherwise there is the potential for distortions that government procurement rules and practice generate in the market somewhat perversely engendering the very same effects that competition rules seek to prevent. This suggests that competition policy in public and open markets needs to be reconfigured if it is to better take into account the effects of the market behaviour of the public buyer and in so doing, promote economic efficiency and social welfare. This would have a major impact and generate significant benefits, to the advantage of citizens—both as consumers and as taxpayers.[85]

The approach taken by this research therefore seeks to contribute to this less explored legal area. It does so by identifying and characterising the nature and operation of the frameworks that regulate the anti-competitive instincts of governments towards domestic interests operating in both public procurement and open markets. It undertakes an integrated research approach at both the multilateral and regional level. This theoretical method of analysis is supported by empirical research into levels of compliance and enforcement when these rules are under a stress test: most notably during a global economic crisis.

The research is ultimately motivated by the premise that public or state restrictions to competition are amongst the most pervasive, entrenched and most problematic sources of distortion to free market dynamics. Promoting competition through free trade is a simple rule of thumb through which special interest group politics can be resisted. Moreover, to abandon competition and the free trade principle in pursuit of the gains from even the most sophisticated of interventions would likely open the door to adverse political consequences that would outweigh any potential gains.[86]

[82] C Cimino, GC Hufbauer and JJ Schott, 'A Proposed Code to Discipline Local Content Requirements', Peterson Institute for International Economics no PB14-6 (February 2014).

[83] See, for example, the WTO *Feed-in-Tariff* dispute and EU case law on PreussenElektra AG, Fenin and Bettercare, and *MOL Magyar Olaj- és Gázipari Nyrt v Commission*.

[84] A Sánchez Graells, 'Distortions of Competition Generated by the Public (Power) Buyer: A Perceived Gap in EC Competition Law and Proposals to Bridge It', University of Oxford Centre for Competition Law and Policy Working Paper CCLP (L) 23 (2009).

[85] Sánchez Graells (n 53) 205–12.

[86] Op cit. Krugman (n 26) 1987.

V. Private Anti-Competitive Behaviour

This book only examines government restraints on competition. While explicitly acknowledging the significance of the anti-competitive behaviour of firms, this book does not undertake a singular analysis of the rules governing private anti-competitive practices in either open or procurement markets. Nor does it undertake a systematic empirical assessment of the anti-competitive behaviour of firms that took place during the 2008–12 crisis, such as cartel activity or bid rigging.

This choice highlights one of the premises for advocating a more holistic approach to competition. For within the jurisdictions of the case study countries, the rules applicable to *private* restraints of competition cannot be extended to control *public* or government activity. For example, in the United States the *Parker immunity doctrine* presumes that the state is exempted from liability if it creates regulation with anti-competitive effects when it exercises legislative authority.[87] In this landmark case, the Supreme Court ruled that the Sherman Act makes no mention of the state as such, and gives no hint that it was intended to restrain state action or an official action directed by a state. Rather, the Sherman Act is applicable to persons, including corporations, and it authorises suits under it by persons and corporations.[88] Moreover, although a US state may maintain a suit for damages under the Sherman Act,[89] the federal state of the USA may not.[90]

In the EU, Article 101 TFEU clarifies the targets of competition law in two stages with the term *undertaking*. Any entity engaged in an economic activity that consists of *offering* goods or services on a given market, regardless of its legal status and the way in which it is financed, is considered an undertaking. To qualify, no intention to earn profits is required, nor are public bodies by definition excluded.[91] In effect, this term is used to describe nearly anyone that is engaged in an economic activity,[92] except employees[93] and public services based on 'solidarity' for a 'social purpose.'

A *public undertaking*, on the other hand, is an undertaking over which public authorities directly or indirectly exercise dominant influence by virtue of their ownership, financial participation or the rules that govern it.[94] *Fenin v Commission*[95]

[87] *Parker, Director of Agriculture, et al v Brown*, 317 US 341 (1943).

[88] ibid, ¶7–15.

[89] *Georgia v Evans*, 316 US 159.

[90] *United States v Cooper Corp* 312 US 600.

[91] The Commission published this definition on DG Competition's website at: http://ec.europa.eu/comm/competition/general_info/u_en.html#t62.

[92] Case C-41/90, *Höfner and Elser v Macrotron GmbH* [1991] ECR I-1979.

[93] See AG Jacobs, *Albany International BV* (1999).

[94] A dominant influence of public authorities is in particular presumed when they: (a) hold the major part of the undertaking's subscribed capital, (b) control the majority of the votes attached to shares issued by the undertaking, or (c) are in a position to appoint more than half of the members of the undertaking's administrative, managerial or supervisory body.

[95] Case C-205/03 P, Advocate General Maduro in *Fenin v Commission*.

highlights that the Community courts' traditional approach for establishing whether or not a public body is an undertaking turned on the concurrent application of two tests: (i) the comparative criterion and (ii) market participation tests. The first test focuses on whether the activity of a public body is capable of being performed by private operators. The potentially all-encompassing scope of this first test is reined in by the market participation test. This determines whether those activities are conducted under market conditions. It distinguishes between conduct undertaken with the objective of capitalisation, and those activities pursued solely pursuant to the principle of solidarity. For where the activities of the Member State are typically those of a public authority, they will not be considered an undertaking subject to Article 101 TFEU.

The results of this approach was that in so far as a public entity undertakes an economic activity that could be separated from the exercise of its public powers, this entity, in relation to that activity, acts as an undertaking. However, if that economic activity could not be separated from the exercise of its public powers, the activities exercised by that entity as a whole remain activities connected with the exercise of those public powers.[96] The fact that the product or a service supplied by a public entity and connected to the exercise by it of public powers was provided in return for contractual remuneration rather than determined, either directly or indirectly—by that entity—was not sufficient to classify the activity as economic or the entity as an undertaking.[97]

Significantly, this TFEU approach effectively operated to push most government procurement activities outside of the application of the competition rules under Articles 101 and 102 TFEU. Government procurement in the EU was seen as an ancillary to a non-economic activity, which prima facie disqualified it from the economic activity regulated under Articles 101 and 102 TFEU. This was regardless of the anti-competitive distortions that government procurement activities may effect, and which may impact both public and open markets. This asymmetrical approach in the competition rules accorded to EU public and open markets undermined a more coherent integrated approach to regulating these markets. Chapter 3 notes post-crisis developments in CJEU rulings such as the *EasyPay* judgment,[98] broke with this historical approach in ruling that for the purposes of the application of EU competition law, an undertaking is any entity engaged in an economic activity.

In Brazil, government procurement is still deemed an ancillary activity with the primary objective of meeting the core interests of the State.[99] Article 3 of Law No 8666/93 clarifies that the goal of bidding is to ensure the equality among the

[96] Case C-113/07 P, *Selex Sistemi Integrati v Commission* [2009].

[97] Case C-138/11, *Compass-Datenbank GmbH v Österreich*.

[98] Judgement in *EasyPay and Finance Engineering*, C-185/14, EU:C:2015/716.

[99] This began with the Philippine Ordinances of 1575. See D Pezzutti Ribeiro Teixeira, 'The Brazilian Experience of Using Public Procurement Policies to Promote the Development of Micro and Small Enterprises from the Legal Point of View', available at www.ippa.org/IPPC4/Proceedings/13ProcurementPreferences/Paper13-3.pdf.

bidders, which means not only equal conditions of competition but also to select the most advantageous proposal to the government. The Brazilian procurement Law No 10520 of 2000[100] is applicable to all direct and indirect public administration and federative levels in all branches of government. Under this framework, state-owned joint capital corporations and governmental agencies may establish their own standards for purchases. When seeking a social mission, the Brazilian state seeks to benefit from the bid as a sustainable economic development activity, creating jobs and income in a context of scarcity. Consequently, procurement has become one of the state's core activities, as assigned by the federal government.

Competition law in Brazil, on the other hand, is governed primarily under Law No 8.884[101] and the federal constitution. In theory, these rules apply economy-wide and contain no express exclusions for particular sectors or firms. Commercial enterprises owned by federal or state governments are covered, as are companies operating in regulated sectors. However, in applying the statute to regulated firms, the competition authority, CADE, avoids creating conflict with the operative regulatory scheme and does not prosecute firms for unilateral conduct mandated or controlled by regulatory agencies.[102]

The OECD has urged CADE to exploit its political and moral authority by fully utilising the powers provided under Article 7 X and the consultation procedure under Resolution 18, to examine anti-competitive restraints imposed by state and local governments.[103] If it were to, CADE could potentially perform a useful integrating function by assessing local regulatory schemes, reflecting the view that anti-competitive restraints imposed by law are often more harmful to competition than any restraints imposed by private agreement. As yet, CADE does not have the power to enforce such requests. The Brazilian agency in charge of investigating and prosecuting anti-competitive conducts, SDE, announced in 2007 that it would focus on collusion investigations involving the public procurement area. These cause an estimated \$12.5–20 million in damages to the government per year. A department in charge of antitrust analysis of public procurement was established to approach other governmental entities dealing with competitive bids and projects budget and review of public accounts to develop a common agenda.[104] These incipient efforts may, in time, lead to assessing the anti-competitive effects that procurement practices can engender on open markets in a manner analogous to private practices. Until then, the fact remains that public procurement is viewed as an ancillary activity, overwhelmingly excluded from the regulation applied to the same economic activities in the private sector, as with the USA and the EU. And as such, any assessment of the operation of the international regulation of private anti-competitive practices requires a different research focus to that undertaken in this book.

[100] Also known as the Reverse Auction Law.

[101] Of 1994, amended in 2000 and 2007.

[102] OECD, *Competition Law and Policy in Brazil* (OECD Policy Brief, 2005).

[103] OECD, 'Competition Law and Policy Developments in Brazil' (2000) 2 *Journal of Competition Law and Policy* 195.

[104] 'Brazil: SDE Focuses on Public Procurement Sector', Felsberg E Associados (10 December 2013).

Public procurement India accounts for roughly 30 per cent of the country's GDP, but as yet there is no single institutional framework governing exclusively public procurement, let alone an integrated competition approach.[105] India's procurement system continues to be decentralised, comprising of an array of entities at various levels of government. India retains preferential treatment in government procurement for small enterprises, Scheduled Caste or Scheduled Tribe entrepreneurs, and traditional handicrafts. India is not a party to the WTO GPA, but became an observer to the Agreement on Government Procurement in 2012, and embarked on a process of formulating a comprehensive government procurement legislation applicable to all parts of the central government, and one that accommodates the requirements of the WTO GPA.

Of relevance to the competition approach underpinning this research, is that the Indian Competition Act 2002 does not distinguish between private and government enterprises except for limited exemptions relating to sovereign functions of government.[106] The Indian Competition Act presumes that any agreement between enterprises or persons (engaged in identical or similar businesses) which, directly or indirectly, results in bid rigging or collusive bidding will have adverse appreciable effect on competition. Under the Act, such agreements are void; if there is any agreement between the coordinating firms resulting in bid rigging, such agreement shall be presumed to be anti-competitive and, consequently, void. The Competition Commission of India (CCI) also has a role in the regulation of public procurement, to intervene if any alleged malpractice causes (or could cause) an appreciable adverse effect on competition in India. The role of the CCI in such cases is also preventive. Moreover, pursuant to Article 19.6 covering the inquiry into certain agreements and dominant position of enterprise, the CCI shall, while determining the 'relevant geographic market', have due regard to, inter alia, national procurement policies. Indeed, by 2013 the CCI had investigated thirteen cases of bid rigging, including for medical equipment, the railway and state lotteries.[107] Nevertheless, it remains the case that public procurement law is fragmented both regionally and sectorally, and is largely separated from competition law along traditional lines, except for the few areas of integration such as bid rigging.

105 The current regulatory framework for India's public procurement includes the General Financial Rules (GFRs), 2005; the Delegation of Financial Powers Rules (DFPR); the Manual on Policies and Procedures for Purchase of Goods issued by the Ministry of Finance; government orders regarding price or purchase preference or other facilities to sellers in the handloom sector, cottage and small-scale industries and to CPSEs; and the guidelines issued by the Central Vigilance Commission to increase transparency and objectivity in public procurement. There are also sectoral laws such as the Telecom Regulatory Authority Act 2000, the Electricity Act 2003, and the Petroleum and Natural Gas Board Act 2006, which also regulate public procurement. In addition, various government instruments and agencies including ministries and departments (e.g. the Public Works Department and the National Highways Authority of India) have their own public procurement system.

106 This includes activity relating to energy, currency, defence and space.

107 AK Chauhan, Director General Competition Commission of India, 'Public Procurement System: Competition Issues', presentation at the Conference of National Productivity Council, Bhubaneswar, 5 February 2013.

VI. Assessing the Legality of the Crisis Measures in Six Case Study Countries

The second area of research that this book undertakes is an assessment of the legality of these anti-competitive state measures in the form of bailouts and buy-nationals implemented during the 2008–12 fiscal crisis. Chapters 4–6 conduct a legal investigation of the relevant data available on the application of crisis measures or stimulus packages implemented during the crisis by: the USA, Brazil, India and three EU Member States—Germany, Ireland and the UK. This assessment of the legality of the bailout and buy-national measures is divided into those that were implemented in the financial services sector as opposed to those implemented in the 'real' or manufacturing economy. These six case studies are included in an attempt to examine the interplay of all variables in order to provide as complete an understanding of an event or situation as possible. This involves an in-depth description of the legal framework being evaluated, the circumstances under which it is applied and the community in which it is located. It seeks a more complete understanding of the regulatory frameworks that have been negotiated by different governments. These qualitative case studies are concerned with identifying not only all the traits found in a particular agreement, but also in its supporting institutions and external policy environments.[108]

The choice of case studies selected—the USA, Brazil, India and three EU Member States: Ireland, Germany and the UK—has been made so as to include as wide a range of examples as possible. It includes a WTO GPA member whose RTAs with provisions regulating competition are separated out along the traditional lines of competition/anti-trust law and government procurement law—the USA. The selection also includes a WTO GPA member with a notified RTA with competition and public procurement laws, which are enforced by a centralised regional body with competence over its Member States in trade and competition policy issues: the EU. The three EU Member States chosen—Germany, the UK and Ireland—offer further contrasts. The UK is a non-euro Member State and the first EU country to signal a financial crisis.[109] Germany is the largest economy in Europe, and the third largest in the world. Due to its large export-oriented manufacturing sector and its specialisation in investment goods, Germany was more exposed to the global trade shock triggered by the financial crisis than most other economies,[110] while at the same time, better equipped to respond than most other economies.

108 FH Giddings, *Principles of Sociology* (London, Macmillan, 1896).

109 On 9 August 2007 the bank BNP Paribas blocked withdrawals from three hedge funds, citing 'a complete evaporation of liquidity'. This led to a panic as investors and savers attempted to liquidate assets deposited in highly leveraged financial institutions. The highly leveraged British bank Northern Rock was forced to request security from the Bank of England, leading to a bank run in September 2007. Having failed to find a private-sector buyer, the British government eventually nationalised the bank.

110 European Economic Forecast (Autumn 2009) 82.

In Ireland, there was both a credit squeeze and a fiscal crisis, which were caused directly, through the costs of recapitalising the banking system as well as indirectly, through the loss of asset-driven revenues. Further, being in the eurozone, Ireland and Germany were also entitled to EU temporary funding programmes, which by September 2012 became the European Stability Mechanism (ESM). This intervention, while not uncontested in Ireland,[111] provided a permanent firewall for eurozone countries to safeguard and provide instant access to financial assistance programmes.

At the other end of the spectrum lie Brazil and India. Both of these case study countries are WTO Members, but neither is a signatory party of the WTO GPA nor party to an RTA with integrated rules to regulate public restraints of competition. As such, these two case studies serve as a type of counterfactual. They illustrate how a government can choose to respond to a crisis when it has minimal regulatory restraints. This can be compared with those governments that have chosen to enact strong rules at regional and multilateral levels, or those choosing to do so only at the multilateral level. In sum, the main objective in selecting this sampling of case studies is to identify and compare the broadest range of different legal scenarios available to produce the richest results possible within the confines of a book on compliance and enforcement in international economic law.

VII. The Enforcement of International Trade Law in a Crisis

After Part II's assessment of the legality of these crisis measures or the extent of their compliance with the international and regional obligations agreed to by the case study countries, Part III of the book addresses issues of compliance and enforcement with regards to the legal nature of these rules. In so doing, the research seeks to ask why governments sometimes obey international trade laws and why they sometimes do not. For if there is no attempt to predict when and why governments comply with their international obligations, it is difficult to advocate multilateralism as opposed to regionalism or even unbridled unilateralism.

Part III examines the nature of these rules from within a discussion of their strength or so-called *degree of legalisation*.[112] This debate positioned the selected legal provisions along a spectrum where one pole is characterised as soft, unenforceable law or best-practice guidelines; while at the other pole laws are characterised as hard law and enforceable law. The research then addresses whether

[111] See Case C-370/12, *Thomas Pringle v The Government of Ireland.*

[112] KW Abbott, RO Keohane, A. Moravcsik, AM Slaughter and D Snidal, 'The Concept of Legalization' (2000) 54 *International Organization* 401; KW Abbott and D Snidal, 'Hard and Soft Law in International Governance' (2000) 54 *International Organization* 421.

these rules are transactional and bilateral, or collective in their nature and enforcement properties.[113] The results of this examination provide significant insight into their enforcement characteristics. It governs who has standing to bring a challenge based on a particular provision, as well as who can impose or benefit from remedies where a provision has been breached. It indicates the limits to what the WTO Members and RTA parties have agreed to in negotiations.[114] Finally, such an empirical and conceptual analysis offers the basis for making informed and evidence-based conclusions about the extent of state sovereignty[115] and domestic regulatory discretion.[116]

In light of Part I and the analysis and conclusions of Part II, Part III examines how international trade law works in crisis, when under a stress test. It asks whether existing enforcement mechanisms have appropriate incentive structures to address the challenges of a global crisis and for preventing a slide into tit-for-tat protectionism. The results of this theoretical and empirical assessment underpin this book's conclusions and recommendations concerning the role and operation of these laws when governments are under pressure to ignore them, along with their raison d'être, and discriminate in favour of domestic actors.

A. Counterfactuals

> It's very hard to know the counterfactual.[117]

This book examines different domestic legislative frameworks and compares their regulatory approaches, but it does not examine counterfactuals. From a policy perspective, 'what if?' questions relate to corresponding policy counterfactuals, such as: what would governments have done to address the crisis if the legal frameworks to prevent public distortions of competition in public procurement and open markets had ensured 100 per cent compliance during 2008–12? It would

[113] J Pauwelyn, 'The Nature of WTO Obligations', Jean Monnet Working Paper No 1/02, NYU School of Law, Jean Monnet Centre (2002); J Pauwelyn, 'A Typology of Multilateral Treaty Obligations: Are WTO Obligations Bilateral or Collective in Nature?' (2003) 14 *European Journal of International Law* 907; JH Pauwelyn, 'Enforcement and Countermeasures in the WTO: Rules Are Rules—Toward a More Collective Approach' (2000) 94 *American Journal of International Law* 335; C Carmody, 'WTO Rules as Collective' (2006) 17 *European Journal of International Law* 419; T Grazzini, 'The Legal Nature of WTO Obligations and the Consequences of their Violation' (2006) 17 *European Journal of International Law* 723.

[114] See RE Hudec, 'Broadening the Scope of Remedies in WTO Dispute Settlement', originally published in F Weiss and J Wiers (eds), *Improving WTO Dispute Settlement Procedures* (London, Cameron May, 2000) 345.

[115] JH Jackson, *Sovereignty and the Fundamental Logic of International Law* (Cambridge, Cambridge University Press, 2006) 58.

[116] This term was defined in the UNCTAD São Paulo Consensus 2004 as 'the scope for domestic policies, especially in the areas of trade, investment and industrial development' that might be 'framed by international disciplines, commitments and global market considerations'.

[117] Mervyn King, the Governor of the Bank of England, before the Treasury Select Committee on the Financial Crisis, March 2009.

be naïve not to assume that if a trade obligation hurts certain producers in the import-competing sectors through reduced tariffs, this interest group will lobby the government for another measure that will protect them. During an economic crisis, these interest groups can be expected to be more active and morally persuasive. This is the policy substitution problem.[118] Given the mercantilist thrust that governments displayed during 2008–12, there are a multitude of alternative policy measures—and therefore counterfactuals—that governments could also have implemented instead of bailouts.

Moreover, some alternative measures may have been more blatantly protectionist, such as increasing tariffs, which was implemented during the depression of the 1930s in the USA under the Smoot–Hawley Tariff Act.[119] It is generally believed that Smoot–Hawley contributed to the early loss of confidence on Wall Street. It raised average tariff rates by 20 per cent, led to retaliation from more than twenty other governments and the failure of overseas banks. US imports from and exports to Europe fell by two-thirds between 1929 and 1932, while overall global trade declined by similar levels in the four years that the legislation was in effect.

Counterfactuals are clearly an important research device. One cited alternative measure is the use of 'green protectionism', or the (non)use of trade rules, with the stated aim of protecting the environment.[120] Indeed, Bagwell and Staiger concluded from their empirical assessment that in the absence of competition rules on domestic subsidies, governments may instead choose to indeed use subsides to erode market access commitments made in previous tariff negotiations.[121] Moreover, trade agreements that are too permissive with respect to subsidies can be self-defeating; but on the other hand, agreements that are too restrictive as regards subsidies could have a chilling effect on trade negotiations.[122] Such hypothetical scenarios provide insight into a situation that could actually happen.

Nevertheless, this book does not attempt to discuss policy counterfactuals. This is not only because of the many plausible alternative instruments that could be described as either blatant or murky protectionism. Rather, this is because these measures were neither reported nor justified by governments as a necessary stimulus measure in a crisis. That is, the objective of this analysis is to assess the legality of 'crisis measures', including how they were implemented, whether they were

[118] D Brou and M Ruta, 'A Commitment Theory of Subsidy Agreements', World Trade Organization. Economic Research and Statistics Division, Staff Working Paper ERSD-2012-15 (September 2012) 4.

[119] Smoot–Hawley Tariff Act, formally United States Tariff Act of 1930, also called Hawley–Smoot Tariff Act, US legislation (17 June 1930).

[120] SJ Evenett and J Whalley, 'The G20 and Green Protectionism: Will We Pay the Price at Copenhagen?', Centre for International Governance Innovation, Policy Brief 14 (April 2009).

[121] K Bagwell, and RW Staiger, 'An Economic Theory of GATT' (1999) 89 *American Economic Review* 215; K Bagwell and RW Staiger, *The Economics of the World Trading System* (Cambridge, MA, MIT Press, 2002).

[122] K Bagwell and RW Staiger, 'Will International Rules on Subsidies Disrupt the World Trading System?' (2006) 96 *American Economic Review* 877.

challenged and how they were defended—in the context of the worst recession since the 1930s. It seeks to understand how best to regulate competition in both government procurement and open markets, given the assumed inevitability of another global depression.

The strategy followed in this book is to provide a textual analysis of existing rules that regulate public restraints of competition in open and public procurement markets. This research takes the international and regional competition and government procurement provisions that have been either (a) negotiated under the GATT/WTO frameworks, or (b) notified to the WTO by the selected case study countries and included in their database of the regional trading arrangements.[123] It assesses these provisions within two conceptual frameworks examining, first, their degree of legalisation, and second, their bilateral or collective nature. The results of this research are then presented from a comparative analysis perspective. The theoretical assessment complements the empirical examination of how these rules operated to condition government responses to the 2008–12 global crisis. Such theories can be empirically tested through country case studies. This conceptual and empirical approach provides deeper insight into the internationally agreed rules to regulate government bailouts and buy-nationals, as well as who breaks them during crisis times. This multidimensional analysis allows for some conclusions to be formed concerning governments' attitudes towards their mutually agreed upon international trade obligations.

VIII. The Outline of the Book

The outline of the book is as follows. In Part I, Chapter 2 sets out competition analysis of the trade policy rules that have been agreed to at the international and then regional level in Chapter 3, which seek to prevent anti-competitive distortions through bailout outs or buy-national measures. Chapter 4 then analyses the nature of these rules, in terms of their degree of legalisation.

This doctrinal analysis of the black-letter rules and jurisprudence is then complemented in Part II, with an empirical examination of the operation of these rules as they operated to constrain the six case study countries from implementing anti-competitive bailout and buy-national measures during the 2008–12 fiscal crisis. The assessments set out in Chapter 5 cover the legality of crisis bailout and buy-national policies directed at both the financial sector and the manufacturing economy in the six case study countries, the USA, Brazil, India, Ireland, Germany and the UK, under both their international and regional competition and public procurement law obligations.

[123] This includes customs unions (CU), economic integration areas (EIA) and free trade agreements (FTAs). See http://rtais.wto.org/UI/PublicMaintainRTAHome.aspx.

Having made findings on the legality of these crisis measures and assessments of each case studies' compliance with its trade commitments, in Part III Chapter 6 examines whether, where violated, these rules were challenged and enforced. Chapter 7 then puts forward some conclusions regarding the legal frameworks regulating the anti-competitive instincts of governments during economic downturns, followed by some more general observations on the nature and enforcement of international trade law under the WTO and RTAs, and how they operate in a crisis.

Part I

The Rules Governing Bailouts and Buy-Nationals

2

The International Framework

I. Introduction

This chapter sets out the applicable trade rules covering competition and public procurement that have been agreed to at the international level. It provides the framework from which to assess the legality of the bailout and buy-national measures implemented in the case study countries. The chapter starts with identifying those GATT/WTO rules that seek to regulate government measures that distort competition in public and open markets. In cultivating a more integrated approach to promoting competition in open and public procurement markets, this chapter also examines the relationship between these two traditionally distinct sets of rules at the international level. It develops a holistic understanding of state measures that distort market competition, which offers greater capacity to address the complex interdependencies of public procurement and open markets. Such an approach should have beneficial competition effects on both economic development and social welfare.

The first section of this chapter demarcates the relevant applicable rules that embed competition policy in both financial markets and the trade in goods, within the GATT/WTO framework, most notably through the National Treatment (NT) and Most-Favoured Nation (MFN) obligations incorporated into the GATT, GATS and WTO Government Procurement Agreement (WTO GPA), along with the Agreement on Subsidies and Countervailing Measures (ASCM). It then discusses the implications of the cumulative nature of the WTO agreements for the settlement of disputes within the WTO Dispute Settlement Body (DSB). It highlights that under the WTO legal framework, even if a government is not a signatory party of the plurilateral WTO GPA, or moreover, even if it has explicitly excluded particular sectors from the coverage of the WTO GPA, or furthermore, even if it has successfully defended a non-compliant government procurement measure under the WTO GPA exceptions, the ASCM nevertheless also conditions a government's use of procurement policy for goods.

This chapter concludes that the ASCM framework clearly addresses those competition distortions that government bailout or buy-national rules and practice can generate in both open and procurement markets. And as such, it provides a somewhat integrated approach to the control of government restrictions of competition in public and private markets for goods. Nevertheless, this examination also indicates that notwithstanding a partially integrated approach, there are weaknesses and gaps to the WTO approach to regulating anti-competitive bailouts and buy-nationals in public procurement and open markets. This legal framework's ability to ensure competitive markets is weakened by existing gaps in rule coverage, gaps in market coverage, as well inconsistencies, most notably in the differing availability of a legal avenue to defend a non-compliant measure on legitimate domestic policy grounds among the different sets of applicable rules.

II. Competition Policy and Non-Discrimination under the GATT

For the trade in goods, competition policy is embodied both within the GATT Article III NT provisions and the Article I MFN obligation. (See Box 1.) On the one hand, the Article III NT requirement prohibits all WTO Members from imposing any internal taxes or rules on imported goods from another WTO Member more onerous than those imposed on a similar domestic product, and in doing so, discriminating in favour of domestic producers. On the other hand, the MFN treatment provision set out under Article I obligates all WTO Members to conduct their trade in goods without discriminating among Member countries. A prohibition of this type of discrimination binds WTO Members together by enforcing the equal treatment of one country vis-à-vis another, fostering trade conducted without political motivations.[1]

Box 1

Article I *Most-Favoured-Nation Treatment*

1. With respect to customs duties and charges of any kind imposed on or in connection with importation or exportation or imposed on the international transfer of payments for imports or exports, and with respect to the method of levying such duties and charges, and with respect to all rules and formalities in connection with importation and exportation, and with respect to all matters referred to in paragraphs 2 and 4 of Article III, any advantage, favour, privilege

[1] Although Art I is seen as the embodiment of the MFN principle, several other MFN-type provisions are contained in the GATT relating to: internal mixing requirements (Art III:7); cinema films (Art IV(b)); transit of goods (Art V:2, 5, 6); marks of origin (Art IX:1); quantitative restrictions (Art XIII:1); measures to assist economic development (Art XVIII:20); and measures for goods in short supply (Art XX(j)).

or immunity granted by any contracting party to any product originating in or destined for any other country shall be accorded immediately and unconditionally to the like product originating in or destined for the territories of all other contracting parties.

Article III *National Treatment on Internal Taxation and Regulation*

1. The contracting parties recognize that internal taxes and other internal charges, and laws, regulations and requirements affecting the internal sale, offering for sale, purchase, transportation, distribution or use of products, and internal quantitative regulations requiring the mixture, processing or use of products in specified amounts or proportions, should not be applied to imported or domestic products so as to afford protection to domestic production.*
2. The products of the territory of any contracting party imported into the territory of any other contracting party shall not be subject, directly or indirectly, to internal taxes or other internal charges of any kind in excess of those applied, directly or indirectly, to like domestic products. Moreover, no contracting party shall otherwise apply internal taxes or other internal charges to imported or domestic products in a manner contrary to the principles set forth in paragraph 1.*

...

4. The products of the territory of any contracting party imported into the territory of any other contracting party shall be accorded treatment no less favourable than that accorded to like products of national origin in respect of all laws, regulations and requirements affecting their internal sale, offering for sale, purchase, transportation, distribution or use. The provisions of this paragraph shall not prevent the application of differential internal transportation charges which are based exclusively on the economic operation of the means of transport and not on the nationality of the product.

It is submitted here, that while trade and competition policy are traditionally viewed as distinct sets of regulation, they share common policy objectives within the WTO framework. For example, both trade and competition policies seek to provide equal opportunities to every participant in the market.[2] Both advocate transparency and fairness in the regulatory process to promote efficiency and the maximisation of consumer welfare; and both seek to foster markets that are contestable and competitive to the benefit of both foreign and domestic interests. Not only do WTO rules and procedures seek to foster competition in markets, but they also promote competition between regulatory regimes.[3] This complementarity is

[2] M Matsushito, Basic Principles of the WTO and the Role of Competition Policy' (2004) 3 *Washington University Global Studies Law Review* 363.

[3] B Hoekman and P Mavroidis, 'Competition, Competition Policy and the GATT. The World Bank', Policy Research Paper 1228 (Washington DC, The World Bank, 1993).

widely accepted;[4] if left unaddressed, behind the border, restrictive practices will ultimately reduce the benefits of tariff reductions and erode support for the liberalisation of trade.

The Article III NT provision operates to ensure that so-called *behind-the-border* internal measures are not used to nullify or impair the effect of negotiated tariff concessions or other multilateral rules applicable to border measures. Moreover, the 'sheltering scope of Article III is not limited to products that are the subject of tariff concessions under Article II'.[5] Article III functions to prevent an expansive category of internal measures[6] from being applied to either imported or domestic products in a discriminatory manner—or 'so as to afford protection to domestic production'. The practices of state trading enterprises are also subject to these provisions when they too concern internal laws, regulations or requirements affecting the conditions of competition between domestic and imported products.[7] This NT obligation covers de facto as well as de jure discrimination.[8]

In sum, competition policy under Article III NT can be seen to protect expectations that are not of any particular trade volume but rather of the equal competitive relationship between imported and domestic products.[9] As a result, determining whether a measure is discriminatory often turns on whether the affected products are 'like', and analytically, the question of determining 'likeness' of products can resemble the relevant product and geographic market definitions that are central to a competition analysis. There is also a distinctive tendency in disputes falling under Article III:2 to consider whether products are directly competitive or substitutable. This approach reflects the influence of economic analysis, which again has had an even greater role in competition analyses.[10]

GATT non-discrimination provisions provide some elements of a competition policy in the absence of a comprehensive competition regime to address

[4] See J Bhagwati et al (eds), *The General Theory of Distortions in Welfare, in Trade, Balance of Payments and Growth: Essays in Honour of CP Kindleberger* (Amsterdam, North Holland, 1971); J Bhagwati and R Hudec (eds), *Fair Trade and Harmonization: Prerequisites for Free Trade?* (Cambridge, MA, MIT Press, 1996).

[5] Appellate Body Report, *Japan–Alcoholic Beverages*, part II, ¶110.

[6] The GATT dispute Italian Discrimination Against Imported Agricultural Machinery, ¶12, BISD 7s/60, L/833, adopted on 23 October 1958, concluded that the application of Art III was intended to cover 'any laws or regulations which might adversely modify the conditions of competition between … domestic and imported products on the internal market'.

[7] Canada–Import Distribution and Sale of Certain Alcoholic Drinks by Provincial Market Agencies, ¶4.26, BISD 35s/37, L/6304, adopted on 22 March 1988; Canada–Import Distribution and Sale of Certain Alcoholic Drinks by Provincial Market Agencies, ¶5.4, 5.15 and 5.31, BISD 39s/27, WT/DS17/R, adopted on 18 February 1998; United States–Measures Affecting Alcoholic And Malt Beverages, ¶5.63, BISD 39s/206, WT/DS23/R, adopted on 19 June 1992.

[8] GATT rules are breached if measures that are on the face of it identical for home and foreign goods are nonetheless in practice much harder for imports to meet. Further, Art III should be understood to apply to both procedural and substantive laws, regulations and requirements. United States–section 337 of the Tariff Act of 1930, ¶5.10.

[9] *Japan–Taxes in Alcoholic Beverages II*, Appellate Body Report.

[10] This is especially in the United States. See ME Janow, 'What Role for Competition Policy in the WTO in the Next Trade Round?' in A Appleton (ed), *The Next Trade Round* (Kluwer, 2003).

anti-competitive practices by both firms and governments.[11] Some have even argued that competition policy considerations are already sufficiently reflected and incorporated in the different parts of the legislation of the WTO. For in addition to Articles I MFN, and Article III NT, the 1994 GATT also requires the Members to 'ensure that monopolies, State enterprises and those with special or exclusive rights make purchasing decisions on the basis of commercial considerations and do not discriminate against imports'.[12] Moreover, because GATT Article II requires *all* laws affecting trade to be non-discriminatory, this presumably includes competition laws.[13]

III. Competition and Public Procurement under the GATT

The GATT negotiating history indicates that early draft texts of the ITO Charter, as proposed by the US negotiators, contained provisions requiring the extension of national treatment to imported goods in the case of government purchases and government contracts. These provisions were deleted from the London Draft Charter as it appeared to the Preparatory Committee that an attempt to reach agreement on such a commitment would lead to exceptions almost as broad as the commitment itself.[14] Accordingly, although government procurement regulation can be characterised as an internal regulatory measure, it was explicitly carved out from the subsequent GATT Article III NT obligations by virtue of GATT Article III:8(a), which states:

> The provisions of this Article shall not apply to laws, regulations or requirements governing the procurement by governmental agencies of products purchased for governmental purposes and *not with a view to commercial resale* or with a view to use in the production of goods for commercial sale. (emphasis added)

[11] Hoekman, and Mavroidis noted: 'In our view the relative payoffs to continuing traditional liberalization of entry into markets will be greater than investment of significant resources into development of competition law disciplines—at both the national and multilateral levels.' B Hoekman, and P Mavroidis, 'Economic Development, Competition Policy and the WTO' (2002) 37 *Journal of World Trade*.

[12] Further, the Agreement on Trade in Services (GATS) prohibits the abuse of a monopoly position in certain situations, and the Agreement on the Trade-Related Aspects of Intellectual Property Rights (TRIPS) sets out rules against anti-competitive practices relating to the licensing of intellectual property rights. One of the most detailed binding multilateral agreements providing for competition rules is the Reference Paper, which prohibits anti-competitive practices that thwart market access in the telecommunication sector. See P Marsden, *A Competition Policy for the WTO* (London, Cameron May, 2003) 53.

[13] MJ Trebilcock, and R Howse, *The Regulation of International Trade*, 3rd edn (New York, Routledge, 2005) 593–94.

[14] The First Session of the Preparatory Committee (London Report), UN Doc EPCT/33-CII-I-66, page 9, ¶(d)(iv) (1948).

Nevertheless, the *Canada–Feed-in Tariffs* (*FIT*) dispute highlights the complications that emerge when determining whether a challenged government purchase is or is not a government procurement—as defined under the GATT Article III:8(a)[15] derogation—and which are of immediate relevance to this chapter. The *FIT* dispute emerged when Japan and the EU challenged the legality of the domestic content requirements set out in the FIT scheme established by the Canadian province of Ontario.[16] The FIT programme pays generators of electricity produced from certain types of renewable energy a guaranteed price for electricity delivered into the Ontario electricity system under 20-year or 40-year contracts.[17] However, only facilities geographically located in Ontario that, inter alia, generate electricity exclusively from specified sources of renewable energy were deemed eligible to participate in the Ontario Power Authority's scheme.

The EU challenged this measure on the grounds that the GATT Article III.8(a) derogation could not apply to the FIT programme[18] given that only those government departments directly using the procured goods or services are immune from Article III's NT obligations.[19] The EU claimed that the meaning of procurement for governmental purposes as set out in Article III:8(a) is narrow. It is restricted to acquisitions made to meet 'the needs' of government. To qualify as a government procurement, any purchase must pass a 'needs' test to ensure that it is indeed intended 'for the direct benefit or use of the government'.[20] The EU challenge also proposed a broad reading of Article III:8(a) when defining 'not with a view to commercial resale or with a view to use in the production of goods for commercial sale'. The EU claimed that if the purchased product is sold or introduced into the market regardless of whether this is done for profit, it should be deemed to be 'with a view to commercial resale', and thus disqualified from the derogation. As such, this interpretation sought to exclude more types of government procurement that distort competition in open markets from the safe haven of the Article III:8(a) derogation.

In its defence, Canada claimed that the EU's interpretation of Article III:8(a) contravened the customary rules of international treaty interpretation.[21] Rather,

[15] Appellate Body Report, *Canada–Measures Relating to the Feed-In Tariff Program* (6 May 2013) WT/DS412/AB/R and WT/DS426/AB/R, ¶1.31.

[16] A FIT is an increasingly employed instrument for promoting investment in renewable energy typically through fixed pricing for the purchases of renewable energy power above the market price for electricity.

[17] The Ontario FIT programme is divided into two streams—the FIT stream and the microFIT stream—for projects having a capacity to produce up to 10 kW of electricity. Participants under the microFIT stream are typically small household, farm or business generation projects. Panel Report, *Canada–Measures Relating to the Feed-In Tariff Program*, WT/DS412/R, WT/DS426/R, 19 December 2012, ¶7.66 (referring to FIT Rules Exhibit (version 1.5.1), s 2.1(a)(iii); and microFIT Rules (version 1.6.1), s 2.1(a)(iv)).

[18] Panel Report, *Canada–FIT*, WT/DS412/R, WT/DS426/R, 19 December 2012, ¶130.

[19] *Canada–Renewable Energy*, third party written submission of the US, paras 13 and 14.

[20] *Canada–FIT*, first written submission by the EU, paras 118–30.

[21] The Appellate Body in the *India–Patents* dispute noted that: '[P]rinciples of interpretation neither require nor condone the imputation into a treaty of words that are not there or the importation into a treaty of concepts that were not intended.' Appellate Body Report, *India–Patent Protection for Pharmaceutical and Agricultural Chemical Products*, WT/DS50/AB/R, ¶45.

not only was the FIT procurement exempt from GATT NT obligations by virtue of Article III:8(a)[22] but, moreover, the FIT regulation did not infringe upon Canada's obligations as a signatory party of the WTO GPA. In effect, Canada's defence was primarily the assertion that when negotiating the coverage of the WTO GPA, Canada had not committed Ontario's electricity purchases in the schedules of entities or markets that fall under the scope of the WTO GPA. Consequently, or so the argument goes, the FIT regulation could not be prohibited by Canada's commitments under either GATT or WTO GPA legal obligations.

On appeal the Appellate Body clarified that the term 'governmental agencies' also refers to those 'arm's-length' entities acting for or on behalf of government in the public realm, within the competences that have been conferred on them to discharge governmental functions. There need not be a so-called charge to the public account. Further, the concepts of 'procurement' and 'purchase' should not to be equated, for procurement is a broader concept than just a purchase:

> Not every procurement needs to be effectuated by way of a purchase, and not every purchase is part of a process of government procurement. … The subject matter of the procurement is a 'product', and it is being procured by a 'governmental agency'.[23]

The Appellate Body found that the scope of the derogation under Article III:8(a) should be limited to products purchased for the use of government, consumed by government, or provided by government to recipients in the discharge of its public functions.[24] This finding is broader than the interpretation submitted by the EU. Further, both the terms 'for governmental purposes' and 'not with a view to commercial resale' qualify and limit the scope of 'products purchased'. In other words, a purchase that does not fulfil the requirements of being made 'for governmental purposes' will not be considered to fall within the derogation of Article III:8(a). This condition is regardless of whether the procurement in question complies with the requirement of being made 'not with a view to commercial resale'[25] because these are cumulative requirements.[26]

Having determined the nature of the measure being challenged, the Appellate Body undertook a like-product analysis. This would allow for some conclusions to be made as to whether Canada's FIT programme was disrupting international competitors' sales of renewable energy generating equipment, as claimed by the EU and Japan. It sought to determine whether the particular product being procured by a governmental agency was similar to the product that was being treated more favourably as a consequence of the offsets set up under the FIT programme.

[22] Appellate Body Report, *Canada–FIT*, WT/DS412/AB/R and WT/DS426/AB/R, 6 May 2013, ¶5.74 stated that Art III.8(a) is a derogation from the Art III NT obligation.

[23] ibid, ¶5.59.

[24] The Appellate Body further noted that the characterisation of the provision as a derogation does not predetermine the question as to which party bears the burden of proof with regard to the requirements stipulated in the provision. *Canada–FIT*, ¶5.57.

[25] ibid, ¶5.59, 5.60, 5.61.

[26] ibid, ¶5.69.

The Appellate Body identified whether the product of foreign origin allegedly being discriminated against was in a competitive relationship with the product being purchased. The Appellate Body concluded that the product being procured was electricity, whereas the product discriminated against for reason of its origin was generation equipment, and that these two products are not in a competitive relationship. Therefore, the scheme was not covered by the Article III:8(a) derogation.

Given that the FIT scheme was found to fall under application of the GATT Article III:4 NT obligations, in favouring domestic over foreign products, it was found to be in violation of GATT Article III:4.

> In the light of our finding that the Minimum Required Domestic Content Levels do not fall within the ambit of Article III:8(a), and in the light of the fact that Canada has not appealed the Panel's finding that the FIT Programme and Contracts are inconsistent with Article III:4 of the GATT 1994 and Article 2.1 of the TRIMs Agreement, the Panel's conclusion … that the Minimum Required Domestic Content Levels prescribed under the FIT Programme and related FIT and microFIT Contracts are inconsistent with Article 2.1 of the TRIMs Agreement and Article III:4 of the GATT 1994 stands.[27]

The Appellate Body then demonstrated the cumulative nature of the WTO agreements by proceeding to assess the legality of the same measure under the ASCM. This move indicated definitively that with or without the GATT Article III:8(a) derogation and, moreover, whether or not a WTO GPA party has excluded a specific procuring entity or market from its Appendix 1 Annexes, there is no safe haven from the application of the ASCM to those government procurement measures that relate to goods. This provides a partially integrated approach to regulating government procurement measures that distort competition in both public and open markets. In sum, this dispute serves to highlight that even if a GPA party deliberately excludes a particular procurement measure from its GPA obligations, this does not generally free it from the obligations of the GATT or ASCM.

A similar dispute subsequently emerged against a local content requirement policy implemented by the Indian government to develop its solar cell industry. In the *India Solar Cells* case, the USA challenged India's measures relating to the domestic content requirements under the Jawaharlal Nehru National Solar Mission (NSM) for solar cells and solar modules as inconsistent under the GATT NT obligation pursuant to Article III:4. In settling the claim under GATT Article III:4, the Panel Report explicitly followed the legal reasoning set out in the *Canada–FIT* Appellate Body Report's interpretation of Article III:8(a) of the GATT 1994.[28] It consequently agreed with the US submission that Article III:8(a) did not apply. Relying on the 2013 decision of the Appellate Body in *Canada–FIT*, the Panel concurred that the product procured (electricity) was not in a competitive relationship with the product being discriminated against (solar cells and modules), and

[27] ibid, ¶5.85.

[28] Panel Report, *India–Certain Measures Relating to Solar Cells and Solar Modules*, WT/DS456/R and Add 1, circulated to WTO Members 24 February 2016, ¶7.115.

therefore such discrimination was not covered by the derogation of Article III:8(a). This finding was upheld on appeal.[29]

IV. GATT Article I:1 Most Favoured Nation and Government Procurement

As a cornerstone principle of the WTO, GATT Article I:1 provides that the MFN obligation applies to any kind of duty or administrative procedure that affects trade in goods. Pursuant to this, WTO Members cannot normally discriminate between their trading partners. If a Member grants a country an advantage such as a lower tariff on one of its products, it must grant this advantage immediately and unconditionally to all WTO Members. The Appellate Body in the *Canada–Autos* dispute emphasised the context and character of the MFN principle:

> Apart from Article I:1, several 'MFN-type' clauses dealing with varied matters are contained in the GATT 1994. The very existence of these other clauses demonstrates the pervasive character of the Most Favoured Nation principle of non-discrimination.[30]

There are various explicit exemptions and conditions to the MFN principle in the GATT[31] that limit or 'dethrone' its all-pervasive character.[32] Yet nowhere is government procurement explicitly excluded from the GATT Article I:1 MFN obligations. Despite the lack of explicit exclusion of government procurement from the Article I MFN obligation, prevailing opinion holds that government procurement is nevertheless exempt from the ambit of the provision. Article I:1 explicitly refers to four types of measures and it is the fourth of these—'with respect to all matters referred to in paragraphs 2 and 4 of Article III' that is of relevance here. To recall, GATT Article III:4 addresses all laws, regulations and requirements affecting their internal sale: offering for sale, purchase, transportation, distribution or use. This, as noted above, is eminently applicable to government procurement qua a law or regulation affecting the internal sale of a product. In other words, the category in question incorporates government procurement measures within the scope of the Article I:1 MFN obligations.

However, the leading interpretation submits that even though procurement is not explicitly exempt from the obligations of Article I:1, or Article III:2 or 4, it

[29] Report of the Appellate Body, *India–Certain Measures Relating to Solar Cells and Solar Modules*, AB-2016-3, WT/DS456/AB/R, 16 September 2016, ¶5.32.

[30] Appellate Body Report, *Canada–Certain Measures Affecting the Automotive Industry*, WT/DS139/AB/R, WT/DS142/AB/R, 31 May 2000, ¶82.

[31] Most notably GATT Art XXIV on regional trading arrangements. GATT Art XXIV provides a conditional exemption from GATT MFN obligations for developing countries, free trade areas and customs unions. See JH Mathis, *Regional Trade Agreements in the GATT* (The Hague, Asser Press, 2002).

[32] GC Hufbauer, J Shelton Erb and HP Starr, 'The GATT Codes and the Unconditional Most Favored-Nation Principle' (1980) 12 *Law and Policy in International Business* 59.

is nonetheless excluded from the scope of Article I:1 by virtue of the derogation for public procurement provided in Article III:8(a). John Jackson notes that: '[G]overnment procurement practices have traditionally been considered unreached by the language of GATT Article I, and the language of GATT Article III and the preparatory work of GATT seem to support this approach.'[33] Mary Footer looks to the context of the treaty negotiation and points out that while early draft texts both for an International Trade Organization (ITO) and the GATT contained provisions requiring the extension of national treatment to imported goods, in the case of government purchases and government contracts these clauses were deliberately not included in the final texts.[34] This position is also supported by Sue Arrowsmith,[35] and by Hufbauer et al.[36] They all submit that Article III:8(a) should be read so as to free government procurement practices entirely from the disciplines of Article I:1, in addition to those of Article III.

It is reasoned here otherwise, however. Rather, that this interpretation is not self-evident and open to debate. The *EC–Vessels* dispute is the only case to offer instruction on this point of law. Here, the Panel was concerned with the different question of whether and how the Article III:8(b) subsidy exemption[37] affects the scope of 'all matters referred to in paragraphs 2 and 4 of Article III'. The Panel considered that the phrase 'matters referred to in' in Article I:1 refers to the subject matter of those provisions in terms of their substantive legal content. If it is explicitly provided that a particular measure is not subject to the obligations of Article III, then the measure does not form part of the 'matters referred to' in Article III:2 and 4 and therefore cannot be covered by the expression 'matters referred to in paragraphs 2 and 4 of Article III' in Article I:1.[38] The Panel thus concluded its analysis by concurring that:

> [T]he relevant drafting history that we are aware of shows that the exclusion of government procurement from the national treatment article would also apply to the most favoured nation clause.[39]

GATT Articles I and III both aim to prohibit less favourable treatment of directly competitive goods. The basic policy of Article III—to eliminate market distortions

[33] JH Jackson, *The Jurisprudence of GATT & WTO* (Cambridge, Cambridge University Press, 2000) 63.

[34] M Footer, 'International Developments: GATT: Developments in Government Procurement Procedures and Practices' (1993) 6 *Public Procurement Law Review*, CS193-204.

[35] S Arrowsmith, *Government Procurement in the WTO* (The Hague, Kluwer, 2003).

[36] Hufbauer et al (n 32).

[37] In a paragraph similar to the government procurement exemption provision in Art III:8(a), the dispute concerned Art III:8(b) which states that: 'The provisions of this Art shall not prevent the payment of subsidies exclusively to domestic producers, including payments to domestic producers derived from the proceeds of internal taxes or charges applied consistently with the provisions of this Article and subsidies effected through governmental purchases of domestic products.'

[38] *EC–Commercial Vessels*, WT/DS301/R, ¶7.83.

[39] ibid, ¶7.87.

caused by internal measures—is as compelling with respect to national treatment type discrimination as it is to most-favoured-nation type discrimination.[40] Therefore, it could be reasoned that the same range of goods should be covered by both obligations. Analysing the differences and complementarities of Articles I and III in enshrining non-discrimination, Horn and Mavroidis[41] submitted that MFN has more stringent requirements with regard to product similarity than NT, since it only refers to 'like' products. National treatment, however, applies not only to 'like' products, but has also been interpreted to apply in the case of 'directly competitive or substitutable goods'. They further note that MFN applies to both internal and border measures, and is therefore wider than NT, which only applies to internal measures. As a result, the authors characterise the two provisions as 'orthogonal' in the sense that MFN refers to the treatment rendered to different foreign products, whereas NT compares the treatment given to foreign products to that of domestic products. This analysis suggests that while the scope of the application of the two articles is similar, the important difference lies rather in how they determine whether the products in question are 'like'.

While this logic may be economically persuasive, it still remains questionable whether the coverage of the two rules should be interpreted to be the same. The two types of discrimination have very different political considerations. Discrimination in favour of a domestic firm cannot be deemed equivalent to discrimination among different WTO Members. The latter is more divisive in undermining the cohesion, solidarity, and non-politicisation of trade among WTO Members than the former. This is recognised in the GATT Article XX, where deviations from the NT standard are under specific conditions permitted, but not with regard to MFN obligations. Under the chapeau of Article XX, there is a requirement, inter alia, that any measure deemed exempt from GATT obligations under one of the Article XX(a)–(j) exceptions must nevertheless not be applied in a manner that would constitute a means of arbitrary or unjustifiable discrimination between countries where the same conditions prevail.

Article XX, in effect, offers a refuge from the requirement for NT, but not from the obligation towards the MFN principle. Moreover, this interpretation of the scope of Article I:1 ignores several Appellate Body Reports that stipulate that if the drafters of an agreement especially intended to exclude a particular aspect from the application of a rule, they would have done so expressly.[42] It is also pertinent to note here the negotiating history of the WTO GPA, which indicates that the

[40] R Hudec, 'The Policy Goals of GATT Art I.1', reprinted in AT Guzman and J Pauwelyn, *International Trade Law* (Austin, TX, Wolters Kluwer Law and Business, 2009) 292.

[41] H Horn and PC Mavroidis, 'Economic and Legal Aspects of the Most-Favored-Nation Clause' (2001) 17 *European Journal of Political Economy* 233.

[42] Appellate Body Report, *European Communities–Anti-Dumping Duties on Imports of Cotton-Type Bed Linen from India*, Recourse to Art 21.5 of the DSU by India, WT/DS141/AB/RW, 8 April 200, ¶84; see also: Panel Report, *EC–Malleable Cast Iron Tube or Pipe Fittings from Brazil*, WT/DS219/R, 7 March 2003, ¶98; Appellate Body Report, *Korea–Definitive Safeguard Measure on Imports of Certain Dairy Products*, WT/DS98/AB/R, 14 December 1999, ¶109.

Tokyo Round closed with the signatories taking a decision with regard to the six plurilateral agreements.[43] In doing so, they sought to ensure that the application of the GATT Article I MFN principle to procurement rules was not to be undermined by the MFN and NT obligations operating as between the limited parties to the Tokyo Procurement Code. The signatories stated that:

> [Any] existing rights and benefits under the GATT of contracting Parties not being parties to these Agreements, *including those derived from Article I*, are not affected by these agreements.[44] (emphasis added)

This provision mirrors Article II:3 of the Marrakesh Agreement:

> The agreements and associated legal instruments included in Annex 4 (hereinafter referred to as 'Plurilateral Trade Agreements') are also part of this Agreement for those Members that have accepted them, and are binding on those Members. The Plurilateral Trade Agreements *do not create either obligations or rights for* Members that have not accepted them. (emphasis added)

Article II:3 of the Marrakesh Agreement confirms that the Procurement Code and now the WTO GPA create a framework of obligations and minimum standards for opening up procurement markets between a limited number of parties. These obligations do not apply on a multilateral basis to the wider membership of the WTO. Article II:3 Marrakesh does not operate to suspend the existing prohibition on discrimination as between the wider WTO membership, pursuant to the GATT Article I:1 MFN obligation. Given that GATT Article I does not include an explicit derogation either for government procurement or for subsidies, and in light of the available negotiating history, this prevailing interpretation deprives WTO Members of the protections of the MFN obligation and diminishes their rights to non-discrimination as between the Members, contra the WTO Dispute Settlement Understanding (DSU) Article 3:2:

> The dispute settlement system of the WTO is a central element in providing security and predictability to the multilateral trading system. The Members recognize that it serves to *preserve the rights and obligations of Members under the covered agreements*, and to clarify the existing provisions of those agreements in accordance with customary rules of interpretation of public international law. Recommendations and rulings of *the DSB cannot add to or diminish the rights and obligations provided in the covered agreements*. (emphasis added)

In such cases of interpretative uncertainty, the WTO DSU requires that any clarification of WTO rules should take place pursuant to customary rules of interpretation, most notably those embodied in Articles 31, 32, and 33 of the Vienna

[43] The historical development of the existing GPA is traced in A Blank and G Marceau, 'The History of the Government Procurement Negotiations since 1945' (1996) 5 *Public Procurement Law Review* 77.

[44] The Code, which came into effect on 1 January 1981 (and was subsequently amended in 1987), was signed by Austria, Canada, the EC, Israel, Finland, Hong Kong, Japan, Norway, Singapore, Sweden, Switzerland and the USA.

Convention on the Law of Treaties (VCLT).[45] For as the Appellate Body has pronounced:

> The duty of a treaty interpreter is to examine the words of the treaty to determine the intentions of the parties. This should be done in accordance with the principles of treaty interpretation set out in Article 31 of the Vienna Convention. But these principles of interpretation *neither require nor condone the imputation into a treaty of words that are not there or the importation into a treaty of concepts that were not intended.*[46] (emphasis added)

Under the General Rule of Interpretation set out pursuant to VCLT Article 31:1, a treaty should be interpreted in accordance with the ordinary meaning to be given to the terms of the treaty, and also in the light of its object and purpose. It is submitted here that to read the Article III:8(a) derogation into 'all matters referred to in paragraphs 2 and 4 of Article III' is to go against the ordinary meaning that should be accorded to the provision. Such an interpretation is opaque and convoluted. There is scant indication of any explicit intentions from the drafters as to this reading, and, moreover, it works against the object and purpose of the GATT. The rationale for this prevailing view seems to be premised chiefly upon an unappealed Panel Report to the WTO *EC–Vessels* dispute. Neither the WTO Panel nor Appellate Body Reports are covered by the rule of *stare decisis* that binds domestic courts to previous reports.[47] This rule was excluded from the pre-Uruguay Round GATT dispute settlement system, and continues to be from the post-Uruguay Round WTO system.[48] Still, WTO Panel and Appellate Body reports have been described as 'stones in the growing edifice even if in theory the builders are free not to continue to build upon them'.[49] The Appellate Body has expressed its deep concern over a Panel's decision to depart from prior Appellate Body rulings on the same question of law because: 'Ensuring "security and predictability" in the dispute settlement system, as contemplated in Article 3.2 of the DSU, implies that, absent cogent reasons, an adjudicatory body will resolve the same legal question in the same way in a subsequent case.'[50]

[45] In the Vienna Convention on the Law of Treaties, s 3: Interpretation of Treaties, Art 31 covers the general rule of interpretation; Art 32 covers supplementary rules of interpretation; and Art 33 covers interpretation of treaties authenticated in two or more languages.

[46] Appellate Body Report, *India–Patent Protection for Pharmaceutical and Agricultural Chemical Products*, WT/DS50/AB/R, 19 December 1997, ¶45.

[47] There is no doctrine of *stare decisis* or binding precedents in international law. Art 59 of the Statute of the International Court of Justice explicitly provides that the decision of the Court has no binding force except between the parties and in respect of that particular case. Additionally, Art 38 states that judicial decisions constitute only 'subsidiary means for the determination of rules of law', United Nations, Statute of the International Court of Justice, 18 April 1946, www.refworld.org/docid/3deb4b9c0.html (accessed 6 December 2016).

[48] For an extended discussion of de facto and de jure and binding and non-binding *stare decisis* in the GATT WTO and international law, see R Bhala, 'The Myth about Stare Decisis and International Trade Law (Part One of a Trilogy)' (1999) 14 *American University International Law Review* 845.

[49] H Lauterpacht, cited in JP Commission, 'Precedent in Investment Treaty Arbitration: A Citation Analysis of a Developing Jurisprudence' (2007) 24 *Journal of International Arbitration* 2, 134.

[50] Appellate Body Report, *United States–Final Anti-Dumping Measures on Stainless Steel from Mexico*, WT/DS344/AB/R, 30 April 2008, ¶160–62.

The Appellate Body in *China–Rare Earth* also confirmed that 'absent cogent reasons'[51] an adjudicatory body must resolve the same legal question in the same way in a subsequent case. If a party asks a panel to deviate from a prior finding on a question of law on the basis of novel legal arguments, a full exploration of those arguments may assist the DSB in the event of an appeal, particularly where those arguments raise complex legal issues. This could be of particular significance with respect to unilateral ad hoc procurement measures such as a 'matching clause', discussed further in Chapter 3.

A. Permitted Exceptions to GATT Obligations

Even if an anti-competitive government measure such as a local content requirement implemented through a buy-national policy is challenged under the DSB and found to be inconsistent with a GATT non-discrimination provision,[52] it may still be permitted as necessary under the General Exceptions pursuant to GATT Article XX. Exceptions from GATT commitments are permitted in tightly prescribed circumstances and only as necessary in the pursuit of specified purposes. These provisions acknowledge and accommodate other policy goals pursued by domestic laws and policy choices, and formulated in response to societal values and preferences. While the various exceptions Members pursue have little in common due to the specificity of domestic circumstances, Article XX seeks to provide a common framework to which these domestic policy choices and laws must conform in order to establish their compatibility to the overall WTO framework.

If a measure is challenged and found to be in violation of a GATT obligation, it is incumbent upon the respondent party to provide an affirmative defence to establish that the 'offending' measure is justified under the scope of one of the domestic policy objectives of Article XX.[53] The impact of international law here is thus not that of a direct regime of governance taking over from the sovereign state but on the governance functions of the state. Despite their acknowledgement of legitimate domestic non-economic policy objectives, these derogations still involve huge entanglements with domestic governance and administration.[54]

In order to justify a discriminatory crisis measure under Article XX, the defending government must first establish that the measure falls under the stated policy objective under the exception, and then it must prove that the measure is

[51] For more discussion on cogent reasons, see Appellate Body Report, *China–Measures Related to the Exportation of Rare Earths, Tungsten and Molybdenum*, WT/DS431/AB/R, WT/DS432/AB/R, WT/DS433/AB/R, 7 August 2014, ¶761.

[52] GATT Panel Report, *US–Section 337*, ¶5.9.

[53] Appellate Body Report, *US–Gasoline*, ¶22–23; Appellate Body Report *US–Wool Shirts and Blouses*, ¶15–16.

[54] JHH Weiler, 'The Geology of International Law' (2004) *Zeitschrift für ausländisches öffentliches Recht und Völkerrecht*, 64(3) 547–562.

necessary.[55] The initial legal focus is therefore on the nexus: the DSB must base its analysis on the finding that there is a rational connection between the challenged measure and the policy objective.[56] To pass this test, a process of 'weighing and balancing' a series of factors must take place to determine the importance of the objective, the contribution of the measure to that objective and the trade-restrictiveness of the measure.[57] This involves, 'in most cases', a *Tinbergian*-type comparison between the challenged measure and possible alternatives.

Yet while this provides a defensive strategy with regulatory discretion for a WTO Member government to pursue domestic goals, this legal framework still subtly reverses 'the internal order of values'.[58] For the burden of proving that a non-compliant measure is necessary resides with the responding party, while the complaining party has the onerous task of identifying any less trade-distorting alternative measure that, in its view, the responding party should have taken.[59] Further, after justifying domestic measures under any of the Article XX exceptions, one more competition test is required under the good faith requirements of the chapeau of Article XX. This test is to ensure that the measure is not to be applied in a manner that would constitute a means of arbitrary or unjustifiable discrimination:

> Subject to the requirement that such measures are not applied in a manner which would constitute a means of arbitrary or unjustifiable discrimination between countries where the same conditions prevail, or a disguised restriction on international trade, nothing in this Agreement shall be construed to prevent the adoption or enforcement by any contracting party of measures.

This competition requirement 'is of necessity, a heavier task than that involved in showing that an exception … encompasses the measure at issue'.[60] Discrimination will be seen as arbitrary or unjustifiable where 'alternative measures exist that would have avoided or at least diminished the discriminatory treatment'.[61] The Panel cited two Appellate Body Reports that also examined whether a WTO-consistent or less trade-restrictive alternative would be available; and whether it would enable the regulating Member to achieve its legitimate policy goals with the same degree of efficiency and efficacy while conducting the analysis under the chapeau of Article XX.[62] This results in two different necessity tests being applied

[55] Appellate Body Report, *US–Gasoline*, p 22.

[56] European Communities–Measures Prohibiting the Importation and Marketing of Seal Products, ¶2.139.

[57] Appellate Body Report, *US–Gambling*, ¶292.

[58] Weiler (n 54).

[59] There are, of course, limits to this exercise, for the responding party need not identify the universe of less-trade-restrictive alternative measures and then show that none of those measures achieves the desired objective, for indeed this would be 'an impracticable and impossible burden'. Appellate Body Report, *US–Gambling*, ¶309–11.

[60] See *US–Gasoline*, WT/DS2/AB/R, ¶23.

[61] Panel Report, *China–Measures Related to the Exportation of Rare Earths, Tungsten, and Molybdenum*, WT/DS431/R, ¶7.664.

[62] Appellate Body Reports, *US–Gasoline*, pp 25–29, DSR 1996:I, 3, pp 23–27, and *US–Shrimp*, ¶171.

to a measure justified under Article XX(a), the first one under a subparagraph, to determine whether the restrictive measure is necessary. The chapeau test then determines whether any discrimination produced by the restriction is necessary.

In the *India–Solar Cells* dispute, India submitted that its local content requirements for solar cells and modules were justified under Article XX(d) because they were integral to its compliance with both domestic and international law obligations to ensure ecologically sustainable growth while addressing India's energy security challenge, and ensuring compliance with its obligations relating to climate change, most notably under the UNFCCC. In examining India's attempt to invoke principles of international environmental law, the Appellate Body rejected the notion that the domestic environmental policies cited by India could constitute 'a "rule" to ensure ecologically sustainable growth'. It followed the Panel in opining that such provisions were 'hortatory, aspirational, declaratory, and at times solely descriptive'.[63] It also rejected the argument that the UNFCCC and the other international instruments cited by India were 'laws or regulations', on the grounds that these instruments had not been incorporated into India's domestic law or given direct effect. The Appellate Body in this case dismissed India's position that the domestic content requirements for solar were justified under this exception. The Appellate Body also dismissed India's justification of its' local content requirements (LCRs) under GATT Article XX(j) exceptions—as essential to the acquisition or distribution of productions in general or local short supply—on the grounds that the solar cell products are in short supply locally. The Appellate Body opined that in determining supply, India should take into account the quantity of available supply of a product from all domestic and international sources. Further, that consideration should be given to all relevant factors, including the availability of imports, the level of domestic production, potential price fluctuations in the relevant market, and the purchasing power of foreign and domestic consumers.

This assessment indicates that a non-compliant measure will be closely examined under the Article XX exceptions, from an allocative efficiency perspective, to ensure that there is no other less-restrictive alternative measure available, and that the non-compliant measures are not applied in a discriminatory manner. Nevertheless, under the GATT there is a legal avenue available for justifying non-compliant measures which are deemed necessary for domestic policy objectives.

[63] The Appellate Body noted that in determining whether a responding party had identified a rule that falls within the scope of 'laws or regulations' under GATT Art XX(d), a panel should consider factors such as '(i) the degree of normativity of the instrument and the extent to which the instrument operates to set out a rule of conduct or course of action that is to be observed within the domestic legal system of a Member; (ii) the degree of specificity of the relevant rule; (iii) whether the rule is legally enforceable, including, eg before a court of law; (iv) whether the rule has been adopted or recognized by a competent authority possessing the necessary powers under the domestic legal system of a Member; (v) the form and title given to any instrument or instruments containing the rule under the domestic legal system of a Member; and (vi) the penalties or sanctions that may accompany the relevant rule.' See B McGivern, Case Note.

V. Buy-Nationals under the Agreement on Subsidies and Countervailing Measures

One of the purposes of the ASCM is to regulate the provision of subsidies to domestic firms. For although the GATT Article III NT requirement prohibits discrimination between domestic and imported products,[64] pursuant to the Article III:8(b) derogation for subsidies, the Article III NT obligation will not apply to subsidies that are granted exclusively to domestic producers, unless they contain a component that introduces discrimination between imported and domestic products.[65]

Following a competition approach, the drafters of the ASCM understood that discriminatory government procurement policies could pose a competition problem very closely related to that of potentially trade-distorting subsidies.[66] This is clear for government procurement is listed alongside direct transfers of funds as one of the four categories of government measures deemed to be a financial contribution pursuant to Article 1:1(iv) ASCM. The negotiators sought to address the need to control government purchasing measures that potentially or actually[67] have adverse effects in the market—albeit only for the market for goods—alongside those financial contributions that governments apply to firms operating in open markets.

The ASCM offers a definition of a subsidy[68] which establishes a system for discriminating between prohibited, actionable and other subsidies. Article 1 stipulates that a subsidy exists if there is a financial contribution by a government or any public body within the territory of a Member,[69] or there is any form of income or price support[70] and a benefit is thereby conferred.[71] The Appellate Body has stressed that the financial contribution is separate from the benefit, and that these two elements together determine whether a subsidy exists.[72] That is, a subsidy exists only when the intervention in question satisfies all three elements of

64 WTO Panel Report, *Indonesia: Certain Measures Affecting the Automobile Industry*, WT/DS54/R, WT/DS55/R, WT/DS59/R, WT/DS64/R, adopted on 23 July 1998, ¶14.33.

65 WTO Panel Report, *Indonesia*, ibid, ¶ 14.43, 14.45, cited in Rubini, *The Definition of Subsidy and State Aid* (Oxford University Press, 2009) 415.

66 MJ Trebilcock and R Howse, *The Regulation of International Trade* (London, Routledge, 2005) 292.

67 The term 'goods' was interpreted by the Panel in the *US–Lumber III* dispute to refer to a 'very broad spectrum of things the government can provide—tangible or movable personal property, other than money and in general encompasses all in-kind contributions'. Report of the Panel, *United States–Preliminary Determinations with Respect to Certain Softwood Lumber from Canada*, WT/DS236/R, 27 September 2002, ('*US–Lumber III*'), ¶7.23–7.24.

68 The GATT and the Subsidies Code of 1979 did not provide an express definition of this term until ASCM Art I.1(iii).

69 Art 1.1(a)(1).

70 Art 1.1(a)(2).

71 Art 1.1(b).

72 Appellate Body, *Brazil–Aircraft*, ¶157, *Canada–Aircraft*, ¶156.

this test.[73] Although a benefit is not explicitly defined, four examples are set out as guidance for calculating benefits under Article 14 ASCM. Under these guidelines, a conferral benefit may occur when a government practice involves a direct transfer of funds—as in a bailout grant, or loan, and potential direct transfers of funds or liabilities, such as bailout loan guarantees, as well as when a government purchases or provides goods or services other than general infrastructure.

A financial contribution must make the recipient 'better off'.[74] The appropriate basis for comparison to identify its trade-distorting potential is the open marketplace. If no advantage can be found—for example, when a government body purchases goods and services at a market price—then there can be no benefit and therefore no subsidy exists.[75] If no benefit can be found, such as when a government body purchases goods and services at a market price, there can be no benefit and therefore no subsidy exists. As Luca Rubini notes:

> [T]he objective of the benefit analysis, which is broadly the same of the definition of subsidy, is fairly simple. It is there to capture those measures that have the potential to distort trade. No more, no less. No comprehensive analysis to conclusively determine whether this potential has translated into actual harm is necessary; no consideration of the redeeming, even if legitimate, objectives of the measures is permitted.

Much controversy was caused, therefore, when the Appellate Body in the WTO *Canada–FIT* dispute declared in the face of substantial existing legal opinion that Ontario's local content requirements were not conferring a benefit under the ASCM Article 3 Prohibition:

> ASCM Article 3
>
> 3.1 Except as provided in the Agreement on Agriculture, the following subsidies, within the meaning of Article 1, shall be prohibited:
>
> (a) subsidies contingent, in law or in fact, whether solely or as one of several other conditions, upon export performance, including those illustrated in Annex I5;
> (b) *subsidies contingent, whether solely or as one of several other conditions, upon the use of domestic over imported goods.*
>
> 3.2 A Member shall neither grant nor maintain subsidies referred to in paragraph 1. (emphasis added)

[73] The Panel Report from *US–Export Restraints as Subsidies* suggests that the introduction of the two-part definition of subsidy, consisting of 'financial contribution' and 'benefit', was intended specifically to prevent the countervailing of benefits from any sort of formal, enforceable government measures, by restricting to a finite list the kinds of government measures that would, if they conferred benefits, constitute subsidies. See Report of the Panel, *United States–Measures Treating Export Restraints as Subsidies*, June 2001, ¶8.73.

[74] Appellate Body Report, *Canada–Aircraft*, ¶157.

[75] This was reinforced by the *EC–Drams* Panel finding that: 'In sum, if the financial contribution is not provided by the government (or directed or entrusted by the government), it is of no concern to us. If the financial contribution is provided (or directed or entrusted) by the government but still does not confer an advantage over what was available on the market, there is no need to discipline such government behaviour which lacks a trade distorting potential.' *European Communities–Countervailing Measures on Dynamic Random Access Memory Chips from Korea*, ¶7.175.

Typically, any financially beneficial intervention that is contingent on export performance or the use of domestic over imported products, such as the local content requirement in a buy-national policy, is viewed as particularly egregious and consequently prohibited under Article 3.[76] The general rationale for this irrebuttable impact standard is that the occurrence of serious negative externalities is presumed for both of these two types of subsidies;[77] there is no need to establish any distortion in any sense. Prohibited subsidies raise serious concerns from a competition perspective, including: political rows, global allocative inefficiencies and obstructing market access. Such a prohibited subsidy must be withdrawn. Indeed, Article 4 ASCM even sets up a rapid (three-month) dispute settlement mechanism for complaints regarding such prohibited subsidies.

The Appellate Body findings in the *Canada–FIT* dispute were subsequently denounced as anticlimactic, confusing when benefits are to be pursued under WTO subsidy law. In addition to the lack of doctrinal agreement as to whether a government procurement that is deemed to confer a subsidy prohibited under the ASCM can be defended under the GATT or WTO GPA exceptions, there is now also further ambiguity as to when an offset will be considered a benefit. Obfuscation is also caused by the combination of the Panel's margin of discretion: first, to determine the sequencing of the agreements being interpreted during a disputel and, second, to exercise judicial economy to curtail the interpretation of several applicable agreements if a measure has already been found to violate one of them. For as the Appellate Body stated in the *Wool Shirts and Blouses* dispute:

> Nothing in [Article 11 of the DSU] or in previous GATT practice requires a panel to examine all legal claims made by the complaining party. … Thus, if a panel found that a measure was inconsistent with a particular provision of the GATT 1947, it generally did not go on to examine whether the measure was also inconsistent with other GATT provisions that a complaining party may have argued were violated. In recent WTO practice, panels likewise have refrained from examining each and every claim made by the complaining party and have made findings only on those claims that such panels concluded were necessary to resolve the particular matter.

However, as the Panel Report to the *India–Autos* dispute observed, the order selected for examination of the claims may have an impact on the potential to apply judicial economy. While some judicial discretion is unavoidable because no law can anticipate every situation or breach, the degree of discretion afforded could be seen to produce a commensurate degree of legal uncertainty. It is also clear that too much uncertainty, coupled with an undefined use of judicial economy, can operate to undermine transparency and good policy-making, and,

[76] ASCM Art 3.2 states: 'A Member shall neither grant nor maintain subsidies referred to in paragraph 1.'

[77] Rubini questions such a presumptive approach erroneously because it suggests that export subsidies and local content requirements have equivalent effects. See L Rubini, *The Definition of Subsidy and State Aid* (Oxford, Oxford University Press, 2009) 402.

moreover, the future use of the WTO DSB to resolve trade disputes falling under these agreements.

A. The Regulation of Bailouts under the ASCM

The ASCM operates as an important competition framework to regulate government distortions or potential distortions of competition and international trade in goods. This is why the legal gap left by the expiration of the provisional Article 8 is so significant. The agreement can no longer expressly permit the possibility that governments can use some subsidies constructively. That, for example, *good* subsidies may remedy market failures or legitimate domestic policy challenges during a severe systemic crisis. The provisional Article 8 rendered certain non-specific subsidies such as R&D, regional development and environmental adaptation subsidies as immune from WTO remedies and the imposition of countervailing duties because they were seen to be only minimally trade distorting. However, since Article 8 was not renewed due to lack of consensus among the WTO Members, unlike the exceptions provided for under GATT Article XX, GATS Article XIV and GPA Article XXIII, the ASCM is allowed to operate without explicit exemptions through which to justify a legitimate but non-compliant domestic policy measure. There is still no doctrinal agreement as to whether a procurement that is deemed to confer a subsidy prohibited under the ASCM could potentially be defended under the GATT Article XX list of exceptions.[78]

Of note, in this regard, is the *Canada–FIT* Appellate Body finding that the decision as to sequencing, or whether to commence the analysis with the claims under the ASCM or under GATT, fell within the Panel's margin of discretion.[79] As a result, it is not clear how a Panel would treat a procurement measure under the ASCM if it had already been successfully defended under a GPA exemption. There is no presumption of compliance with the ASCM if a measure has been permitted under the WTO GPA, or vice versa. This uncertainty undermines a fully integrated framework for regulating public restrictions of competition in public and private markets for goods. All that is known is that the relationship between the GATT and other Annex 1A agreements, which includes the ASCM, shall be considered on a case-by-case basis.[80] This detracts from legal certainty and transparency in the use of domestic policy measures to address democratically endorsed domestic policy objectives within the framework of the WTO. It also detracts from use of the DSB for fear of legal interpretations that may have unforeseen repercussions for the future legality of other domestic measures. This has consequences for the enforcement of the ASCM.

Other, practical, methodological complexities exist. Under the WTO GPA, procurement is defined pursuant to Article II as procurement for governmental

[78] See eg BJ Condon, 'Climate Change and Unresolved Issues in WTO Law' (2009) 12 *Journal of International Economic Law* 895.

[79] Appellate Body Report, *Canada–FIT*, ¶5.8, citing Appellate Body Report, *EC–Bananas III*, ¶204.

[80] Appellate Body Report, *Brazil–Desiccated Coconut*, ¶13.

purposes of goods, services, or any combination thereof. That is, for the purposes of the coverage of the WTO GPA, it does not matter whether the procurement is for goods or services or both. Rather it is the value thresholds and the particular entities at central and sub-central levels of government, set out in the Appendix, that are the major determinants of the coverage of the agreement. This results in further discrepancies between the applicable agreements. If a challenged procurement measure falls under the scrutiny of the ASCM, the scope of those obligations applies only to the goods part of a procurement that may include both goods and services elements. Yet governments can procure services in combination with physical goods, such as processing, assembly or labelling. Identifying and unbundling the goods-only portion of a build–operate–transfer project[81] in order to determine if a benefit has been conferred under the ASCM is complex. In the *US–Large Civil Aircraft* dispute, the Panel considered whether excluding purchases of services from the scope of ASCM Article 1:1(a)(1) would run counter to the overall object and purpose of the Agreement by creating 'an enormous loophole in the coverage of the SCM Agreement and provide WTO Members with a roadmap for distorting trade in goods through "service contracts" with their goods producers'.[82] The Panel considered that:

> [T]he question of whether or not a transaction is properly characterized as a 'purchase of services' depends on whether or not the work performed was principally for the benefit or use of the government (or unrelated third parties), or rather principally for the benefit or use of the 'service' 'seller' itself.[83]

However, on appeal the Appellate Body concluded the Panel's interpretation that 'transactions properly characterized as purchases of services are excluded from the scope of Article 1.1(a)(1)(i) of the SCM Agreement' to be moot and of no legal effect.[84] It is consequently evident that while the WTO GPA works coherently as a stand-alone agreement, both legal and methodological difficulties arise when regulating the same procurement measure under the other applicable WTO agreements.

VI. Competition Policy under the GATS: Bailouts and Buy-Nationals

The GATS regime also includes non-discrimination provisions to prevent government restrictions of competition in services markets. This framework has a

[81] For further information on the World Bank definition of build–operate–transfer (BOT), see http://ppp.worldbank.org/public-private-partnership/agreements/concessions-bots-dbos.

[82] Panel Report, *United States–Measures Affecting Trade in Large Civil Aircraft* (2nd complaint), WT/DS353/R, 31 March 2011, ¶VII.12.

[83] ibid, ¶VII.79.

[84] Appellate Body Report, *US–Large Civil Aircraft* (2nd complaint), 12 March 2012, ¶620.

narrower scope of application because although GATS Article XVII contains a NT provision to prohibit discriminatory government measures,[85] it functions in a different and less ambitious manner than under the GATT Article III.[86] Rather than serve as a principle of general application, it is to be applied only when a specific commitment has been made and recorded in the national schedules that form an integral part of the GATS Agreement. The GATS interpretation of the no less favourable treatment standard is built into the NT provision of the Agreement itself.[87] Where GATS NT provisions are applicable, they are limited to imported goods or services or foreign firms supplying services on the domestic market.[88]

As regards MFN, it was found during the *EC–Bananas* dispute that the GATS MFN 'no less favourable' requirement, with regard to formally identical or formally different treatment and conditions of competition, should be understood to be relevant to the interpretation of the MFN obligation of Article II of the GATS.[89] Article VIII GATS regulating monopolies and exclusive service suppliers also includes an explicit MFN requirement in paragraph 1.

The GATS regime also permits exceptions to these non-discrimination principles, under Article XIV, including those necessary to protect public morals under the scope of paragraph (a). There is a close similarity between the Article XIV GATS exceptions and those exceptions under GATT Article XX noted above.[90] The chapeau language is almost replicated, and to a lesser extent the text of the provisions. However, the language of the public order exception under Article XIV GATS identifies the maintenance of public order as an additional justification. A footnote to these exceptions under Article XIV(a) states that the public order exception may be invoked only when a genuine and sufficiently serious threat is posed to one of the fundamental interests of society. This provides greater regulatory autonomy than under the GATT as evinced by the DSB findings in the *US–Gambling* dispute.[91]

[85] Under Art XVII.3 'formally identical or formally different treatment shall be considered to be less favourable if it modifies the conditions of competition in favour of services or service suppliers of the Member compared to like services or service suppliers of any other Member'.

[86] GATS Art XVII applies in respect of 'all measures affecting the supply of services'. Art XXVIII defines a 'measure' to mean 'any measure by a Member, whether in the form of a law, regulation, rule, procedure, decision, administrative action, or any other form'. See Appellate Body Report, *EC–Regime for the Importation, Sale and Distribution of Bananas*, ¶220.

[87] Para 3 of GATS Art XVII states that: 'Formally identical or formally different treatment shall be considered to be less favourable if it modifies the conditions of competition in favour of services or service suppliers of the Member compared to like services or service suppliers of any other Member.'

[88] The definition of the service suppliers of other Members set out in Art XXVIII includes natural persons of other Members and, broadly speaking, local subsidiaries or branches of foreign-owned or controlled companies. That is, the NT provision does not apply to the treatment of goods and services destined for the supply of foreign markets through exportation.

[89] *EC–Regime for the Importation, Sale and Distribution of Bananas*, WT/DS27/R/USA, ¶7.298–7.304.

[90] The Appellate Body Report findings in the *US–Gambling* case confirmed the relevance of Art XX GATT to the interpretation of Art XIV: see ¶291.

[91] See Panel Report, *US–Gambling*, ¶6.467; and Appellate Body Report, *US–Gambling*, ¶323.

Compared to GATT, the GATS follows a relatively flexible approach, allowing countries to take policy goals into account in shaping specific commitments. This is in part due to the absence of border measures; without these, market access and NT obligations assume a fundamentally different and more flexible role.[92] It could therefore be expected that the invocation of these exceptions will be less frequent than under GATT. On the other hand, the regulation of services often deals with domestically sensitive issues and transcends concerns of market access, requiring different, more detailed language than under GATT 1994. For instance, the GATS general exceptions also include provisions relating to the protection of fair competition in all areas of particular importance to the regulation of services.

A. The GATS Annex on Financial Services

Within the GATS Annex on Financial Services, a prudential provision is included which stipulates that:

> Notwithstanding any other provisions of the Agreement, a Member *shall not be prevented from taking measures for prudential reasons*, including for the protection of investors, depositors, policy holders or persons to whom a fiduciary duty is owed by a financial service supplier, or to ensure the integrity and stability of the financial system. Where such measures do not conform with the provisions of the Agreement, they shall not be used as a means of avoiding the Member's commitments or obligations under the Agreement. (emphasis added)

While only applicable to those Members who signed up to the Annex on Financial Services (see Chapter 6), paragraph 2 acts as a safe haven for any measure falling within its ambit that might otherwise violate other provisions of the GATS. Its first sentence indicates that a signatory may impose any subsidy measure for 'prudential reasons'. This is even if these measures would otherwise violate other GATS provisions, including the market access or non-discrimination provisions. Paragraph 2 offers an indicative list of prudential reasons that includes both protection of persons and the preservation of the system. Again, this offers Members considerable discretion to implement diverse measures.

Unlike the exceptions set out under Article XX GATT discussed above, paragraph 2 does not require the implementing Member to prove the measure is either 'necessary' or 'the least trade restrictive reasonably available' to maintain, for example, the integrity of the system. Arguably, however, the requirement that a measure adopted for prudential reasons should not be used as a means of avoiding other obligations under the Agreements functions in place of the chapeau to prevent any anti-competitive abuse of this provision.[93] In other words, while the

[92] T Cottier, P Delimitatsis and N Diebold, 'Art XIV Exceptions', available at: http://ssrn.com/abstract=1280215.

[93] See EH Leroux, 'Trade in Financial Services under the World Trade Organization' (2002) 36(3) *Journal of World Trade* 413, 430–31.

exception confers Members certain leeway to depart from their commitments in order to regulate for prudential reasons, it imposes certain limits to do so in order to avoid the adoption of measures disguised as prudential but which in effect are purely or primarily protectionist.[94] The prudential exception does not make any requirements on notification or consultation, and subject to the stipulations of the chapeau, it can be applied for an indefinite period of time.

While broad, the discretion offered to financial bailout measures under paragraph 2 of the Annex is not, however, limitless. The second sentence has been described as an 'anti-avoidance' provision, designed to prevent abuse of opportunities provided in the first sentence. It sets a good-faith standard which prevents the implementation of measures with primarily protectionist effects,[95] or as a means of avoiding other GATS obligations. Paragraph 4 also indicates that not only is the WTO DSM applicable if a 'prudential' measure violates a Member's obligations or commitments under the GATS, but also that Panels must have the necessary expertise in the specific financial service under dispute.

B. The GATS and Subsidy Control: Bank Bailouts

Article XV GATS recognises that subsidies, such as bank bailout measures, may in some circumstances have distortionary effects on the trade in services. However, beyond this, the current GATS provision merely permits, but does not compel, WTO Members to enter into negotiations with a view to developing the necessary rules to avoid distortions caused by subsidies. As discussed, the trade in services is not covered by the ASCM, whereas under GATS Article XV, footnote 7 sets out the need for a future work programme that shall determine how, and in what time frame, negotiations on such multilateral disciplines will be conducted.

Another soft provision is the consultation mechanism incorporated in Article XV:2, which states that:

> Any Member which considers that it is adversely affected by a subsidy of another Member may request consultations with that Member on such matters. Such requests shall be accorded sympathetic consideration.

However, no further details are provided on what can be considered sympathetic consideration.

As such, beyond displaying good faith towards the theoretical notion of removing distortionary subsidies to the trade in services, this provision provides little

[94] See the IEL blog at http://worldtradelaw.typepad.com/ielpblog/2010/05/global-trade-watch-on-the-prudential-carve-out.html.

[95] See Leroux (n 93) and A von Bogdandy and J Windsor, 'Annex on Financial Services', in R Wolfrum, P-T Stoll and C Feinäugle (eds) *Max Planck Commentaries on World Trade Law, WTO—Trade in services* (Leiden and Boston, MA, Martinus Nijhoff, 2008) vol 6, 640–666.

compulsion to force Members even to enter into negotiations as regards subsidy control in the GATS.

C. The GATS and Government Procurement

The scope of application is at first sight straightforward as regards government procurement measures and the rules on the international trade in services. For GATS Article XIII:1 explicitly excludes government procurement from the application of the GATS obligations, Instead, GATS Article XIII:2 provides that new multilateral negotiations on government procurement of services should commence within two years of the GATS coming into force. The Working Party on GATS rules duly began discussions in December 1995 on the government procurement of services—along with two other mandated issues on establishment of an emergency safeguards mechanism for services and disciplines on subsidies. However, to date it has not made any substantive progress of relevance to this research.

Subsidies are mentioned under GATS Article XV, which recognizes that, in certain circumstances, subsidies may have distortive effects on trade in services. However, beyond a requirement that Members shall enter into negotiations with a view to developing the necessary multilateral disciplines to avoid such trade-distortive effects, this provisions merely requires an exchange of information on Members subsidies provided to domestic services suppliers that relate to trade in services. Notwithstanding this, a subsidy that is applied to services markets will still be subject to non-discriminatory obligations under GATS Article II, if that service has been scheduled under the GATS.

Further, even though government procurement is explicitly excluded from the core provisions of the GATS, the GATS remains highly relevant for procurement coverage under the WTO GPA. This is because the WTO GPA itself deals only with government procurement policies; it cannot address measures such as trade restrictions that affect the ability of foreign enterprises to sell services to governments.[96] There thus remains a 'relationship of correspondence' between the GATS and the WTO GPA:[97] any access to procurement markets under the WTO GPA is conditioned and constrained by the GATS schedules and, consequently, by the application of the MFN principle operating within the GATS.[98]

In sum, this overview indicates that while the GATS has excluded both subsidies and government procurement from its coverage, there are various complexities to these formal exclusions. Not only is procurement increasingly a combination of goods and services, but the WTO GPA and GATS are intimately

[96] See K Dawar, 'The WTO Government Procurement Agreement: The Most-Favoured Nation Principle, the GATS and Regionalism' (2015) 42 *Legal Issues of Economic Integration* 257.

[97] Blank and Marceau (n 43) 48.

[98] K Dawar (n 96) 257–280.

connected through their relationship of correspondence, which conditions the services markets that can be incorporated into each party's WTO GPA schedules. Nevertheless, it remains the case that a direct challenge to a government measure that imposes anti-competitive restrictions on another Member's market access to its public procurement of services, or open markets for services, is not yet possible under the GATS.

VII. The WTO Government Procurement Agreement and Competition

As discussed above, the GATT Article III:8(a) NT derogation expressly excludes government procurement. In search of a framework for liberalising procurement markets and setting minimum standards, certain GATT contracting parties negotiated a Government Procurement Code during the Tokyo Round.[99] The Code erected a rudimentary framework to open and regulate government procurement markets among its relatively limited membership.[100] The Procurement Code was unprecedented in applying the fundamental non-discrimination obligations discussed above to procurement of goods above a certain threshold by central government entities of those signatory countries. It laid down procedural provisions, including transparency requirements and multilateral dispute settlement procedures as well as special and differential treatment for developing countries. The Code also indicated that governments required legitimate flexibilities to promote domestic policy objectives and thus permitted exclusions of certain products provided they were identified at the time of the coverage negotiations.

While the Procurement Code was a landmark in creating international disciplines for government procurement, it remained limited in membership and narrow in scope and coverage. The Code was only applicable to the procurement of goods the value of which fell above a certain threshold. Moreover, it only applied to the purchasing of central government entities, rather than including sub-central government purchasing. So, in the case of the USA, only federal procurement above a fixed value threshold was subject to the obligations of the Code. There were both substantive and procedural ambiguities in the text that DSB reports were unable to resolve.[101] For instance, the GATT *Sonar Mapping System* dispute indicated that

[99] It was signed on 12 April 1979, as part of the text of the Tokyo Round Agreements negotiated under the GATT. It became effective on 1 January 1981, and was first amended by the Protocol of 2 February 1987, which came into force on 14 February 1988. GATT, BISD 33S/190 [1987].

[100] The Code was signed by twelve GATT parties: nine developed countries—Austria, Canada, the EC (consisting of Belgium, France, the Netherlands, Germany, Luxembourg, the UK, Ireland, Denmark, Italy, Greece), Finland, Japan, Norway, Sweden, Switzerland, the USA—and three developing countries—Israel, Singapore and Hong Kong.

[101] M Footer, 'International Developments: GATT: Developments in Government Procurement Procedures and Practices' (1993) 6 *Public Procurement Law Review* CS193.

the coverage of the agreement excluded 'services' except where 'incidental to the supply of products'; yet also that it did include the procurement of products incidental to the procurement of services.[102] The *Trondheim Toll System* dispute further suggested that the requirement for domestic bid challenge procedures did not include the need for disappointed bidders to challenge any aspect of the procurement process under the administrative decisions taken by any contract-awarding authorities along with appropriate remedies and interim measures.[103]

The 1994 and 2011 WTO GPA negotiators continued to address these concerns by significantly expanding the scope and coverage of the previous treaty to include the procurement of services as well as goods and to cover sub-central entities and a number of utilities as well. Under the WTO GPA, procurement is defined pursuant to Article II as:

> Procurement for governmental purposes:
>
> (a) Of goods, services, *or any combination thereof*. (emphasis added)

That is, as discussed above with reference to the ASCM, for the purposes of the coverage of the WTO GPA, it does not matter whether the procurement is for goods or services or a combination of both. Rather it is the value thresholds and the particular entities at central and sub-central levels of government, set out in the Appendix, that are the major determinants of the coverage of the agreement. The coverage of the Agreement is set out for each signatory party in its Appendix I. This Appendix is divided into five Annexes concerning the specific coverage of the obligations.[104] These Annexes are negotiated along four basic parameters consisting of: (i) the value of procurement—covering only contracts estimated to exceed a certain value threshold; (ii) the identity of the procuring entity—covering only those listed by each party in its annexes; (iii) the type of goods or services procured—consisting of all goods, apart from some expressly excluded by each party, and only services listed by each party in its annexes; and (iv) the origin of the goods or services—including only countries that are GPA parties.[105] The five Annexes typically also contain General Notes that further qualify the application of the Agreement.

The enforceability of the GPA was also strengthened in response to noted arbitration deficiencies. A new provision required domestic bid challenge procedures, as well as the application of the WTO Dispute Settlement Mechanism for inter-state disputes over the implementation of the agreement. The drafters of the WTO GPA text created some more negotiating momentum through including a

[102] United States–Procurement of a Sonar Mapping System (GPR.DS1/R).

[103] Norway–Tendering Procedures on Trondheim Toll Ring Project (BISD 40S/319).

[104] The Annexes address (1) central government entities covered by the Agreement; (2) covered sub-central government entities; (3) 'other' covered entities (eg utilities); (4) services coverage; and (5) coverage of construction services.

[105] A Reich, 'The New GATT Agreement on Government Procurement: The Pitfalls of Plurilateralism and Strict Reciprocity' (1997) 31 *Journal of World Trade* 125.

commitment to review the agreement with a view to further increasing its scope and coverage.[106] Subsequently, albeit seventeen years later, the signatories to the 1994 GPA agreed to adopt a revised GPA text in 2011. For while the 2011 text of the agreement had been provisionally adopted in 2006, it could not enter into force until a conclusion was also reached in the related negotiations on the extension of the market access parameters.[107]

A. Competition Policy under the WTO GPA

As with the GATT, competition policy is also embedded into the WTO GPA legal framework. Article III of the WTO GPA sets out both NT and MFN requirements for the signatory parties' procurement measures in one short article that requires that all the signatory parties provide immediately and unconditionally treatment that is no less favourable than that it accords to domestic products, services and suppliers. In addition to these non-discrimination requirements, the WTO GPA also explicitly prohibits the use of offsets, under Article V, with limited exceptions of developing countries. These non-discrimination requirements are bolstered by minimum standards to ensure the tender process is open and competitive, including commitments to publish and widely advertise sufficient information about procurement opportunities.

Transparency provisions are also included that incorporate four main aspects: (i) ensuring adequate publicity for contract opportunities; (ii) ensuring public availability and knowledge of rules governing award procedures; (iii) providing the basis for a rules-based procurement system by limiting the discretionary power of procurement authorities; and (iv) providing opportunities for interested parties to verify and enforce the correct rules.[108] Additional rules under Article X require technical specifications and tender documentation to prevent anti-competitive discrimination in the design of contract specifications curtailing

[106] Art XXIV:7 subparagraphs (b) and (c) stipulate: '(b) Not later than the end of the third year from the date of entry into force of this Agreement and periodically thereafter, the Parties thereto shall undertake further negotiations, with a view to improving this Agreement and achieving the greatest possible extension of its coverage among all Parties on the basis of mutual reciprocity, having regard to the provisions of Art V relating to developing countries. (c) Parties shall seek to avoid introducing or prolonging discriminatory measures and practices which distort open procurement and shall, in the context of negotiations under subparagraph (b), seek to eliminate those which remain on the date of entry into force of this Agreement.'

[107] See 'Decision on the Outcomes of the Negotiations under Art XXIV:7 of the Agreement on Government Procurement, GPA/112 of 16 December 2011', available at www.wto.org/english/tratop_e/gproc_e/negotiations_e.htm.

[108] See S Arrowsmith, 'The Revised Agreement on Government Procurement: Changes to the Procedural Rules and Other Transparency Provisions' in S Arrowsmith and RD Anderson (eds), *The WTO Regime on Government Procurement: Challenge and Reform* (Cambridge, Cambridge University Press, 2011) ch 10.

competition. The prescription of technical specifications should be based, where appropriate, in terms of performance and functional requirements, rather than on design or descriptive characteristics, logos or patents. They should also be based, where existing, on international standards, otherwise, on national technical regulations, recognised national standards, or codes, 'or equivalent'.[109]

As with the GATT and the GATS, there are also general and security exceptions to the WTO GPA requirements included under Article XXIII. These are subject to similar certain non-discrimination requirements to GATT Article XX and GATS Article V, through the requirement that the application of a necessary but non-compliant government intervention does not constitute arbitrary discrimination.

B. Enforcing the Rules: The WTO GPA Dispute Settlement Mechanism

It is one thing for a country to sign up to a treaty and quite another to enforce compliance with it.[110] The WTO GPA contains a two-track system of dispute resolution—as an inter-governmental body, the WTO legal framework does not provide standing for individuals or companies to bring a complaint under the DSU concerned with the implementing measures of the agreement.[111] First, at the domestic level there is another avenue for private parties to challenge a bid believed to breach the rules of a particular procurement tender process. It is widely acknowledged that an effective domestic review mechanism for disappointed bidders establishes an invaluable transparency, self-policing and accountability mechanism within the government procurement system itself.[112] The most effective means of enforcement of the procurement rules is to enable citizens themselves—as the suppliers that deal with the government's procuring agencies—to police compliance with the provisions of the agreement. As beneficiaries of the regime, they are in the best position to detect violations and they will typically have the most incentive to challenge them.

Second, at the plurilateral level, there is an avenue for inter-party dispute resolution over the application of the agreement. The WTO dispute settlement system also has the authority to settle disputes arising over implementation of the

[109] Art X:3.

[110] Guzman and Pauwelyn (n 20) 115.

[111] The WTO's Dispute Settlement Understanding is contained in Annex 2 of the 'Final Act Embodying the Results of the Uruguay Round of Multilateral Trade Negotiations', 15 April 1994, Legal Instruments, *Results of the Uruguay Round of Multilateral Trade Negotiations, I* (GATT Secretariat (1994) 33 ILM 1140–272).

[112] See, for example: SL Arrowsmith, J Linarelli and D Wallace, Jr, *Regulating Public Procurement: National and International Perspectives* (The Hague, Kluwer Law International, 2000) ch 12 'Enforcement and Remedies'; DI Gordon, 'Constructing a Bid Protest Process: Choices Every Procurement Challenge System Must Make' (2006) 35 *Public Contract Law Journal*; George Washington University Law School Public Law Research Paper no 200.

WTO GPA.[113] Any government that is a party to the WTO GPA, and considers that a benefit accruing to it from the provisions of the agreement are being nullified or impaired—directly or indirectly—may duly notify the WTO DSB. As discussed further in Part III of this book, the DSB then has the authority to settle the dispute within the terms of the WTO DSU.[114] However, because the WTO GPA is a plurilateral agreement outside of the WTO's multilateral 'covered agreements', there is no possibility of suspending benefits from another WTO agreement as a remedy under the WTO GPA. This reduces the potential remedies available for enforcing these rules in the event of non-compliance.

VIII. Conclusions

This chapter's examination of the WTO regulation that seeks to prevent public distortions of competition in open and procurement markets indicates that GATT Article III contains explicit derogations for both the government procurement of goods and subsidies. These derogations have traditionally, but not unquestionably, been exported to exempt both subsidies and procurement measures from the scope of Article I MFN. However, as the *Canada–FIT* and *India–Solar Cell* WTO disputes highlighted, the lines between public procurement and other trade measures and markets are often blurred, particularly when governments seek to promote new markets or correct market failures in open markets.

The plurilateral GPA similarly incorporates non-discrimination requirements to prohibit anti-competitive distortions to trade that favour domestic bidder/producer interests in procurement markets. These are strengthened by the inclusion of minimum standards to ensure the tender process is open and competitive, and requirements to guarantee that technical design specifications do not curtail competition. It also explicitly prohibits the use of offsets in Article V, although with limited exemptions to this for developing country signatory parties. The Agreement's security and general exceptions are available to all the signatory parties but, again, these are subject to the non-discrimination requirement. Exceptions are only permitted if they are justified as necessary to protect specified public policy objectives, and do not discriminate in their application.

At first sight, this approach seems to be comprehensive and integrated in covering goods, services or any combination thereof. However, under the plurilateral GPA the coverage of procurement markets and the number of signatory parties are relatively low. The Agreement regulates public distortions of competition in

[113] Art XX of the WTO GPA states that provisions of the WTO DSU Understanding on Rules and Procedures Governing the Settlement of Disputes under the WTO Agreement are also to be applicable to the disputes concerning the WTO GPA.

[114] See Art XXII Consultations and Dispute Settlement.

procurement markets but the rules only apply to those covered procurements set out in the Annexes to the Agreement and those above the negotiated de minimis value thresholds. The *Canada–FIT* dispute was significant in demonstrating that whether or not a government is a signatory party of the WTO GPA, and whether or not it has explicitly excluded particular sectors from the coverage of the GPA, the ASCM will remain applicable to all WTO Members' procurement measures. That is, the WTO GPA does not provide a safe haven to the procurement of the signatory parties excluded from the Appendices and Annexes; it merely provides a framework for liberalising international procurement markets.

The ASCM framework on the other hand, will address any challenged distortions that government purchasing rules and practice can generate in the market for goods, in addition to other types of government-conferred benefits. As a result of this cumulative nature of the WTO agreements, the ASCM does provide a somewhat integrated approach to the control of government restriction of competition in public and private markets—but not for services. That is, the WTO legal framework partially acknowledges that these discriminatory government practices can engender the same effects that competition rules seek to prevent and therefore requires a coherent approach to both sets of regulation.

Nevertheless, this chapter submits that given the significant role of the ASCM in regulating competition in both public and private markets, there are gaps and ambiguities that require clarification for the benefit of both the WTO Members and for the strength of the legal framework itself. This is most notably with regard to the coverage of services, and equally the availability of general exceptions to these obligations for certain subsidies. For while certain discriminatory procurement policies may be sanctioned through the GATT and GPA General and Security exceptions, this option is not self-evident for the ASCM, even though its application is cumulative. Legal uncertainty is a constraint on domestic decision-making, and coherent economic management. Uncertainty as to the probable outcome of a dispute over a domestic measure seeking to address legitimate policy objectives may also produce regulatory chill or impact on the level of implementation and enforcement of the agreement itself. This ultimately serves to detract from the WTO's efforts to preserve competition in both public procurement and open markets.

As a point of comparison with this focus on the GATT/WTO framework, the following chapter examines whether and how regional trade agreements seek to regulate anti-competitive state practices in open and procurement markets.

3

The Regional Rules

I. Overview

Building on the analysis of the international competition policy rules in the previous chapter, this chapter identifies the regional laws that the case study countries have agreed upon to prevent unilateral bailout and buy-national policies. Chapter 3 begins by examining the black letter law of the procurement and competition/State aid rules the case study countries have agreed upon in selected RTAs. The chapter continues this book's holistic approach, to understand more about the interface between these two traditionally distinct market regulations. The objective here is to assess those rules aimed at preventing anti-competitive bailout and buy-national measures in both public procurement and open markets at the regional level. Therefore, only those RTAs that feature both sets of regulation are directly instructive. The taxonomy and selection of agreements for analysis in this research thus differ in important ways from existing studies.[1]

After conducting an assessment of the RTA provisions that have included subsidy control and procurement regulation, the chapter confirms that the TFEU regulatory framework has the most comprehensive integrated regime to regulate government measures that distort competition in both procurement and open markets. The chapter consequently uses the TFEU and the WTO framework discussed in the previous chapter as points of analytic comparison.

Chapter 3 closes by highlighting the main doctrinal findings from this black-letter law assessment, noting the main gaps and weaknesses in the existing legal frameworks to prevent state measures that distort the conditions of competition in both public and private markets. The chapter concludes that with the qualified exception of the TFEU in the EU, an integrated framework to condition public restraints of competition has yet to be established at the regional level. The results of this chapter highlight the weaknesses of these regional laws in reining in the

[1] H Horn, PC Mavroidis and A Sapir, *Beyond the WTO? An Anatomy of EU and US Preferential Trade Agreements* (Brussels, Bruegel, 2009).

anti-competitive behaviour of the public sector in both open markets as well as public procurement markets.

II. Selecting the RTAs for Assessment

Table 3.1 sets out the eighteen RTAs concluded by the case study countries that include provisions to prevent anti-competitive state measures in *both* public and private markets. Table 3.1 indicates that four of these RTAs are signed by the USA, and a further 11 by the EU, including the TFEU itself. India is a party to two agreements, while Brazil is a party to only one of the RTAs identified through the WTO RTA database. All of these agreements are in force and all of them were signed after the year 2000.

Table 3.1 breaks down the relevant substantive provisions in these 18 RTAs of interest to this research.[2] In the area of public restrictions of competition, the table indicates whether the agreement includes:

— subsidy/State aid/public aid rules applicable to goods;
— subsidy/State aid/public aid rules applicable to services;
— exceptions and exclusions from the scope of the obligation;
— a requirement for a dispute settlement mechanism.

The specific government procurement provisions of interest to this research include

— MFN and NT non-discrimination obligations for government procurement rules for goods;
— MFN and NT non-discrimination obligations for government procurement rules for services;
— offset prohibitions;
— exemptions for subsidies;
— exceptions and carve outs;
— a requirement for a domestic bid challenge mechanism;
— a requirement for a state-to-state dispute settlement mechanism.

[2] This analysis excludes an examination of the frameworks regulating agriculture, investment and intellectual property rights.

Table 3.1: Selected RTA provisions regulating public restraints of competition

RTA	Subsidy / state aid rules for goods	Exceptions	Exclusions	Dispute settlement	Subsidy / state aid rules for services	Procurement provisions in services	Procurement of goods provisions: NT and MFN	Procurement bid challenge mechanism	Offsets prohibition	Exceptions	Subsidies in procurement	Dispute settlement
NAFTA	✓	✓	✓	✓	✗[3]	✗	✓	✓	✓	✓	✗	✗
US–Australia	✗	✗	✗	✗	✗	✗	✓	✓	✓	✓	✗	✓
US–Chile	✗	✗	✗	✗	✗	✗	✓	✓	✓	✓	✗	✓
US–Morocco	◊[4]	✗	✗	✗	✗	✗	✓	✓	✓	✓	✗	✓[5]
TFEU	✓[6]	✓	✓	✓	✓	✓	✓	✓	✓	✓	✗	✓
EC–Albania	✓[7]	✗	✗	✗	✗	✗	✓	✗	✗	✗	✗	✓[8]

(continued)

[3] Chapter Twelve: Cross-Border Trade in Services Art 1201: Scope And Coverage 2(d).

[4] Reference to Voluntary Export Restraints in WTO ASCM Art 18.

[5] Art 20 Direct violation and (c) a benefit the Party could reasonably have expected to accrue to it under Chapter Nine (Government Procurement).

[6] Art 87 (1) of the EC Treaty declares, 'save as otherwise provided in this Treaty, any aid granted by a Member State or through State resources in any form whatsoever which distorts or threatens to distort competition by favouring certain undertakings or the production of certain goods shall, in so far as it affects trade between Member States, be incompatible with the common market'.

[7] During the first 10 years after the date of entry into force of this Agreement, any public aid granted by Albania shall be assessed taking into account the fact that Albania shall be regarded as an area identical to those areas of the Community described in Art 87(3)(a) of the Treaty establishing the European Community but without prejudice to WTO ASCM obligations.

[8] Art 43 (SAA Arts 117 and 118): the Joint Committee shall, for the purpose of attaining the objectives of this Agreement, have the power to take decisions within the scope of this Agreement in the cases provided for therein. The decisions taken shall be binding on the Parties, which shall take the measures necessary to implement the decisions taken.

Table 3.1: *(Continued)*

RTA	Subsidy / state aid rules for goods	Exceptions	Exclusions	Dispute settlement	Subsidy / state aid rules for services	Procurement provisions in services	Procurement of goods provisions: NT and MFN	Procurement bid challenge mechanism	Offsets prohibition	Exceptions	Subsidies in procurement	Dispute settlement
EC–Bosnia Herzegovina	✓[9]	✗	✗	✗	✗	✗	✪[10]	✗	✗	✗	✗	✗
EC–Macedonia	✓[11]	✗	✗	✓	✗	✗	✪[12]	✗	✗	✗	✗	✗
EC–Montenegro	✓[13]	✗	✗	✓[14]	✗	✗	✪[15]	✗	✗	✗	✗	✗

(continued)

[9] As with Albania but including an additional Protocol 3 on state aid to the steel industry.

[10] Art 26 (SAA Art 41): state monopolies Bosnia and Herzegovina shall adjust any state monopolies of a commercial character so as to ensure that, following the entry into force of this Agreement, no discrimination regarding the conditions under which goods are procured and marketed exists between nationals of the Member States of the EU and of Bosnia and Herzegovina.

[11] Art 69 Competition and other economic provisions: 1. The following are incompatible with the proper functioning of the Agreement, insofar as they may affect trade between the Community and the former Yugoslav Republic of Macedonia: (iii) any public aid which distorts or threatens to distort competition by favouring certain undertakings or certain products.

[12] Title VI Approximation of Laws and Law Enforcement. The former Yugoslav Republic of Macedonia shall endeavour to ensure that its laws will be gradually made compatible with those of the Community. Deadlines will be set for competition law, intellectual property law, standards and certification law, public procurement law.

[13] Art 73.1(iii): any state aid which distorts or threatens to distort competition by favouring certain undertakings or certain products.

Protocol 5 on state aid to the steel industry: The Parties recognise the need that Montenegro addresses promptly any structural weaknesses of its steel sector to ensure the global competitiveness of its industry.

[14] If one of the Parties considers that a particular practice is incompatible with the terms of para 1, it may take appropriate measures after consultation within the Stabilisation and Association Council or after 30 working days following referral for such consultation. Nothing in this Article shall prejudice or affect in any way the taking, by the Community or Montenegro, of countervailing measures in accordance with the GATT 1994 and the WTO Agreement on Subsidies and Countervailing Measures and the respective related internal legislation.

[15] Following the EC–Bosnia Herzegovina provision: the purchasing of state monopolies is subject to NT obligations.

Table 3.1: *(Continued)*

RTA	Subsidy / state aid rules for goods	Exceptions	Exclusions	Dispute settlement	Subsidy / state aid rules for services	Procurement provisions in services	Procurement of goods provisions: NT and MFN	Procurement bid challenge mechanism	Offsets prohibition	Exceptions	Subsidies in procurement	Dispute settlement
EC–Egypt	✓	✗	✗	✓	✗	✗	✪[16]	✗	✗	✗	✗	✗
EC–Israel	✓	✗	✗	✓[17]	✗	✓	✓[18]	✓	✓	✓	✗	✓
EC–Jordan	✓[19]	✓	✗	✓	✗	✗	✪[20]	✗	✗	✗	✗	✗
EC–Chile	✗[21]	✗	✗	✓[22]	✗	✗	✓	✓	✓	✓	✗	✓

(continued)

[16] Art 38: the Parties agree on the objective of a progressive liberalisation of public procurement. The Association Council will hold consultations on the implementation of this objective.

[17] The parties agreed under Art 36.2. to adopt by decision the necessary rules for the implementation of para 1. Until these rules are adopted, the provisions of the Agreement on interpretation and application of Arts VI, XVI and XXIII of the GATT shall be applied as the rules for the implementation of para 1(iii).

[18] Chapter 2 Public Procurement, Art 35: the Parties shall take measures with a view to a mutual opening of their respective government procurement markets and the procurement markets of undertakings operating in the utilities sectors for purchase of goods, works and services beyond the scope of what has been mutually and reciprocally covered under the Government Procurement Agreement concluded in the framework of the WTO.

[19] EC–Jordan, Chapter 2: Competition and other Economic Matters, Art 53 1: the following are incompatible with the proper functioning of the Agreement, in so far as they may affect trade between the Community and Jordan: (c) any public aid which distorts or threatens to distort competition by favouring certain undertakings or the production of certain goods.

[20] Art 58: the Parties agree on the objective of a gradual liberalisation of public procurement. The Association Council will hold consultations on the implementation of this objective.

[21] EC–Chile NT, Art 77.4: the provisions of the NT Article shall not prevent the payment of subsidies exclusively to domestic producers, including payments to domestic producers derived from the proceeds of internal taxes or charges applied consistently with the provisions of this Article and subsidies effected through governmental purchases of domestic products.

[22] Antidumping and countervailing measures, Art 78.1: if a Party determines that dumping and/or countervailable subsidisation is taking place in its trade with the other Party, it may take appropriate measures in accordance with the WTO Agreement on Implementation of Article VI of the GATT 1994 and the WTO Agreement on Subsidies and Countervailing Measures.

Table 3.1: ***(Continued)***

RTA	Subsidy / state aid rules for goods	Exceptions	Exclusions	Dispute settlement	Subsidy / state aid rules for services	Procurement provisions in services	Procurement of goods provisions: NT and MFN	Procurement bid challenge mechanism	Offsets prohibition	Exceptions	Subsidies in procurement	Dispute settlement
EC–Mexico	◊[23]	✗	✗	✗	✗	✗	✪[24]	✗	✗	✗	✗	✗
EC–South Africa	✓	✓[25]	✗	✓[26]	✗	✗	✓	✗	✗	✗	✗	✗
Mercosur	✓[27]	✗	✗	✗	✗	✗	✪[28]	✗	✗	✗	✗	✗

(continued)

[23] Art 5 Trade in goods: in order to achieve the objective laid down in Art 4, the Joint Council shall decide on the arrangements and timetable for a bilateral, progressive and reciprocal liberalisation of tariff and non-tariff barriers to trade in goods, in accordance with the relevant WTO rules, in particular Art XXIV of GATT, and taking account of the sensitive nature of certain products. This decision shall include, in particular, the following matters: (e) anti-dumping and countervailing measures;

[24] Art 10 Public Procurement 1: the Parties shall agree to the gradual and mutual opening of agreed government procurement markets on a reciprocal basis.

[25] Art 41 Public Aid 1: in so far as it may affect trade between the Community and South Africa, public aid favouring certain firms or the production of certain goods, which distorts or threatens to distort competition, and which does not support a specific public policy objective or objectives.

[26] Art 42 Remedial measures: 1. If the Community or South Africa considers that a particular practice is incompatible with the terms of Art 41, and that such practice causes or threatens to cause serious prejudice to the interests of the other Party or material injury to its domestic industry, the Parties agree, where it is not adequately dealt with under existing rules and procedures, to enter into consultations with a view to finding a mutually satisfactory solution. Such consultations will be without prejudice to the Parties' rights and obligations in terms of their respective laws and international commitments. Art 44 Review: 1. In the absence of any rules or procedures for the implementation of Art 41, the provisions of Arts VI and XVI of GATT 1994 as well as the WTO Agreement on Subsidies and Countervailing Measures shall apply to public aid or subsidies.

[27] Art 4 provides for the application of 'their domestic legislation to restrict imports whose prices are influenced by subsidies, dumping or any other unfair practice'. Mercosur incorporates the WTO Agreement on Subsidies and Countervailing Measures into its legal structure. There are additional requirements and disciplines for investigation and application of trade-defence measures.

[28] A Decision to adopt the 'Protocol on Government Procurement in Mercosur' was taken in December 2004 but the Protocol is not yet in force. The Protocol aims to provide Party's suppliers non-discriminatory treatment for government procurement by public entities; it includes basic principles such as MFN, NT and transparency.

Table 3.1: *(Continued)*

RTA	Subsidy / state aid rules for goods	Exceptions	Exclusions	Dispute settlement	Subsidy / state aid rules for services	Procurement provisions in services	Procurement of goods provisions: NT and MFN	Procurement bid challenge mechanism	Offsets prohibition	Exceptions	Subsidies in procurement	Dispute settlement
India–Japan	✗[29]	✓[30]	✓	✗	✓[31]	✓[32]	✓[33]	✗[34]	✗	✓[35]	✗	✗

(continued)

[29] Art 21 Export Subsidies and Domestic Support: neither Party shall introduce or maintain any export subsidies or domestic support, which are inconsistent with its obligations under the WTO Agreement, on any agricultural good which is listed in Annex 1 to the Agreement on Agriculture.

[30] Art 11 Exceptions: 1. For the purposes of this Agreement except Chapters 6 and 9, Arts XX and XXI of the GATT 1994 are incorporated into and form part of this Agreement, *mutatis mutandis*. 2. For the purposes of Chapters 6 and 8, Arts XIV and XIV *bis* of the GATS are incorporated into and form part of this Agreement, *mutatis mutandis*. 3. Nothing in this Agreement shall be construed to prevent a Party from taking any action which it considers necessary for the protection of its essential security interests to protect critical public infrastructure, including communications, power and water infrastructure, from deliberate attempts to disable or degrade such infrastructure. Note: Nothing in this paragraph shall be construed so as to derogate from the rights and obligations of the Parties under the WTO Agreement. 4. Nothing in this Agreement shall be construed to require a Party to accord the benefits of this Agreement to the other Party, or to the goods or service suppliers of the other Party or investors that are enterprises of the other Party, where the Party adopts or maintains measures in any legislation or regulations which it considers necessary for the protection of its essential security interests with respect to a non-Party, or goods or service suppliers of a non-Party or investors that are enterprises of a non-Party, that would be violated or circumvented if the benefits of this Agreement were accorded to such goods or service suppliers or such enterprises of the other Party or to their investments.

[31] Art 70 Subsidies: 1. Each Party shall review the treatment of subsidies related to trade in services taking into account the development of the multilateral disciplines pursuant to paragraph 1 of Article XV of the GATS. 2. In the event that either Party considers that its interests have been adversely affected by a subsidy of the other Party, the Parties shall, upon request by the former Party, enter into consultations with a view to resolving the matter. 3. During the consultations referred to in paragraph 2, the Party granting a subsidy shall, if it deems fit, consider a request of the other Party for information relating to the subsidy programme such as: (a) domestic laws and regulations under which the subsidy is granted; (b) form of the subsidy (e.g. grant, loan, tax concession); (c) policy objective and/or purpose of the subsidy; (d) dates and duration of the subsidy and any other time limits attached to it; and (e) eligibility requirements of the subsidy including those with respect to potential beneficiaries. 4. The dispute settlement procedures provided for in Chapter 14 shall not apply to this Article.

[32] Art 57.3: Arts 59 and 60 shall not apply to any measure by a Party with respect to government procurement.

[33] Art 111 Non-Discrimination: with respect to any measure regarding government procurement, each Party shall provide to the goods, services and suppliers of the other Party treatment no less favourable than that it accords to non-Party's goods, services and suppliers in accordance with its laws and regulations.

[34] Art 113 Further Negotiations: the Parties shall enter into negotiations to review this Chapter with a view to achieving a comprehensive Chapter on Government Procurement including the provisions of challenge procedures, when India expresses its intention to become a Party to the Agreement on Government Procurement in the Annex 4 to the WTO Agreement (hereinafter referred to as 'the GPA').

[35] Art 115 Exceptions: 1. The provisions of this Chapter shall not be applicable to: (a) with respect to India, state governments and their entities and local governments; and (b) with respect to Japan, local governments. 2. Nothing in this Chapter shall be construed to prevent any Party from taking any action or not disclosing any information that it considers necessary for the protection of its essential security interests relating to the procurement of arms, ammunition, or war materials, or to procurement indispensable for national security or for national defence purposes.

Table 3.1: *(Continued)*

RTA	Subsidy / state aid rules for goods	Exceptions	Exclusions	Dispute settlement	Subsidy / state aid rules for services	Procurement provisions in services	Procurement of goods provisions: NT and MFN	Procurement bid challenge mechanism	Offsets prohibition	Exceptions	Subsidies in procurement	Dispute settlement
India–Korea	✓[36]	✓[37]	✓	✓[38]	×[39]	×[40]	✓[41]	✖	✖	✖	✖	✖

✓—Substantive provision
◊—Reference to other agreements
✖—No provisions
✪—Agree on general objectives

[36] Art 2.20 Subsidies: The Parties reaffirm their commitments to abide by Arts VI and XVI of GATT 1994 and the *Agreement on Subsidies and Countervailing Measures* contained in Annex 1A to the WTO Agreement.

[37] Art 2.9 General and security exceptions: 1. For the purposes of this Chapter, Arts XX and XXI of GATT 1994 and its interpretative notes are incorporated into and made a part of this Agreement, *mutatis mutandis*. 2. Nothing in this Chapter shall be construed to require a Party to accord the benefits of this Chapter to the other Party, or the goods of the other Party where a Party adopts or maintains measures in any laws and regulations which it considers necessary for the protection of its essential security interests with respect to a non-Party, or goods of a non-Party that would be violated or circumvented if the benefits of this Chapter were accorded to such Party or goods.

[38] Chapter 14 Dispute Settlement.

[39] Article 6.2 Scope and coverage: 3. This Chapter does not apply to: (b) subsidies or grants, including government-supported loans, guarantees and insurance; or to any conditions attached to the receipt or continued receipt of such subsidies or grants, whether or not such subsidies or grants are offered exclusively to domestic services, service consumers or service suppliers; Art 6.16 Subsidies: 1. The Parties shall review the treatment of subsidies in the context of developments in multilateral fora of which both Parties are party. 2. In the event that either Party considers that its interests have been adversely affected by a subsidy or grant provided by the other Party, upon request, the other Party shall enter into consultations with a view to resolving the matter. 3. During the consultations referred to in paragraph 2, the subsidising Party may, as it deems fit, consider a request of the other Party for information relating to the subsidy scheme or programme such as: (a) its laws and regulations under which the measure is introduced; (b) form of the measure, including grant, loan or tax measure; (c) policy objective and/or purpose of the measure; (d) dates and duration of the programme or subsidy and any other time limits attached to it; and (e) eligibility requirements of the measure, including criteria applied with respect to the potential population of beneficiaries. 4. Chapter Fourteen (Dispute Settlement) shall not apply to any requests made or consultations held under this Article or to any disputes that may arise between the Parties under this Article.

[40] Art 6.2 Scope and coverage: 3. This Chapter does not apply to: (a) government procurement.

[41] Art 13.12: Government procurement: 1. The Parties, recognising the importance of government procurement in their respective economies, shall endeavour to promote cooperative activities between the Parties in the field of government procurement. 2. The cooperation pursuant to paragraph 1 may include, but is not limited to the following areas: (a) promoting the exchange of information and views on government procurement policies and regulatory framework; (b) providing each other with accumulated knowledge, experience and information; (c) facilitating the exchange of knowledge, experience and information on e-Procurement; and (d) designating contact points for information exchange. Article 13.13 Renewable energy resources: 1. The Parties, recognising the importance of development of renewable energy resources in their respective economies, agree to cooperate in research, design and development of various renewable energy technologies, including solar, wind, bioenergy, and others as mutually agreed.

III. The USA's RTAs

Of the four relevant RTAs concluded by the USA, only the NAFTA incorporates rules to regulate and remedy the provision of subsidies[42] and this is confined to goods and not services.[43] NAFTA Chapter 19 on the Review and Dispute Settlement in Antidumping and Countervailing Duty Matters establishes the rules of procedure for investigations and reviews, along with an agreement to consult on developing more effective rules and disciplines concerning the use of government subsidies[44] through a division in each party's Secretariat dedicated to operationalising the chapter. In addition to the general exceptions to these obligations, GATT Article XX exceptions are also incorporated and clarified.[45] NAFTA Article 1502 on Monopolies and State Enterprises further notes in paragraph 3 that each party *shall* ensure that monopolies and state enterprises do not act in an anti-competitive or discriminatory manner towards the firms or investments of the other parties. However, it is significant that paragraph 4 explicitly carves out government procurement from these obligations.[46]

The NAFTA elsewhere incorporates comprehensive provisions to prevent discrimination in government procurement of goods. The NT and non-discrimination provisions set out under Chapter Ten, Article 1003 prohibit a party from discriminating against the suppliers of another party to favour domestic suppliers. Article 1006 also prohibits offsets or local content requirements. These, and other obligations relating to tender procedures, are enforced through the requirement for domestic bid challenge procedures under Article 1017. In addition to the General Exceptions,[47] the US schedules preclude all classes of research and development, telecommunications services, all classes of utilities, transportation, travel and relocation services. In sum, the regulatory framework for preventing anti-competitive state measures in public and private markets remains based on a traditional unintegrated approach within this front-runner US RTA.

[42] Although the US–Morocco RTA makes a reference to WTO ASCM Art 18 when addressing voluntary export restraints.

[43] Chapter 12 on Cross Border Trade in Services explicitly excludes subsidies from the coverage of the chapter in Art 1201.2(d).

[44] Art 1907 Consultations.

[45] NAFTA Art 2101 states that: 'GATT Art XX and its interpretative notes, or any equivalent provision of a successor agreement to which all Parties are party, are incorporated into and made part of this Agreement.' Further, that: 'The Parties understand that the measures referred to in GATT Art XX(b) include environmental measures necessary to protect human, animal or plant life or health, and that GATT Art XX(g) applies to measures relating to the conservation of living and non-living exhaustible natural resources.'

[46] Art 502.4. Para 3 does not apply to procurement by governmental agencies of goods or services for governmental purposes and not with a view to commercial resale or with a view to use in the production of goods or the provision of services for commercial sale.

[47] NAFTA Art 1018 Exceptions relating to security, public morals, human, animal or plant life, intellectual property rights and relating to goods or services of handicapped persons, of philanthropic institutions or of prison labour.

The other three US RTAs that are of relevance and examined here, namely the US–Australia, the US–Chile and the US–Morocco agreements, all take the traditional position of separating the regulation of competition in public procurement and on the open market. They can therefore be viewed together because of their similarity in choosing not to incorporate provisions that seek to prevent anti-competitive State aid for either goods or services markets. Nevertheless, all three agreements include comprehensive provisions to prevent anti-competitive buy-national policies under their government procurement rules. The procurement provisions of all three agreements provide for NT and MFN obligations for the procurement of goods and all prohibit the use of offsets. These provisions are enforced through a requirement for bid challenge procedures and the dispute settlement mechanism of the agreement is also applicable to the procurement provisions. But once again, subsidies to procurement suppliers are explicitly excluded from the coverage of the provisions. This definitively separates the two sets of regulation as regards ensuring competitive product markets in both procurement and open markets.

IV. Brazil's RTAs

The only RTA signed by Brazil that includes provisions to prevent government measures that distort competition in both public and private markets is under Mercosur. Article 4 provides for the application of the parties' domestic legislation to restrict imports of goods whose prices are influenced by subsidies, dumping or any other unfair practices:

> The States Parties shall ensure equitable trade terms in their relations with third countries. To that end, they shall apply their domestic legislation to restrict imports whose prices are influenced by subsidies, dumping or any other unfair practice. At the same time, States Parties shall co-ordinate their respective domestic policies with a view to drafting common rules for trade competition.

Mercosur also incorporates the WTO Agreement on Subsidies and Countervailing Measures into its legal structure and includes additional requirements and disciplines for investigation and application of trade-defence measures.

The stated aim of the 2004 'Protocol on Government Procurement in Mercosur' is to provide a party's suppliers with non-discriminatory treatment for government procurement by public entities. It therefore includes basic principles such as MFN, NT and transparency. However, this Protocol is not in force. This results in an incipient integrated framework to harness anti-competitive state practices in both public procurement and open markets in a coherent manner.

In sum, Brazil has not committed itself definitively to prohibit public distortions of competition in the form of buy-nationals in its regional procurement commitments, and nor has it moved beyond its commitments not to impose subsidies, such as bailouts, under the WTO ASCM

V. India's RTAs

For the research presented in this book, India's relevant RTAs are with Korea and Japan. However, neither of these agreements provide comprehensive coverage of both subsidies and procurement. As Table 3.1 indicates, in the India–Japan RTA, subsidy control for goods is confined to prohibiting only those export subsidies or domestic support measures on any agricultural good listed in Annex 1 to the Agreement on Agriculture and which are anyway conditioned by its obligations under the WTO Agreement.[48]

In the area of services India and Japan have agreed to review the treatment of subsidies related to trade in services, taking into account the development of the multilateral disciplines. Moreover, if either party considers that its interests have been adversely affected by a subsidy of the other party, consultations can be requested with a view to exchanging information on the subsidy programme and ultimately resolving the matter. However, the dispute settlement procedures provided for this agreement do not apply to this subsidy in services provision.

The procurement provisions set out under Article 111 require that for any measure regarding government procurement, each party shall accord the goods, services and suppliers of the other party treatment no less favourable than that it accords to any non-party's goods, services and suppliers in accordance with its laws and regulations. However, following the GATS approach, under the services chapter Article 57:3 stipulates that Article 59 on market access and Article 60 on national treatment shall not apply to any measure by a party with respect to government procurement. Significantly, offsets are not prohibited. However, the exceptions qualify this with the note that these obligations do not extend to state or local government procurement entities, or practices relating to security interests.[49] These procurement provisions are not subject to the agreement's dispute settlement mechanism, and nor are there any immediate requirements for either party to establish a domestic bid challenge mechanism.[50]

[48] Art 21 Export Subsidies and Domestic Support: 'Neither Party shall introduce or maintain any export subsidies or domestic support, which are inconsistent with its obligations under the WTO Agreement, on any agricultural good which is listed in Annex 1 to the Agreement on Agriculture.'

[49] Art 115 Exceptions: '1. The provisions of this Chapter shall not be applicable to: (a) with respect to India, state governments and their entities and local governments; and (b) with respect to Japan, local governments. 2. Nothing in this Chapter shall be construed to prevent any Party from taking any action or not disclosing any information that it considers necessary for the protection of its essential security interests relating to the procurement of arms, ammunition, or war materials, or to procurement indispensable for national security or for national defence purposes.'

[50] Art 113 Further Negotiations: 'The Parties shall enter into negotiations to review this Chapter with a view to achieving a comprehensive Chapter on Government Procurement including the provisions

The India–Korea RTA subsidy provisions for goods differ in that they reaffirm both parties' commitments under the WTO Agreement on Subsidies and Countervailing Measures,[51] rather than the Agreement on Agriculture as with the India–Japan agreement. Subsidies are not covered by the obligations of the services chapter. Rather, the parties agreed to review the treatment of subsidies in the context of developments in multilateral fora of which both parties are party. Following the India–Japan approach, if either party considers that its interests have been adversely affected by a subsidy or grant provided by the other party, they may request further information and consultations with a view to resolving the matter. However, the dispute settlement chapter does not apply to any disputes under this provision.[52]

Procurement is explicitly excluded from the services chapter. However, there is one provision that recognises the importance of government procurement in the parties' respective economies and shall endeavour to promote relevant cooperative activities. The field of cooperation is specifically targeted towards the research, design and development of renewable energy technologies and resources in both parties' respective economies.[53] However, yet again, these provisions are not covered by the dispute settlement mechanism chapter for the agreement, which limits their enforceability.

of challenge procedures, when India expresses its intention to become a Party to the Agreement on Government Procurement in the Annex 4 to the WTO Agreement (hereinafter referred to as "the GPA").'

[51] Art 2.20: Subsidies The Parties reaffirm their commitments to abide by Arts VI and XVI of GATT 1994 and the *Agreement on Subsidies and Countervailing Measures* contained in Annex 1A to the WTO Agreement.

[52] Art 6.2: Scope and Coverage 3: 'This Chapter does not apply to: (b) subsidies or grants, including government-supported loans, guarantees and insurance; or to any conditions attached to the receipt or continued receipt of such subsidies or grants, whether or not such subsidies or grants are offered exclusively to domestic services, service consumers or service suppliers'; Art 6.16: Subsidies: '1. The Parties shall review the treatment of subsidies in the context of developments in multilateral fora of which both Parties are party. 2. In the event that either Party considers that its interests have been adversely affected by a subsidy or grant provided by the other Party, upon request, the other Party shall enter into consultations with a view to resolving the matter. 3. During the consultations referred to in paragraph 2, the subsidising Party may, as it deems fit, consider a request of the other Party for information relating to the subsidy scheme or programme such as: (a) its laws and regulations under which the measure is introduced; (b) form of the measure, including grant, loan or tax measure; (c) policy objective and/ or purpose of the measure; (d) dates and duration of the programme or subsidy and any other time limits attached to it; and (e) eligibility requirements of the measure, including criteria applied with respect to the potential population of beneficiaries. 4. Chapter Fourteen (Dispute Settlement) shall not apply to any requests made or consultations held under this Art or to any disputes that may arise between the Parties under this Art.'

[53] Art 13.12: Government Procurement: '1. The Parties, recognising the importance of government procurement in their respective economies, shall endeavour to promote cooperative activities between the Parties in the field of government procurement. 2. The cooperation pursuant to paragraph 1 may include, but is not limited to the following areas: (a) promoting the exchange of information and views on government procurement policies and regulatory framework; (b) providing each other with accumulated knowledge, experience and information; (c) facilitating the exchange of knowledge, experience and information on e-Procurement; and (d) designating contact points for information exchange.' Art 13.13: Renewable Energy Resources: '1. The Parties, recognising the importance of development of renewable energy resources in their respective economies, agree to cooperate in research, design and development of various renewable energy technologies, including solar, wind, bioenergy, and others as mutually agreed.'

VI. The EU's RTAs

The EU has competence to negotiate trade agreements for its Member States, pursuant to TFEU Article 207.[54] According to the Treaties, EU Member States, through the Council, authorise the European Commission to start and conduct the negotiations while the Council monitors the talks before voting to sign and conclude the deals. With the entry into force of the Lisbon Treaty in 2009, trade was reinforced as an exclusive competence of the EU.[55]

As Table 3.1 indicates, the external RTAs signed by the EU all include provisions to prevent anti-competitive State aid/subsidies except the agreements with Chile and Mexico. The EU's agreements with the Balkan countries of Albania, Bosnia Herzegovina, Macedonia and Montenegro promote convergence with EU laws in the area of State aid. For example, Article 73 of the RTA[56] between the EU and Montenegro addresses competition and other economic provisions as follows:

> 1. The following are incompatible with the proper functioning of this Agreement, insofar as they may affect trade between the [Union] and Montenegro:
>
> ....
>
> iii) any State aid which distorts or threatens to distort competition by favouring certain undertakings or certain products.
>
> 2. Any practices contrary to this Article shall be assessed on the basis of criteria arising from the application of the competition rules applicable in the [Union], in particular from Articles [101. 102, 106 and 197 of the TFEU] and interpretative instruments adopted by the [Union] institutions.

The EUROMED agreements follow a more general requirement towards State aid, based on the template of Article 53.1 of the EC–Jordan RTA, but without referencing compatibility with the European framework:

> Article 53
>
> 1: The following are incompatible with the proper functioning of the Agreement, in so far as they may affect trade between the [Union] and Jordan: ... (c) any public aid which distorts or threatens to distort competition by favouring certain undertakings or the production of certain goods.

These EUROMED agreements are, however, asymmetrical from a competition approach. They provide greater subsidy control than procurement regulation.

[54] The EU common commercial policy is based on Art 207 TFEU, while the negotiation of trade agreements is conducted in accordance with the rules set out in Art 218 TFEU.

[55] However, in practice, two kinds of FTAs can be distinguished: regular trade agreements covering exclusive EU competences, and 'mixed' agreements with broader coverage—encompassing not only EU exclusive competences but also shared and even Member State exclusive competences—and thus require a different legal basis. Mixed agreements need to be signed, concluded and ratified by both Member States—and thus national parliaments—and the EU.

[56] This is Article 38 of the Interim Agreement on trade and trade related matters between the European Community and the Republic of Montenegro, 2007, L345/2.

In the case of the EC–Egypt and the EC–Jordan agreements, the procurement obligations are limited to consultations on the progressive liberalisation of government procurement.[57] The EC–Israel agreement is more balanced in that the procurement provisions aim to further open their respective procurement markets beyond that already agreed to by both parties under the WTO GPA framework.[58]

At the other end of the spectrum, the EC–Mexico RTA is underdeveloped as regards both sets of regulation; while the EC–Chile agreement is weighted towards preventing discrimination in government procurement markets. Subsidy control in the EC–Chile agreement is explicitly excluded from the NT obligations, in Article 77.4, along with subsidies that are achieved through governmental purchases of domestic products:

> The provisions of the National Treatment Article *shall not prevent the payment of subsidies exclusively to domestic producers*, including payments to domestic producers derived from the proceeds of internal taxes or charges applied consistently with the provisions of this Article and subsidies effected through governmental purchases of domestic products. (emphasis added)

The EC–South Africa agreement presents a more integrated regulatory model. It contains both State aid control for goods—supported by dispute settlement procedures—as well as NT and MFN obligations for the procurement of goods—although not for services. However, the procurement regulation does not include a prohibition on offsets, nor requirements for domestic bid challenge procedures or state-to-state dispute settlement provisions. This weak enforcement mechanism greatly undermines the potential strength of this model's provisions.

A. State Aid Control under the TFEU

Notwithstanding the strictness of EU subsidy control, State aid still represent about 1 per cent of EU GDP, excluding crisis-related measures.[59] Various EU trade measures have also been challenged under the WTO ASCM.[60] This is somewhat counter-intuitive in light of Article 107 TFEU, which stipulates that:

> 1. Save as otherwise provided in the Treaties, any aid granted by a Member State or through State resources in any form whatsoever which distorts or threatens to distort

[57] EC–Egypt RTA, Art 38; EC–Jordan RTA, Art 58.

[58] EC–Israel RTA, Art 35.

[59] OECD DAF/COMP/GF(2010)5.

[60] See: *European Communities—Measures Relating to the Development of a Flight Management System* (Complainant: United States); *European Communities—Countervailing Measures on Dynamic Random Access Memory Chips from Korea* (Complainant: Korea, Republic of): *European Communities—Measures Affecting Trade in Commercial Vessels* (Complainant: Korea, Republic of); *European Communities—Aid for Commercial Vessels* (Complainant: Korea, Republic of); *European Communities and Certain Member States—Measures Affecting Trade in Large Civil Aircraft* (Complainant: United States); *European Communities and Certain Member States—Measures Affecting Trade in Large Civil*

competition by favouring certain undertakings or the production of certain goods shall, in so far as it affects trade between Member States, be incompatible with the internal market.

Despite this outright prohibition, State aid is provided pursuant to the list of exemptions set out in the subsequent paragraphs of Article 107. These provisions permit, in paragraph 2, any State aid having a social character or disaster relief; along with an expansive list of subsidy measures that may ex ante be considered compatible with the internal market in paragraph 3, such as aid to promote the economic development of areas where the standard of living is abnormally low. The assessment of the compatibility of an aid is seen as a balance between its negative effects on trade and competition within the internal market and its positive effects in terms of a contribution to the achievement of well-defined objectives of common interest. The Commission has established common principles for an economic assessment of the compatibility of State aid to assist Member States,[61] in addition to clarifying evaluation in the field of State aid.[62]

In essence, this State aid framework is more permissive with regard to subsidy measures promoting secondary non-economic policy objectives than the WTO ASCM, yet more rigorous in assessing each measure. Indeed, the ex ante notification and the ex post monitoring and enforcement mechanisms set out under Article 108 serve to make EU State aid control convincing and somewhat inspirational, not only relative to other regional arrangements but to the WTO ASCM framework. Under TFEU Article 108(3), the Commission shall be informed of any plans to grant or alter State aid with sufficient time to enable it to submit comments. If the Commission considers that any such proposed measure is not compatible with the internal market, it has the power to decide whether and when the non-compliant State aid should be removed.[63] The Member State concerned cannot legally put its proposed measures into effect until this procedure has resulted in a final decision. The monitoring mechanism also requires that the Commission, in cooperation with the Member States, constantly reviews all systems of existing aid.[64] Once again, if the Commission finds that aid granted

Aircraft (Second Complaint) (Complainant: United States); *European Communities—Expiry Reviews of Anti-dumping and Countervailing Duties Imposed on Imports of PET from India* (Complainant: India); *EU and Certain Member States—Certain Measures Affecting the Renewable Energy Generation Sector* (Complainant: China); *EU—Certain Measures on the Importation and Marketing of Biodiesel and Measures Supporting the Biodiesel Industry* (Complainant: Argentina), *EU—Cost Adjustment Methodologies and Certain Anti-Dumping Measures on Imports from Russia* (Complainant: Russian Federation).

[61] Common Principles for an Economic Assessment of the Compatibility of State Aid under Art 87.3: http://ec.europa.eu/competition/State_aid/reform/economic_assessment_en.pdf (accessed 3 March 2014).

[62] See 'The Draft Methodological Guidance Paper—Concepts and Recommendations', available at: http://ec.europa.eu/competition/consultations/2013_state_aid_modernisation/draft_guidance_paper_en.pdf (accessed 20 April 2014).

[63] Pursuant to Art 107 TFEU.

[64] Established in Art 108(2).

by a state or through state resources is not compatible with the internal market, it possesses the power to decide whether and when the Member State concerned should remove or redesign the non-compliant State aid measure. If the Member State concerned does not comply with this decision within the prescribed time, the Commission or any other interested state may refer the matter to the Court of Justice of the EU (CJEU).[65] A Member State is obliged to take the 'necessary measures' to comply with a CJEU judgment.[66] If the Member State does not do so, penalty payments may then be imposed.[67]

As Part III of this book opines, while far from perfect, this independent monitoring, enforcement and adjudication system serves to increase both compliance with and enforcement of these regional rules far beyond that presently conceivable within the WTO. As such they remain an inspirational model.

B. An Integrated Competition Approach under the TFEU?

In what could at first sight appear to be a wholly integrated approach to regulating public restraints of competition in public procurement and open markets under the TFEU, public procurement measures are subject to the same State aid control rules set out under Article 107. This provision refers to any aid granted by a Member State or through state resources *in any form whatsoever* that distorts or threatens to distort competition by favouring certain undertakings. A procurement transaction will fall within the scope of State aid control and may be prohibited if it is deemed to favour certain undertakings by giving them an economic advantage and as such displays all four of the characteristics set out in Article 107. That is: (i) it must be financed directly or indirectly through state resources; (ii) it must confer an economic advantage above the de minimis threshold of €200,000[68] to undertakings exercising an economic activity; (iii) the advantage is selective[69] and distorts or threatens to distort competition; and (iv) it has an effect on intra-Community trade.

[65] On application by a Member State, the Council may, acting unanimously, decide that aid which that state is granting or intends to grant shall be considered to be compatible with the internal market, in derogation from the provisions of Art 107 or from the regulations provided for in Art 109, if such a decision is justified by exceptional circumstances. If, as regards the aid in question, the Commission has already initiated the procedure provided for in the first subparagraph of this paragraph, the fact that the state concerned has made its application to the Council shall have the effect of suspending that procedure until the Council has made its attitude known. Art 108(2) third paragraph.

[66] Pursuant to Art 260 TFEU.

[67] Pursuant to Art 260(2) TFEU.

[68] Granted to an undertaking over any period of three years without prior Commission approval. Commission Regulation (EC) No 1998/2006 of 15 December 2006 on the application of Arts 87 and 88 of the Treaty to de minimis aid, [2006] OJ L379.

[69] Except in the case of the provision of general infrastructure with public funds, where no selectivity element would be present as regards the users of the infrastructure.

As a result of this cumulative assessment, in those procurement cases where there is an economic advantage, the remaining conditions concerning selectivity, distortion of competition and effect on trade are also likely to be met. Public contracts are generally financed, either completely or partially, out of state resources, and most public contracts are directly or indirectly attributable to public bodies included in the broad definition of 'state' for the purposes of Article 107(1) TFEU. The determination of whether or not there has been an economic advantage under the State aid 'which the recipient undertaking would not have received under normal market conditions' becomes the pivotal test in assessing most procurement contracts under Article 107(1).

Although this provision seems applicable to a public undertaking if it promotes an 'economic activity' in market conditions by participating or interacting in the market, Court of First Instance (CFI) and ECJ case law indicates otherwise. Contentiously, the CFI and ECJ earlier determined that procurement activities will not be considered 'economic' activities unless the subsequent use of the purchased goods amounts to an 'economic' activity.[70] Those findings led to a bifurcation in regulating public and private anti-competitive behaviour. For only the activities of public undertakings as *offerors* of goods or services in the market are subject to competition rules.[71] All other commercial activities of the public sector do not qualify per se as 'economic activities' unless they cross the path of its scope of application when performing subsequent downstream economic activities. Moreover, the different activities carried on by a given entity do not need to be analysed together. Findings from the *Selex* case indicate that EC competition rules are applicable to the activities of an entity, which can be severed from those in which it engages as a public authority.[72]

Under the existing TFEU framework, if a public purchase corresponds to a normal commercial transaction and the authorities are paying a market price for the works, goods or services procured, it is to be presumed that no State aid is involved. This is because the same choice would have been made by a so-called 'disinterested' or market economy buyer.[73] Subsequently, this become known as the *Altmark* test. In effect, a presumption that compliance with government procurement regulations is a guarantee that the compensation is not excessive.[74]

[70] Judgment of the Court of First Instance in Case T-319/99, *FENIN v Commission*, para 36; confirmed on appeal by Judgment of the Court in Case C-205/03 P, *FENIN v Commission*, para 26; and Judgment of the Court of First Instance in Case T-155/04 *Selex v Commission* [2006] ECR II-4797, para 65, confirmed on appeal by Judgment of the Court in Case C-113/07 P *Selex v Commission* [2009] ECR, nyr, paras 102 and 114.

[71] See A. Sánchez Graells, *Competition and the Public Buyer: Towards a More Competition-Oriented Procurement System* (Cantoblanco, 2009) 173–79.

[72] Case T-155/04, *Selex v Commission* [2006] ECR II-4797, para 54.

[73] Case T-14/96, *BAI v Commission* [1999] ECR II-139, paras 71–76.

[74] See Judgement of the Court of 24 July 2003, in Case C-280/00, *Altmark Trans GmbH* [2003] ECR I-7747.

This was reconfirmed in the *London Underground Public–Private Partnership* case where the Commission found that:

> [W]hen these types of infrastructure arrangements are concluded after the observance of an open, transparent and non-discriminatory procedure, it is, in principle, presumed that the level of any market sector support can be regarded as representing the market price for the execution of the project. This conclusion should lead to the assumption that, in principle, no State aid is involved.[75]

Those EUCJ findings were consolidated by the European Commission into a rebuttable presumption that no State aid incompatible with the TFEU will exist where the award of the contract is a pure procurement transaction, and also if the procurement procedure is compliant with EU public procurement directives.[76] It will be suitable for achieving best value for money, inasmuch as no economic advantage that would go beyond normal market conditions will usually arise under these circumstances.[77] It follows from this that the legality of a Member State's government procurement policy is primarily sourced not under Article 107(1) TFEU but in a series of legislative measures in the form of directives.[78] As a result, the *Altmark* test simply served to deactivate the prohibition on any aid that in any form distorts or threatens to distort competition by favouring certain undertakings or the production of certain goods within the internal market.[79]

Since the crisis, the Court of Justice of the EU (CJEU) issued a revised interpretation of the concept of an undertaking for the purposes of the application of EU competition law to encompass economic agents engaging in a combination of both economic and non-economic activities.[80] In a significant step, the 2015 *EasyPay* case, the CJEU determined that an activity will be considered as economic—unless it has links with another activity that fulfils an exclusively social function, based on the principle of solidarity and entirely non-profit making. Moreover, such an activity must, by its nature, its aims and the rules to which it is subject, be 'inseparably' connected to it.[81] As such, the *EasyPay* judgment departed from previous case law[82] to confirm that for the purposes of the application of EU

[75] Decision N264/2002 London Underground Public Private Partnership, p 36, ¶79.

[76] Assessment of the Commission of 30 May 2007, in case N 46/2007 *Welsh Public Sector Network Scheme*, COM(2007) 2212 final, para 18.

[77] The ECJ has pronounced that under European government procurement rules, the awarding authority must follow transparent open procedures *ensuring fair conditions of competition for suppliers*. See eg ECJ judgment of 12 December 2002 in Case C-470/99, *Universale Bau* [2002] ECR I-11617, 89.

[78] These directives were recently revised under Directive 2014/24/EU approved by the European Parliament and European Council on 26 February 2014 on public procurement, which repeals Directive 2004/18/EC [2014] OJ L94, 65–242.

[79] See A Sánchez Graells, 'Public Procurement and State Aid: Reopening the Debate?' (2012) 21(6) *Public Procurement Law Review* 205–12.

[80] Judgment in *EasyPay and Finance Engineering*, C-185/14, EU:C:2015:716.

[81] See Sanchez-Graells, Albert and Herrera Anchustegui, Ignacio, Revisiting the Concept of Undertaking from a Public Procurement Law Perspective—A Discussion on EasyPay and Finance Engineering (26 November 2015). Available at SSRN: https://ssrn.com/abstract=2695742.

[82] Judgment in *FENIN v Commission*, C-205/03 P, EU:C:2006:453; Judgment in *Selex Sistemi Integrati v Commission*, C-113/07 P, EU:C:2009:191.

competition law, an undertaking is any entity—even a procurement agency—engaged in an economic activity, irrespective of its legal status and the way in which it is financed. And further, that any activity consisting in offering goods and services on a given market is an economic activity.[83]

Another legal development promoting a competition approach was the 2014 High Court in England ruling on the application of the UK competition rules to tender design of an exclusive concessions contract tendered to Luton Operations to run a bus service between the airport bus terminal and central London.[84] In this case, the contracting authority was found to have abused its dominant position by negotiating a seven-year deal with the successful bidder when there would have been sufficient capacity for a second operator after three years. The long exclusivity generated a higher return for Luton Operations was held to be bad for consumers and an abuse of dominance in the buying market.

This is line with the aim of the EU procurement directives[85] to create a level playing field for firms seeking to compete for public contracts and to increase the efficiency of public expenditure on the basis of the Treaty provisions regarding freedom of establishment and free movement of services. Those government procurement contracts that do not fall within the scope of these directives, such as contracts with a value below certain thresholds and service concessions, are still subject to the general principles of the TFEU concerning transparency and non-discrimination.[86] This was also confirmed by the ECJ.[87] As a result, on the one hand, compliance with government procurement rules excludes the existence of an 'undue economic advantage' in the award of a public contract and, consequently, determines the inapplicability of Article 107 because the award of the public contract will not constitute State aid.[88] Yet on the other hand, however, recipients of legal and authorised State aid cannot be excluded automatically from public tenders.[89] This has raised questions about the ability of these procurement

[83] See *Stadt Halle* (C-26/03).

[84] *Arriva the Shires Ltd v London Luton Airport Operations Ltd* [2014] EWHC 64 (Ch).

[85] Directives are provided for in Art 288 TFEU which states that a Directive is a measure of general application which requires Member States to *achieve certain results* but leaves to each Member State the precise *form and method of implementation*. Concessions: Directive 2014/23/EU; General: Directive 2014/24/EU; Utilities: Directive 2014/25/EU. Directive 89/665/EEC—the Public Sector Remedies Directive on the coordination of the laws, regulations and administrative provisions relating to the application of review procedures to the award of public supply and public works contracts, [1989] OJ L395/33; and Directive 92/13/EEC—the Utilities Remedies Directive coordinating the laws, regulations and administrative provisions relating to the application of Community rules on the procurement procedures of entities operating in the water, energy, transport and telecommunications sectors, [1992] OJ L76/7. The Directives on remedies were amended by Directive 2007/66/EC.

[86] ECR I-10745 and the Commission Interpretative Communication on the Community rules applicable to contract awards not or not fully subject to the provisions of the Government Procurement Directives [2006] OJ C179, 2.

[87] Case C-324/98 *Telaustria and Telefonadress* [2000].

[88] See Assessment of the Commission of 30 May 2007, in Case N-46/2007, *Welsh Public Sector Network Scheme*, COM(2007) 2212 final; and N Tosics and N Gaál, 'Government Procurement and State Aid Control—The Issue of Economic Advantage' [2008] *EC Competition Policy Newsletter* 15.

[89] See judgment of the Court in Case C-94/99, *ARGE* [2000] ECR I-11037.

procedures to guarantee a market price. It is also of significance that the Commission cannot, in these cases, pronounce ex ante that State aid would not be provided through a particular tender procedure. That is, despite the comparative strength of State aid control in the EU, the European Commission is still unable definitively to limit the use of government procurement as a means to grant disguised State aid or provide a coherent approach to prevent government restrictions of competition in public and open markets.

The revised Directive 2014/24/EU could be seen to offer further leverage to promote competition based on Article 18. This rule stipulates that procurements should not be designed with the intention of artificially narrowing competition through discriminating for or against certain economic operations.[90] Nevertheless a somewhat tautological traditions persists, which presumes that if a tender award follows the government procurement rules it will not prima facie constitute State aid. As a result, there is limited scope for joint enforcement of State aid and government procurement rules. This formalistic approach relies on government procurement rules to provide transparency and due process, but without definitively preventing the provision of economic advantages. This approach provides simplicity and legal certainty. But this must be balanced against the loss of welfare gains through potential distortions to competition in these markets.

In sum, this section indicates that while stronger and more integrated than the regional frameworks erected in other RTAs, historically the regulation as developed within the EU still displays features that work to undermine an integrated approach to regulating public restrictions of competition in both procurement and open markets and which limit the ability of the rules to prevent government procurement contracts being used to provide disguised State aid as fully as they could.

VII. TFEU State Aid Rules under WTO Commitments

Given that the TFEU establishes the strongest legal framework to control government subsidies that distort or threaten to distort competition within the internal market, it might be assumed that such stringent ex ante control of State aid would likely conform to WTO obligations under the ASCM. Intuitively, it is difficult to see how a government support measure that does not affect trade between Member States under the TFEU would still constitute a challengeable subsidy under the WTO ASCM. Yet the EU has long been a regular and major target of countervailing duty measures and challenges within the WTO.[91] Indeed, several areas exist where

[90] See A Sánchez Graells, *Public Procurement: A 2014 Updated Overview of EU and National Case Law*. Forthcoming 2nd edn at e-Competitions (2014) (1st edn: e-Competitions: National Competition Laws Bulletin, No. 40647, 8 December 2011). Available at SSRN: https://ssrn.com/abstract=1968371.

[91] For example: *EC and Certain Member States–Large Civil Aircraft* DS316; *EU– Certain Measures on the Importation and Marketing of Biodiesel and Measures Supporting the Biodiesel Industry* DS459, *EU*

the EU State aid regime does not conform completely to the requirements of the WTO ASCM, and may result in a violation of its multilateral commitments.[92]

Of immediate relevance for this discussion are the Court rulings in the EU dispute *PreussenElektra.* Under the TFEU, an EU Member State's measure requiring private regional electricity suppliers to purchase electricity produced from renewable energy producers in their area of supply and at prices fixed above market prices was challenged before the ECJ. However, unlike the *Canada–FIT* Panel findings, here the ECJ pronounced that the measure conferring an economic advantage did not involve a direct or indirect transfer of state resources.[93] This interpretation suggests that if an 'independent' financial institution is instructed by a Member State government to grant 'a financial contribution' that benefits certain actors operating in the private sector, it will not—*ceteris paribus*—be deemed State aid under current TFEU case law. However, the *Canada–FIT* dispute findings indicate that this measure could be considered a subsidy provided by a government agency under the WTO ASCM.

A. Matching Clauses

Another noteworthy conflict between the TFEU and the WTO can be seen in the EU's use of 'matching clauses' in its State aid regime. These regulatory provisions authorise increased subsidies if foreign competitors have directly or indirectly received, or are going to receive, aid of an equivalent intensity for similar projects, programmes, research, development or technology. A matching clause is included under section 5.1.7 of the European Commission R&D&I Framework,[94] with the stated aim of addressing actual or potential, direct or indirect distortions of international trade. While this may appear reasonable, it must be recalled that a matching clause is also a unilateral self-help measure prohibited under Article 23 DSU in the WTO.[95] The findings from the *Korea–Dairy* dispute further indicate that, at least in theory, a Member need not provide evidence of its economic or legal interest in order to challenge such a measure.[96] Despite their inclusion in treaties, matching clauses have yet to be activated. However, their very existence places a

and Certain Member States–Certain Measures Affecting the Renewable Energy Generation Sector DS452; *European Communities–Aid for Commercial Vessels* DS307; *European Communities–Countervailing Measures on Dynamic Random Access Memory Chips from Korea* DS299; *European Communities–Export Subsidies on Sugar* DS283;

[92] C-D Ehlermann and M Goyette, 'The Interface between EU State Aid Control and the WTO Disciplines on Subsidies' (2006) 4 *European State Aid Law Quarterly* 695.

[93] Case C-379/98, *PreussenElektra* [2001] ECR I-2099, para 58. This was also confirmed in Case C-345/02, *Pearle and Others* [2004] ECR I-7139 and Case C-677/11 *Doux Élevage SNC v UKL-ARREE.*

[94] Section 5.1.7 of the European Commission R&D&I Framework. See also European Commission DG Competition Issue Paper, 'Revision of the State Aid Rules for Research and Development and Innovation' (Brussels, 12 December 2012).

[95] Panel Report, *Canada–Aircraft Credits and Guarantees,* ¶7.170.

[96] Panel Report, *Korea–Dairy,* ¶7.14.

downward regulatory pressure on subsidy control. They would, prima facie, not be permitted if public procurement and subsidies were included under the scope of the application of GATT Article I MFN, as submitted in Chapter 2.

VIII. Conclusions

Chapter 3's assessment of the relevant RTAs signed by the case study countries indicates that, with the exception of the TFEU, all the RTAs were limited in their ability to prevent the anti-competitive distortions produced by state bodies in both private and public markets in a coherent and integrated manner. While some RTAs prioritised State aid control, others were more focused on procurement provisions with dispute settlement mechanisms. Most of the RTAs either explicitly or implicitly excluded subsidies from procurement provisions and procurement from competition issues. This indicates a lop-sided or asymmetrical approach to regulating public restrictions of competition in open and public markets.

The most striking examples of the different inter-governmental regimes that exist can be seen between the WTO and the EU frameworks. WTO rules do not provide explicit exceptions or ex ante control. Given the permitted exceptions to EU State aid control and the ambiguity surrounding the applicability of the GATT Article XX exceptions to the obligations of the ASCM, the interface between the EU and WTO rules regarding subsidies and procurement displays some obvious gaps. This gap is exacerbated because WTO subsidy control is ex post, either through a challenge within the DSB or a countervailing duty applied unilaterally by the effected Member. However, TFEU State aid control takes place both ex ante and ex post. Any Member State planning to grant an aid must notify the measure to the Commission and wait for a clearance decision before implementing the aid. Ex post, the Commission keeps existing aids under review to ensure continuing conformity.

Yet even under the TFEU, the applicability of State aid control to public procurement contracts is curtailed by the presumption that the use of competitive, transparent and non-discriminatory public tenders is sufficient to presume that no State aid is provided to the economic operator selected as a result of the procedure. This is a significant limitation to consolidating an integrated framework to prevent unnecessary government distortions to competition in both public and private markets.

Having set out an analysis of strengths and limitations of the black-letter law regulating subsidies and government procurement in the WTO and selected RTAs, the next chapter proceeds to assess the legality of the crisis measures in the case study countries under these international and regional rules.

4

Characterising the Rules

I. Introduction

This chapter concludes Part I's analysis with a comparative characterisation of the international provisions regulating bailouts and buy-nationals in the markets for both goods and services. It starts by analysing these provisions in terms of their degree of legalization,[1] as an appropriate but limited starting point. For the purposes of this research, further analysis is necessary in terms of the bilateral or collective characteristics of these provisions. This assessment provides insight into enforcement and compliance with these rules—the so-called '*couple diabolique obligation-sanction*'.[2] Determining the legal nature of these provisions serves to clarify their associated rules on standing, in terms of who can invoke responsibility for a breach of a law and the sort of claims they can make.

This chapter begins this exploration by introducing the terminology used for characterising these provisions. It presents the analytical categories of 'soft' and 'hard' law in order to situate the results of the previous two chapters' assessment within the analytical framework put forward by Abbott and Snidal.[3] The research then supplements this initial assessment with the conceptual framework developed initially to understand the enforcement nature of public international law provisions[4] and more latterly applied to the body of international economic law within the WTO.[5]

[1] KW Abbott and D Snidal, 'Hard and Soft Law in International Governance' (2000) 54 *International Organization* 421.

[2] P Weil, 'Le droit international en quête de son identité', (1992) 237 *Récueil des Cours de l'Academie de Droit International* 13, 53. Cited in J Brunnée, 'Enforcement Mechanisms in International Law and International Environmental Law' in U Beyerlin et al (eds), *Ensuring Compliance with Multilateral Environmental Agreements: A Dialogue Between Practitioners and Academia* (Leiden, Brill, 2005).

[3] Abbott and Snidal (n 1).

[4] Sir G Fitzmaurice, 'The Foundations of the Authority of International Law and the Problem of Enforcement' (1956) *Maryland Law Review* 19, 1–13; J Crawford, Special Rapporteur, 'Third Report on State Responsibility', Document A/CN.4/507 and Add 1–4.

[5] J Pauwelyn, 'A Typology of Multilateral Treaty Obligations: Are WTO Obligations Bilateral or Collective in Nature?' (2003) 14 *European Journal of International Law* 907; J Pauwelyn, 'The Nature of WTO Obligations', Jean Monnet Working Paper no 1/02, NYU School of Law, Jean Monnet Centre (2002).

The findings of this chapter suggest that while there might be a persuasive case to interpret collective obligations or legal infrastructure into the WTO system, the selected provisions examined in this book are binding obligations more realistically characterised as 'transactional' and 'bilateral' rather than 'collective' or 'integral' in their legal nature. And as such, their enforcement is also overwhelmingly bilateral. The chapter concludes that whether or not there is a normative case for advocating the inclusion of more collective or 'solidarity' measures within either the WTO or RTAs, the existing legal infrastructure remains primarily bilateral. This theoretical claim is subsequently taken into the empirical research undertaken in Part II for verification, and used to support the discussion on compliance and enforcement in Part III.

II. Assessing the Provisions

One established method of analysing trade obligations is to divide legal provisions into two main categories depending on whether a rule seeks to safeguard a government's right to regulate, or whether it seeks to set positive standards among the parties to the agreement.[6] This dichotomy has since been refined to employ the term negative integration for that part of economic integration that consists of the removal of discrimination, and positive integration for the formation and application of coordinated and common policies in order to fulfil economic and welfare objectives other than the removal of discrimination.[7] This negative/positive dichotomy has also been used to assess social protection provisions in trade agreements. A negative provision is viewed as a right to regulate and includes exceptions based on GATT Article XX and any modifications to the GATT Article XX chapeau, as discussed in Chapter 2, along with any provisions concerned with regulating potential conflicts with obligations arising for other international agreements. Positive regulation consists of provisions allowing the parties to take directly protective measures. Others further divide positive regulation into two main thematic groups: those clauses that establish standards, sometimes enforceable; and those clauses providing for cooperation on social matters.[8]

[6] This was employed by Jan Tinbergen in the context of European economic integration during the 1950s. See J Tinbergen, *Centralization and Decentralization in Economic Policy* (Amsterdam, 1954) 76.

[7] See eg J Pelkmans, 'The Institutional Economics of European Integration' in M Cappelletti, M Seccombe and J Weiler (eds), *Integration Through Law: Europe and the American Federal Experience* (New York, Walter de Gruyter, 1986) 321, n 2. See also F Ortino, *Basic Legal Instruments for the Liberalisation of Trade: A Comparative Analysis of EC and WTO Law* (Oxford, Hart Publishing, 2004) 17–18.

[8] L Bartels, 'Social Issues: Labour, Environment and Human Rights' in S Lester and B Mercurio (eds), *Bilateral and Regional Trade Agreements: Commentary, Analysis and Case Studies* (Cambridge, Cambridge University Press, 2007); L Bartels, 'Applicable Law in WTO Dispute Settlement Proceedings' (2001) 35 *Journal of World Trade* 499.

From this broad-brush perspective, competition policy provisions in the WTO could be viewed as negative integration in seeking a level playing field for domestic and foreign market actors through non-discrimination provisions, while procurement laws are also positive integration attempts to coordinate and harmonise domestic rules by setting minimum requirements for transparency and non-discrimination in tendering public contracts. Such a characterisation provides a blunt understanding of how provisions place obligations upon the parties, opening up debates on sovereign non-intervention and domestic regulatory discretion. Yet theoretical ambiguity remains over the legal strength or 'bite' of a particular obligation. This is better understood by analysing whether the institutional mechanism for enforcing a particular provision is supported by a binding dispute settlement mechanism and remedies may be provided to an aggrieved party. This serves to clarify whether the provision is softer for being enforced through a 'power-oriented' or 'diplomacy' approach, as contrasted with the harder 'rule-oriented' approach.[9]

A. The Soft Law–Hard Law Continuum

The debate about the role of soft and hard international law stands in stark contrast to the positivist approach that questions whether international law is even law due to its the lack of secondary rules, compulsory jurisdiction of courts, legislature and centrally organised sanctions. Jan Klabbers[10] notes that during the 1970s theorists began to point out that most of the norms set out in international agreements are susceptible to enforcement through tribunals and courts entrusted to respect the obligations of the agreements. Moreover, other norms exist of 'various degrees of cogency, persuasiveness and consensus'. These norms are also incorporated into international agreements but their inclusion does not create enforceable rights and duties.[11] This latter group of norms could be termed 'soft' laws, and should be distinguished from 'hard' laws consisting of rules that states expect will be carried out and complied with. Other terms were floated, including 'non-binding agreements', 'de facto agreement', 'non-legal norms', 'weak law', 'para-legal' and even 'imperfect law'. Some were even linear and deterministic in designating soft law as a 'transitional stage in the development of norms where their content is vague and their scope imprecise'.[12] For when international lawyers began speaking of 'soft law' it was

[9] JH Jackson, *The Jurisprudence of GATT and the WTO: Insights on Treaty Law and Economic Relations* (Cambridge, Cambridge University Press, 2000) 121.

[10] J Klabbers, 'Reflections on Soft International Law in a Privatized World', 2. Available from: www.helsinki.fi/eci/Publications/Klabbers/JKSoft_law_and_public.pdf (accessed 28 January 2017).

[11] RR Baxter, 'International Law in Her Infinite Varieties' (1980) 29 *International and Comparative Law Quarterly* 549.

[12] A McNair, in GJH van Hoof, *Rethinking the Sources of International Law* (Utrecht, Rijksuniversiteit, 1983) 187.

> deftly, using the epistemological possibility of speaking in different terms of law's binding nature and creating a category next to the familiar 'hard' law (which, while alone, never was called 'hard', of course).[13]

Klabbers views the 1990s as a period of 'justificatory zeal' where international lawyers sought to present soft law within a primarily binary lexicon of legal/illegal and binding/non-binding. Since then the analysis of soft law has become more sophisticated and self-confident. The work of Guzman and Meyer, for example, portrays the positive role of soft law within international negotiations, where diverse parties can seek to respond to complex cross-border issues that challenge domestic sovereignty. Soft law is used to solve coordination games in which the existence of a focal point is enough to generate compliance. Soft law can also be a rational choice when the marginal costs of the expected loss from violations exceed the marginal benefits of deterred violations. Soft law is now one sensible option when states are uncertain about the future appropriateness of hard rules in changing circumstances. Lastly, the use of soft law can also emerge from the non-binding decisions and interpretations of binding rules made by international tribunals or what Guzman and Meyer call international common law. They conclude that international law comes in a large variety of guises and is best understood as positioned along a continuum, or spectrum, running between fully enforceable binding treaties and fully political unenforceable positions. And if viewed in this way: 'Soft law is something that dims in importance as the commitments of States get weaker, eventually disappearing altogether.'[14]

B. Degrees of Legalisation

Further categorisation of soft and hard law was introduced by applying three conceptual dimensions to determine variations in degrees of legalisation among international instruments: (i) obligation; (ii) precision in the text of the rule; and (iii) delegation.[15] Within this rubric, the concept of obligation refers to the degree to which states are legally bound by rules or commitments. A hard obligation is a legally binding rule. If the treaty does not formally characterise itself as *not*-legally binding, it is the language employed within the various clauses that will indicate the extent to which such intent exists. This is exemplified by words of obligation, most commonly 'shall,' 'will' 'must' but also 'agree to' and 'undertake to', for instance. If, on the other hand, international agreements are obligations of a non-binding form, such as political declarations, codes of conduct and guidelines, they are soft law instruments.[16] The use of phrases such as 'the Parties shall endeavour

[13] Klabbers (n 9).

[14] AT Guzman and TL Meyer, 'International Soft Law' (2010) 2 *Journal of Legal Analysis* 171–225.

[15] Abbott and Snidal (n 1).

[16] The Conference on Security and Co-operation in Europe Final Act, Helsinki, 1 August 1975; available at www.hri.org/docs/Helsinki75.html.

to…' or 'the Parties may…' does not impose any restrictions or obligations on the signatory parties.[17] There are also instances where international instruments that go as far as to negate explicitly any intent to create legally binding obligations. For instance, the parties to the 1975 Helsinki Final Act explicitly signified that it was not an 'agreement… governed by international law'.

This appears to confirm the binary nature of international law. However, there is more nuance and fluidity in operation. For not only may soft laws have big impacts but also the non-binding character of soft law may change or strengthen once it begins to interact with binding agreements. A binding hard law may also soften due to a treaty's lack of complementary enforcement power or dispute settlement mechanism.[18] In other words, while some provisions of treaties create little or no obligation, they can be inserted in a form of instrument that presumptively creates rights and duties. Conversely, 'instruments of lesser dignity may influence or control the conduct of States or individuals to a certain degree, even though their norms are not technically binding'.[19]

For Abbott et al, precision refers to the degree of ambiguity of the language defining the parties' obligations in the legislative text. Ambiguous provisions in a treaty may be deprived of the character of hard law despite their legally binding form.[20] Ambiguity or a low level of precision in international rules may also demand greater interpretation when determining compliance. This places pressure on the courts to interpret law, rather than the legislature. For example, in the WTO the dispute settlement mechanism has a mandate to interpret the GATT/WTO-covered agreements in a stable and predictable manner, even when these texts are at best ambiguous. However, even when negotiators have used 'creative ambiguity' to achieve a settlement, WTO dispute settlement bodies are not required to determine if such ambiguity is deliberate. What is required is a determination of whether the meaning of a text is ambiguous after applying the customary rules of treaty interpretation and in light of the evidence and arguments presented by the parties to the dispute.[21]

[17] Enabling clauses such as 'The parties shall cooperate…' are soft in that they do not set out benchmarks by which to assess whether a party has or has not cooperated.

[18] J Pauwelyn, R Wessel and J Wouters (eds), *Informal International Lawmaking* (Oxford, Oxford University Press, 2012).

[19] Baxter (n 10) 565.

[20] An oft-cited example of the disabling nature of legal vagueness is the 1992 Rio Framework Convention on Climate Change. Here, the US interpretation found the ambiguity of the core articles to imply that there is nothing in any of the language which constitutes a commitment to any specific level of emissions at any time. Available at http://unfccc.int/kyoto_protocol/items/2830.php.

[21] WTO DSU Art 3.2 states: 'The dispute settlement system of the WTO is a central element in providing security and predictability to the multilateral trading system. The Members recognize that it serves to preserve the rights and obligations of Members under the covered agreements, and to clarify the existing provisions of those agreements in accordance with customary rules of interpretation of public international law. Recommendations and rulings of the DSB cannot add to or diminish the rights and obligations provided in the covered agreements.'

The WTO DSB ruled out the possibility of declaring that there is no applicable WTO law, by invoking the concept of *non liquet* because, for example, the texts are imprecise or contradictory. For to do otherwise would, in effect, award the case to the respondent. However, such a possibility would also likely lessen the intrusiveness of WTO jurisprudence.[22] Yet, the WTO's highly judicial mode of decision-making was adopted precisely because of the problems of the political/diplomatic approach under GATT.[23] As one commentator observed, while the WTO DSB is the most powerful of all the economic organisations that exist, a tension has developed between this dispute settlement system and the rest of the organisation.[24]

A less obvious source of imprecision can be located in the availability of many legal mechanisms to limit the binding force of a commitment, such as exceptions, exemptions, derogations and safeguards/escape clauses,[25] as well as whether there are remedies for a breach. Under a safeguard, for instance, states are exempted from fulfilling the treaty obligations upon the occurrence of particular events and/or upon the judgment of the party. The rationale behind circumventing obligations is that parties would be more disposed to offer trade concessions if there were a way to 'escape' temporarily from their obligations in the case of emergency. There are trade-offs, however. The inclusion of a *rebus sic stantibus* clause[26] can also produce a legally fragile environment, which is only slightly mitigated by secondary obligations such as notifications and due process requirements attached to the use of safeguards. In the WTO system, systemic weaknesses are compounded by the fact that Article XIX also contains several vague phrases including 'unforeseen developments' and 'serious injury', the meaning of which has also had to be subsequently teased out in disputes with the accompanying accusations of judicial activism.[27]

This category of precision could usefully be explicitly extended to include transparency issues. Lack of transparency shelters non-compliant measures. By way of pertinent illustration, one study of the impact of international agreements on government procurement practices concluded that in opaque policy areas where

[22] C Barfield, 'WTO Dispute Settlement System in Need of Change', AEI Briefing Paper (2002) www.aei.org/publications/pubID.14115/pub_detail.asp.

[23] DZ Cass, *The Constitutionalization of the WTO* (Oxford, Oxford University Press, 2005) 135.

[24] JH Jackson, 'The Future Scope of WTO—Issues as Seen in the Sutherland Report' (2006) www.rieti.go.jp/en/events/bbl/06032301.html.

[25] This book accepts the terms 'escape clauses' and 'safeguards' can be used interchangeably but prefers to use the term 'safeguards' due to the research focus on the GATT/WTO and its internal terminology.

[26] This clause indicates that an agreement be ruled non-applicable if circumstances change fundamentally from the time of the signing of the treaty. But it cannot be used if one of the parties produced the change through a breach in its treaty obligations, or if there was a time limit set in the treaty which has not yet been reached; see International Law Definitions, at www.hfienberg.com/irtheory/intlaw-definitions.html.

[27] See eg *Korea–Definitive Safeguard Measure on Imports of Certain Dairy Products*; *United States–Fur Felt Hats*, or in the later Agreement on Safeguards.

treaty violations are difficult to observe and prove, international agreements are largely ineffective in constraining national governments.[28] This confirms previous findings of discrimination or *home bias* in public procurement tenders.[29] The European Commission published research to indicate that 99 per cent of all local authority contracts tendered within the EU are awarded to domestic firms. In postulating that this figure could not be solely be due to cost and quality differences alone, the Commission concluded that, 'discrimination in public procurement is very difficult to detect or prove'. Indeed, the study indicated that while 46 per cent of EU businesses reported that they believed local preferences influence the outcome of public procurement procedures to a 'high extent', none could provide concrete evidence of discrimination.[30] There is therefore a case for explicitly including the issue of transparency within the proposed concept of precision, or supplementing the typology with this additional category. For if due to entrenched transparency weaknesses, it is difficult to prove violations of international rules, signatory parties may continue to discriminate in favour of domestic interests with impunity. To some extent, this is the method of promoting social values through the 'legal labyrinths of arcane tendering procedures, murky supplier qualifications'[31] that some commenters advocate, even when these social values have not been based on transparent democratic oversight.

The final category put forward by Abbott et al is of delegation and refers to the degree to which states have delegated the power to a third party to implement the treaty rules. The focus here is not on the form or content of an agreement but rather on the extent to which parties give authority to designated third parties, including courts, arbitrators and administrative organisations to implement the agreement. At one end of the delegation continuum sits developed institutional bureaucracies, such as the international criminal tribunals, entrusted with the powers of interpreting agreed norms, enforcing compliance and resolving disputes in cases of non-compliance. Some dispute settlement bodies, most notably the CJEU under the TFEU, have developed to interpret treaty provisions in an extensive and teleological manner. Interpretation is undertaken with an expansive view to achieving the goals of the treaty. Others, including the WTO DSB, have been more circumspect and have taken a more literal reading of the treaty texts.[32]

[28] SJ Rickard and DY Kono, 'Think Globally, Buy Locally: International Agreements and Government Procurement' (on file with author).

[29] F Trionfetti, 'Discriminatory Government Procurement and International Trade' (2000) 23 *The World Economy* 57; A. Shingal, 'Services Procurement under the WTO's Agreement on Government Procurement: Whither Market Access?' (2011) 10 *World Trade Review* 527.

[30] European Commission, 'Green Paper on the Modernisation of EU Public Procurement Policy: Towards a More Efficient European Procurement Market' (2011).

[31] JL Dunoff, 'Linking International Markets and Global Justice' (2009) 107 *Michigan Law Review* 1039.

[32] See, for example, the debate on applicable law in the WTO: J Trachtman, 'The Domain of WTO Dispute Resolution' (1999) 40 *Harvard International Law Journal* 333; JP Pauwelyn, 'Public International Law in the WTO System: How Far Can We Go? (2001) 95 *American Journal of International Law*; Bartels (n 7).

For pursuant to DSU Article 3.2, the DSB has to be mindful to neither add to nor diminish the rights and obligations provided in the covered agreements.[33]

Towards the softer end of the delegation continuum sits non-binding arbitration, such as the pre-WTO GATT system. For the GATT was not designed to be an international organisation, but for what John Jackson termed 'a reciprocal-tariff reduction agreement' with ancillary related clauses to make such reductions meaningful and to provide non-discriminatory trade among participating nations. Lasting difficulty was caused when the complementary institutional structure of the International Trade Organisation was not established; the GATT treaty language itself contains only sketchy institutional clauses, including those regarding dispute settlement, and these 'birth defects' have troubled world trade rules ever since.[34]

This book does not seek to devalue through omission non-binding regulatory frameworks addressing competition in public procurement and open markets, such as the UNCITRAL Model Laws,[35] ICN or OECD guidelines, or indeed the pre-GATT framework.[36] Rather, this book focuses on WTO and RTA provisions and thereby excludes the expanding universe of instruments that exist in this area. That is, in terms of their degrees of legalisation, the previous chapters had already concluded *prima facie* that the set of WTO provisions assessed in this book, while not fully homogeneous, are typically hard-binding obligations, enforced by a dispute settlement mechanism that interprets ambiguities in the provisions as they relate to the dispute in hand.

The degree of obligation laid down in these selected RTAs with government procurement provisions is typically more limited than in the GPA. Nevertheless, binding language provides an obligation to the parties to prevent discrimination in procurement processes. The strongest regional framework selected for analysis is established, monitored and enforced under the EU's TFEU; while the weakest model appears under Mercosur. This, despite incorporating binding obligations, has yet to be fully implemented due to the low level of enforcement power delegated to the regional institution. Horn, Mavroidis and Sapirs' discussion of

[33] D Palmeter and PC Mavroidis, 'The WTO Legal System: Sources of Law' (1998) 92 *American Journal of International Law* 398.

[34] See Jackson (n 8) 119.

[35] L Jiang, 'Developing Multilateral Rules on Government Procurement: The Value of Soft Law' in S Arrowsmith and R Anderson (eds), *The WTO Regime on Government Procurement: Challenge and Reform* (Cambridge, Cambridge University Press, 2011); R Hunja, 'The UNCITRAL Model Law on Procurement of Goods, Contruction and Services and Its Impact on Procurement Reform' in S Arrowsmith and A Davies (eds), *Public Procurement: Global Revolution* (London, Kluwer Law International, 1998); J Linarelli, 'The WTO Agreement on Government Procurement and the UNCITRAL Model Procurement Law: A View from Outside the Region' [2006] *Asian Journal of WTO & International Health Law and Policy* 1.

[36] See eg: CR Yukins, 'A Case Study in Comparative Procurement Law: Assessing UNCITRALS's Lessons for US Procurement' (2006) 3 *Public Contract Law Journal* 457; SJ Evenett, '"Soft Law" and International Economic Regulation: The Case of Mergers and Acquisitions', Oxford University, GEP Newsletter (2005).

selected US and EU RTAs notes a further complication with this typology. Particularly in RTAs, these provisions may be enforced not only through a formal judicial dispute settlement mechanism, but also through more political means—although the existence of a provision may still be important in coordinating expectations concerning their implicit agreement. In such a situation it is not the legal strictness of the language that matters to the enforceability of the provision, rather that this strictness helps parties maintain their non-formal enforcement of the agreement.[37]

As a result, assessing the binding nature of these provisions is but an initial starting point to this specific examination. Evaluating the degree of legalisation of these provisions does not immediately identify who has legal standing to bring a challenge to a violation of the provision, how a breach is proved, or the remedies and countermeasures available. With the aim of understanding more about the operational and enforcement qualities of these provisions, the following section characterises the nature of the provisions that aim to prevent anti-competitive government measures in public procurement and open markets in terms of whether they are bilateral/reciprocal or collective/integral.

III. The Nature of Legal Obligations

Various commentators have noted that within the body of international law, legal obligations traditionally 'run bilaterally' between states.[38] The bilateral nature of these legal obligations can also be applied to the patterns of responsibility and enforcement attached to these rules through the principle that each state must protect its own rights. As the ICJ in its *Reparation for Injuries* Opinion proclaimed: '[O]nly the party to whom an international obligation is due can bring a claim in respect of its breach.' And further, that only the state personally and materially injured by a breach of international law is entitled to resort to reprisals to enforce compliance.[39]

In the face of such bilateralist proclivity, several international disputes have indicated that in certain cases a distinction can and should be made between the types of obligations an international rule could provide depending on the importance of the rights involved.[40] This is reflected in the ILC 2001 Draft Articles on

[37] H Horn, PC Mavroidis and A Sapir, 'Beyond the WTO? An Anatomy of EU and US Preferential Trade Agreements' (Brussels, Bruegel Blueprint Series, 2009) vol VII.

[38] Philip Allott argued that this bilateralism displays civil law characteristics even to the extent of resembling relations between feudal landowners. P. Allott, *Eunomia. New Order for a New World* (Oxford, New York, Oxford University Press, 1990) 296.

[39] Reparation for injuries suffered in the service of the United Nations, Advisory Opinion: ICJ Reports 1949, 182.

[40] *Barcelona Traction case*, ICJ Reports (1970) 32–33 (¶33–34). For other ICJ pronouncements in respect of *erga omnes* obligations, see *Namibia Opinion*, ICJ Reports (1971) 16, 56 (¶126); *Case*

the Responsibility of States for Internationally Wrongful Acts. The Commentary recognised that a broader range of states may have a legal interest in invoking responsibility and ensuring compliance with the obligation in question. In certain situations, *all* states may have such an interest, even though none of them is individually or specially affected by the breach. Indeed, embracing of the concept of international crimes of state and crafting of the so-called *mise-en-oeuvre* of state responsibility[41] presented a significant landmark overcoming the traditional bilateralist bias in favour of embodying community interest in international law.

The following section contrasts the characteristics of bilateral and collective obligations to evaluate what action can be taken to secure the performance of different obligations from a non-compliant government. The chapter then applies this framework to assess the selected WTO and regional provisions to determine what action can be taken if these are breached. For while these ILC draft provisions give rise to international obligations for states, special rules may also determine which other state or states are entitled to invoke the international responsibility arising from their breach, and what remedies they may seek. It is a matter of interpretation as to whether the rules in question are *lex specialis* and intended to be exclusive.[42]

A. Bilateral and Collective Obligations

> Every treaty in force is binding upon the parties to it and must be performed by them in good faith.[43]

Compliance with a binding obligation is often viewed as one of the most important benchmarks from which to assess the effectiveness of a law. Much of the analysis undertaken in the areas of compliance[44] and enforcement[45] follows the classification that makes a distinction between *bilateral* or *multilateral* treaty obligations. It further divides multilateral treaties into the categories of reciprocal, interdependent or integral depending on the consequences arising from

Concerning East Timor, ICJ Reports (1995) 90, 102 (¶29); and *Application of the Convention on the Prevention and Punishment of the Crime of Genocide. Bosnia and Herzegovina v Yugoslavia (Preliminary Objections)*, ICJ Reports (1996) 625 (¶4), 628 (¶6).

41 Commentary to the ILC.

42 Art 55 of the ILC Draft Articles explicates the residual character of the Draft Articles. See eg Art 33 of the European Convention on Human Rights. Also see Art 396 of the Treaty of Versailles, the subject of the decision in the SS *Wimbledon* case.

43 Art 26 VCLT *Pacta Sunt Servanda*.

44 This research maintains the conventional distinction between compliance with obligations by individual Members and the procedural issues of enforcement, recognition and execution of decisions of the WTO DSB.

45 For example, the role of arbitrators in determining reasonable period of time; contract theory; reputation costs; imposing remedies collectively; the multilateral enforcement of DSB findings; and early determination of injuries once nullification and impairment have been established.

their breach.[46] To recall, under traditional international law, a multilateral treaty is perceived as assembled from a collection of bilateral relationships. The multilateral treaty serves to provide a network of bilateral treaties running reciprocally between the individual contracting parties. Under such a regime, while a signatory party is obligated to comply with the rules vis-à-vis all the other parties, it can only breach them as regards another party within these isolated reciprocal relationships.[47] Further, it is only as an individual injured signatory party suffering the consequences of a breach that a state is entitled to claim for damages permitted in international law.

In contrast to this bilateral model are those treaties that are established to serve an interest in common to all states and are consequently legally indivisible or *erga omnes* obligations. A violation of an *erga omnes* obligation affects the subjective rights of all states and therefore each state is an injured party and has a right to obtain cessation of the unlawful conduct, reparation and guarantees of non-repetition. This is regardless of any material or tangible interest. A violation of *erga omnes* obligations normally does not cause any material or moral damage to any particular state and therefore compensation is not always admissible in international law. In the area of fundamental freedoms, for example, such obligations cannot be complied with selectively by a state. Consequently, even if a state's violation of an *erga omnes* obligation does not affect the material interests of any other state or its nationals, all other states possess a recognised subjective right in the respect of these obligations. This distinction was confirmed in the Permanent Court of International Justice (PCIJ) *Wimbledon* case.[48] France alone had suffered financially assessable injury as a consequence of Germany's breach of international law, and therefore France alone was entitled to obtain compensation. Nevertheless, the PCIJ declared admissible the applications also submitted by Japan, Italy and the UK. This was on the grounds that each of the four applicant powers had a clear interest in the execution of the provisions relating to the Kiev Canal, since they all possessed fleets and merchant vessels flying their respective flags. This was regardless of the fact that they may be unable to adduce a prejudice to any pecuniary interest.'[49]

The reverse claim was raised in the *South West Africa* cases. In this dispute, the ICJ initially rejected South Africa's claim that the conflict alleged by the applicants was not a dispute the Court could have adjudicated upon—because no material interest of the applicants or their nationals was involved. The Court went on to

[46] The conceptual distinction between reciprocal/bilateral and integral/multilateral obligations has been traced back to Gerald Fitzmaurice during the discussions that emerged in the International Law Commission over the codification of the VCLT. It was further developed by James Crawford in his Third Report to the ILC on state responsibility. See J Pauwelyn, 'A Typology of Multilateral Treaty Obligations' (n 4).

[47] The VCLT is most frequently cited as an example of a bilateral treaty.

[48] *Wimbledon*, PCIJ, Ser A, no 1 (1923) 20.

[49] ibid.

confirm that a *legally protected interest* need not necessarily relate to anything material or tangible and can be infringed even though no prejudice of a material kind has been suffered.[50] The Court nevertheless also clarified that any subjective rights 'must be clearly vested in those who claim it by some text or instrument, or rule of law'.[51] It was consequently found that Ethiopia and Liberia were not individually injured by the apartheid regime in South West Africa; only the people of South West Africa as a whole.

The effect of conferring singular or individual rights upon states arising from a breach of a multilateral obligation would tend either to treat those states incorrectly as proprietors of the right, or give undue preference to subjective feelings of affront.[52] The ILC Final Draft Articles, adopted in August 2001,[53] set out this distinction but did not provide an illustrative list of such obligations.[54] The category of *erga omnes* laws was described as multilateral obligations 'owed to the international community as a whole'.[55] Any party in the international community can challenge a breach of a multilateral obligation *erga omnes*, although full remedies are only granted to those injured states that are 'specially affected' by the breach.[56]

The category of *erga omnes partes* multilateral obligations[57] are those owed not to all States but to the signatory parties to a particular treaty only and established for the protection of a collective interest of the group.[58] This distinction provided the basis for crafting Article 42 on individually injured parties, while Article 48 is crafted on those parties that while not individually harmed, can be seen to have a legal interest in the compliance with the obligations set out in a particular rule.[59] Ultimately, proposals to incorporate 'collective counter-measures' that can be taken at the request of and on behalf of an injured state, as well as 'solidarity measures' to be taken in the general interest where there was no individual injured state, were both jettisoned. For some this indicated that evidently the limits even of progressive development of state responsibility had been reached.[60]

[50] It declared that the Members of the League of Nations 'were understood to have a legal right or interest' in the observance by South Africa of its obligations deriving from the mandate over South West Africa, regardless of any prejudice of a material kind.

[51] The ICJ found that this was a condition which was not satisfied in the cases under scrutiny.

[52] Crawford (n 3) fn 39, General Assembly, Official Records, Fifty-fifth Session, Supplement no 10 (A/56/10).

[53] ILC Report on the work of its fifty-third session (23 April–1 June and 2 July–10 August 2001), General Assembly, Official Records, Fifty-fifth Session, Supplement no 10 (A/56/10). Draft Articles, 43–59; Commentary, 59–365.

[54] ICJ Reports (1995) 90, 102, ¶29.

[55] Final Draft Articles, Art 48, ¶1(b).

[56] Full remedies include cessation, non-repetition, reparation and countermeasures. Art 42 (b) states: 'A State is entitled as an injured State to invoke the responsibility of another State if the obligation breached is owed to … (b) A group of States including that State, or the international community as a whole, and the breach of the obligation: (i) Specially affects that State; or (ii) Is of such a character as radically to change the position of all the other States to which the obligation is owed with respect to the further performance of the obligation.'

[57] Final Draft Articles, Art 48, ¶1(a).

[58] Commentary (n 52) fn 238, 320–21, ¶(7).

[59] Crawford (n 3).

[60] ibid.

For bilateralism limits collective responses to breaches of international law and protects the principle of state sovereignty. But in doing so, it ossifies international law's so-called *epiphenomenal* quality, which according to some is just 'a nice way of saying it is stupid'.[61]

> The role of international law within international society has been marginal, residual, and intermittent. It has been one element in the willing and acting of the state-societies as they made their fevered calculations of so-called *power* and *interest*, as they sought one advantage after another, one equilibrium after another. International law has been neither very threatening nor very useful to the politicians and the diplomats. … It has performed the role of an old servant in a family of ancient lineage, a venerable legal adviser to great landowners whose most treasured possession is now a colourful past, full of glory and shame. International law is the faithful friend of a family overtaken by time.[62]

It is naïve to advocate bilateralism on the grounds that it contributes to the orderly external appearance of the law—facilitating a precise identification of who has a right or claim against whom, and who may enforce it through the principle of reciprocity. It is rather opined here that the relative absence of international solidary measures perpetuates a 'value-poverty' in international law, allowing governments to behave in ways that they would be morally restrained from internally.[63] There is a continual and palpable tension between the 'relative normativity' and primitive 'every-man-for-himself' nature of trenchant bilateralism highlighted by Prosper Weil[64] and the increasing recognition of and importance attached to community interests, including the agreed-upon goal of a fair and competitive level playing-field under the WTO trading system.

The following section therefore assesses whether the selected trade provisions identified in previous chapters could be considered as either bilateral or collective in their nature. It then analyses the implications that these findings might have for their enforcement.

IV. The Nature of Selected WTO Obligations

The distinction between reciprocal and integral obligation does not normally apply to treaties in their entirety; rather individual provisions can be characterised by the different rules that govern them as far as legal standing and countermeasures are concerned.[65] In other words, WTO rules should not be perceived

[61] DJ Bederman, 'Constructivism, Positivism and Empiricism in International Law' (2001) 89 *Georgetown Law Journal* 469.

[62] Allott (n 37) 296.

[63] B Simma, 'From Bilateralism to Community Interest in International Law', *Collected Courses of the Hague Academy of International Law*, vol 250 (Leiden, Brill, 1994).

[64] P Weil, 'Towards Relative Normativity in International Law?' (1983) 77 *American Journal of International Law* 413.

[65] See J Pauwelyn, 'Enforcement and Countermeasures in the WTO: Rules are Rules—Towards a More Collective Approach' (2000) 94 *American Journal of International Law*.

as a monolithic bloc that is either bilateral or collective in nature. This section therefore assesses the nature of the selected provisions regulating anti-competitive state spending in both open and procurement markets within the wider context of the WTO dispute settlement mechanism. This should determine the implications attached to this distinction between bilateral and multilateral obligations in terms of their attached rights of standing, available remedies and countermeasures.

The WTO system is designed to promote mutually agreed reductions of trade barriers—through the reciprocity principle, and non-discriminatory treatment among Members—through the MFN principle. While the MFN principle serves as a primary defence against trade discrimination and the distortion of competition, there are two types of reciprocity of immediate interest to this chapter: open and restrictive reciprocity. Open reciprocity does not demand any direct response to an antecedent action. It rather imposes on the receiving side a certain obligation for repayment in the future. Open reciprocity characterises the negotiations followed under the GATT. Restrictive reciprocity, on the other hand, places much greater emphasis on a simultaneous exchange of strictly equivalent benefits and obligations. This restrictive approach characterises the negotiations followed under the WTO GPA, discussed below.

The wedding of reciprocity and non-discrimination serves to remove the prisoner's dilemma attached to adverse terms-of-trade effects associated with unilateral tariff reductions. Together they preserve the value of concessions that a Member achieves in a current negotiation against erosion in a future negotiation to which it may not be a party. Reciprocity and non-discrimination are thus cornerstone principles of the multilateral trading system. More specifically, reciprocity is the rule by which several parties manage to maintain a balance and symmetry of treatment by granting the same or equivalent rights and benefits to each other. Reciprocity is therefore *conditional* in that it is contingent on rewarding actions and, moreover, ceases when such actions cease; for while the act of giving is voluntary, the act of the recipient in obligatory.

Chapter 2 discussed how under that GATT, the MFN obligation is embodied in GATT Article I:1. This is an *unconditional* MFN provision because it obligates parties to extend to all other parties, immediately and without discriminatory conditions, the most favourable trade market access concessions it has granted, or may grant, to any third party. Unconditional MFN requires non-discrimination even when reciprocity is violated; MFN treatment is offered to all Members without regard to equal participation in the exchange of market access concessions that led to a particular MFN agreement. And as such, this unconditionality may encourage countries not to reciprocate, thereby causing a free-rider problem. As elucidated by Bagwell and Staiger:

> More important, the Most Favoured Nation obligation protects the value of concessions against future erosion through discrimination. If country A receives a concession from country B and is not entitled to Most Favoured Nation treatment from B, then the value of the concession can be undermined if country B later makes an even better concession to country C on the same goods (or close substitutes). Faced with this uncertainty,

country A would offer less for the concession in the first place (as would country B for the reciprocal concession), and fewer valuable deals would be struck.[66]

This free-rider problem attached to unconditional MFN status may in some cases undermine incentives to expand on WTO multilateral agreements in other trade areas. For unlike the GATT unconditional MFN provision, within the WTO's plurilateral agreements, the MFN principle requires only *conditional* treatment. From the outset, under the various plurilateral codes, including the Government Procurement Code, non-discriminatory treatment was made conditional on an explicitly strict reciprocal exchange of rights and obligations. This included market access concessions among parties to the agreement. That is, MFN clauses vary so that they can serve different purposes at different times. Unlike the GATT, public procurement was always an example of an agreement that places access concessions on a *strict* reciprocity and on a *conditional* MFN basis. The strictness of the reciprocity principle and conditionality of the WTO GPA MFN obligation is formally set out in an appendix to the Agreement, which as noted, forms an integral part of the Agreement.

Moreover, even the extension of a bilateral act under the unconditional MFN obligation of GATT Article I does not transform bilaterally *negotiated* concessions into collectively *applied* ones. The unconditional MFN principle does not imply that WTO obligations are more appropriately regarded as collective. Rather it implies that unless otherwise justified, the Members can expect a benefit negotiated bilaterally will be extended collectively to promote the objective of non-discrimination. This reasoning is contra Chios Carmody,[67] for whom the principal object of the WTO rules is the protection of *collective expectations* about the trade-related behaviour of governments. These expectations form a common interest over and above the interests of individual WTO Member states. Therefore, these collective expectations require a collective enforcement approach, including collective remedies and countermeasures attached to protect the governments and traders who collectively hold expectations about future trade.

Within this paradigm, the vital role of the dispute settlement system is therefore to re-establish the distribution of these expectations in the face of non-compliance with WTO rules. Pursuant to dispute findings[68] and DSU Article 3.8,[69] any particular breach of a provision under the covered agreements has a multilateral effect

[66] K Bagwell and RW Staiger, *The Economics of the World Trading System* (Cambridge, MA, MIT Press, 2002) 62.

[67] C Carmody, 'WTO Rules as Collective' (2006) 17 *European Journal of International Law* 425.

[68] ibid. Carmody notes the WTO violation cases referring to expectations under GATT Art XXIII:1(a), see *EC–Computer Equipment*, *EC–Trade Description of Sardines*, WT/DS231/AB/R (26 September 2002), *India–Patent Protection*, *Korea–Alcoholic Beverages* and *Canada–Measures Affecting the Export of Civilian Aircraft*, WT/DS70/AB/R (2 August 1999). Likewise, for cases involving expectations in non-violation claims under GATT Art XXIII:1(b), see *Japan–Measures Affecting Consumer Photographic Film and Paper*, WT/DS44/R (21 March 1998), *EC–Measures Affecting Asbestos and Asbestos-Containing Products*, WT/DS135/AB/R (12 March 2001).

[69] DSU Art 3.8 stipulates: 'In cases where there is an infringement of the obligations assumed under a covered agreement, the action is considered *prima facie* to constitute a case of nullification or

in disturbing expectations and affecting a wider number of operators beyond. It is therefore incomplete to interpret each bilateral relationship in isolation without taking into account the greater 'context' of other bilateral relationships entered into and subsequently made applicable to 'all' via MFN. All WTO Members have something to gain from enforcing WTO rules and the objective that these collective obligations are owed to all WTO Members. For as the Appellate Body has stated:

> With the increased interdependence of the global economy… Members have a greater stake in enforcing WTO rules than in the past since any deviation from the negotiated balance of rights and obligations is more likely than ever to affect them, either directly or indirectly.[70]

Whether or not this argument is normatively persuasive, a closer examination of the text of DSU Article 3.8 does not readily lead to such a conclusion. Instead this Article appears to presume a nullification of benefits once breach is established. In cases where there is an infringement of the obligations assumed under a covered agreement, the action is considered prima facie to constitute a case of nullification or impairment. This means that there is normally a presumption that a breach of the rules has an adverse impact on other Members, and in such cases it shall be up to the Member against whom the complaint has been brought to rebut the charge. Nowhere does the text suggest that all or any WTO Members have a right to complain about any WTO breach. That is, Article 3.8 DSU does not provide for collective standing but rather a presumption to the effect that a breach will, at first sight, be considered to constitute a case of nullification and impairment or adverse impact on other Members. The EU contested this presumption in its appeal during the *EC–Bananas III* dispute, on the basis that the USA has never exported a single banana to the European Community, and therefore, could not suffer any trade damage. The Appellate Body opined that Article 3.8 is concerned with what happens after a violation is established; it was not concerned with the standing required in order to be allowed to invoke a breach.[71]

The Appellate Body has also ruled on more than one occasion that the object and purpose of the GATT 1994 as reflected in Article III non-discrimination obligations is to avoid protectionism, requiring equality of competitive conditions and protecting *expectations* of equal competitive relationships.[72] The Panel, during the *US–Superfund* dispute, examined whether measures with only an insignificant effect on the volume of exports do still nullify or impair benefits. They concluded that the first sentence should not be interpreted to protect *expectations on export*

impairment. This means that there is normally a presumption that a breach of the rules has an adverse impact on other Members parties to that covered agreement, and in such cases, it shall be up to the Member against whom the complaint has been brought to rebut the charge.'

[70] Appellate Body Report, *EC–Bananas III*, ¶136.
[71] Ibid, ¶250–53.
[72] Appellate Body Reports, *Philippines–Distilled Spirits*, ¶221, *Korea–Alcoholic Beverages*, ¶120.

volumes, but rather to protect *expectations on the competitive relationship* between imported and domestic products.[73] As a result:

> A change in the competitive relationship contrary to that provision must consequently be regarded *ipso facto* as a nullification or impairment of benefits accruing under the General Agreement. A demonstration that a measure inconsistent with Article III.2 first sentence, has no or insignificant effects would therefore in the view of the Panel not be a sufficient demonstration that the benefits accruing under that provision had not been nullified or impaired even if such a rebuttal were in principle permitted.'[74]

In other words, to read collective obligations into Article 3.8 DSU is to confuse expectations on trade volumes, which is a commercial strategy, with expectations related to competitive treatment, which is fair play. This is an erroneous line of legal reasoning. This argument also displays a tendency to confuse a general interest in enforcing a law under *pacta sunt servanda*[75] and the legal interest of a Member that is based upon the original reciprocal basis for achieving concessions.[76] For as was found during the *Korea–Government Procurement* dispute: '[T]here is a difference in perspectives of the reasonable expectations of one party as opposed to the mutual understanding of all the parties.'[77] Neither the collective Membership of the WTO Treaty, nor the collective dimension to the unconditional MFN principle can negate the inherently bilateral character of trade and negotiated trade obligations. For while a breach of a WTO trade obligation may have economic effects on more than one WTO Member, this will not necessarily affect the rights of *all* other WTO Members in the same collective manner as a breach of an integral *erga omnes* obligation, such as a violation of a nuclear disarmament treaty would. Moreover, it belittles the gravity of these *erga omnes* values to suggest so.

The bilateral relationships negotiated in the GATT/WTO and then multilateralised through the unconditional MFN requirement are also enforced bilaterally in the event that the benefits that accrue to a particular Member are found to have been nullified by another Member. Each claim by each Member is considered individually by the DSU. In the event that the challenged measure is found to be non-compliant, the losing defending Member faces bilateral state-to-state countermeasures against it if it does not comply with the recommendations of the Panel or Appellate Body.[78] And while paragraph 6 of Article 21 DSU indicates a collective approach to the issue of implementation of recommendations

[73] This claim was under Art III.2.

[74] GATT Panel Report on *US–Superfund*, ¶5.1.9.

[75] Art 26 VCLT.

[76] Even the way GATT and GATS concessions are renegotiated under GATT Art XXVIII and GATS Art XXI proves the reciprocal nature of WTO obligations. Essentially, only other WTO Members with a substantial trade interest must be involved and agree to the renegotiated list of concessions. Renegotiation, once again, happens largely on a bilateral level. Pauwelyn (n 63).

[77] Panel Report, *Korea–Measures Affecting Government Procurement*, ¶7.75.

[78] DSU Art 22.

or rulings that may be raised at the DSB by any Member at any time following their adoption,[79] this, as discussed below, is one of the very few collective rights provided in the text of the provisions of WTO-covered agreements. The WTO's rules are overwhelmingly reciprocal in nature and bilateral in their modality of enforcement. Indeed, if WTO obligations were of the predominantly integral type, any inter se suspension[80] of these obligations would necessarily affect the rights of all other WTO Members and thus fall afoul of the *pacta tertiis principle*,[81] as well as the general rule that countermeasures may suspend only rights of the violating state, not of any third state.[82]

An examination of WTO disputes only serves to highlight the predominantly bilateral character of its rules and legal infrastructure. The argument for applying the term collective to the overwhelming majority of WTO provisions seems to be primarily based on scant, or selective but over-quoted findings. The most cited is sourced in the *EC–Bananas* Appellate Body report, which opined, as noted above, that 'no legal interest' is required to bring a case in the WTO. If quoted alone this statement is misleading because it was swiftly followed and significantly qualified by the acknowledgement that (a) the USA was a producer of bananas and hence a potential exporter, (b) the US market for bananas was potentially affected by the EC regime in terms of world supplies and prices, and (c) the GATT claims were inextricably interwoven with those under GATS for which the USA did unmistakably have standing.[83] The Appellate Body concluded with a further qualification for legal standing:

> Taken together, these reasons are sufficient justification. … This does not mean, though, that one or more of the factors … would necessarily be dispositive in another case.[84]

Standing to bring a challenge in the WTO DSU needs to be supported by establishing that a breach has occurred, even if there is no requirement to prove that actual trade flows have been diverted,[85] rather some proof of trade opportunities being affected is sufficient. This is not the same as affected collective expectations. Determining a breach of WTO rules is a purely bilateral matter and, as noted, often dependent on a bilateral like-product analysis between the complaining

[79] The opening sentences of Art 21.6 read: 'The DSB shall keep under surveillance the implementation of adopted recommendations or rulings. The issue of implementation of the recommendations or rulings may be raised at the DSB by any Member at any time following their adoption.'

[80] See K Dawar, 'Disconnection Clauses: An Inevitable Symptom of Regionalism?', available at: http://www.ssrn.com/link/SIEL-2010-Barcelona-Conference.html.

[81] This is confirmed in Art 58 of the Vienna Convention.

[82] See Art 49.1 of the ILC Final Draft Articles: 'An injured State may only take countermeasures against a State which is responsible for an internationally wrongful act …'.

[83] Appellate Body Report, *EC–Bananas*, ¶136–37.

[84] ibid, ¶138.

[85] See, for example, the Panel Report on *US–Taxes on Petroleum and Certain Imported Substances*, ¶5.2.2, referring to GATT Art III as a provision 'not only to protect current trade but also to create the predictability needed to plan future trade'.

party's exports and domestic products.[86] If a breach is found, a bilateral remedy is sought for the complainant, who can ultimately suspend bilateral concessions if the recommendations for cessation are not implemented in a reasonable time. If other WTO Members have the same non-compliant measure, a new state-to-state complaint must be lodged by those with standing, and they must also establish there has been a breach leading to a nullification and impairment of their benefits under the provision. Once this has been established, bilateral remedies will also be sought for the complainant.

Even the rights of third parties to disputes are stringently applied in the WTO. This was illustrated in the *China–Rare Earths* dispute when Canada requested enhanced third party rights for itself and the other third parties in the proceedings. This request was pursuant to the discretion afforded to the Panel under Article 12.1 DSU to grant 'enhanced' third-party rights in a dispute, but only provided that any such enhanced rights are consistent with the provisions of the DSU and the principles of due process.[87] Canada submitted that all the third parties to this dispute had 'significant direct legal and systemic interests' in its outcome given that it concerned the prohibition and permission of export restrictions and that they were all significant producers and consumers of the materials or analogous material involved in this dispute. Canada also cited several disputes as evidence of the tendency of panels to grant enhanced third-party rights on an ad hoc basis. Canada further reasoned that third-party enhanced rights would not disturb the balance between parties and third parties, again, underlining the undisputedly bilateral nature of the dispute.

That is, with the exception of presenting a written and/or oral submission in a special session, Canada's request was primarily for transparency and access to relevant documents.[88] Nevertheless, unlike the *EC–Bananas* findings that are so central to this argument, the Panel denied this more recent request. Implicitly underlining the bilateral nature of the WTO enforcement structure, the Panel most notably found that although Canada may have a 'direct legal and systemic interest' in the provisions under which this measure was challenged, such an interest does not distinguish Canada from any other third party to this case, or *indeed any other WTO Member*. The reasoning provided was that while enhanced third-party rights had been approved previously on grounds—such as whether the third

[86] *United States–Measures Affecting Alcoholic and Malt Beverages*; *United States–Taxes on Automobiles*; *Japan–Taxes on Alcoholic Beverages*; *European Communities–Measures affecting Asbestos and Asbestos-Containing Products*.

[87] See Appellate Body Reports, *US–1916 Act*, ¶150; *EC–Hormones*, ¶154; and *US–FSC*, ¶243.

[88] The enhanced rights specifically requested were that the third parties: (i) receive copies of the parties' written submissions, their oral statements, rebuttals, and answers to questions from the Panel and each other, through all stages of the proceedings; (ii) are present for the entirety of all substantive meetings of the Panel with the parties; (iii) make a second written submission, and/or to present an oral statement, in a special session set aside for this purpose, during the second substantive meeting, should such a special session be held; and (iv) review the draft summary of its own arguments in the descriptive part of the Panel Report. Panel Report, *China–Rare Earths*, ¶7.1.

parties enjoyed certain economic or social benefits that were directly implicated by the measure at issue, and whether enhanced third-party rights had been granted in previous similar disputes relating to the measure or similar measures—they had also been denied when third parties failed to demonstrate such connections. And Canada, along with Carmody, failed to provide a convincing case.[89]

Having established that the infrastructure of the WTO provisions and applicable dispute settlement system are predominantly bilateral in character, the following section evaluates the selected provisions from within the terms of this typology.

V. WTO GPA Provisions

The conditionality of the MFN obligation and the bilateral nature of provisions prohibiting public restrictions of competition in government procurement markets are evident within the plurilateral WTO GPA. Negotiations are complex, based on a request-and-offer approach where an initial offer from all the parties is submitted to the WTO GPA Committee. On the basis of those submissions, the parties start bilateral negotiations. The WTO GPA follows the GATS negotiating approach but with added complexities. Within the GATS negotiations, the issue concerns whether to include a service or not in the Schedule of Specific Commitments and to determine to what extent a party will commit to that inclusion.[90] In the case of the WTO GPA negotiations, not only must the parties decide which services and goods and construction services are covered by the obligations, but they must also negotiate which contracting authorities will be included in Annexes I–III, and the value of the thresholds that will trigger the scope of application of the agreement in each case and category of procurement.

Of further relevance is that the WTO GPA does not include an Annex to limit the application of restrictions to the MFN principle.[91] Instead, as noted in Chapter 2, parties to the WTO GPA commonly qualify the scope of the coverage of their obligations within the General Notes. The bilateralism of these obligations is thus heightened because if a party considers that another's commitments are insufficient, it may exclude it from one of the sectors included, or from contracting authorities covered. Thus, while reciprocity and non-discrimination are at the core of the GPA, large exclusions are allowed within the Annexes from both the NT and MFN obligations. For example, the US General Notes excludes

[89] Panel Report, *China–Raw Earths* ¶7.9.

[90] That is, the choice is whether to negotiate specific services with a full commitment where MFN and NT apply fully; or with a partial commitment, where MFN and NT obligations are subject to conditions; or without commitments where only MFN in applicable.

[91] In contrast to this, restrictions to the MFN principles are permitted under Art II:2 GATS if listed and subject to the conditions set out in the Annex on Art II exemptions.

small and medium-sized enterprises[92] from the scope of application of the GPA, thereby excluding the NT obligation. It also excludes Japan from the award of contracts by entities recorded in Annex III that are responsible for the generation and distribution of electricity, thereby excluding the MFN obligation for these types of procurement as regards Japan. There is, as a result, little element of collective obligation attached to these provisions or their enforcement.

VI. WTO ASCM Provisions

WTO drafters, in rare cases, agreed that each Member possesses a legal right in the compliance by any other contracting parties with the obligations imposed by the rule. In the case of violation, each is to be considered as an injured state, regardless of any actual or potential adverse impact on its economic interests.[93] Indeed, this is theoretically the case for prohibited subsidies as defined under the ASCM. As discussed in Chapter 2, the two categories of prohibited subsidies set out under Article 3 are presumed to distort international trade and have adverse effects on the interest of other Members. These subsidies are seen as so egregious that they may be challenged through the WTO DSM on the basis of special accelerated procedures. If the subsidy is found to be prohibited it must be withdrawn without delay. Prohibited subsidies may also be subject to countervailing measures if subsidised imports are causing injury to the domestic industry.

ASCM Article 4.1 stipulates that:

> Whenever *a Member* has reason to believe that a prohibited subsidy is being granted or maintained by another Member, such Member may request consultations with such other Member. (emphasis added)

That is, pursuant to Article 4.1, the trade effects of the prohibited subsidy become immaterial for the purpose of bringing a claim and of reacting to breaches because any Member that 'has reason to believe that a prohibited subsidy is being granted or maintained by another Member' can request the establishment of a panel. Thus, in a seemingly collective manner, all Members are entitled to resort to the dispute settlement system regardless of the effects of the alleged violation. The findings of the *US–FSC* dispute further emphasised that 'trade effects', 'adverse effects' or 'trade impacts' are immaterial:

> Other Members are not obliged to make a case regarding the adverse effects to successfully challenge such measures. They are required simply to establish the existence of a measure that is, as a matter of principle, expressly prohibited. As an empirical matter they

[92] In the USA, the typical cap on an SME is 500 employees, compared with 250 employees in the EU.

[93] T. Grazzini, 'The Legal Nature of WTO Obligations and the Consequences of their Violation' (2006) 17 *European Journal of International Law* 723.

> undoubtedly do have adverse effects. But that is not the legal basis upon which action may be taken to challenge them under the ASCM.[94]

In the *Brazil–Aircraft* dispute, the countermeasures adopted in response to violations of Article 4 ASCM aimed 'at removing a measure which is presumed under WTO Agreement to cause negative trade effects, irrespective of who suffers those trade effects and to what extent'.[95] As the FSC dispute further explicated, the obligation concerning prohibited subsidies

> is an *erga omnes* obligation owed in its entirety to each and every Member. It cannot be considered to be 'allocatable' across the Membership. Otherwise, the Member concerned would be only partially obliged in respect of each and every Member, which is manifestly inconsistent with *an erga omnes* per se obligation. Thus, the US has breached its obligation to the EC in respect of all the money that it has expended, because such expenditure in breach—the expense incurred—is the very essence of the wrongful act.[96]

In theory, *erga omnes* obligations are attached to violations of these specific WTO provisions and that all Members could be considered ipso facto injured states. Each Member is entitled to refer the dispute to the DSB, even if the measure concerned has no actual or potential adverse impact upon it. Indeed, a violation of Article 3 ASCM 'entails an irrebuttable presumption of nullification or impairment. It is therefore not necessary to refer to it'.[97] This is not the case for actionable subsidies, where countervailing measures can be resorted to only if the subsidy in question is causing or potentially causing injury to another Member on a bilateral basis.

However, any linear movement towards interpreting a collective enforcement approach to prohibited subsidies was waylaid by the subsequent findings of the Arbitration Report to the *US–Upland Cotton* dispute.[98] Here, pursuant to Article 7.10 ASCM, the Arbitrator was called upon under paragraph 6 of DSU Article 22 to determine whether Brazil's countermeasures to US cotton subsidies were commensurate with the degree and nature of the adverse effects determined to exist. This involved considering whether the proposed countermeasures should include a calculation of the effects of the 'global impact' of eliminating the subsidies at issue, as argued by Brazil. Or, conversely whether countermeasures should be limited to the adverse impact of the subsidy on Brazil alone.[99] In making this determination, the Arbitrators pointed out that the specific type of 'adverse effect' at issue, within the meaning of Article 5 ASCM, was under paragraph (c) serious prejudice. This clause was drafted specifically with reference to the interest of

[94] *US–FSC*, ¶5.39. See also *Canada–Export Credit and Loans for Regional Aircraft*, WT/ DS222/ARB, ¶3.29.

[95] *Brazil–Aircraft*, ¶3.33–3.40, 6.1–6.5.

[96] *US–FSC*. ¶6.10.

[97] *Brazil–Export Financing Programme for Aircraft*, Art 22(6), WT/DS46/ARB, 28 August 2000, ¶3.48(a).

[98] *United States–Subsidies on Upland Cotton*, Recourse to Arbitration by the United States under Art 22.6 of the DSU and Art 7.10 of the SCM Agreement, WT/DS267/ARB/2, 31 August 2009.

[99] ibid, ¶4.66.

'another Member,' rather than all Members.[100] This is not an *ergo omnes* obligation. The Arbitrators reinforced this by quoting the observations of the initial Panel Report:

> The text of Article 7.2 of the *SCM Agreement* makes it clear that the dispute settlement procedures set forth in Article 7 of the *SCM Agreement* may only be invoked by a Member where that Member believes that it has itself suffered serious prejudice as a result of the subsidization. *From this, the only logical inference is that the serious prejudice under examination by a WTO panel is the serious prejudice experienced by the complaining Member.*[101] (emphasis added)

The Arbitrators concluded that even if 'significant price suppression' was determined to exist in relation to the world market, the finding in essence relates to the interests of Brazil and reflects 'serious prejudice' to the interests of Brazil specifically.[102] As a result, determining whether Brazil's proposed countermeasures were 'commensurate with the degree and nature of the adverse effects determined to exist' involved determining whether they were commensurate with the impact on Brazil of the price suppression resulting from the granting of the prohibited subsidies on the world cotton market.

Thus, until further interpretation to the contrary, any collective character attributed to prohibited subsidies under Article 3 ASCM, is limited in practice. The relationship between Members remains bilateral in character:

> [T]the conclusion we have reached is not in any sense, a matter of 'entitling' the EC to act 'on behalf' of Members other than itself. [The EC] is proposing countermeasures relating to the redress of rights and obligations as between those two Members.[103]

Moreover, even if the other prohibited subsidy provisions defined under ASCM Article 3 have been endowed with collective obligations, an examination of the disputes brought under Article 4.1 indicates that in practice the legal infrastructure supporting the enforcement of the obligation remains wholeheartedly bilateral. As discussed, cases are brought bilaterally. The costs and benefits of bringing a dispute are not shared collectively. For not even in the most egregious subsidies cases will all other Members necessarily suffer from any resulting negative consequences on their production.

VII. Characterising the Selected RTA Provisions

Chapter 3's examination of the relevant RTAs signed by the case study countries indicated that with the qualified exception of the TFEU, all the selected RTAs were

[100] ibid, ¶4.75.
[101] ibid, ¶4.86, quoting Panel Report, *US–Upland Cotton*, ¶7.1403.
[102] ibid, ¶4.88.
[103] *US–FSC*, ¶6.63.

both limited and asymmetrical in integrating the control of anti-competitive distortions produced by state bodies in both private and public markets. While some prioritised State aid control, others were more focused on procurement provisions supported by domestic bid challenge systems. These RTAs typically either explicitly or implicitly excluded subsidies from procurement provisions and procurement from competition issues.

With the exception of the TFEU framework, all of the provisions examined in Chapter 3 were deemed bilateral in their nature and enforcement properties, where applicable. For example, the strongest US RTA of the four examined here—the NAFTA—is the only US RTA to incorporate binding rules to regulate and remedy the provision of subsidies;[104] and this is confined to goods and not services.[105] NAFTA Chapter 19 on the Review and Dispute Settlement in Antidumping and Countervailing Duty Matters establishes the rules of procedure for investigations and reviews, along with an agreement to consult on developing more effective rules and disciplines concerning the use of government subsidies[106] through a division in each party's Secretariat dedicated to operationalising the chapter. However, various provisions indicate the bilateral nature of these provisions. Article 1904 on the Review of Final Antidumping and Countervailing Duty Determinations, states that each party shall replace judicial review of final antidumping and countervailing duty determinations with a *binational* panel review. That is, not even a panel including Members that are not party to the dispute is envisaged. Only an involved party on its own initiative may request review of a final determination by a panel.[107] This tilts their enforcement towards a power/diplomacy-based model of dispute settlement, highlighted by Jackson, and away from 'rule-oriented' approach.[108] In sum, there is no possibility presented in the dispute settlement provisions for collective enforcement of these obligations.

In the regulation of government procurement markets, NAFTA Article 1003 provides binding articles on NT and non-discrimination and prohibits the use of offsets as regards the specified procurements markets set out in the Annexes and qualified further in the General Notes.[109] The provisions provide for a domestic bid challenge mechanism that is open to all suppliers. The procurement chapter also has recourse to the treaty dispute settlement procedures under Article 2004:

> Except for the matters covered in Chapter Nineteen (Review and Dispute Settlement in Antidumping and Countervailing Duty Matters) and as otherwise provided in this

[104] Although the US–Morocco RTA makes a reference to the WTO ASCM Art 18 when addressing voluntary export restraints.

[105] Chapter 12 Cross Border Trade in Services explicitly excludes subsidies from the coverage of the chapter in Art 1201.2(d).

[106] Art 1907 Consultations.

[107] Art 1903 Review of Statutory Amendments also states that: '[A] Party to which an amendment of another Party's antidumping or countervailing duty statute applies may request in writing that such amendment be referred to a *binational* panel for a declaratory opinion as to whether the amendment does not conform to Art 1902(2)(d)(i)' (emphasis added).

[108] JH Jackson, *The Jurisprudence of GATT and the WTO: Insights on Treaty Law and Economic Relations* (Cambridge, Cambridge University Press, 2000) 121.

[109] Set out in NAFTA Annex 1001.2b and Annex 1001.2c.

> Agreement, the dispute settlement provisions of this Chapter shall apply with respect to the avoidance or settlement of all disputes between the Parties regarding the interpretation or application of this Agreement or *wherever a Party considers that an actual or proposed measure of another Party is or would be inconsistent with the obligations of this Agreement or cause nullification or impairment* in the sense of Annex 2004. (emphasis added)

Consequently, under Article 2006(1) providing for consultations, *any* party may request in writing consultations with any other party regarding any actual or proposed measure or any other matter that it considers might affect the operation of the procurement commitments set out under the Agreement. This would suggest a collective dimension to the enforcement of what are bilateral rules. However, the bilateral nature of this obligation is reinforced in Article 2013 setting out the rules on third-party participation in a treaty with only three signatory parties.

> A Party that is *not* a disputing Party, on delivery of a written notice to the disputing Parties and to its Section of the Secretariat, shall be entitled to attend all hearings, to make written and oral submissions to the panel and to receive written submissions of the disputing Parties. (emphasis added)

Bilateral characteristics are also evident in the rules for selecting a Panel. Article 2011 states, inter alia, that if the disputing parties are unable to agree on the chair, the complainant party shall select as chair, an individual who is not a citizen of that party. Further, if a complainant party fails to select its panellists within a specified period, the panellists shall be selected from citizens of the other disputing party.

In sum, the research into the RTAs of the USA, Brazil, India and the EU indicates that, where included, the nature of these provisions is overwhelmingly bilateral, as is their enforcement. Again, the significant exception to this characterisation is in the EU under the framework of the TFEU.

VIII. The TFEU and the Role of the European Commission

> By creating a Community of unlimited duration, having its own institutions, its own personality, its own legal capacity and capacity of representation on the international plane and, more particularly, real powers stemming from a limitation of sovereignty or a transfer of powers from the States to the Community, *the Member States have limited their sovereign rights*, albeit within limited fields, *and have thus created a body of law which binds both their nationals and themselves.* The integration into the laws of each Member State of provisions which derive from the Community, and more generally the terms and the spirit of the Treaty, *make it impossible as a corollary, to accord precedence to a unilateral and subsequent measure over a legal system accepted by them on a basis of reciprocity.*[110] (emphasis added)

[110] Case 6/64, *Costa v ENEL* [1964] ECR 585, 593–94.

It has been noted that in the supranational vision underlying the EU, the 'community' as a transnational regime is meant to tame the national interests with a new discipline.[111] The EU treaties serve to protect collective higher values including respect for human dignity, liberty, democracy, equality, the rule of law and human rights. These values are seen as indivisible collective values in common to the Member States. The ECJ reasoned in favour of the supremacy of the rules to protect collective values in the landmark *Van Gend en Loos* dispute:

> The [Union] constitutes a new legal order of international law for the benefit of which the States have limited their sovereign rights, albeit within limited fields, and the subjects of which comprise not only Member States but also their nationals.[112]

The collective nature of these rules was confirmed early on when the doctrine of direct effect was challenged. The dispute revolved over whether Article 18 TFEU[113] had direct application in a Member State with the effect that on the basis of this Article, nationals could lay claim individual rights that the courts must protect.[114] Controversially, the then-ECJ took a teleological interpretive approach to reading the Treaty text with the aim of determining the underlying, evolving aims of the *enterprise* as a whole. Thus, rather than adopting the narrow literal interpretation of a provision as prescribed by the WTO DSU, the CJEU typically examines the whole context in which a provision is situated and what it seeks to achieve. As a result, the ECJ has exhibited a 'meta-teleological' approach, which puts less emphasis on specific objectives and aims of legislation than integration and unity in European law.[115] This has not been without criticisms of judicial activism. Such moves have been denounced as seeking inspiration in guidelines that are essentially political and not therefore judicially applicable. Or further, that: 'This is the root of judicial activism which may be an usurpation of power … in the face of society's declining taste for a precipitated process of integration.'[116]

Thus, while not without tension between the state and the community of states as governments continue to pursue their national interests and maximise their benefits, EU norms nevertheless *trump* conflicting Member State norms and in so doing possess a collective or integral dimension. For Joseph Weiler, this hierarchy of norms is not rooted in a hierarchy of normative authority or in a hierarchy of

[111] JHH Weiler, 'The State über Alles: Demos, Telos and the German Maastricht Decision', in *Festschrift für Ulrich Everling* (Baden-Baden, Nomos, 1995) vol II, 1651, 1682.

[112] Case 26–62 *NV Algemene Transport- en Expeditie Onderneming van Gend & Loos v Netherlands Inland Revenue Administration*, Judgment of the Court, 5 February 1963, Summary, para 3. Referred to here as: Case 26/62 *Van Gend en Loos* [1963].

[113] Then EEC Art 12, para 1: 'Within the scope of application of this Treaty, and without prejudice to any special provisions contained therein, any discrimination on grounds of nationality shall be prohibited.'

[114] See Case 26/62 *Van Gend en Loos* [1963].

[115] G Conway, *Limits of Legal Reasoning and the European Court of Justice* (Cambridge, Cambridge University Press, 2012).

[116] H Rasmussen, *On Law and Policy in the European Court of Justice* (Leiden, Nijhoff, 1986) 62.

real power. Rather, European federalism is constructed with a top-to-bottom hierarchy of norms, but with a bottom-to-top hierarchy of authority and real power. This resulting asymmetry is fraught because Europe's constitutional architecture has never been validated by a process of constitutional adoption by a European constitutional demos. Hence, as a matter of both normative political principle and empirical social observation, the European constitutional discipline does not enjoy the same kind of authority as may be found in federal states rooted in a classic constitutional order. It is a constitution without some of the classic conditions of constitutionalism.[117] Despite this lack of constitutional authority, and unlike the WTO, the EU institutions are granted exclusive competence to regulate specific areas, including external trade, and as a result the Member States have no competence to deviate from them.

As Chapter 3 noted, in the area of subsidies Article 108 TFEU requires EU Member States to notify all planned State aid measures to the Commission and to obtain the Commission's approval *prior* to implementation.[118] Thus insofar as transparency is a sine qua non for treaty compliance, subsidy control is more convincing in the EU than the WTO or in the other selected RTAs. In addition to an ex ante surveillance mechanism, the Commission provides a powerful normative dynamic by publishing a State aid scoreboard assessing the impacts of State aid and State aid control.[119] The Commission can declare that a specific measure does not constitute permitted aid or decide whether to approve of a specific measure, and it can also unilaterally decide to launch an ex officio investigation into certain alleged State aid measures.[120] Furthermore, in one of the most important displays of collective obligations, the standing requirement for making a complaint to the Commission under the TFEU reaches far beyond that of the Member States. It includes competitors or other interested parties who believe that a certain measure constitutes State aid and therefore have a legal right to complain to the Commission.

[117] See JHH Weiler, 'Federalism and Constitutionalism. Europe's Sonderweg' in K Nicolaidis and R Howse (eds), *The Federal Vision: Legitimacy and Levels of Governance in the US and the EU* (Oxford, Oxford University Press, 2001).

[118] Except for those measures that the Commission has exempted from notification.

[119] In the first quarter of the year, the Commission sends a spreadsheet to the Member States, for completion with the figures of the actual State aid expenditure for each of the listed measures granted during the previous year. The data received from the Member States are of varying quality and the Scoreboard team spends a lot of time checking the data and adding missing amounts. Problems have been reported in obtaining data from regional and local public authorities. Many Member States are late in providing the data, but only one infringement procedure has been launched for not respecting the deadline set by Implementing Regulation No 794/2004. See European Court of Auditors Special Report 15/2011, 'Do the Commission's Procedures Ensure Effective Management of State Aid Control?'.

[120] Under Art 4.5 of the Procedural Regulation, all decisions must be adopted within two months following the receipt of a complete notification. The notification will be considered as complete if, within two months from its receipt, or from the receipt of any additional information requested, the Commission does not request any further information. If the Commission asks for further information, a new two-month period starts when the Member State submits the information requested.

As regards government procurement rules, Chapter 3 noted that within the TFEU, public purchases are also subject to State aid control under Article 107. This provision refers to any aid granted by a Member State or through state resources *in any form whatsoever* that distorts or threatens to distort competition by favouring certain undertakings. There are also detailed secondary rules at the EU level in the form of EU Directives that govern public purchases of goods, services and infrastructure in all EU Member States.[121] Herein lies the problem. While procurement falls under the scope of the obligations of Article 107, the use of competitive, transparent and non-discriminatory public tenders has traditionally been considered sufficient to presume that no State aid is provided to the economic operator selected as a result of the procedure. This removes the possibility that the Commission can identify and pronounce ex ante that State aid would not be provided through a particular tender procedure.

In the case *MOL Magyar Olaj- és Gázipari Nyrt. v The Commission*, a dispute arose involving the amendment of the 2007 Mining Act in Hungary. This amendment had increased the mining fee rate to 30 per cent, except for MOL—a Hungarian oil and gas company extracting hydrocarbons—which remained subject to the rates set in the 2005 agreement. In June 2010, the Commission adopted a decision that this measure constituted State aid that was incompatible with the common market and requested Hungary to recover approximately €96.6 million and €6.6 million for 2008 and 2009, respectively, from MOL.[122] Subsequently, MOL brought an action before the General Court for annulment of the Commission Decision. The General Court controversially ruled in MOL's favour, finding that MOL did not gain unfairly from the fixed mining royalty payments to the government. In its reasoning, the Court noted inter alia that the Mining Act allows any undertaking to apply for the extension of its mining rights on one or more fields on which it has not started extraction within five years of issuance of the authorisation. Since the criteria laid down by the Mining Act for the conclusion of an extension agreement are objective and applicable to any potentially interested operator that fulfils those criteria, the Court felt that no undue advantage to MOL could be established. This ruling raised some points of criticism of the regulation of competition in public procurement tenders under the Directives. Most notably for this research is the questionable margin of assessment permitted to domestic authorities when determining the rate of the extension fee and whether undertakings could potentially derive a competitive advantage from this in being able to submit abnormally low bids permitted by this discretion.

Article 69.1 of Directive 2014/24/EU on Abnormally Low Tenders requires that economic operations explain to contracting authorities the costs proposed when

[121] Concessions: Directive 2014/23/EU; General: Directive 2014/24/EU; Utilities: Directive 2014/25/EU.

[122] Decision 2011/88/EU on State aid C1/09 (ex NN 69/08) granted by Hungary to MOL Nyrt ([2011] OJ L34, 55).

tenders appear to be abnormally low in relation to the works, supplies or services, including whether or not State aid was involved. If the contracting authority can establish that the reason the tender is abnormally low is because the tenderer has obtained State aid, it can reject the tender on those grounds alone.[123] This offers another unilateral legal avenue to address public restraints of competition in procurement markets. As such this could be challenged under WTO DSU Article 3.2 and the ASCM, but not, as discussed, under Article I:1 GATT. In practice, however, there is little incentive for a contracting authority to trigger it because their procurement budget is gaining from the subsidies given by another public body at home, in another Member State or elsewhere. An additional disincentive is that the contracting authority is required to provide proof to a level that is not clear and in a context where the enforcement system of State aid rules has given exclusive competence to the Commission. It is of little surprise that, to date, this provision has not been applied.[124]

It can be contended that an integrated approach to regulating government measures that distort competition in public procurement and open markets in undermined by the CJEU interpretations in various disputes. Procurement falling under the scope of Article 107 is evaluated and monitored by the Commission, offering a strong transparent compliance and a collective enforcement mechanism. This is not the case for those procurements regulated by one of the applicable directives. This is confirmed by the rulings of cases such as *Altmark*[125] and *Mol v The Commission*.[126]

IX. Summary Conclusions

Part I of this book has looked at the first two levels of research into the international rules regulating state behaviour in public and private markets. In doing so, the research set out the relevant rules in the WTO and in the RTAs of the case study countries as regards preventing anti-competitive state measures in government procurement and State aid policies to assess them in terms of (a) their level of integration and (b) the nature of their enforcement.

[123] The tender may be rejected on the ground that State aid was responsible for the low price of the bid only after consultation with the tenderer where the latter is unable to prove, within a sufficient time limit fixed by the contracting authority, that the aid in question was compatible with the internal market within the meaning of Art 107 TFEU.

[124] See with reference to the 2004 Directive, G Skovgaard Olykke, 'The Legal Basis Which Will (Probably) Never Be Used: Enforcement of State Aid Law in a Public Procurement Context' [2011] *European State Aid Law Quarterly* 457.

[125] Case C-280/00, *Altmark Trans GmbH* [2003] ECR I-7747; Judgment of the General Court (Second Chamber), 12 November 2013 *MOL Magyar Olaj- és Gázipari Nyrt. v European Commission.* Case T-499/10.

[126] Decision 2011/88/EU (n 121).

The first level of analysis into the degree of integration or coherence between these two interdependent but hitherto distinct sets of regulation produced mixed results. Within the WTO, in addition to the GATT non-discrimination principles, the plurilateral GPA regulating procurement measures among the parties and the ASCM seek to prevent anti-competitive subsidies in a variety of forms including through government purchases, of all the WTO Members. This is a partial acknowledgement of the interdependence of open and government procurement markets. Nevertheless, unlike the GPA, the ASCM no longer includes specified exceptions to be permitted. The applicability of the GATT Article XX exceptions to the ASCM is to be determined only on a case-by-case basis. This produces legal uncertainty and undermines coherence and an integrated approach to regulating anti-competitive state measures in procurement markets under the WTO GPA and ASCM.

The research further concluded that there are cogent reasons for re-examining the scope of Article I:1 MFN with regards to the matters referred to in Article III:4 and its accompanying derogation for government procurement and subsidies under Article III:8(a)(b). At present, procurement measures and subsidies are seen to be excluded from the MFN obligations by virtue of Article III:8(a)(b) despite the lack of explicit intention of the Members to do so. This argument is based substantially on the convoluted interpretations from one panel report. While this may appear to be of marginal importance due to the coverage of the GPA and ASCM agreements, the potential use 'matching clause' or other similar unilateral provisions to permit or disqualify government subsidies in certain cases may well increase the salience of this issue.

Of the selected RTAs, only the TFEU takes an integrated approach to regulating public restraints of competition in public and private markets under Article 107 TFEU. The European courts have taken an expansive and teleological interpretive approach, promoting the core values of the community above those of the Member States. Yet, this integrated approach is undermined by the fact that the use of competitive, transparent and non-discriminatory public tenders, as prescribed by the Procurement Directives, is considered sufficient to presume that no State aid has been provided. However, these procurement procedures cannot guarantee a market price and the European Commission cannot pronounce ex ante that State aid has not been provided through a particular tender. This reduces transparency and questions the legitimacy of those tender processes not falling under Article 107 TFEU. Significantly for this research, it also splits the integrated approach to regulating public restraints of competition into two asymmetrical sets of regulation.

The second level of research regarding the legal nature of these selected provisions concluded that in the WTO, the provisions are binding obligations. Further, the institutional infrastructure supporting the agreements is overwhelmingly bilateral in nature. This has implications for the enforcement of these rules, determining who has standing and the remedies available to injured Members. The individual provisions selected for analysis were also overwhelmingly bilateral, even as regards prohibited subsidies under the ASCM. The enforcement of these provisions has also hitherto been undeniably bilateral. Even requests for enhanced third-party rights are carefully deliberated, and not always permitted.

At the regional level, all the RTAs examined were also bilateral in nature and enforcement infrastructure, again with the notable exception of the TFEU. The EU has collective values that are higher than the bilateral relationships between the Member governments as depicted under the WTO. This collective project has been subject to much tension in its development due to what has been seen as judicial activism during dispute settlement. Nevertheless, the role of the Commission is pioneering because it provides a collective approach to compliance and enforcement of the provisions regulating public restraints of competition provides more transparency, legal certainty and compliance than in any other intergovernmental trade agreement. Notwithstanding this, as noted, there are limits to the integrated nature of this approach. The collective approach applied to State aid control is not applied to those procurements seen to be in compliance with the procurement Directives. This, in effect, deactivates the prohibition on distortionary State aid, in favour of the 'legal labyrinths of arcane tendering procedures, murky supplier qualifications'.[127] As such, it detracts from transparency and compliance.

Part I's theoretical examination therefore concludes that there are 'gaps' in coverage of binding international government procurement and competition rules that are typically not filled at the regional level rules, with the singular exception of the TFEU. The integrated approach provided under the ASCM in the WTO system offers a unitary framework for regulating all WTO Member government's measures, with a potential to distort trade in both government procurement and open markets. Nevertheless, it has certain shortcomings and interpretative ambiguities that act to undermine its ability to regulate subsidies, including crisis measures. It does not cover the trade in services; the burden of proof under the ASCM is typically onerous, and moreover, its remedies are prospective. Further, it is supported by a primarily bilateral enforcement mechanism for state-to-state dispute resolution under the WTO DSM. And additionally, it is not certain whether a non-compliant subsidy measure can be defended under the GATT Article XX General Exceptions, even if the non-compliant measure was seen as necessary to protect a legitimate domestic policy objective under the WTO GPA.

Yet while the WTO GPA does cover both goods, services and a combination thereof, and it also includes general exceptions that can be used to defend a non-compliant procurement measure, it is, however, unable to regulate the procurements of those WTO Members who are not signatory parties to the GPA; or the procurements of GPA parties that are not included in negotiated schedules; or moreover, those procurements of the WTO GPA parties that fall below the negotiated financial thresholds above which the rules apply.[128] The inability of parties

[127] JL Dunoff, 'Linking International Markets and Global Justice' (2009) 107 *Michigan Law Review* 1039.

[128] In this sense, these GPA thresholds can be seen as setting a de minima.

to cross-retaliate under the other covered agreements of the WTO further undermines its potential strength. The WTO GPA therefore has very different weaknesses and gaps in its scope, coverage and available remedies than those identified under the WTO ASCM. And as noted, a non-compliant procurement measure, even if it is exempted for public policy reasons under the WTO GPA, will also be examined under the ASCM without public policy exemptions, due to the cumulative nature of the WTO agreements.

In terms of the enforcement nature of these international provisions, Part I concludes that these provisions, while hard binding rules in terms of their degree of legalisation, should be generally described as bilateral in nature. Market access obligations are negotiated bilaterally and generally applied through the MFN provision, although in the WTO GPA even the reciprocity requirement is pragmatically applied. Furthermore, even in the case of those exceptional provisions that display a collective quality, most notably here under Article 3.1 ASCM, the institutional infrastructure supporting enforcement is unambiguously bilateral. This limits standing only to those governments with a direct interest in the non-compliant measure.

The RTAs examined in Part I were also overwhelmingly bilateral in their enforcement. The TFEU is the only significant exception to this. However, while the collective enforcement qualities are provided for under Article 107, which regulates State aid including through procurement measures, this collective and integrated model is undermined by case law. Current interpretations indicate that a particular procurement cannot be considered unlawful State aid if it complies with procurement directives. These rulings split the integrated approach to regulating these interdependent markets back into two asymmetrical regimes.

To apply and test the findings of Part I's theoretical legal examination, the remainder of this book addresses the operation of these selected rules in regulating discriminatory anti-competitive government distortions to public procurement and open markets. It takes as its evidentiary base the stress test of the economic crisis years of 2008–12. This was when governments were under abnormally high levels of pressure to protect domestic interest groups, including through implementing discriminatory and WTO non-compliant trade measures. This timeframe allows for an examination of the strengths and weaknesses of the system when they are most salient. It serves to illuminate how violations of international and regional trade obligations to tackle market failures were defended during a global economic crisis, to prevent a tit-for-tat trade war and promote a coordinated recovery.

Part II

The Case Studies International Trade Law in a Crisis: Who Makes it and Who Breaks it?

5

Assessing the Legality of Bailouts and Buy-Nationals

I. US Fiscal Bailout Measures

> The bubble burst because banks stopped trusting each other—long before the rest of us stopped trusting banks.[1]

In the United States, the banking sector historically developed without direct government support or ownership. The financial services sector has been fragmented—both geographically and into different retail functions. Indeed, interstate banking only developed in the 1980s and 1990s, along with the emergence of holding companies to allow banks to combine their activities in disparate markets.[2] When the Glass–Steagall Act of 1933, which had prohibited universal banking and associating retail banking with investment banking in securities markets, was repealed in 1999,[3] the trend towards deregulating financial markets was confirmed. As a result of these deregulatory moves,[4] the market for asset-backed securities swelled dramatically, and most notably for insured and bundled mortgages. This new regulatory climate encouraged home ownership, even for those on a low income, through so-called subprime mortgages and mortgage guarantees insured by the government-sponsored Federal National Mortgage Association—Fannie Mae—and the Federal Home Loan Mortgage Corporation—Freddie Mac. These two entities held approximately 60 per cent of mortgage-backed securities. In June 2008, their combined debt and obligations totalled \$6.6 trillion.[5]

When, in late 2006, the house price index started to fall, it became clear that these securities-backed mortgages were not risk free and, furthermore, that the insurers of these securities had insufficient reserves to cover the increasing

[1] P Seabright, as cited by J Vickers, 'The Financial Crisis and Competition Policy: Some Economics' [2008] December, *Global Competition Policy* 1.

[2] This was particularly so after the Riegle–Neal Interstate Banking Act of 1994.

[3] The Glass–Steagall Act was repealed by the Gramm–Leach–Bliley Act of 1999.

[4] Including the Commodities Futures Modernization Act of 2000.

[5] RD Congleton, 'On the Political Economy of the Financial Crisis and Bailout of 2008–2009', Public Choice 2009 140, 300–02.

delinquencies on residential mortgages. By 2008 Bear Stearns had to be rescued by JP Morgan on the condition of a 'backstop' guarantee from the US government on future losses, thus establishing the precedent of a bailout guarantee for failing investment banks.[6] What followed was a series of large subsidies made possible through deposit guarantees, shortly followed by comprehensive rescue packages. These bailout measures aimed to address the financial sector as a whole because financial subsectors were also suffering. The first measure (set out in Appendix 1) is a prime example. The American International Group (AIG) was bailed out by the US government for $182 billion, indirectly saving several financial institutions exposed to AIG derivatives.[7]

Tailor-made rescue packages were then designed for the big US mortgage lenders Fannie Mae and Freddie Mac. A significant part of the Troubled Asset Relief Program (TARP)—$250 billion—was also used to purchase equity in nine financial institutions. This capital injection was accompanied by strict requirements relating to executive compensation and corporate governance, while giving incentives to the institutions to pay the government back. TARP was widely denounced by liberals, conservatives, Republicans, Democrats and the public. Indeed, one Member of Congress is quoted as saying: 'I don't think it is too much of a stretch to say this may be the day America died.'[8] A Bloomberg poll in October 2009 asked how TARP had affected the economy: 43 per cent of respondents said it had weakened the economy; 21 per cent said it had made a difference; only 24 percent said it helped, with 12 per cent unsure one way or another. Commentators in newspapers from the *Wall Street Journal* to the *New York Times* disparaged TARP. And while the markets responded favourably to the announcement of TARP, suggesting that the launch of the bailout programme indeed helped restore investors' confidence in the financial system, the market reacted negatively to the receipt of TARP bailout funds. Moreover, banks that received larger bailouts experienced greater stock price declines.[9]

A. The Legality of US Fiscal Measures under the GATS

The financial rescue measures (see Appendix 1: measures 1–4) adopted by the US government are beneficial subsidies transferred to domestic banks as service suppliers. These measures therefore fall under the purview of the GATS: all of the measures were designed to confer a benefit to a specific financial services undertaking and in so doing distort the conditions of competition between the subsidised undertaking and those companies that were not equally subsidised.

[6] C Woll, 'The Power of Inaction', (Cornell University Press, 2014) 87.

[7] Including Goldman Sachs, Morgan Stanley and Bank of America as well as several European banks.

[8] A member of US Congress is quoted as saying this on 3 October 2008, the day TARP was enacted. Cited in M Ncube, 'Bank Bailout under TARP in the US', BSG-WP-2016/010, January 2016.

[9] ibid.

The United States had scheduled NT commitments towards US branches, agencies, securities affiliates, and other operations of foreign banks. Further binding commitments were also made in market access and NT, corresponding to all subsectors included in the Annex on Financial Services in the GATS, and in line with the Understanding on Commitments in Financial Services.[10] Some exceptions have been set out within the US GATS Schedule. Most notably, all directors of a national bank must be US citizens, unless the bank is an affiliate or subsidiary of a foreign bank.[11] Further, that credit union, savings bank, home loan or thrift businesses may not be provided through branches of corporations organised under a foreign country's law and foreign banks cannot be members of the Federal Reserve System.[12]

So, although GATS Article XV does not impose any obligations to remove any subsidies in the services sector, it does not leave such subsidies unregulated; GATS Article XVII:1 national treatment is applicable. This provision requires that governments accord NT to all financial service providers with a commercial presence in their country to the extent that any treatment could have anti-competitive effects within that country.[13] That is, Article XVII applies to subsidies in the same way that it applies to all other measures. Any subsidy that is a discriminatory measure within the meaning of Article XVII would have to be either scheduled as a limitation on NT or brought into conformity with that Article. A binding commitment under Article XVII with respect to the granting of a subsidy does not require a Member to offer such a subsidy to a services supplier located in the territory of another Member.[14] Only when the bailout 'subsidy' is provided to both the parent company and/or to any specific subsidiaries or branches is Article XVII applicable. However, if the subsidy is only provided to the parent company, since most of the parent company of foreign supplies under Mode 3 are located outside the US jurisdiction, Article XVII would not apply.

Yet even if the US fiscal measures were to be challenged under Article XVII:1 GATS on the grounds that the bailouts were specific, targeted and not horizontally available to all banks, the USA could still defend its measures under the 'Understanding on Commitments in Financial Services'. Part C of the Understanding requires that NT is to be granted during the 'normal course of ordinary business'. Given that the US fiscal stimulus measures were designed to alleviate the effects of a systemic subprime crisis, it is likely that these circumstances would have been

[10] Foreign banks may establish a commercial presence in the US market either by establishing federal- or state-licensed branches, agencies, or representative offices, or by establishing or acquiring a national or state subsidiary bank. WTO document GATS/EL/90/Suppl.3, 26 February 1998.

[11] In which case, only a majority of the board need be US citizens.

[12] WTO Trade Policy Review: United States. Report by the Secretariat, WT/TPR/S/200 (2013) 108.

[13] Art XXVII:3 also notes that formally identical or formally different treatment shall be considered to be less favourable if it modifies the conditions of competition in favour of services or service suppliers of the member compared to like services or service suppliers of any other member.

[14] See Guidelines for the Scheduling of Specific Commitments under the General Agreement on Trade in Services (GATS), adopted March 2001, S/L/92, ¶15–16.

pronounced as 'outside' of the parameters deemed to be in the normal course of ordinary business. If this is defined as an exception to NT, the burden of proving that the crisis measure was outside the normal course of ordinary business rests on the responding Member.

Of further applicability is the Annex on Financial Services. Under the 'prudential carve out' provisions of paragraph 2 of the Annex, except for being subject to a 'good faith' means–ends policy analysis, it is the right of the USA or any other signatory to the GATS Annex on Financial Services to adopt any measure aimed at the protection of investors, consumers of financial services or financial stability in general. The broad conception of the prudential carve-out provision was highlighted during the *Argentina–Financial Services* dispute. Here, the Panel noted the provision was left intentionally broad as the result of a delicate compromise. Therefore, a narrow interpretation of the scope of application of the provision or of the conditions under which the prudential exception can successfully be invoked would go against the balance of rights and obligations of the Agreement.[15] This exception[16] does not prescribe or illustrate the type of measures that can be adopted. Consequently, even if these measures were challenged it can be asserted that paragraph 2 would serve as a legitimate defence for the USA's financial bailout measures, and the USA would shoulder the burden of proof.

In effect, unless it could be shown that there is no relationship between these crisis measures and the financial bailout of these ailing financial institutions, or that the US government enacted the measure in 'bad faith' to avoid other obligations of the GATS, contra the last sentence of the prudential carve-out, more than 80 per cent of the approximate $12 trillion of US federal crisis relief would likely escape the WTO's purview because it falls within the safe harbour of the GATS Annex. And this will remain the case for as long as the GATS continues to operate a comprehensive framework for the regulation of financial subsidies.

B. The Legality of the US Fiscal Measures under US RTA Obligations

Table 3.1 in chapter 3 sets out the eighteen RTAs concluded by the case study countries that include provisions to prevent anti-competitive state measures. Table 3.1 indicates that four of these RTAs are signed by the USA, a further eleven by the EU, including the TFEU, India is a party to two agreements, while Brazil is a party to only one of the RTAs identified through the WTO RTA database. All of these agreements are in force and all of them were signed after the year 2000.

[15] Report of the Panel, *Argentina–Measures Relating to Trade in Goods and Services*, WT/DS453/R, 30 September 2015, ¶7.849.

[16] Art 2(a) of the Annex confirms the prudential measure is an exception.

Of the four relevant RTAs concluded by the US, only the NAFTA incorporates rules to regulate and remedy the provision of subsidies,[17] for example in the form of bailouts, but this is confined to goods and not services.[18] As a result, the rescue measures aimed at the financial sector were not subject to the constraints of any regional rules.

(i) *Summary of Legality of US Bailout Measures under International and Regional Law*

The above assessment indicates that given that the bailouts were only provided to parent companies, and that the USA had not signed up to any hard rules prohibiting subsidies in the financial sector, the $12 trillion provided to US banks was not in violation of any rules under the GATS. Despite the emerging governance of international organisations such as the Financial Stability Board and a dizzying array of international agreements aimed at introducing standards for supervisory and macroprudential oversight the international regulatory framework for financial markets is best characterised as soft, non-binding law. It has little enforcement power or 'compliance pull' beyond reputational mechanisms.[19] As such, it has been unable either to prevent crises or regulate the bailout subsides and promote competition in these markets. Not only was the banking industry not held to account at the time of the crisis, but the situation has remained largely unchanged. For in January 2017, a decade after the emergence of the financial turmoil, the Basel Committee on Banking Supervision was still unable to agree to a series of reforms intended to make it harder for banks to avoid the higher Basel III capital requirements that were put in place after the financial crisis.[20]

C. The US Auto-Industry Stimulus Measures

Hot on the heels of the banking sector bailout measures, in December 2008, the US government introduced the Auto Industry Financing and Restructuring Act (AIFR) (Appendix 1, measure 5).[21] These funds were sourced from TARP, which was established to implement $700 billion of emergency funding appropriated under the 2008 Emergency Economic Stabilization Act (EESA). Under the EESA,

[17] Although the US–Morocco RTA makes a reference to the WTO ASCM Art18 when addressing voluntary export restraints.

[18] Chapter 12 Cross Border Trade in Services explicitly excludes subsidies from the coverage of the chapter in Art 1201.2(d).

[19] See C Brummer, 'How International Financial Law Works (and How it Doesn't)' (2011) 99 *Georgetown Law Journal* 257.

[20] See. 'Basel Postpones Bank Reform Vote Amid Policy Differences: Global Financial Supervisors Fail to Agree on Latest Capital Rules' *Financial Times*, 3 January 2017, www.ft.com/content/589f1ce0-d1a1-11e6-9341-7393bb2e1b51.

[21] HR 7321.

the financial institutions deemed eligible to apply for emergency funding were broadly defined to:

> … cover any institution, including, but not limited to, any bank, savings association, credit union, security broker or dealer, or insurance company, established and regulated under the laws of the United States or any State, territory, or possession … and having significant operations in the United States, but excluding any central bank of, or institution owned by, a foreign government.[22]

However, by October 2008, revisions had been made to this programme to allow for the bulk of the funds to be used to purchase government equity stakes in financial institutions, rather than purchasing their illiquid assets. The result was the Capital Purchase Program (CPP) established under TARP to provide for the purchase of senior preferred stock and warrants from any Qualifying Financial Institution (QFI). The scope of QFIs was set more narrowly than under the EESA in that to qualify, the applicant must be established and operating in the United States.[23] That is, it may not be controlled by a foreign bank or company. This, as a result, operated to prevent any foreign affiliated financing companies in the USA from participating in the CPP.

In the event, only two auto companies received financial rescue packages under these TARP-funded schemes. Thus, while the CPP was directed at financial institutions, this measure directly benefited manufacturing industries, rather than the financial institutions themselves. In a slight of hand, the Federal Reserve formally approved GMAC Financial Services LLC's bid to become a bank holding company in December 2008. GMAC was then eligible to apply to the CPP as a Qualified Financial Institution and received an initial loan funding of \$5 billion, followed in May 2009 by an additional \$7.5 billion in funding under the AIFP programme.[24] As regards Chrysler, the US Treasury Department provided \$1.5 billion for a special purpose entity created by Chrysler Financial to serve as a conduit to receive TARP funding under the AIFP.

(i) The Legality of the AIFP and CPP Auto Bailouts under the WTO

If challenged as an injurious subsidy under the WTO DSM by a government of a foreign-affiliated auto producer, the TARP-funded bailouts would likely be found to fall under the ASCM's basic definition of actionable subsidies for the

[22] Emergency Economic Stabilization Act, HR 1424–22, ss 3(5) and 101.

[23] The CPP was made available to bank holding companies, financial holding companies, insured depository institutions, and savings and loan holding companies that engage solely or predominantly in activities that are permissible for financial holding companies under relevant law.

[24] The Federal Reserve and the US Treasury Department suspended certain bank holding company rules and other requirements under the CPP and AIFP programmes for the specific purpose of allowing 'Big Three'-affiliated automotive financing companies, such as GMAC and Chrysler Financing, to qualify for a total of \$12.5 billion in direct TARP funding assistance to date. See CC Bensen, 'US Automotive Industry Bailout Programs: Avoiding WTO Potholes on the Road to Economic Recovery' (2009) available at: http://alsb.roundtablelive.org/resources/documents/np%202009%20benson,%20c.pdf.

following reasons. Firstly, these guarantees were both a financial contribution by a government or other public body, Secondly, these rescue packages were provided on terms that were significantly more favourable than what was available on the market because these markets were frozen.[25] This confers a benefit under the provisions of ASCM Article 1.1(b). Furthermore, these loan guarantee subsidies were specific under ASCM Article 2 provisions.[26] To be actionable under this provision, a subsidy must be specific to an enterprise or industry or group of enterprises or industries, or if the granting authority or authorising law explicitly limits access to a subsidy to certain enterprises. A subsidy will not be found to be specific if the authorizing law or the agency granting the subsidy establishes objective criteria or conditions for a company to be eligible for the subsidy.[27] These rescue packages were funded by AIFP, which was established for the explicit purpose of targeting $17.4 billion in TARP funding directly to the *domestic* automotive industry. This likely qualifies them as specific measures to assist domestic automotive producers and consequently actionable.

A complainant WTO Member could also argue that these rescue packages constitute highly distortive subsidies and are so prejudicial that they pose a per se threat of serious prejudice and necessarily create an imminent or foreseeable risk of future serious prejudice to the WTO interests of other Members. These so-called 'dark amber' subsidies were originally listed under Article 6.1 ASCM because they pose a per se threat of serious prejudice due to their extremely distorted nature. Under the original 1994 WTO Agreements, Article 6.1 had a five-year period of provisional application.[28] During that time, those dark amber subsidies that were automatically deemed to cause serious prejudice included, inter alia, subsidies to cover operating losses sustained by an industry and direct forgiveness of debt—in effect, bailouts.

Although these subsidising initiatives are no longer automatically presumed to cause serious prejudice, a significant textual and negotiating history remains to suggest that most WTO Members view these subsidies as extremely trade distorting and injurious. The USA, for instance, tabled a formal proposal to the WTO Negotiating Group on Rules to this effect, just before the onset of the crisis in

[25] While the US Treasury information does not provided data on the Auto SSP loan guarantees, the EISA programme, for example, provided below-market interest rates, deferral of payments for up to five years after the start of operations of the new facilities, and stretching out payments for up to 25 years. See 'CRS Report for Congress on Federal Loans to the Auto Industry under the Energy Independence and Security Act' (13 November 2008) 14–15.

[26] The ASCM Agreement also states under Art 2.1 that a subsidy limited to certain enterprises located within a particular geographical region is considered to be specific.

[27] There are also cases where the conditions for conferring a subsidy appear to be non-specific, but will nevertheless be deemed specific 'as applied' if other factors are also in play. Such factors include, for example, the actual use of a subsidy programme by only a limited number of certain enterprises, the predominant use by certain enterprises, and the manner in which discretion is exercised in granting the subsidy.

[28] Pursuant to Art 31 ASCM, those subsidies presumed to cause serious prejudice under Art 6.1 ASCM subsidies and non-actionable subsidies for R&D, environment and regional aid under Arts 8 and 9, expired on 1 January 2000.

June 2007, which was not subsequently referred to. This US proposal included a draft ASCM text that would classify all but the total ad valorem subsidisation of a product exceeding 5 per cent as prohibited subsidies under Article 3 ASCM. This would have consequences in that no proof of adverse effects would be required for a WTO challenge. In other words, if such auto bailouts were challenged on the basis of these dark amber provisions in a WTO dispute settlement proceeding and the DSB were to accept this line of legal reasoning, the subsidising government would have the burden of showing that serious prejudice had *not* resulted from the subsidy.[29]

In sum: it is possible that a challenge could have been made that the AIFP and CPP auto bailout measures constitute dark amber subsidies, so trade distorting that they pose a per se threat of serious prejudice and necessarily create an imminent or foreseeable risk of future serious prejudice to the WTO interests of other Member countries. However, no such challenge was brought to the WTO DSM based on a violation of the ASCM.

(ii) The Legality of the US Auto Industry Bailouts under RTA Obligations

US RTAs do not regulate subsidies in goods within their competition provisions. Nevertheless, the general non-discrimination rules will apply to the auto industry measures unless exempted. For example, NAFTA's Article 300 on Scope and Coverage stipulates that the chapter applies to trade in goods of a Party, including goods covered by Annex 300-A, which is Trade and Investment in the Automotive Sector. Thus Article 301 NT is applicable:

1. Each Party shall accord national treatment to the goods of another Party in accordance with Article III of the *General Agreement on Tariffs and Trade* (GATT), including its interpretative notes, and to this end Article III of the GATT and its interpretative notes, or any equivalent provision of a successor agreement to which all Parties are party, are incorporated into and made part of this Agreement.
2. The provisions of paragraph 1 regarding national treatment shall mean, with respect to a state or province, treatment no less favorable than the most favorable treatment accorded by such state or province to any like, directly competitive or substitutable goods, as the case may be, of the Party of which it forms a part.

As indicated in Appendix 1, Measure 5 explicitly targets US auto-makers, discriminating against even those licensed financing companies operating in the USA to provide a loan to US customers to buy a vehicle in the USA, due to their affiliation with a foreign bank or company. This could be challenged as a violation of NT commitments towards the other parties to the RTA. However, given that under NAFTA Article 301 incorporates the NT in accordance with GATT Article III NT, a strong defence could be made on the part of the USA that this textual incorporation

[29] See 'Expanding the Prohibited Red Light Subsidy Category, Draft Text Proposal from the United States to the WTO Negotiating Group on Rules', TN/RL/GEN/146 (5 June 2007).

necessarily includes Article III:8(a)'s explicit exemption from the scope of the application of the NT obligations for subsidies.

Moreover, even if a claim were to be made against the AIFP subsidies it would likely be difficult to obtain redress under these RTA provisions. For although the language of the NAFTA NT provision is arguably in the form of hard law due to words such as 'shall' rather than 'may', these provisions are nonetheless weakened because they are bilateral in nature and enforcement capabilities. Further compounding the diplomatic nature of these regional obligations is the economic reality that motor vehicles and parts account for a larger share of intraregional trade in North America than any product sector.[30] A bailout to any one of the 'Big Three' US automakers will presumably have positive ripple effects throughout the regional supply chain.[31]

D. The US Auto Supplier Support Program

The US Auto Supplier Support Program (Auto SSP initiative)[32] was announced in March 2009. It provided $3.5 billion in guarantees and financing for auto parts suppliers who might otherwise be unable to access credit. The US Treasury noted that supplier instability created greater uncertainty for the auto companies that rely on the parts they ship:[33]

> This cycle of frozen credit markets, growing supplier uncertainty and growing auto company uncertainty has the potential to unravel the industry and short-circuit restructuring efforts at companies like GM and Chrysler.[34]

[30] When the NAFTA negotiations began, all three trade ministers understood that the elimination of trade barriers and investment incentives would not prompt huge segments of the automotive industry to shut down in one North American location and move to another. Three-way auto trade in 2003 was $125 billion, representing 20% of total trade among NAFTA partners. Between 1993 and 2003, the value of NAFTA auto trade almost doubled, accounting for 18% of the total growth in NAFTA trade over this period. J Schott, 'The Automotive Industry', available at: www.dpc.senate.gov/hearings/…/schott-chapter.pdf.

[31] A response to these developments is put forward in B Hoekman, 'Supply Chains, Mega-Regionals and Multilateralism: A Road Map for the WTO', EUI Working Paper RSCAS 2014/27.

[32] Appendix 1, measure 6.

[33] The US Treasury Factsheet notes that suppliers that ship to auto companies generally receive payment for those shipments about 45–60 days later. In a normal credit environment, suppliers can either sell or borrow against those receivables in the interim period to pay their workers and fund their ongoing operations. However, in the crisis environment, due to the uncertainty about the ability of the auto companies to honour their obligations, banks were unwilling to extend credit against these receivables. To help address this problem, the Supplier Support Program provided selected suppliers with financial protection on monies they were owed by domestic auto companies and the opportunity to access immediate liquidity against those obligations. US Treasury Fact Sheet Auto Supplier Support Program, 'Stabilizing the Auto Industry at a Time of Crisis', www.treasury.gov/initiatives/financial-stability/TARP-Programs/automotive-programs/Documents/supplier_support_program_3_18.pdf (accessed 28 May 2013).

[34] ibid.

The programme was designed to ensure that automakers received the parts and components they needed to manufacture vehicles and that suppliers had access to liquidity on their receivables. This enabled, for example, suppliers to obtain a legal guarantee that they would receive payment for their auto parts even in the event that the auto company they supplied filed for bankruptcy. Participating suppliers were also able to sell their receivables into the programme at a modest discount. This provided suppliers with the funding necessary to operate their businesses and helped to unlock credit more broadly in the supplier industry.

The scheme was run through US auto companies that had agreed to participate in it. Those suppliers to those companies that had agreed to maintain qualifying commercial terms had the opportunity to request government-backed protection. If granted, the supplier paid a small fee for the right to participate in the programme. The programme was open to any US-based supplier that shipped to a participating auto manufacturer on qualifying commercial terms. The decision as to which US-based suppliers and which receivables were to receive protection was made by the participating auto companies. On 9 April 2009, the Treasury made the following funds available: $3.5 billion for General Motors' parts suppliers and $1.5 billion for Chrysler's. Ultimately, only $413 million was loaned out and all of that was returned.

(i) The Legality of the Auto Supplier Support Program under WTO Obligations

If challenged under the WTO DSM by a government of a foreign-affiliated auto producer as a violation of the ASCM, the Auto SSP financial guarantees would arguably be found to fall under the ASCM's basic definition of actionable subsidies for the same reasons as the auto bailouts, discussed above.

The Auto SSP subsidies were not contingent on either export performance or domestic content requirements, and are therefore not prohibited subsidies. Nevertheless, it might be possible to demonstrate that these guarantees were also actionable subsidies that cause adverse effects, under Article 5's category (iii) serious prejudice to the interests of a WTO Member that was also a major automotive producer. Again, the *US–Upland Cotton* Panel Report demonstrates that challenges based on the threat of serious prejudice are possible, as long as some early indication of one or more of the serious prejudice factors materializes—in this case as a result of the Auto SSP guarantees and funds.

As previously noted, a complainant WTO Member could also argue that the Auto SSP guarantees and funding base constitute highly distortive dark amber subsidies and are so prejudicial that they pose a per se threat of serious prejudice and necessarily create an imminent or foreseeable risk of future serious prejudice to the WTO interests of other Members. No such challenge was brought against the Auto SSP guarantees and funds to the WTO DSM. Chapter 6 examines whether any WTO Member claimed it was adversely affected by such subsidies and sought remedies through the application of countervailing duties.

(ii) The Legality of the Auto Supplier Support Program under RTA Obligations

The guarantees provided under the Auto SPP arguably operated as a subsidy to the automotive industry. However, to recall, US RTAs typically do not contain competition provisions regulating subsidies to goods. As regards NT violations, given that the programme was only open to US-based suppliers, it thus discriminated against foreign autoparts suppliers facing similar difficulties within the US automotive market. Nevertheless, NAFTA NT obligations also incorporate Article III of the GATT and its interpretative notes, or any equivalent provision of a successor agreement to which all parties are party, into the agreement. This would presumably serve to exclude subsidies from its coverage due to the GATT Article III.8 derogation.

E. The US 'Cash for Clunkers' Scheme

The January 2009 National Incentive Program for Voluntary Retirement of Fuel-Inefficient Vehicles, 'Cash for Clunkers' (section 247), was designed to accelerate fuel savings nationwide by providing incentives to registered owners of high-fuel-consumption automobiles to replace such vehicles with more fuel-efficient automobiles or public transportation.[35] Eligible drivers received a reimbursement voucher for the purchase of a new or used vehicle. The car traded-in would then be taken apart for scrap. Vouchers for public transit fare credits in the equivalent dollar amount were also made available. This programme lasted from July 2009 to August 2009. Significantly, the 'Cash for Clunkers' rules did not mandate that the voucher must be spent on domestically produced cars.

(i) The Legality of 'Cash for Clunkers' under the WTO

The 'Cash for Clunkers' rules offered a financial contribution by the government or public body. The government provided vouchers redeemable for cash value when a consumer turned in an old vehicle and purchased a newer, fuel-efficient one. There was thus an indirect transfer of funds from the government to the dealers who were able to sell the new vehicle as a result of the voucher programme. As such, the 'Cash for Clunkers' scheme conferred a benefit to the automotive industry. Auto companies should have been able sell more vehicles with the

[35] If the retired vehicle was made before 1998, the voucher would amount to $2,000, while vehicles from 1999–2001 would get $3,000 and any vehicles made after 2002 would get $4,500. Owners of eligible vehicles would receive a redeemable voucher for the purchase of a new or used fuel-efficient automobile. Cars that have a fuel economy rating of less than 18 miles per gallon are deemed to be high fuel consumption automobiles. A fuel-efficient automobile is technically one that has a fuel economy rating that exceeds the Corporate Average Fuel Economy (CAFE) target for that class by at least 25% and meets or exceeds federal emissions standards. See C Brunel and GC Hufbauer, 'Money for the Auto Industry: Consistent with WTO Rules?', Petersen Institute for International Economics (February 2009).

scrapping programme than before, so they were in a better position than they would otherwise have been in the marketplace. The 'Cash for Clunkers' subsidy could also be defined as specific. The scrapping programme applied to the automobile industry, so the access to the vouchers was explicitly limited to certain US enterprises only.

Notwithstanding this, there are no criteria or conditions governing the eligibility for vouchers such as these. These vouchers and other types of incentives for scrapping old cars are made available directly to consumers not the auto companies. They do not fall under the scope of the ASCM because they are general in nature and not extended directly to particular auto-producing enterprises. And while these firms may benefit indirectly from such incentives through increased opportunities for new sales to the consumers who take advantage of such tax benefits by scrapping their older cars, so do related industries such as petroleum, road building and other service industries. It would be difficult to demonstrate that these programmes are sufficiently specific so as to qualify. The incentive is conferred on the consumer, not on the manufacturer. The scheme permits the consumer to choose between auto manufacturers, subject to the public interest environmental requirements regarding emissions or fuel efficiency. That is, they can be seen as neutral regarding the whole industry, both domestic and international.

In the unlikely event that these vouchers were deemed to be specific subsidies that affected only certain auto industry companies via the customer vouchers, it would still be difficult to prove that the 'Cash for Clunkers' vouchers were actionable subsidies. As noted, these are subsidies under the definition of ASCM Article 1 but are permitted if they do not cause adverse effects to the interests of other Members. ASCM Article 15.1 provides that a determination of injury shall be based on positive evidence and involve an examination of (a) the volume of subsidised imports and the effect of the subsidised imports on prices in the domestic market for like products and (b) the subsequent impact of these imports on the domestic producers of such products. Any change in circumstances causing an injurious subsidy must be clearly foreseen and imminent. The factors to be considered include the following:

(i) the nature of the subsidy and the trade effects likely to arise therefrom;
(ii) a significant rate of increase of subsidised imports into the domestic market, indicating the likelihood of substantially increased importation;
(iii) sufficient freely disposable, or an imminent, substantial increase in, capacity of the exporter, indicating the likelihood of substantially increased subsidised exports to the importing Member's market, taking into account the availability of other export markets to absorb any additional exports;
(iv) whether imports are entering at prices that will have a significant depressing or suppressing effect on domestic prices and would likely increase demand for further imports and inventories of the product being investigated.

In sum: even if a Member claimed that the 'Cash for Clunkers' programme caused adverse effects to their auto industry, it would be extremely difficult to establish.

The programme was very short. Moreover, it would be difficult to determine that a car under the 'Cash for Clunkers' price threshold is 'like' or directly competitive and substitutable with a car priced over the threshold, and thus deemed a discriminatory measure. However, if it were possible to establish either material injury to a domestic industry or a threat of material injury, the scheme could have been challenged at the WTO, which it was not, and importing Members would have had the right to impose countervailing duties on those cars as like-products, which they did not.

(ii) The 'Cash for Clunkers' Programme under RTA Obligations

As with the assessment of the legality of US financial and auto subsidies, under these bilateral and regional obligations, the competition and procurement chapters do not seek to regulate subsidies. And as discussed with reference to the US auto bailouts, the NAFTA provisions incorporate the GATT NT standard, which, it should be recalled, excludes subsidies from the scope of its Article III non-discrimination requirements pursuant to Article III:8(b).

F. Buy National: The American Recovery and Reinvestment Act

The American Recovery and Reinvestment Act of 2009 (ARRA) was comprised of a $787 billion stimulus package involving federal tax reductions, along with expenditures on infrastructure, education, healthcare, energy and other projects. The ARRA's Buy American provision, enacted as section 1605, built on aspects of two previous US domestic content laws. The first statute: the 'Buy American Act' was first enacted in 1933 and applies only to US federal government procurements and construction projects covered by the Federal Acquisition Regulation (FAR). The second statute, the Buy America law, was first enacted in 1964 and applies principally to Federal Transit Administration (FTA) grants provided to states and localities. While both the Buy American Act and the Buy America law require that final products delivered to the government be made domestically, the 1964 Buy America law has a deeper reach than the Buy American Act.[36]

Section 1605 of the ARRA combines the coverage of both statutes. Its general requirement to use only iron, steel and other manufactured goods produced in

[36] A further comparison of the two statutes' treatment of manufactured goods and construction materials, which generally are parts and supplies incorporated directly into the final manufactured product or construction material, reveals that: under Buy America 100% of the components should be made in the USA for the final manufactured good or construction material to qualify as US-made. By contrast, the Buy American Act requires only 51% of the components of supplies and construction materials be made domestically for the final product to qualify as US-made. In like manner, under Buy America, the cost of domestic materials must be 25% more expensive than foreign materials for a cost-based waiver, while under the Buy American Act the cost differential is just 6%, or 12% for a small business.

the US, applies to federal ARRA-funded public building and works projects, as well as all state and local ARRA grant-funded public buildings and works projects. Additionally, section 1605 tracks the statutory language of the Buy America law and applies that law's more exacting rules of origin requirements.

Section 1605 of the Recovery Act: Use of American Iron, Steel, and Manufactured Goods.

(a) None of the funds appropriated or otherwise made available by this Act may be used for a project for the construction, alteration, maintenance, or repair of a public building or public work *unless all* of the iron, steel, and manufactured goods used in the project are produced in the United States.
(b) Subsection (a) shall not apply in any case or category of cases in which the head of the Federal department or agency involved finds that–
    (1) applying subsection (a) would be inconsistent with the public interest;
    (2) iron, steel, and the relevant manufactured goods are not produced in the United States in sufficient and reasonably available quantities and of a satisfactory quality; or
    (3) inclusion of iron, steel, and manufactured goods produced in the United States will increase the cost of the *overall* project by more than 25 per cent.
(c) If the head of a Federal department or agency determines that it is necessary to waive the application of subsection (a) based on a finding under subsection (b), the head of the department or agency shall publish in the Federal Register a detailed written justification as to why the provision is being waived.
(d) This *section shall be applied in a manner consistent with United States obligations under international agreements.* (emphasis added)

Section 1605 paragraph (a) uses the term 'all' with respect to the required use of iron, steel, and manufactured goods produced in the United States. Nevertheless, under paragraph (b) the head of a federal department or agency may waiver these Buy American requirements in three circumstances: (i) non-availability, (ii) unreasonable cost or (iii) inconsistency with the public interest. The first circumstance recognises that supply chains not only vary by product but are constantly evolving in response to global supply and demand, resulting in complex production landscapes with components and end-products being manufactured and assembled in a large number of countries. It therefore provides that if iron, steel or manufactured goods are not produced in the USA in sufficient and reasonably available quantities and of satisfactory quality, the domestic content requirement may be put aside.[37]

For the second waiver, under Article 3(b), the ARRA mandates a 25 per cent test as the standard for cost-based waivers, as with the Buy America approach. For iron, steel and other manufactured construction material, the contracting officer must compare the offered price using foreign-manufactured construction material to the estimated price if only domestic-manufactured construction

[37] A broad ICT exemption from Buy American requirements already exists for US government procurement for foreign, commercial-off-the-shelf (COTS) information technology. Pub L No 108-447 § 517; Pub L No 108-199, § 535(a).

material were used.[38] The cost of using domestic-manufactured construction material may be found to be unreasonable only if it increases the overall offered price by more than 25 per cent. For unmanufactured construction material, the test is the same except the threshold is 6 per cent.[39] Offers that do not qualify for domestic status will have a price premium added for the purposes of pricing evaluation. The FAR regulations also require procuring agencies to publish a notice in the Federal Register including a detailed justification for the exemption.

The so-called 'saving clause' was added at paragraph (d) to preserve the USA's existing international commitments otherwise affected by the Act.[40] The scope of this amendment is nevertheless quite limited because—first and foremost—those international agreements do not apply to federal grant funds destined for states and localities, which indeed significantly channelled much of the ARRA funds. Second, those international agreements typically apply neither to federal small business procurements nor to public works procurements valued at less than $7.4 million. And moreover, they only have limited application to federal defence procurements.

The following sections assess the legality of the ARRA's Buy America Act (BAA) requirements under the WTO and the USA' commitments within its RTAs.

(i) *The Legality of the Buy America Act under the WTO GPA*

As Chapter 2 discussed, government procurement is regulated in the WTO in the plurilateral GPA, to which the US is an original signatory party. In order to comply with the WTO GPA requirements, the Members of the WTO GPA were explicitly exempted from the BAA procurement requirements, under the 'saving clause' of section 1605(d). The Interim Final Guidance[41] exempts GPA and FTA parties to the extent that the sub-federal entities are bound by international agreements, where the project is above a threshold of 5 million Special Drawing Rights[42] (SDRs).[43]

[38] FAR 25.604(c)(1), 74 *Federal Register*, 14627.

[39] FAR 25.605, 74 *Federal Register*, 14627.

[40] The Conference Report advises: 'Section 1605(d) is not intended to repeal by implication the President's authority under Title III of the Trade Agreements Act of 1979. The conferees anticipate that the Administration will rely on the authority under 19 USC 2511(b) to the extent necessary to comply with US obligations under the WTO Agreement on Government Procurement and under US free trade agreements and so that section 1605 will not apply to least developed countries to the same extent that it does not apply to the parties to those international agreements. The Conferees also note that waiver authority under section 2511(b)(2) has not been used.' Section 2511(b)(2), which is part of the Trade Agreements Act of 1979, gives the President the power to relax Buy American requirements for countries that are not GPA contracting parties, if those countries are not 'major industrial countries' but assume GPA obligations.

[41] Office of Management and Budget 2 CFR Part 176 Requirements for Implementing Sections 1512, 1605, and 1606 of the American Recovery and Reinvestment Act of 2009 for Financial Assistance Awards. *Federal Register*, vol 74, no 77, Thursday, 23 April 2009.

[42] Special Drawing Rights is a form of international money, created by the International Monetary Fund, and defined as a weighted average of various convertible currencies.

[43] Revised Appendix US States, Other Sub-Federal Entities, and Other Entities Subject to US Obligations under International Agreements (November 2012) www.ustr.gov/sites/default/files/REVISED%20Appendix.pdf.

Thus, though the reach of the WTO GPA and the RTAs to US sub-central procurements is already partial, to the extent they do cover sub-central procurements, they too are exempted from the BAA restrictions.

The rules of origin followed for BAA procurements are that the domestic manufacture test applies to any manufactured construction material and manufactured end-products, without regard to the origin of components. In contrast, to determine product origin for GPA and FTA procurements, the substantial transformation test is used. The reason for the different rules as between Buy American and trade agreements provisions can be found in GPA Article IV and analogous FTA articles. GPA Article IV forbids GPA contracting parties from applying rules of origin in covered government procurements 'which are different from the rules of origin applied in the normal course of trade and at the time of the transaction in question'. Substantial transformation is the rule of origin applied in the normal course of trade. The Trade Agreements Act of 1979 requires the use of the substantial transformation test in procurements subject to GPA and FTA liberalisation. Therefore, the Buy America provisions apply to procurements that are not subject to liberalisation under any trade agreement, and as a result in this case the USA is free to choose which rules it wants to determine product origin.

In sum, the BAA provision of the Recovery Act, as implemented by the Interim Final Guidance, appears to be fully consistent with US obligations under the plurilateral GPA, since GPA parties are explicitly carved out from the requirements of the BAA.

(ii) The Canada–US 2010 Agreement on Government Procurement

The conclusion reached as regards the legality of the BAA under the WTO GPA was of little comfort to Canada. For despite the 'saving clause' set out under the BAA section 1605(d), Canadian companies would continue to be excluded from sub-national procurement opportunities funded by that legislation. A committee was immediately established to conduct an analysis of the impact of the BAA on both Canadian businesses and government procurement markets in both Canada and the United States.[44] Indicating the urgency of the matter, the Committee held six meetings on the Canada–US Agreement on Government Procurement (AGP) between March and April 2010. Canada sought to address not only the specific issues related to the ARRA, but also other long-standing trade irritants in government procurement between Canada and the USA:

> [G]iven the normal length of time required to negotiate international agreements, reaching an accord in six months is an impressive accomplishment. When you take into account that the agreement also required the provinces to sign on, reaching an agreement with that group in six months is, frankly, quite mind-boggling.[45]

[44] See the United States–Canada Agreement on Government Procurement Report of the Standing Committee on International Trade, Lee Richardson, MP Chair (May 2010) 40th Parliament, 3rd Session.

[45] Shirley-Ann George, Senior Vice-President, Policy, Canadian Chamber of Commerce: Evidence, Meeting no 4, 18 March 2010.

The Committee noted that, in addition to the stipulations of the BAA, in some cases US state and local governments were not considering foreign bids on procurement contracts, even when foreign companies were eligible to compete for those contracts. The Committee speculated that this was because the government agencies were unsure if they could use Canadian-made inputs, or because some US municipal governments decided to buy from US suppliers so as to avoid the need to carry two sets of inventories: one of US-made goods for ARRA-financed projects; and one which included Canadian-supplied goods for projects for which the ARRA did not apply. Difficulties were reported resulting from those eligibility requirements, such as the case of a Toronto firm that won a contract to supply a California healthcare centre with plastic piping, only to have that piping removed from the plastic on arrival because it was made in Canada and thought to contravene the ARRA.[46]

In the event, under the 2010 AGP Canada made an unprecedented market access concession to provide US companies with a degree of permanent access to procurement markets in all provinces and territories except Nunavut. Although in practice many sub-national procurement contracts in Canada were open to bidders from either country prior to the entry into force of the AGP, the Canadian government agencies had been under no obligation to offer US businesses access to procurement contract opportunities. Following the conclusion of the AGP, the US was the only WTO GPA signatory country to which Canada's sub-national procurement commitments initially applied—again underlining the erosion of the MFN principle within the WTO GPA schedules.[47]

In exchange, the United States simply extended its 1994 WTO GPA commitments on sub-national procurement, which cover thirty-seven US states, to Canada. The US did not therefore increase its market access commitments under the Schedules of the WTO 1994 GPA. The fact that the US had previously opened its sub-national procurement in thirty-seven states to all GPA parties except Canada highlights the flexibility of the MFN obligation under the GPA. US negotiators had refused to exempt Canadian businesses from the small business set-asides or other exemptions, and in retaliation Canada refused to expand its WTO GPA commitments to include sub-national procurement in 1994. Canada's negotiators argued that those set-asides prevented Canadian businesses from enjoying the same degree of access to US federal procurement markets as the US had to Canadian federal procurement markets. Thus, in order to simply qualify for the full legal protection the US already offered to other GPA parties, Canada had to give access to Canadian provincial and territorial government procurement without making any progress on the issue of small business set-asides or other US exemptions at the WTO.

[46] Parliament of Canada Committee Report on the Canada-US Agreement on Government Procurement. Available at: www.parl.gc.ca/HousePublications/Publication.aspx?DocId=4416059&File=9.

[47] Canada renegotiated its market access commitments again under the revised 2011 GPA and accompanying schedules.

Evidently, the detrimental economic effects on Canadian businesses from the BAA gave the United States leverage to resolve a long-standing trade spat involving the WTO GPA, but this was bilateral in nature and did not involve making any reciprocal concessions. On the Canadian side, some denounced the agreement as 'egregiously one-sided' particularly with regard to relative number of local preferences maintained by the USA. Furthermore, the obligation to establish a bid challenge mechanism for aggrieved US bidders, who feel denied their appropriate degree of access to municipal procurement in Canada, was not complemented by reciprocal obligations in the USA.[48] Others felt that Canada had set itself up for failure in the way it approached its negotiations with the USA. Given that Canada was the only country that truly wanted an agreement on procurement, it began in a poor negotiating position, which was difficult to translate into a fair deal.[49]

(iii) The Legality of the Buy America Act under the GATT

Chapter 1 noted the traditional perspective that government procurement is excluded from the application of both Article I MFN and Article III:4 NT provisions by virtue of the Article III:8(a) exclusion of government procurement from Article III:4's NT obligations. Consequently, if the BAA were to be challenged at the WTO, the scope of the GATT obligations would not be seen to cover a procurement measure and consequently the BAA provisions could not be challenged as a violation of MFN or NT under the GATT.

The more recent *Canada–Feed-in Tariff* (*FIT*) and *India–Solar Cells* disputes offer some guidance as to the scope of the Article III:8 derogation, which is of relevance to government procurement regulation. As challenged, both India's Jawaharlal Nehru National Solar Mission policy and the *FIT* programme imposed a 'Minimum Required Domestic Content Level' on electricity generators utilising solar PV and wind-power technologies that compelled them to purchase and use certain types of renewable energy generation equipment sourced in Ontario in the design and construction of their facilities. The Panel likened these 'Minimum Required Domestic Content Level' to the domestic content requirements challenged in *Indonesia–Autos*. Here the Panel opined that 'by definition, [domestic content requirements] always favour the use of domestic products over imported products, and therefore affect trade'.[50]

In other words, a buy-national measure that explicitly prevents the 'purchase' of a like product from certain Members not party to the WTO GPA would be deemed in violation of the NT requirement articulated in Article III:4 unless the measure falls under the NT derogations under Article III:8(a) or (b). To determine

[48] Evidence, Meeting no 5, 23 March 2010.

[49] Carl Grenier stated in Evidence, Meeting no 4, 18 March 2010: 'Canada approached the United States, basically telling them, "We needed a deal at any cost." If you say that to anyone, you'll get one. We did get one, and that cost is high.'

[50] Panel Report, *Indonesia–Certain Measures Affecting the Automobile Industry*, WT/DS54/R, WT/DS55/R, WT/DS59/R, WT/DS64/R, adopted 23 July 1998, ¶14.82.

whether the challenged measures fall within the ambit of in Article III:8(a) it must be ascertained:

(i) whether the challenged measures can be characterised as 'laws, regulations or requirements governing procurement';
(ii) whether the challenged measures involve 'procurement by governmental agencies'; and
(iii) whether any 'procurement' that exists is undertaken 'for governmental purposes and not with a view to commercial resale or with a view to use in the production of goods for commercial sale'.

Under requirement (i), it is clear that the ARRA and the BAA component can be characterised as laws, regulations or requirements governing procurement. The question of whether the challenged measure involves procurement by government agencies, requirement (ii), could be raised, however. Their conformity may be affirmed with reference to the unadopted GATT panel report, *United States–Procurement of a Sonar Mapping System*. This Panel opined that the following factors were relevant in deciding whether procurement was made by the entities subject to this Agreement: 'payment by government, governmental use of or benefit from the product, government possession and government control over the obtaining of the product.' The GATT Panel concluded: in the light of the government's payment for, ownership and use of the sonar mapping system and given the extent of its control over the obtaining of the system, the acquisition of the sonar mapping system was government procurement within the meaning of Article I:1(a), first sentence, and not 'private' procurement outside the Agreement as proposed in the alternative by the European Community.[51] Under the logic of this assessment, the BAA requirements would most likely be seen to govern 'procurement by government agencies' because even when using intermediary contractors, the government pays for, uses and controls the obtaining of the construction materials.

To conform to requirement (iii), the BAA needs to show that the goods procured under the Recovery Act are 'purchased for governmental purposes'. Here the *Canada–FIT* dispute offers more interpretive guidance. The Panel determined the ordinary meaning of 'governmental purposes' as relatively broad.[52] However, it is instructive that the expression 'governmental purposes' is immediately followed by the words 'and not with a view to commercial resale or with a view to use in the production of goods for commercial sale'. The words 'and not' after 'governmental purposes' qualifies this expression by indicating that the procurement of products purchased with a view to commercial resale are excluded from the operation of Article III:8(a).[53] These interpretations were not challenged by

[51] GATT Panel Report, *US–Sonar Mapping*, ¶4.5.

[52] Incorporating 'les besoins des pouvoirs publics' and 'las necesidades de los poderes públicos', respectively in the French and Spanish versions, WT/DS412/R WT/DS426/R, 70, ¶7.139.

[53] WT/DS412/R WT/DS426/R, 71, ¶7.140.

the Appellate Body. Consequently, it can be assumed that in the absence of any evidence to the contrary, the goods purchased under the BAA were not for commercial resale.[54] Rather, the object of the US government's financial contribution under section 1605 was the very purchasing of goods or services with a local content requirement as a domestic response to the economic crisis. As such, the BAA fulfils the three requirements of Article III:8(a) and is exempt from Article III:4 NT requirements, and in light of prevailing case law interpretation, also from the MFN requirements of Article I:1.

(iv) The Legality of Buy America under the ASCM

At face value, it could be assumed that because section 1605(d) provides that the BAA provisions be consistent with international obligations, they would not likely violate the ASCM. Further, section 176.90 of the Office of Management and Budget's Interim Final Guidance[55] on the non-application to acquisitions covered under international agreements states in paragraph (a):

> The Buy American requirement set out in §176.70 shall not be applied where the iron, steel, or manufactured goods used in the project are from a Party to an international agreement, listed in paragraph (b)(2) of this section, and the recipient is required under an international agreement, described in the appendix to this subpart, to treat the goods and services of that Party the same as domestic goods and services. This obligation shall only apply to projects with an estimated value of $7,443,000 or more and projects that are not specifically excluded from the application of those agreements.

However, it is very difficult to conclude that an offset or local content requirement prohibited under ASCM Article 3 would not be a 'benefit' if it were designed to have a positive impact within a stimulus package. In the event that a WTO member were to challenge ARRA section 1605 provisions under the ASCM, the Panel would first assess the measure to determine whether it can be defined as a subsidy within the meaning of ASCM Article 1.1. As the Appellate Body in *Canada–Aircraft* succinctly recalled:

> The definition of 'subsidy' in Article 1.1 has two discrete elements: 'a financial contribution by a government or any public body' and 'a benefit is thereby conferred'. The first element of this definition is concerned with whether the government made a 'financial contribution', as that term is defined in Article 1.1(a). The focus of the first element is on the action of the government in making the 'financial contribution'. That being so, it seems logical that the second element in Article 1.1 is concerned with the 'benefit … conferred' on the recipient by that governmental action.[56]

[54] The Panel also noted that to the extent that the language of Art XVII:2 serves as context for the interpretation of Art III:8(a), it helps to confirm that a 'procurement … of products purchased for governmental purposes' under Art III:8(a) cannot also be a 'procurement … of products purchased … with a view to commercial resale or with a view to use in the production of goods for commercial sale'.

[55] Office of Management and Budget (n 41).

[56] Appellate Body Report, *Canada–Aircraft*, ¶156.

As regards the first element, some ambiguity arises under Article 1.1(a)(1), which defines a subsidy as a financial contribution by a government body within the territory of a Member, where inter alia, a government provides goods or services *other* than general infrastructure, or purchases goods. Because general infrastructure projects such as public construction works are provided under the BAA, this provision may therefore provide a carve-out for section 1605-type stimulus spending. However, if the object of the US government's financial contribution under section 1605 was not the public construction itself, but rather the purchasing of goods or services with a local content requirement, as submitted above, the situation changes. For this could be deemed to override the carve-out and section 1605 requirements would then fall under the scope of the ASCM's Part II, III and IV obligations.

Another argument to secure the placing of section 1605 procurement measures within the ASCM definition of prohibited subsidies is that given that the WTO DSB has yet to interpret whether or not intergovernmental subsidies are immune from the ASCM requirements, it is an open question whether the ARRA's billion-dollar financing from federal government to local government constitutes subsidies falling under the scope of the ASCM requirements.[57] This is an untried legal avenue. However, it could potentially lead to the conclusion that section 1605 is a financial contribution within the terms of Article 1. Following this, and as set out by the Appellate Body in *Canada–Aircraft*, under ASCM Article 1.1(b), there is a second legal requirement to qualify for the definition of a subsidy. This is whether there is a 'benefit … conferred' on the recipient by that governmental action. This second element requires an evaluation of whether a benefit has been conferred with reference to the marketplace value.[58] There is some indication of the potential benefit that section 1605 could confer in the OMB's Final Interim Guidance on Evaluating Proposals of Foreign Iron, Steel, and/or Manufactured Goods.[59] Here paragraph (e) stipulates that if the use of domestic iron, steel and/or relevant manufactured goods would increase the cost of the overall project by more than 25 per cent, then the award official shall determine that the cost of the domestic iron, steel and/or relevant manufactured goods is unreasonable. This implies that the 'benefit' provided by section 1605 has a threshold of up to 25 per cent above the market rate of the overall project.

The *Canada–Aircraft* dispute further indicates that a WTO Member may challenge a subsidy programme of another Member 'as such' or, alternatively, 'as

[57] See www.globaleconomicgovernance.org/blog/2009/03/resist-us-protectionism-the-top-trade-priority-for-the-g20/.

[58] Art 14 ASCM Calculation of the Amount of a Subsidy in Terms of the Benefit to the Recipient. Art 14(d) supports this interpretation: 'The provision of goods or services or purchase of goods by a government shall not be considered as conferring a benefit unless the provision is made for less than adequate remuneration, or the purchase is made for more than adequate remuneration. The adequacy of remuneration shall be determined in relation to prevailing market conditions for the good or service in question in the country of provision or purchase (including price, quality, availability, marketability, transportation and other conditions of purchase or sale).'

[59] § 176.110.

applied'. In order to do this, the Panel emphasised that it 'must first determine whether the … programme per se mandates the grant of prohibited export subsidies in a manner inconsistent with Articles 3.1(a) and 3.2 of the SCM Agreement'.[60] As regards section 1605 requirements, it is clear that this is a mandatory statute when the benefit conferred is below the 25 per cent market value threshold. The findings in *United States–Tobacco* recalled that panels have consistently ruled that legislation which mandated action inconsistent with the General Agreement could be challenged 'as such'. This is unlike legislation which merely gave the discretion to the executive authority to act inconsistently which could only be challenged 'as applied'.[61] In light of these findings, a challenge to section 1605 would be to an 'as applied' subsidy programme because it requires mandatory compliance unless the benefit conferred through buying domestic iron, steel and or manufactured goods increases the overall project costs by more than 25 per cent.

Having determined that section 1605 requirements fall within Article 1.1's definition of a subsidy, it follows that Article 3.1(b) explicitly prohibits subsidies contingent, whether solely or as one of several other conditions, upon the use of domestic over imported goods. The Interim Final Guidance requires that domestic iron, steel and manufactured goods be 'substantially transformed in the United States' which may de facto make the subsidy contingent upon the use of domestic over imported goods:

> Domestic iron, steel, and/or manufactured good—(1) Is wholly the growth, product, or manufacture of the United States; or (2) In the case of a manufactured good that consists in whole or in part of materials from another country, has been substantially transformed in the United States into a new and different manufactured good distinct from the materials from which it was transformed. There is no requirement with regard to the origin of components or subcomponents in manufactured goods or products, *as long as the manufacture of the goods occurs in the United States.*[62] (emphasis added)

As noted in Chapter 1, Part II ASCM 'Prohibited Subsidies' provides in Article 3 that a Member shall neither grant nor maintain subsidies contingent, whether solely or as one of several other conditions, upon the use of domestic over imported goods. The 25 per cent price benefit that section 1605 confers appears directly contingent on the use of domestic over imported goods because 'none of the funds' may be used under section 1605 'unless all of the iron, steel, and manufactured

[60] Panel Report, *Canada–Aircraft*, ¶9.124.

[61] Panel Report, *United States–Measures affecting the Importation, Internal Sale and Use of Tobacco*, adopted by the Council on 4 October 1994 (DS44/R) ¶118. See also: Panel Report, *United States–Taxes on Petroleum and Certain Imported Substances*, adopted on 17 June 1987, BISD 34S/136, 160; Panel Report, *EEC–Regulation on Import of Parts and Components*, adopted on 16 May 1990, BISD 37S/132, 198–99; Panel Report, *Thailand–Restrictions on Importation of and Internal Taxes on Cigarettes*, adopted on 7 November 1990, BISD 37S/200, 227–28; Panel Report, *United States–Measures Affecting Alcoholic and Malt Beverages*, adopted on19 June 1992, BISD 39S/206, 281–82, 289–90; Panel Report, *United States–Denial of MFN Treatment as to Non-Rubber Footwear from Brazil*, adopted on 19 June 1992, BISD 39S/128, 152.

[62] Office of Management and Budget (n 41).

goods used in the project are produced in the United States'. To recall, a prohibited measure must be withdrawn unless the implementing Member can justify the measure under an exception or carve-out. The ASCM does not contain exceptions equivalent to those under Article XX GATT or the WTO GPA Article XXIII.

To reiterate the problem once again, it is unclear whether a crisis measure in the form of a subsidy prohibited under the ASCM agreement could potentially be defended under GATT Article XX public morals exceptions because the Appellate Body has ruled that the relationship between the GATT and other Annex 1A agreements, which includes the ASCM, shall be considered on a case-by-case basis. This uncertainty may have a chilling effect on enforcement within a bilaterally based international organisation

G. Nullification and Impairment

The aim of GATT Article XXIII is to prohibit WTO Members from upsetting the legitimate expectations of other Members under the agreement. It is therefore theoretically possible for a challenge to be made that the BAA requirements nullified or impaired a WTO commitment to the extent that it upset the legitimate expectations of a WTO member, pursuant to Article XXIII:1(b). In this case, it would need to be shown that procurements under the BAA policy actually shifted the effected purchases from the open or private market to the protected public sector to such an extent that the balance of tariff concessions are nullified or impaired for a particular WTO member or members.

Pursuant to GATT Article XXIII:1(c), a measure could also theoretically be challenged for nullification or impairment as a result of 'the existence of any other situation'. However, because such a challenge has never been brought, there is no jurisprudence to offer guidelines on the scope of this provision. The lack of interpretative guidance concerning the definition of 'any situation' in the General Agreement and in subsequent GATT practice also results in legal uncertainty. This reduces the legal predictability of GATT dispute settlement proceedings. Indeed, not even the term 'non-violation complaint' has been precisely defined by the contracting parties, nor have the differences been explicated between 'non-violation complaints' based upon Article XXIII:1(b) and 'situation complaints' based upon Article XXIII:1(c). Neither has the relationship between 'situations' within the terms of Article XXIII:1(c) and 'situations' referred to in other safeguard clauses, such as Articles XII, XVIII and XIX, been addressed. This uncertainty means the procedural rules on the operation of these obligations become even more important. It is advocated as an area for further formal deliberation with a view to greater interpretative guidance.

The relevant case law from the *Korea–Procurement* dispute indicates that there are three elements to an Article XXIII non-violation complaint: (1) the application of a measure by a WTO Member; (2) a benefit accruing under the relevant WTO agreement; and (3) nullification or impairment of the benefit as a result of the application of the measure. The burden of proof is a detailed justification of all three elements in order to establish a rebuttable presumption that the claim is true. Section 1605, along with accompanying implementing regulation conditioning procurement, is likely to be deemed a measure applied by the USA. Benefits accruing under WTO agreements include any concessions or other forms of market access liberalization now nullified or impaired by BAA domestic content requirements. It is conceivable that significant increases in demand for domestic steel from the US government upset the balance of concessions accruing under the GATT. This may have resulted in a price increase, reducing demand on the open market and a reallocation of products from the private sector to the protected public sector. However, to establish this, a sophisticated empirical assessment of the relevant market using competition principles is required. This, while difficult, is not impossible; but no challenge was made.

II. Brazil's Bailout Measures in the Financial Sector

The first signs of the crisis emerged in Brazil in June 2008, with declining capital flows and falling commodity prices.[63] The Brazilian financial system suffered from the financial crisis mainly through either capital flight from the stock market and/or a reduction in the domestic supply of credit. The reduction of supply of credit experienced by the big Brazilian banks resulted in lack of credit supplied to medium and small banks. As a consequence, they were not able to fulfil the credit demands of the big exporters or consumers and a credit crunch emerged. In response, the government enacted a stimulus package amounting to a $20.4 billion injection into the economy, equivalent to 1.2 per cent of Brazil's GDP in 2009. It aimed to boost aggregate demand and mitigate the negative impact of the crisis through three major channels, namely, additional government spending, 47.5 per cent of total spending, with additional tax cuts and subsidies accounting for a further 15.2 per cent of the total injection.

As Appendix 2, measure 1 indicates, the Brazilian government decided to use the three major federal public banks—Banco do Brasil (BB), Caixa Econômica Federal (CEF) and the state-owned development bank Banco Nacional de Desenvolvimento Econômico e Social (BNDES)—to expand credit and to play a countercyclical role in a context of tightening credit conditions by private banks. These financial institutions controlled by the Brazilian federal government, were authorised, directly or indirectly, to acquire ownership interest in private and

[63] The Brazilian financial sector is the largest and most sophisticated among Mercosur countries. The financial sector is fairly concentrated, with the ten largest institutions accounting for over 65% of financial sector assets. See eg LF De Paula and R Sobreira, 'The 2008 Financial Crisis and Banking Regulation in Brazil', UFRGS, Artigo Aceito para Apresentação no III Encontro da Associação Keynesiana Brasileira de 11 a 13 de Agosto 2010.

public financial institutions in Brazil, including insurance companies, social welfare institutions and capitalisation companies, with or without the acquisition of the capital stock control. Subsidies accounting for 15.5 per cent of the stimulus package were established, which is equivalent to $3.1 billion or 0.2 per cent of GNP.

Initially, the government capitalised the BNDES with R$100 billion to ensure resources for private and public investments (Appendix 5, measure 2), which amounted to a subsidy of $0.9 billion or 0.06 per cent of GNP, allowing BNDES to increase its credit by 85 per cent in 2009. A further liquidity assistance line allowed Banco Central do Brasil (BCB) to acquire credit portfolios from financial institutions. The policy aim was to extend authority for the BCB to assist Brazilian financial institutions facing cash shortages, mainly small to mid-sized banks. The guarantees for these transactions ranged from 120 to 140 per cent for credits with clients that had transactions involving more than one financial institution or loans secured by the public-sector payroll. The BCB demanded guarantees for other credits from 150 to 170 per cent of the assets underlying the transaction.[64]

In addition to these initiatives, in June 2008 the Ministry of Finance provided an additional R$19 billion in credit lines for various sectors, via BNDES and BB. Then, in August 2009, the government made a further contribution of R$500 million to the endorsement funds of BB and BNDES. This guaranteed loans to small and mid-size enterprises. State-owned banks also established new credit lines to maintain the supply of credit to individuals and companies in a context of high liquidity preference by private banks to avoid a sharp drop in economic activity. Under the new liquidity assistance line, BCB was allowed to acquire credit portfolios from financial institutions. The aim was to extend authority for the BCB to assist Brazilian financial institutions facing cash shortages, again mainly small and mid-sized banks. The financial institutions would be able to repurchase their assets by paying the value of the assets plus the variation in the benchmark rate, plus 4 per cent per year. The asset resale value would be adjusted on a daily basis. The financial institutions could accelerate the repurchase of these assets, fully or in part.[65]

A. The Legality of Brazil's Financial Rescue Measures under the GATS

Appendix 2, measures 1–5 constitute subsidies to enable public banks to provide credit that would otherwise not be available. As discussed above, subsidies are not regulated under the GATS. Nevertheless, if Brazil had made commitments for the banking sector within its schedules these measures would fall under the general non-discrimination principles. Yet during the conclusions of the negotiations of

[64] ibid.
[65] ibid.

the GATS agreement in 1994, certain WTO members, including the USA, wanted to continue the negotiations on financial services specifically. These concluded in 1997 with the Fifth Protocol to the General Agreement on Trade in Services. However, when the Protocol entered into force in 1999, several members, including Brazil, postponed their acceptance of the Protocol.

Brazil's GATS commitments are mostly in the area of commercial presence under Mode 3,[66] although horizontal market access limitations have been scheduled regarding commercial presence, along with the movement of natural persons under Mode 4, investment and subsidies. Under Mode 4 market access is guaranteed only to specialised staff working under temporary contracts, and special conditions apply to the appointment of managers to affiliates of foreign companies.[67] Brazil has made no GATS commitments under Mode 1 cross-border supply. Brazil has also retained the right to require foreign service suppliers to be organised as legal entities under Brazilian law. The installation of new financial institutions is subject to case-by-case approval. The participation of foreign capital in financial institutions is subject to conditions of national interest, international agreements and reciprocity. Failing these conditions, the establishment of new branches of financial institutions or an increase in foreign participation is not allowed. Cross-border supply of insurance services is also not allowed, although the purchase of insurance from outside Brazil may be authorised under special conditions.

In sum, under Brazil's financial services commitments,[68] the establishment of new branches and subsidiaries of foreign financial institutions is permitted only when subject to a case-by-case authorisation by the executive branch, by means of a presidential decree. Moreover, applying investors may also be required to fulfil additional specific conditions.[69] Otherwise, commercial presence is not allowed. Given that subsidies are not regulated under the GATS and Brazil does not have to observe the GATS NT principles when implementing its financial stimulus measures, these crisis measures were not actionable under the WTO DSU. Brazil is also not required to withdraw or justify competition-distorting financial rescue measures under the carve-outs provided in the Annex or the Understanding.

[66] As well as increases in the participation of foreign persons in the capital of financial institutions incorporated under Brazilian law. http://tradeinservices.mofcom.gov.cn/en/f/2008-08-22/54080.shtml.

[67] WTO TPR Brazil, WT/TPR/S/283 (2013).

[68] For the purpose of these commitments, financial institutions are defined as multiple banks, commercial banks, investment banks, consumer-finance companies, real estate finance companies, leasing companies, brokers and dealers. Each may perform only those activities permitted by the National Monetary Council, the Central Bank and/or the Securities Commission. Financial instruments, such as securities, futures and options, when registered for negotiation on an exchange, cannot be traded in an over-the-counter market. All members of senior-level management of financial services suppliers must be permanent residents in Brazil. Representative offices may not engage in commercial business. See: http://tradeinservices.mofcom.gov.cn/en/f/2008-08-22/54080.shtml.

[69] Foreign persons may participate in the privatisation programme of public-sector financial institutions and in each case commercial presence will be granted, also by means of a presidential decree. http://tradeinservices.mofcom.gov.cn/en/f/2008-08-22/54080.shtml.

B. The Brazilian Auto Industry Stimulus Measures

The Brazilian automotive industry was booming when the crisis arrived.[70] The crisis resulted in a severe decrease in production, with suppliers experiencing an even greater reduction than assemblers. The main impact was on vehicle exports, with a 46 per cent decrease in exports in March 2009 as compared to March 2008.[71] Along with the other major car-producing countries, domestic car sales within Brazil are very dependent on income and credit. When the crisis weakened credit operations, sales went down. The Brazilian government responded by restoring credit levels, discussed in Chapter 5. Appendix 4, measures 8 and 9 indicate that a special credit line of $1.7 billion was set up for assemblers and those banks that finance car sales credit operations, along with tax reductions to lower federal government taxes on cars, trucks, buses and light commercial vehicles.[72] Under the Incentive Programme for Technological Innovation and Consolidation of the Productive Chain of Motor Vehicles (INOVAR-AUTO),[73] qualifying companies could benefit from tax credits (IPI) based on expenses incurred in the country.[74] These expenses must be related to specific outcomes, such as research and development.[75]

The INOVAR-AUTO regime established three categories under which eligible companies could benefit from the programme's incentives.[76] Under Category 1, companies must manufacture automotive products in Brazil; Category 2 covers companies that trade automotive products in Brazil; and Category 3 includes companies with investment plans approved by the Ministry of Development, Industry and International Trade.[77] In other words, this measure promoted domestic producer interests. The conditions for admission to the regime include energy-efficiency targets, minimum levels of expenditures in innovation and research and development, and percentage of vehicles included in the certification programme on energy efficiency.

[70] In 2008, Brazil was the sixth largest producer of vehicles in the world, with an annual production of 3.22 million cars.

[71] In 2008, car production was at its peak and investments were planned to reach a production capacity of 5 million vehicles. O Salerno, 'The Global Economic Crisis Sectoral Coverage. Automotive Industry: Trends and Reflections', WP 278, International Labour Office, Geneva (2010).

[72] 7% for 'popular cars' (up to 1,000cc), 6.5% for cars with 1,001–2,000cc engines, 5.5% for flex-fuel (dual-fuel) and ethanol-only engines, 5% for trucks, 7.5% for light commercial vehicles;

[73] Created by Provisional Executive Order no 563 and partially regulated by Executive Decree no 7716, both dated 3 April 2012.

[74] The programme aims at supporting technological development, innovation, safety, environmental protection, energy efficiency and quality of cars, trucks, buses and auto parts.

[75] The expenses must be related to research; technological development; technological innovation; strategic raw materials; tooling; collections to the National Fund for Scientific and Technological Development (FNDCT) as provided for in regulations, and capacity-building of providers.

[76] Decree no 7.716, 3 April 2012.

[77] Decree no 7.819, 2 October 2012.

(i) Brazil's Auto Industry Stimulus Measures under WTO Obligations

As with the US measures, these measures would likely be considered specific subsidies because they confer a benefit from a government body to a confined sector of the economy. The eligibility for benefiting from these measures was confined to companies that manufacture automotive products in Brazil; companies that trade automotive products in Brazil; or companies with investment plans approved by the Ministry of Development, Industry and International Trade. If these specific subsidising measures could be shown to cause adverse effects, they would be actionable under the WTO ASCM. Again, as the following chapter discusses, no challenge was brought.

(ii) Brazil's Auto Measures under RTA Obligations

As with the auto bailout measures implemented by the USA, these Brazilian initiatives would also likely be considered specific subsidies because they confer a benefit from a government body to a confined sector of the economy. However, as Chapter 4 indicated, none of Brazil's RTA provisions contain binding rules on competition issues. The Fortaleza Protocol—the competition rules in MERCOSUR—does not contain State aid control, and has de facto been unenforced.

Along with the sugar sector, the automotive industry is excluded from the free movement of goods within Mercosur. The regional agreement on automotive policy ratified by the Member States in 2000 and 2001 did not enter fully in force as intended. Subsequently, a working group was established in 2010 to draft a new common automotive policy. However there is no indication that this working group has been convened.[78] Further, during the period under review, Brazil did not participate in any disputes within Mercosur. This suggests that it is improbable that Brazil's auto-industry measures would be challenged under its RTA commitments.

C. Brazil's Buy-National Measures

The Buy Brazil Act of 15 December 2010 amended federal laws governing government procurement at the federal, state and municipal levels, as well as for public entities.[79] Under this law, foreign companies may participate in international tenders, but a preference has been introduced for goods and services produced in Brazil of up to 25 per cent.[80] The Brazilian procurement law previously

[78] WT/TPR/OV/W/4, 40.

[79] On 19 July 2010, the Brazilian government amended Law no 8666 with a provisional measure ('Medida Provisória' MP 495). Both houses of the Brazilian Congress passed the so-called 'Buy Brazil Act' Law 12.349/10 of 15 December 2010.

[80] The new law gives Brazil the possibility for specific strategies to support Brazilian production such as in the information and communication technology (ICT) sector. Federal agencies and para-statal structures have to give preferences to locally produced ICT products and services based on non-transparent criteria.

prohibited differentiating between domestic and foreign companies in the tendering procedures, but maintained a preference for goods and services produced in Brazil when bids are equivalent in terms of price, quality and delivery time.[81] Under the 2010 Buy Brazil Act preferences are given to products: (i) made in Brazil; (ii) made or provided by Brazilian corporations; and (iii) made or provided by corporations that have invested in research and technology development in Brazil.[82] While the Act directly discriminates against competing foreign-owned firms, government can disregard preferences if there is no local production or capacity to provide the services in Brazil.

In order to qualify for the preferences, foreign companies have to set up a Brazilian company in line with the requirements of the new law and to invest directly in the country. However, the Act does not exclude possible joint ventures or partnerships between foreign and Brazilian companies. It extends any advantage made to Brazilian firms to the international partners of government procurement treaties signed by Brazil. At present, this includes only other Mercosur countries, and that remains unratified.

(i) The Legality of the Buy Brazil Act under WTO Obligations

Brazil is not a party to the WTO GPA; ergo the WTO GPA rules cannot form the basis of a claim against Brazil. As with the analysis of the BAA above, it is uncontroversial that procurement is exempt from the GATT Article III NT obligations, pursuant to Article III:8(a). However, as with the BAA, a claim could be made under the ASCM on the grounds that the subsidy provided under the Buy Brazil Act is contingent upon the use of domestic over imported goods. To recall, Article 3 stipulates that subsidies that are contingent, whether solely or as one of several other conditions, upon the use of domestic over imported goods are prohibited.

Moreover, if there was compelling evidence that the Buy Brazil Act requirements nullified or impaired a WTO commitment to the extent that it upset the legitimate expectations of a WTO member, it could also form the basis of a challenge pursuant to Article XXIII:1(b). Again, as discussed with reference to the BAA, there is no guidance in the case law as to whether the Brazilian government would be able to defend domestic policies that violate the ASCM under Article XX

[81] The federal constitution establishes as a general rule that government procurement must be preceded by a bid process. The general rules for bids are defined in the following federal laws: Law no 8666/93 for administrative contracts (goods and services supplies), Law no 8987/95 for public services provided through concessions or permissions and Law 11079/04 for services provided through public-private partnerships. Law no 8666 of 21 June 1993 establishes for federal, state and municipal levels the rules for administrative contracts and governmental procurement related to works, services, acquisitions, sales and leases.

[82] The margin of preference depends on a market study with criteria such as job creation and income generation, effect on the collection of taxes and development and technological innovation made in Brazil.

exceptions. As each dispute is to be assessed on a case-by-case basis, there is little legal certainty about the legal scope of domestic crisis policy-making. Perhaps it was this uncertainty that prevented any WTO Member affected by these domestic content requirements from challenging them under the DSU.

(ii) The Legality of the Buy Brazil Act under RTAs

Brazil is a signatory to Mercosur, which adopted a Protocol on Government Procurement in 2003.[83] As Chapter 3 set out, the Protocol established mechanisms for improving the transparency of government procurement in addition to MFN and NT clauses. This stipulates that service and goods providers from any of the four Member States must be afforded the same treatment as that given to national firms or, when applicable, that offered to individuals or firms from third countries under MFN. This treatment extends to services or goods provided by private-sector firms that may be affiliates of non-Mercosur companies, so long as the firm itself is legally established in a Mercosur country.[84]

As a result, under the Protocol, Mercosur Member States agreed to open their procurement markets above specified thresholds[85] for goods, services and public works by federal and sub-federal governments, albeit subject to negotiated country-specific reservations. The Protocol established a threshold of $3 million for public work tenders/projects for Brazil, with reservations in respect of procurement by sub-federal government. Brazil's list includes the main bodies of the executive branch of the central government, excluding the majority of public enterprises and all regulatory agencies.[86]

However, in order for it to enter into force, the Protocol requires parliamentary ratification by two of the four members; this has not taken place and the Protocol has yet to be ratified. In December 2004, the relevant regulations were submitted and were amended but were still waiting approval when a revision of the Protocol was adopted in 2006,[87] which also has not yet entered into force. As such, Brazil's buy-national policy does not violate any living law, although if the Protocol were to enter into force, the Mercosur Protocol on Government Procurement does accord preference margins to Mercosur Member States. This could form the basis for a claim against Buy Brazil Act procurements.

[83] The Protocol on Government Procurement was adopted by the Council of the Common Market in December 2003.

[84] TA O'Keefe, *Latin American and Caribbean Trade Agreements* (Leiden, Martinus Nijhoff, 2009) 193–95.

[85] These thresholds are $75,000 for Brazil, $150,000 for Argentina and $200,000 for Paraguay and Uruguay.

[86] WT/TPR/S/140.

[87] MERCOSUR CMC/DEC/55/04. Information available from the Directorate-General of Customs: www.aduanas.gub.uy/.

III. The Legality of India's Bailouts and Buy-Nationals

The Indian stock market experienced the effects of the global crisis as early as January 2008. Systemic shocks produced a reversal of inflows from foreign institutional investors (FIIs) into the country, transforming $17.7 billion net equity investment inflows from FIIs during 2007 into a net disinvestment of $13.3 billion during the period from January 2008 to February 2009. The blame was directed towards the massive de-leveraging of US banks after the financial meltdown, when FIIs withdrew funds from all over the emerging markets in order to meet the liquidity requirements of their principals in the USA.[88]

By mid-September 2008, India's money markets had dried up of funds in foreign credit markets, leading to a virtual halt of external commercial borrowing for India, including access to short-term trade finance. The collapse of the stock market ruled out the possibility of companies raising funds from the domestic stock market. Indian banks also lost access to funds from abroad, as interbank borrowing seized up in the USA and Europe. Instead, banks had to send funds to their branches abroad in those countries. All these put heavy pressure on domestic banks, leading to a liquidity crisis from mid-September to end-October 2008 and this was reflected in the interbank call money markets where the call money rates rose to 20 per cent.[89]

The combined fiscal deficit of the centre and states, including off-budget bonds, was estimated to pass 11 per cent of GDP for 2008–09, a huge rise from 2007–08 at about 5 per cent of GDP.[90] The growth in GDP moved down to 5.8 per cent (year-on-year) during the second half of 2008–09 from 7.8 per cent in the first half. Government consumption growth, however, rose steeply at 35.9 per cent from just 0.9 per cent in the first half and 7.4 per cent in 2007–08. The sharp rise in government consumption growth cushioned the sharp drop in aggregate demand and prevented a much sharper fall in GDP growth in the second half of 2008–09.

The total fiscal stimulus administered by India was set at 6 per cent of GDP. The Indian government sought to increase liquidity with the banks, infusing about Rs2,00,000 crores into the domestic money market to alleviate the pressures brought on by deterioration in the global financial environment. With infusion of this adequate liquidity the banks could provide credit and continue to finance working capital and fixed investment projects.

[88] KK Vohra, 'India's Response to the Global Financial Crisis and Current Issues in Deposit Insurance', DICJ, Kyoto (18 February 2016).

Deposit Insurance and Credit Guarantee Corporation', DICJ, Kyoto, 18 February 2016.

[89] N Bajpai, 'Global Financial Crisis, its Impact on India and the Policy Response', Working Paper no 5 (July 2011).

[90] KP Kannan, 'National Policy Responses to the Financial and Economic Crisis: The Case of India' Centre for Development Studies, Trivandrum (2008).

A. India's Bailout Measures in the Financial Sector

The Indian government notified the WTO that by December 2008 it had introduced what it termed a 'broad stimulus package including fiscal measures to counter recessionary trends'. As a result of this, three successive fiscal stimulus policies were implemented in India between early December 2008 and March 2009. Appendix 3, measures 1–4 indicate that these measures included:

- across-the-board central excise duty reduction by 4 percentage points;
- additional spending of Rs 200 billion;
- additional borrowing by state governments of Rs 300 billion for expenditure;
- assistance to certain export industries in the form of interest subsidy on export finance,
- refund of excise duties/central sales tax, and other export incentives; and
- a 2 percentage point reduction in central excise and service tax.

In addition to increasing liquidity, the lending rates of banks were also lowered to reduce the cost of borrowing. The rate at which banks borrow from the Reserve Bank of India was cut five times by 4 percentage points from 9 to 5 per cent in October 2008. Several Indian banks subsequently reduced their prime lending rate (PLR) to around 12–12.5 per cent, with the aim of creating more demand for credit by companies as well as the demand for consumer goods, including cars and property.

(i) The Legality of India's Banking Measures under the GATS

To recall, GATS Article XV does not impose any obligations to remove any subsidies in the services sector. Nevertheless, this does not leave subsidies completely unregulated: GATS Article XVII:1 is applicable and requires that governments accord NT to all financial service providers with a commercial presence in their country to the extent that any treatment could have anti-competitive effects within that country. In principle, India should therefore have extended aid to foreign banks with a commercial presence in their jurisdiction to comply with these obligations.

However, India has made limited commitments regarding the financial sector under its GATS commitments. Foreign banks are allowed to access the Indian market only through domestic branches. Restrictions are also imposed on the number of banking licences,[91] and on the value of the banking system's assets in the hands of foreign banks.[92] The commitments made by India under financial services are therefore limited. In banking, no commitments are made in Modes 1, 2 and 4. In Mode 3, the granting of branch licenses to foreign banks is subject to a cap of twelve per year for both new and existing banks.

[91] Twelve per year, both for new entrants and existing banks.
[92] 15% of total assets.

Notwithstanding this, as with the other banking bailouts, even if India's fiscal measures to the banking sector were to be challenged under Article XVII:1 GATS on the grounds that the bailouts were targeted and not horizontally available to all banks, it is likely that India could defend its measures under the 'Understanding on Commitments in Financial Services', which includes, in Part C, the requirement that NT be granted in the 'normal course of ordinary business'. Given that these fiscal stimulus measures were designed to alleviate the effects of a systemic sub-prime crisis, it is likely that these circumstances would have been pronounced as outside of the parameters deemed to be in the normal course of ordinary business. The burden of proof would also have been on the challenging Member to show otherwise. India is not a party to the Annex on Financial Services.

(ii) The Legality of the Stimulus Package under RTAs

As with most RTAs, the India–Sri Lanka CEPA has carved subsidies out from the scope of the services chapter, with the stipulation that the disciplines of the services chapter do not apply to subsidies. The agreement does, however, provide room for revision of subsidy disciplines subject to the developments in the multilateral context. Under the India–Sri Lanka CEPA, the Article on subsidies explicitly states that the dispute settlement mechanism does not apply to subsidies. In line with GATS Article XV, which refers to exchange of information on subsidies, the India–Sri Lanka CEPA outlines in detail the kind of information to be shared. The India–Singapore CECA, the India–Korea CEPA and SATIS also include similar provisions.

In sum, India was not prevented from providing liquidity to its domestic banks by its RTA obligations.

B. India's Bailouts in the Auto industry

The government of India's rescue package for the auto industry (Appendix 3 measure 5) was restricted to imposing a higher depreciation rate of 50 per cent for commercial vehicles, such as trucks, buses and vans, bought during the period January–March 2009. In addition to this, an extra line of credit was made available to non-banking financial companies (NBFCs) for purchase of commercial vehicles and assistance by it for purchase of buses for urban transport systems under the governmental urban renewal scheme. There was also a reduction in the excise duty on cars and utility vehicles with an engine capacity of 2000 cc and above, along with a reduction in excise duty for small cars from 16 to 12 per cent and for hybrid cars from 24 to 14 per cent in the 2008 budget. All these steps were expected to boost demand for commercial vehicles which had been badly hit by economic slowdown.

(i) The Legality of India's Bailouts to the Auto Industry

None of the auto industry measures was explicitly directed towards domestic rather than foreign car manufacturers, therefore a direct violation claim under the ASCM could not be raised at the WTO DSB.

C. Buy India

India did not notify the WTO of any specific buy-national policy as a component of the stimulus packages imposed. Nevertheless, as discussed in Chapter 1, the government of India has historically used procurement policy to promote domestic firms and sectors, including SMEs and solar energy. Analysis of the *India–Solar Cells* and *Canada–FIT* disputes indicates that local-content requirements imposed through procurement would likely be assessed under GATT Article III to identify whether the challenged measure is a procurement under the definition of Article III:8(a) derogation, as well as the TRIMs agreement and a potential claim under the ASCM. Moreover, these challenges can be raised whether or not India is a party to the WTO GPA, and whether or not, as a party to the WTO GPA, India had excluded the specific procurement being challenged from its schedules.

IV. Regulating Crisis Bailouts under the TFEU

The legislative options open to Member States of the EU during the financial crisis were primarily conditioned ex ante by the legal framework of the TFEU, which seeks to establish an internal market for the provision of financial services by adopting harmonisation measures. After setting out the legal framework governing State aid in the EU, this chapter first sets out the crisis measures that were enacted for both the financial and the manufacturing sectors, in Ireland, the UK and Germany. It then assesses the legality of these measures under the TFEU and the Temporary Framework established by the European Commission in response to the crisis. It concludes by assessing the legality of the EU's State aid control under the WTO's subsidy control measures under the ASCM.

A. State Aid Control under the TFEU

Article 107 TFEU stipulates that:

> 1. Save as otherwise provided in the Treaties, *any aid* granted by a Member State or through State resources *in any form* whatsoever which *distorts or threatens to distort competition* by favouring certain undertakings or the production of certain goods *shall, in so far as it affects trade between Member States, be incompatible with the internal market.* (emphasis added)

This appears to be an outright prohibition, and yet State aid is nevertheless provided pursuant to the list of exemptions set out in the subsequent paragraphs of Article 107. These provisions permit, in paragraph 2, any State aid having a social character or disaster relief; along with an expansive list of subsidy measures that may ex ante be considered compatible with the internal market in paragraph 3, such as aid to promote the economic development of areas where the standard of living is abnormally low. The assessment of the compatibility of an aid is seen as a balance between its negative effects on trade and competition within the internal market and its positive effects in terms of a contribution to the achievement of well-defined objectives of common interest. The Commission has established common principles for an economic assessment of the compatibility of State aid to assist Member States,[93] in addition to clarifying evaluation in the field of State aid.[94] There are several banking directives for the transposition into Member States and subsequent coordination of national legislations.[95] While neither the Treaty nor these banking directives contain any specific provisions or exemptions for the financial services sector, a 1981 judgment of the ECJ had confirmed the application of general competition rules to the financial services sector in 1981.[96]

This State aid framework is unequivocally more rigorous than subsidy control for services under GATS, which is as yet non-existent. Under the TFEU, the ex ante notification and the ex post monitoring and enforcement mechanisms set out under Article 108 serve to make EU State aid control convincing, not only relative to other regional arrangements but under the WTO framework. Under TFEU Article 108(3), the Commission shall be informed of any plans to grant or alter State aid in goods or services, with sufficient time to enable it to submit comments. If the Commission considers that any such proposed measure is not compatible with the internal market, it has the power to decide whether and when the non-compliant State aid should be removed.[97] The Member State concerned cannot legally put its proposed measures into effect until this procedure has resulted in a final decision. The monitoring mechanism also requires that the Commission, in cooperation with the Member States, constantly reviews all systems of

[93] Common Principles for an Economic Assessment of the Compatibility of State Aid under Art 87.3: http://ec.europa.eu/competition/State_aid/reform/economic_assessment_en.pdf (accessed 3 March 2014).

[94] See: 'The Draft Methodological Guidance Paper—Concepts and Recommendations', available at: http://ec.europa.eu/competition/consultations/2013_state_aid_modernisation/draft_guidance_paper_en.pdf (accessed 20 April 2014).

[95] The First Banking Directive (77/780/EEC), Second Banking Directive (89/646/EEC), Own Funds Directive (89/299/EEC), Solvency Ratio Directive (89/647/EEC), Large Exposure Directive (92/121/EEC) and Consolidated Supervision Directive (92/30/EEC) are consolidated into a single Directive: the European Parliament and Council Directive 2000/12/EC, [2000] OJ L126, as amended by the European Parliament and Council Directive 2000/28/EC, the Banking Consolidation Directive, [2000] OJ L257.

[96] Credit institutions had argued that they provided services of general economic interest and as a result Treaty rules on competition should not, or only restrictively, apply to them. However, the application of competition rules to the financial services sector was confirmed by the EUCJ in its judgment in Case 172/80 *Zucher v Bayerische Vereinsbank* [1981] ECR I-2021.

[97] Pursuant to Art 107 TFEU.

existing aid.[98] Once again, if the Commission finds that aid granted by a state or through state resources is not compatible with the internal market, it possesses the power to decide whether and when the Member State concerned should remove or redesign the non-compliant State aid measure. If the Member State concerned does not comply with this decision within the prescribed time, the Commission or any other interested state may refer the matter to the CJEU.[99] A Member State is obliged to take the 'necessary measures' to comply with a CJEU judgment.[100] If the Member State does not do so, penalty payments may then be imposed.[101]

Yet despite the strictness of EU subsidy control, State aids still represent about 1 per cent of EU GDP, excluding crisis-related measures.[102] Various EU trade measures have also been challenged under the WTO ASCM,[103] which is somewhat counter-intuitive in light of Article 107 TFEU. The fact is that State aid is regularly provided—whether or not there is a crisis—pursuant to the list of exemptions set out in the subsequent paragraphs of Article 107. The assessment of the compatibility of an aid is seen as a balance between its negative effects on trade and competition within the internal market and its positive effects in terms of a contribution to the achievement of well-defined objectives of common interest. The Commission has established common principles for an economic assessment of the compatibility of State aid to assist Member States,[104] in addition to clarifying evaluation in the field of State aid.[105]

In essence, this State aid framework is actually more permissive with regard to subsidy measures promoting secondary non-economic policy objectives than

[98] Established in Art 108(2).

[99] On application by a Member State, the Council may, acting unanimously, decide that aid which that state is granting or intends to grant shall be considered to be compatible with the internal market, in derogation from the provisions of Art 107 or from the regulations provided for in Art 109, if such a decision is justified by exceptional circumstances. If, as regards the aid in question, the Commission has already initiated the procedure provided for in the first subparagraph of this paragraph, the fact that the state concerned has made its application to the Council shall have the effect of suspending that procedure until the Council has made its attitude known. Art 108(2) third paragraph.

[100] Pursuant to Art 260 TFEU.

[101] Pursuant to Art 260(2) TFEU.

[102] OECD DAF/COMP/GF(2010)5.

[103] See: *European Communities–Measures Relating to the Development of a Flight Management System* (Complainant: United States); *European Communities–Countervailing Measures on Dynamic Random Access Memory Chips from Korea* (Complainant: Korea, Republic of): *European Communities–Measures Affecting Trade in Commercial Vessels* (Complainant: Korea, Republic of); *European Communities–Aid for Commercial Vessels* (Complainant: Korea, Republic of); *European Communities and Certain Member States–Measures Affecting Trade in Large Civil Aircraft* (Complainant: United States); *European Communities and Certain Member States–Measures Affecting Trade in Large Civil Aircraft* (Second Complaint) (Complainant: United States); *European Communities–Expiry Reviews of Anti-dumping and Countervailing Duties Imposed on Imports of PET from India* (Complainant: India); *EU and Certain Member States–Certain Measures Affecting the Renewable Energy Generation Sector* (Complainant: China); *EU–Certain Measures on the Importation and Marketing of Biodiesel and Measures Supporting the Biodiesel Industry* (Complainant: Argentina), *EU–Cost Adjustment Methodologies and Certain Anti-Dumping Measures on Imports from Russia* (Complainant: Russian Federation).

[104] Common Principles for an Economic Assessment of the Compatibility of State Aid under Art 87.3: http://ec.europa.eu/competition/State_aid/reform/economic_assessment_en.pdf (accessed 3 March 2014).

[105] See Draft Methodological Guidance Paper (n 92).

the WTO ASCM's coverage of goods, yet more rigorous in its assessment of each measure. Indeed, the notification, monitoring and enforcement mechanisms set out under Article 108 serve to make EU State aid control convincing and somewhat inspirational, not only relative to other regional arrangements but to the WTO ASCM framework.

The European Commission must be informed of any plans to grant or alter State aid in sufficient time to enable it to submit comments.[106] If the Commission considers that any such proposed measure is not compatible with the internal market, it has the power to decide whether and when the non-compliant State aid should be removed.[107] The Member State concerned cannot legally put its proposed measures into effect until this procedure has resulted in a final decision. The monitoring mechanism also requires that the Commission, in cooperation with the Member States, constantly reviews all systems of existing aid.[108] Once again, if the Commission finds that aid granted by a state or through state resources is not compatible with the internal market, it possesses the power to decide whether and when the Member State concerned should remove or redesign the non-compliant State aid measure. If the Member State concerned does not comply with this decision within the prescribed time, the Commission or any other interested State may refer the matter to the CJEU.[109] A Member State is obliged to take the 'necessary measures' to comply with a CJEU judgment.[110] If the Member State does not do so, penalty payments may then be imposed.[111]

B. The EU Response to the Financial Crisis

The European Commission's response to the financial crisis came in the form of four Communications (see Appendix 4). The Commission's rationale for intervention was based on the assumption that a banking failure would cause systemic reactions throughout the financial and manufacturing sectors. Action was consequently directed at different levels. The European Central Bank (ECB) and non-eurozone national central banks provided greater liquidity to the banking system and cut interest rates; while the European Economic Recovery Plan launched a €200 billion discretionary fiscal stimulus package comprising of a €170 billion budgetary expansion by Member States and €30 billion EU funding to increase demand and stimulate confidence.

A European Financial Stabilisation Mechanism (EMS) was established, based on a European Council Decision[112] amending Article 136 TFEU. This was immediately contested. In Ireland, a challenge was brought against the EMS on

106 TFEU Art 108(3).
107 TFEU Art 107.
108 Established in TFEU Art 108(2).
109 See n 97 above.
110 Pursuant to TFEU Art 260.
111 Pursuant to TFEU Art 260(2).
112 Decision 2011/199/EU of 25 March 2011.

the grounds that the amendment of Article 136 TFEU by Article 1 of Decision 2011/199 constitutes an unlawful amendment of the TFEU. Further, that by ratifying, approving or accepting it, Ireland would undertake obligations incompatible with the Treaties on which the EU is founded.[113]

Article 1 of Decision 2011/199 provides:

The following paragraph shall be added to Article 136 of the [FEU] Treaty:

1. The Member States whose currency is the euro may establish a stability mechanism to be activated if indispensable to safeguard the stability of the euro area as a whole. The granting of any required financial assistance under the mechanism will be made subject to strict conditionality.

Pringle's claim was that this provision did not provide for the lawful adoption of the Decision pursuant to the simplified revision procedure provided by Article 48(6) TEU because it entailed an alteration of the competences of the EU. This is contrary to the third paragraph of Article 48(6) TEU. Consequently, the Decision was inconsistent not only with provisions of the TEU and TFEU concerning economic and monetary union but also with the general principles of EU law. *Pringle* argued that by accepting the ESM Treaty, Ireland would undertake obligations that directly encroach on the exclusive competence of the Union in relation to monetary policy. Indeed, the objective of creating an autonomous and permanent international institution was to circumvent the economic and monetary prohibitions and restrictions laid down by the provisions of the TFEU. Further, the ESM Treaty was incompatible with the general principle of effective judicial protection and with the principle of legal certainty.

In determining whether the Decision encroached on the Union's exclusive competence in the area of monetary policy pursuant to Article 3(1)(c) TFEU,[114] the Court interpreted the TFEU provisions relating to the Union's exclusive competence,[115] and those relating to the Union's economic policy,[116] and the general principle of effective judicial protection.[117] The Court found nothing capable of affecting the validity of the Decision amending Article 136 TFEU with regard to a stability mechanism for Member States whose currency is the euro. Further, its examination of the relevant provisions of the TEU and TFEU and the general principles of effective judicial protection found they did not preclude the conclusion of a Treaty such as the EMS. The EMS was thereby deemed legitimate and subsequently provided up to €500 billion to individual Member States whose currency is the euro and who were in exceptional difficulty, which includes Ireland but not the UK.

[113] Case C-370/12, *Thomas Pringle v The Government of Ireland.*

[114] This requires amendment using the ordinary revision procedure provided for under Art 48(2)–(5) TEU.

[115] Namely Arts 3(1)(c) TFEU and 127 TFEU on the Union's monetary policy and Art 3(2) TFEU on the Union's competence for the conclusion of an international agreement.

[116] Namely Arts 2(3), 119–23, 125 and 126 TFEU.

[117] Namely Arts 4(3) and 13 TEU.

C. The Temporary Framework for State Aid

By November 2008, a European Economic Recovery Plan had been adopted by the European Commission, along with the Temporary Framework for State Aid.[118] The Temporary Framework aimed to reduce the negative impact of the banking crisis in the real economy by providing Member States with additional possibilities to grant State aid including to companies in the automobile sector. This complemented the Communications on State aid measures to support the banking sector previously adopted by the Commission, thereby enabling Member States to support financial institutions that specialised in car finance:

- grants under the de minimis Regulation which enabled Member States to offer aid of up to €200,000 per company over any period of three fiscal years[119] without it being deemed State aid;[120]
- State aid of up to €500,000 per company for the next two years was made available to relieve them from current difficulties;[121]
- grant loans or guarantees offered by Member States to the car industry on market conditions;[122]
- co-financing for active social protection measures from the European Adjustment Globalisation Fund to support the workers made redundant as a result of major structural changes in the world trade.[123]
- two years' reduction of up to 15 per cent of the annual premium to be paid for new guarantees for large car-sector companies and up to 25 per cent for SMEs operating in the car sector.[124]
- State aid was also permitted in the form of subsidised interest rates applicable to all types of loans[125] but particularly for the production of green products.

The General Block Exemption Regulation (GBER) 2008[126] also offers Member States additional possibilities to support the car industry though measures

[118] [2009] OJ C16, 1.

[119] Or state guarantee amounting to €1.5 million.

[120] [2006] OJ L379, 5.

[121] Further, if an auto industry company has already received de minimis aid prior to the entry into force of the Temporary Framework or will so during the validity of the Temporary Framework, the sum of the aid received under the Temporary Framework and de minimis aid received under the De Minimis Regulation must not exceed €500,000 between 1 January 2008 and 31 December 2010.

[122] Under the Reference Rates Communication and Communication on Guarantees. See [2008] OJ C14, 6; [2008] OJ C155, 10; [2008] OJ L406, 20, 1.

[123] [2008] OJ L406, 1.

[124] This allowed these companies to apply a premium fixed in the communication for another eight years. The maximum loan amount must not exceed the total annual wage bill of the beneficiary; while the state guarantee could not exceed 90% of the loan, it could cover both investment and working capital loans.

[125] In order to help bridging the difficulties of car companies in accessing financing, the Commission accepted that a reduced interest rate could be applied for interest payments until the end of 2012 for public or private loans. The reduced interest rate was calculated on the basis of the central bank overnight rate instead of the one-year interbank offered rate.

[126] This was extended until 30 June 2014.

that constitute State aid but can be granted without prior notification and authorisation.[127] Under GBER, Member States can support the auto industry through, for example: research, development and innovation; regional development; training of employees; aid to SMEs; risk capital; environmental protection; and measures promoting entrepreneurship, newly created companies in assisted regions and female entrepreneurship.[128] Important alternative avenues to grant State aid measures include the possibility for Member States to offer certain types of environmental aid to the auto industry. Subject to the Guidelines on State aid for environmental protection of 2008, aid can be granted, for example, to companies that improve the environmental performance of their production process; for environmental studies; for the acquisition of new green transport vehicles under certain conditions; for energy saving; and for sustainable biofuels, which indirectly benefits car manufacturers developing motors using biofuels.[129]

There is also the possibility to grant aid for Research & Development & Innovation (R&D&I),[130] which allows Member States to grant the auto industry aid for research and development projects for cars, including for the development of green technology. R&D&I aid is also permitted for the loan of highly qualified personnel; for technical feasibility studies; for process and organisational innovation in services; and for innovation clusters which can help car manufacturers to invest in open research and testing infrastructure. An auto industry company may benefit from R&D&I aid if it is having difficulty revamping its operations and if it can be shown that such aid will contribute to its future viability.[131] The R&D&I provisions also contain a matching clause, as discussed in Chapter 3. Regional aid may also be granted to the auto industry if it promotes the economic, social and territorial cohesion of the EU by addressing the handicaps of the disadvantaged regions through supporting investments and job creation linked to such investments. In disadvantaged regions, Member States can grant car-sector investment aid for setting up a new establishment, extending an existing establishment, diversifying the establishment's output into new products or introducing fundamental change in the overall production process.[132] The Guidelines on State aid to promote risk capital investments in SMEs enable Member States to grant aid high-growth-prospect auto companies.[133] Emergency assistance is also available.[134]

[127] Member States need only inform the Commission ex post that such aid was granted.

[128] The auto industry is deemed to include car producers, their suppliers and their distributors.

[129] [2008] OJ C82, 1.

[130] The Framework for State aid for Research and Development and Innovation, [2006] OJ C323, 1.

[131] Guidelines on State Aid for Rescuing and Restructuring Firms in Difficulty of 2004, [2004] OJ C244, 2.

[132] [2006] OJ C54, 13.

[133] Including aid to risk capital investors or venture capital funds for their risk capital investment, fiscal incentives to investment funds and/or their managers or investors and the constitution of investment funds ('venture capital funds') [2006] OJ C194, 2.

[134] Member States can, before preparing a comprehensive restructuring plan, grant to a car-sector company either a loan or a state guarantee on a commercial loan for a duration of six months. By granting such aid, Member States gain time, thereby allowing the company to prepare a restructuring plan or to repay the aid/stop using the state guarantee.

So, in addition to these existing legally sanctioned avenues to provide aid to the auto industry, the Temporary Framework aimed to facilitate the access to credit. It therefore benefited the manufacturers of cars as well as parts suppliers. Likewise, it encouraged car-sector companies to invest in a sustainable future, including development of green products. As noted, the legality of these temporary measures was based on Article 107(3)(b) TFEU. This provision allows the Commission to declare as compatible with the Common Market aid 'to remedy a serious disturbance in the economy of a Member State'. The measures applied to all companies including companies in difficulty that were not in difficulty on 1 July 2008, but only entered into difficulty thereafter due to the global financial and economic crises.[135] Member States were obliged to notify the schemes containing these measures but once the scheme was approved, they could grant individual aid immediately without further notification.

V. Member State Bailouts in the Financial Sector

A. The Irish Financial Sector Bailouts

As Appendix 4.1 indicates, in Ireland all the measures created in response to the crisis were in the financial sector. The Irish financial rescue package[136] included a guarantee arrangement to safeguard all deposits (retail, commercial, institutional and interbank), covered bonds, senior unsecured debt and dated subordinated debt (see Appendix 4.1, measures 1–7).[137] The six banks initially covered by the scheme were Allied Irish Bank, Bank of Ireland, Anglo Irish Bank, Irish Life and Permanent, Irish Nationwide Building Society and the Educational Building Society.

However, the scheme was subsequently opened up to certain foreign banks' subsidiaries in Ireland 'with a significant and broad based footprint in the domestic economy'.[138] Financial support could be provided to these credit institutions for up to two years in order to maintain the stability of the financial system in Ireland.[139] The scheme also provided the power to direct the commercial conduct

[135] State aid for car manufacturers already in difficulty before this or whose difficulties are mainly due to structural problems rather than the crisis, would fall under the Guidelines on State Aid for Rescuing and Restructuring Firms (n 129).

[136] The legislative framework underpinning the guarantee arrangement for depositors and lenders to Irish financial institutions is the Credit Institutions (Financial Support) Act 2008.

[137] Commission Decision of 13 October 2008 in Case NN 48/2008, *Ireland–Guarantee Scheme for Banks in Ireland*, COM(2008) 6059.

[138] Notably the Ulster Bank, First Active, Halifax Bank of Scotland, IIB Bank and Postbank. Commission Decision of 13 October 2008 in Case NN 48/2008, *Ireland–Guarantee Scheme for Banks in Ireland*, COM(2008) 6059, ¶7.

[139] Commission Decision of 13 October 2008 in Case NN 48/2008, *Ireland–Guarantee Scheme for Banks in Ireland*, COM(2008) 6059, ¶23.

and competitive behaviour of covered credit institutions to minimise any potential competitive distortion. In particular, the rate of expansion of their activities must not exceed certain limits. These credit institutions must comply with all directions given, and requirements made, by the Minister of Finance or Irish Regulatory Authority.[140] Whether or not this was perceived to be a rubber-stamping exercise, this Member State did defer to the regional notification requirements.

The European Commission approved this scheme despite explicitly pointing out that the commercial terms of the guarantee were not in line with the market economy investor principle; and also that the guarantee conferred selective advantage to the banks concerned and should be regarded as State aid within the meaning of Article 107(1) TFEU. However, the European Commission assessed the scheme under Article 107(3)(b) TFEU. The European Commission noted that some fundamentally sound banks were experiencing liquidity difficulties and this could have serious funding repercussions for the real economy. It concluded that the scheme did intend to remedy a serious disturbance in the Irish economy.

The Commission then undertook an assessment of the three conditions of (i) appropriateness, (ii) necessity and (iii) proportionality, as set out in the Banking Communication. First, the guarantee scheme was deemed an appropriate measure to restore confidence in the financial markets and overcome a market failure for wholesale funding that affects even healthy credit institutions. Second, the guarantee was limited to the minimum necessary in scope[141] and time to reach the objective. Third, the Commission pronounced that the distortions of competition were properly balanced via various safeguards against the positive effects of the scheme. As a result of this means–ends assessment, the Irish support scheme for financial institutions was determined by the European Commission to be compatible with the TFEU.

B. The Auto Industry Rescue Measures in Ireland

Despite the depth of the financial crisis in the banking sector and the availability of various measures to offer State aid to the auto industry in Ireland, as an EU Member State, none were implemented.

[140] They must conduct their affairs in a manner that progressively reduces the risk undertaken by the guarantee. Appropriate balance sheet management, application of improved structures to ensure long-term stability of funding, restructuring executive management responsibilities, and improving liquidity, solvency and capital ratios are examples of such measures which have to be taken by the covered institutions. Finally, in the event of a default of a covered institution, it will have to draw up a restructuring plan within six months and comply with the directions.

[141] The Commission considered the 'drying-up of interbank lending due to an erosion of confidence between financial institutions' in the context of the current wide spread crisis and held that inclusions of retail deposits, wholesale deposits and subordinated debts were necessary. Commission Decision of 13 October 2008 in Case NN 48/2008, *Ireland–Guarantee Scheme for Banks in Ireland*, COM(2008) 6059, ¶61–64.

VI. The UK Financial Sector Bailouts under the TFEU

As with the Irish liquidity measures undertaken by independent banks, the European Commission deemed those UK rescue measures (see Appendix 4.2) to fall outside the scope of State aid control. Nevertheless, the legality of the 'rescue merger' announced for HBOS in September 2008 was publically questioned by the UK Office of Fair Trading in overseeing the first phase of the merger decision. The concept of the rescue merger, also referred to as the *failing-firm defence*, enabled the European Commission to clear a concentration even though a dominant position is created or strengthened in its aftermath—provided that there is no causal link between the concentration and the dominant position. That is, as long as the merger does not lead to a deterioration of the competitive structure of the market, it will be approved. The HBOS controversy was based on the merger's potentially anti-competitive effects. A calculation was made that in the personal current account market the merger would combine shares of 19 and 14 per cent, and in the Scottish market for SME business it would combine shares of around 10 and 35 per cent—creating a balanced duopoly with the RBS. Nevertheless, in an unprecedented manner, the government still intervened.[142]

With the support of the Bank of England, HM Treasury and the Financial Services Agency, the law was amended to enable the merger to take place without a second-phase merger investigation. Subsequently it emerged that HBOS's assets were more toxic than Lloyds had expected. This led to further government intervention through the state taking a controlling 40 per cent stake in the bank. The UK government introduced a £37 billion bailout plan, of which £17 billion went to the newly combined Lloyds TSB and HBOS. A further £20 billion was invested in the similarly troubled Royal Bank of Scotland, taking over 58 per cent of the bank's shares.

The European Commission investigated this decision as a notification for State aid. It determined that the merger could go ahead as long as the necessary 'compensatory measures' were implemented to deter irresponsible behaviour. That is, there was no call for restoring competition, rather a requirement to divest itself of 632 branches.[143] And although Lloyds had acquired 14 per cent of HBOS, it was controversially found that the merger could continue if it sold only 4.6 per cent, despite this resulting in a maintaining ten point higher market share than its next biggest rival, RBS.

142 This was the first case of such an intervention since the reforming Enterprise Act of 2002, which was designed to take mergers out of political decision-making.

143 This divestiture, known as Project Verde, would bring a 4.6% share of personal current accounts which were attached to the branches. Current accounts are important for (the absence of) competition because consumers are very reluctant to switch. Banks can then lever profits by cross-selling insurance, savings products, loans and mortgages. See B Lyons. 'Competition Concerns Means Lloyds Should Be Required to Float HBOS Following Failure to Divest Branches to the Coop' (2013) http://competition-policy.wordpress.com/2013/04/25/competition-concerns-mean-lloyds-should-be-required-to-float-hbos-following-failure-to-divest-branches-to-the-co-op/.

As part of its response to the financial crisis, the UK government had already set up an Independent Commission on Banking (ICB). The ICB investigation found strong evidence that smaller challengers to the 'big four' banks have to fight to overcome switching costs by providing both higher deposit rates and lower borrowing rates, which resulted in lower margins.[144] The ICB recommended that a much larger divestiture was necessary to create a credible competitor. Yet even given its own 40 per cent ownership stake, the UK government asserted that it would not press Lloyds to enhance the divestiture as required by the European Commission.[145] In this instance, the ability of the UK government to circumvent all existing checks and balances was unambiguously unnerving.

A. The Auto Industry Rescue Measures in the UK

The only measure implemented directly for the auto industry was a variation of the US 'Cash for Clunkers' scheme discussed above, known in the UK as the Scrappage Incentive Scheme. The UK government provided a £300 million subsidy for the car scrappage scheme to operate between May 2009 and March 2010. This provided individual UK car owners a subsidy towards the purchase of new car (or van) when they traded in their ten-year-old (or older) car or van for scrappage. Car owners received a subsidy of £1,000 from the government, while an additional £1000 sum was offered by the approved car dealer. The scheme was voluntary for both car owners and dealers.

As with the analysis for the US 'Cash for Clunkers' scheme, the UK Scrappage Incentive Scheme is unlikely to be deemed a specific subsidy because it was not extended directly to automotive-producing enterprises. Moreover, the consumers benefiting from the scheme were not compelled to buy domestically produced cars. However, in the event that such a programme was found to provide a benefit that spread across both individual consumers and the car industry, once again, due to the short length of the programme it would also be difficult to prove that these subsidies were actionable because they caused adverse effects. In the unlikely event it were possible to establish either material injury to a domestic industry or a threat of material injury, the subsidy would have been actionable at the WTO and importing Members would have had the right to impose countervailing duties on those cars, as discussed further in Chapter 7.

VII. The Financial Bailout Measures in Germany

The single regulator of financial services in Germany is the German Federal Financial Supervisory Authority (BaFin), which is an independent agency governed by

[144] In fact, challengers need at least a 6% share of personal current accounts. The high loan to deposit ratio also makes funding difficult for challengers.

[145] Lyons (n 141).

public law, run by an administrative Council, and chaired by the Federal Ministry of Finance. BaFin is fully financed by assessments and fees from the companies it supervises. However, the German central bank retains supervisory roles in regulating banks, including prudential audits and financial crisis management. As the crisis unfolded, several BaFin-supervised institutions were found to be severely undercapitalised. These institutions had not been monitored primarily because the originate-to-distribute business model BaFin had adopted was not directly addressed in the act for the Strengthening of the Financial Market and Insurance Supervision.[146]

A. The Legality of the Financial Bailout Measures in Germany

Appendix 4.3 indicates the twenty-six government measures notified to the WTO by the EU, which were implemented by the German government in response to the fiscal crisis. Between 2008 and 2013 the German government spent 8.8 per cent of GDP on rescue measures to the financial sector, mostly in the first two years of the crisis.[147] In November 2008, Commerzbank became Germany's first commercial lender to turn to the government for capital, taking €8.2 billion to prop up its flagging finances and a 25 per cent stake in the company. This State aid was approved by the European Commission. By 18 March 2009 Germany's rescue plan for Commerzbank added a further €10 billion to the original rescue package of November 2008, taking the grand total government capital injection to this bank to €18.2 billion.

On 9 April 2009, following the entry into force of the Financial Market Stabilization Supplementary Act, SoFFin made an offer to buy Hypo Real Estate Holding AG ('Hypo'). SoFFin offered €1.39 per share (€290 million), 10 per cent above the statutory minimum of €1.26 (there is no minimum acceptance level for the bid). SoFFin gave Hypo's shareholders from 17 April 2009 until 4 May 2009 to accept this takeover offer. The bid followed the acquisition by SoFFin of an 8.7 per cent stake in Hypo at €3.00 per share on 28 March 2009. Bayerische Landesbank ('BayernLB') then sought €5.4 billion plus an additional €1 billion for a capital increase, The €5.4 billion payment from the rescue programme was met with an additional €1 billion capital injection provided by BayernLB's public-sector owners with the state of Bavaria contributing €700 million and the state's savings banks €300 million.

As with the Irish and UK liquidity measures undertaken by independent banks, the European Commission deemed these twenty-four German rescue measures

[146] WW Eubanks, 'The European Union's Response to the 2007–2009 Financial Crisis', Congressional Service Report, 7-5700 R41367 (2010).

[147] H Maurer and P Grussenmeyer, 'Financial Assistance Measures in the Euro Area from 2008 to 2013: Statistical Framework and Fiscal Impact', European Central Bank Statistics Paper Series no 7 (2015) 9. www.ecb.europa.eu/pub/pdf/scpsps/ecbsp7.en.pdf.

to fall outside the scope of State aid control and hence compatible with the TFEU. The European Commission approved of the German loan programme (KfW-Sonderprogramm 2009) The €15 billion loan programme provided for interest rate reductions on loans to finance investments and working capital of up to €50 million. This was to be granted to undertakings with a turnover of less than €500 million. The programme was administered by the Kreditanstalt für Wiederaufbau (KfW), the main public development bank in Germany, in close cooperation with the undertakings' own bankers. The EU Commission's approval was in accordance with the Temporary Framework. On 19 February 2009, as a second measure, the EU Commission also authorised under the temporary Federal framework scheme (Bundesregelung Kleinbeihilfen) permission for German authorities at federal, regional and local level to grant aid in the form of reduced interest rates on loans granted before 31 December 2010 and to provide subsidised guarantees for investment and working capital loans granted before 31 December 2010.

B. The German Auto Rescue Measures

The automotive industry in Germany was extremely vulnerable during the financial and economic crisis. Up to the crisis, German brands had acquired many foreign makes, including Rover, Mini, Triumph, Bentley, Rolls-Royce, Bugatti, Lamborghini, Chrysler, Skoda and SEAT. 2007 was a year of very strong growth, with new car registrations up 17%, but registrations of major German brands increased by 22 per cent.[148] Even during the crisis, sales continued to increase for German brands domestically, but they did slow significantly. After October 2008, production levels declined rapidly. Compared with 2009, passenger cars declined 31 per cent and commercial vehicles decreased 59 per cent. The German auto market was the third largest in the world, after the USA and Japan, at the start of the crisis. Industry-wide employment was 780,000 before the crisis, and by September 2009 30,000 jobs had been cut.[149] Observers compared the auto crisis as well as the entire financial crisis as the worst problem Germany had faced since World War II. In the period from January to March 2009, Daimler reported losses of €1.4 billion, and responded by reducing production at several of its plants, reducing working hours and cutting salaries by 8.75 per cent for 60,000 employees, with no bonuses in 2008 for 141,000 employees. To dampen its financial problems, Daimler acquired about €2 billion from an Abu Dhabi strategic investment fund in exchange for 9 per cent of its shares. BMW reported having to cut some 8,000 jobs only a few months after the start of the crisis. Opel made unsuccessful several attempts at receiving direct subsidised loans from the German government, in order to save the jobs of 25,000 Opel employees in Germany. However,

[148] *Germany Autos*, 2009.

[149] H Herbst, 'How Long Can Germany Keep Auto Jobs?' *Bloomberg Businessweek*, 28 September 2009, retrieved from http://www.businessweek.com.

Opel is owned by GM, a US company. Ultimately, the loan was not approved and following the US government's bailout of GM, GM itself provided support of €1.9 billion for Opel's restructuring costs.[150]

C. The German Car Scrappage Programme: Umweltpramie

In 2009 the German government introduced a scrappage programme that, as with the US and UK initiatives, offered consumers €2,500 euros to surrender their old 'clunkers'. It turned out to be very effective and helped spur more than 1.3 million new car sales. The German equivalent of 'Cash for Clunkers' was more flexible than the US programme. The Umweltpramie scheme requirements include that a car be nine years old; that the person trading-in the vehicle be the owner for at least the past year, that the trader buys a new car within the allotted timeframe, that the programme's budget of €5 billion was not exhausted, and that the car meet at least the Euro 4 emissions tier.[151] This German programme had no specific trade-in vehicle mileage requirements, nor did it have a tiered system of incentive payments. For any new car, the payment was €2,500.[152] The programme's budget was raised from €1.5 billion to €5 billion.[153] These funds were exhausted by September 2009.

(a) Legality of the German Car Scrappage Scheme

Following a similar legal analysis to that of the legality of the US 'Cash for Clunkers' scheme, it is clear that the Umweltpramie rules offer a financial contribution by the government or public body to consumers if they turn in an old vehicle and purchase a newer fuel-efficient one. This is an indirect transfer of funds from the government to the dealers who are able to sell the new vehicle as a result of the voucher programme, and also to other related industries such as petroleum, road building and auto service industries. However, they do not fall under the scope of the WTO's ASCM because they are general in nature and not extended directly to particular automotive-producing enterprises. The incentive is conferred on the consumer, not on the manufacturer. The scheme permits the consumer to choose between auto manufacturers. That is, they can be seen as neutral regarding the whole industry, both domestic and international, and as a result in compliance with international trade rules.

150 M Sheahan, 'GM to Restructure Opel Without European Aid' *International Business Times*, 16 June 2010, retrieved from http://www.ibtimes.com.

151 Bundesamt fur Wirtschaft und Ausfuhrkontrolle, 2009. The Euro 4 emissions requirement is the currently enforceable vehicle emissions requirement in the EU.

152 J Ewing, 'Cash for Clunkers: Car-Scrapping Plans—Germany's Lessons' *Spiegel Online*, 7 May 2009, retrieved from http://www.spiegel.de

153 E Kirschbaum, 'German "Cash for Clunkers" Out of Gas Just Before Vote' *Reuters*, 2 September 2009, retrieved from http://www.reuters.com.

VIII. The Legality of the Rescue Measures under the TFEU

Given the vast resources spent on these rescue measures in these three countries, a significant part of the crisis funding initiatives implemented in Ireland, the UK and Germany appear to constitute subsidies or State aid within the meaning of Article 107(1) TFEU. Within the TFEU's competition regime, State aid that distorts or threatens to distort competition within the internal market is prohibited under Article 107(1) unless authorised by the European Commission ex ante based on one or more of the common interest objectives set out under Article 107(2) and (3). Unlike other regional agreements, control of State aid among the Member States is an important component of the EU's competition rules. The Commission has been endowed with unparalleled powers under the EU State aid rules. While the Commission's decisions are subject to judicial review by the EU courts, the EUCJ has repeatedly argued that it is not for the EU judiciary to substitute its economic assessment for that of the Commission.[154] Judicial review is therefore confined to an assessment of the Commission's compliance with procedural rules.[155]

Prior to the onset of the crisis in 2008, the Commission based its approval of State aid to troubled financial institutions on the provision permitting as compatible with the internal market, rescue and restructuring (R&R) aid under Article 107(3)(c):

> Aid to facilitate the development of certain economic activities or of certain economic areas, where such aid does not adversely affect trading conditions to an extent contrary to the common interest.[156]

The Commission adopted six decisions and authorised six individual rescue packages on the basis of the R&R Guidelines.[157] The Commission viewed all of

[154] See Case T-149/95, *Ducros v Commission* [1997] ECR II-2031, ¶63.

[155] See Cases T-228 and 233/99, *Westdeutsche Landesbank Girozentrale and Another v Commission* [2005] ECR II-2123, ¶97.

[156] This legal avenue was clarified in the 2004 Community Guidelines on State Aid for Rescue and Restructuring Firms in difficulty, the 2008 Commission Notice on the Application of Art 87 and 88 of the Treaty to State aid in the Form of Guarantees and in the most recent State Aid Draft Methodological Guidance Paper—Concepts and Recommendations. Available at: http://ec.europa.eu/competition/consultations/2013_state_aid_modernisation/draft_guidance_paper_en.pdf (accessed 20 April 2014).

[157] Commission Decision of 5 December 2007 in Case NN 70/2007 (ex CP 269/07), *United Kingdom Rescue Aid to Northern Rock*, COM(2007) 6127 final; Commission Decision of 30 April 2008 in Case NN 25/2008 (ex CP 15/08), *WestLB risk shield, Germany*, COM(2008) 1628 final; Commission Decision of 4 June 2008 in Case C 9/2008 (ex NN8/2008, CP 244/2007), *Sachsen LB, Germany*, COM(2008) 2269 final; Commission Decision of 31 July 2008 in Case NN 36/2008, *Denmark–Roskilde Bank AS*, COM(2008) 4138; Commission Decision of 1 October 2008 in Case NN 41/2008, *UK–Bradford & Bingley* (see also Press Release IP/08/1437); Commission Decision of 2 October 2008 in Case NN 44/2008 *Germany–Hypo Real Estate Holding AG* (see Press Release IP/08/1453).

these cases as 'individual problems' requiring 'tailor made remedies that can be addressed under the rules for companies in difficulty'.[158] This was the legal basis upon which the Bank of England granted emergency liquidity assistance to the ailing Northern Rock bank in 2007. The UK Treasury announced a guarantee arrangement for all existing accounts and subsequently all new retail deposits in Northern Rock. The Commission adopted a decision on these UK measures to save Northern Rock, including the initial provision of emergency liquidity assistance by the Bank of England that was provided against high-quality collateral, bearing a premium interest rate and without a government indemnity.[159] It concluded that given that the Bank of England acted independently and this assistance was distinct from other measures, this liquidity assistance did not constitute State aid within the meaning of Article 107(1) TFEU.

The Commission pronounced that the later Northern Rock rescue measures, including guarantees and further extensions, did, however, constitute State aid. The Commission assessed the measures' compatibility under both Article 107(1) and 107(3) exemptions. The Commission found that contrary to the UK authorities' defence under Article 107(1),[160] an aid that benefited only one operator or one sector could not address the kind of situation targeted by this clause. Consequently, it concluded the measures to rescue Northern Rock were designed to resolve the problems of a single recipient rather than serious and systemic economic disruption.[161] Nevertheless, the Commission still subsequently authorised these measures—but with reference to both Article 107(3) and an exception for the banking sector set out in the R&R Guidelines.[162] This exception holds that while rescue aid must be given in the form of loans and guarantees lasting no more than six months, an allowance is made for the banking sector to ensure the credit institution can continue to operate in the short term in accordance with the prudential legislation in force.[163]

By the following year, the crisis was understood to be systemic and the vast amount of liquidity and restructuring measures required led the Commission to change legal course and to invoke Article 107(3)(b) permitting:

> Aid to promote the execution of an important project of common European interest or to remedy a serious disturbance in the economy of a Member State

[158] Commission Decisions in Case NN 25/2008, *WestLB risk shield, Germany*, ¶42; and Case C 9/2008 *Sachsen LB, Germany*, ¶95.

[159] See MEMO/07/545, 'State aid: Commission Approves UK Rescue Aid Package for Northern Rock—Frequently Asked Questions', 5 December 2007, Brussels.

[160] The UK authorities submit that a systemic crisis was possible because of the reaction of the market and the behaviour of depositors.

[161] Commission Decision of 5 December 2007 in Case NN 70/2007 (ex CP 269/07), *United Kingdom Rescue Aid to Northern Rock*, COM(2007) 6127 final.

[162] R&R Guidelines, §25(a).

[163] The UK authorities committed to present a restructuring plan for Northern Rock going beyond the short-term rescue by 17 March 2008.

The Commission clarified the use of Article 107(3)(b) TFEU in the Banking Communication,[164] Appendix 4.5 pronouncing that the provision should be used as a legal basis for rescue measures aimed at addressing the crisis and restoring market confidence in the financial sector.[165] This legal basis would not, however, affect the existing narrow interpretation of what constitutes a 'serious disturbance' in the economy of a Member State. Based on previous administrative practice of the European Commission,[166] three elements must be assessed under the Article 107(2)(b) exemption: (i) that the disturbance at stake must affect the whole of the economy of the Member State concerned and not merely a region thereof; (ii) that the complex assessments of an economic and social nature related to the term 'serious disturbance' fall within the exercise of the wide discretion that the Commission enjoys; and (iii) that being a derogating provision, Article 107(2)(b) needs to be interpreted strictly.[167]

Despite the narrow interpretation of 'serious disturbance' accorded to Article 107(2)(b), this clause still offered the Commission far greater flexibility in the types of State aid it could permit due to the broad interpretative scope of the words 'aid to … remedy a serious disturbance in the economy of a Member State' as compared with the specific nature of aid to develop 'certain' economic activities or economic areas. The latter concept does not ipso facto easily translate into vast amounts of State aid throughout the Member States cutting across both the financial and real economy with the objective of stemming a systemic banking crisis. The choice of this provision was also politically motivated; it pre-empted recourse by the Member States to the provisions of Article 108(2):

> On application by a Member State, the Council may, acting unanimously, decide that aid which that State is granting or intends to grant shall be considered to be compatible with the internal market, in derogation from the provisions of Article 107 or from the regulations provided for in Article 109, if such a decision is justified by exceptional circumstances.

Article 108(2), if invoked, could seemingly allow the Member States themselves to take control of State aid supervision through the Council and effectively sideline the Commission over State aid control for as long as the 'exceptional circumstances' justified it.

As it was, between October 2008 and December 2010 the Commission 'took control' of State aid in the Member States, approving more than 200 State aid

[164] The Communication from the Commission on the application, from 1 August 2013, of State aid rules to support measures in favour of banks in the context of the financial crisis ('Banking Communication') OJ C 216, 30.7.2013, p1–15.

[165] Typically, in its decisions, the Commission would find the existence of State aid based on the market economy investor principle (MEIP), but would consider the measure as justified under Art 107(3)(b) TFEU.

[166] See Commission Decision in Case NN 70/07, *Northern Rock* [2008] OJ C43/1; Commission Decision in Case NN 25/08, *Rescue aid to WestLB*, [2008] OJ C189/3; Commission Decision in Case C 9/08, *SachsenLB* [2009] OJ L104/34.

[167] See Cases C-57 and 61/00, *Freistaat Sachsen and others v Commission* [2003] ECR I-9975, ¶167, 169.

decisions relating to the financial sector either in the form of schemes or ad hoc support, on the basis of Article 107(3)(b) TFEU. The Commission also approved guarantee schemes in twenty different Member States, each with the objective of supporting the short- and medium-term financing needs of solvent financial institutions that faced increasing difficulty in accessing liquidity. Guarantees were open to all systemically relevant solvent financial institutions in the state concerned, including subsidiaries of foreign institutions, thereby avoiding prima facie violations of NT obligations under GATS XVII.1. This led some to accuse the Commission of simply 'blowing in the wind'.[168]

Whether or not this was merely window-dressing, the Commission did take the helm by insisting on formally evaluating State aid with the aim of minimising distortions of competition. The pricing of guarantees was set at the estimated market rates because under crisis conditions guarantees to cover such vast contingencies were unavailable on the commercial market. The Commission also undertook a type of means–ends analysis when reviewing each Member State's proposal for State aid measure for (a) its appropriateness to achieve the objective of remedying the serious disturbance in the economy, by being targeted on restoring financial stability; (b) its necessity in time and scope; and (c) its proportionality in that the positive effects of aid are carefully weighed against the resulting distortions of competition and limit such distortions to a minimum. At the very least this initiative provided the Member States with a framework through which to evaluate their crisis interventions.

IX. The Interface between EU State Aid Control and the ASCM

The EU is the only WTO Member that seeks to control government subsidies that distort or threaten to distort competition within its internal market. However, this discussion also noted that it cannot be assumed that permitted State aid will always conform to WTO obligations under the ASCM. There are several areas where the EU State aid regime does not conform completely to the requirements of the WTO ASCM, and which as a result may lead to a violation of its commitments.[169] To the extent that an EU Member State's measure does not distort competition in the internal market but does distort competition externally, the WTO will be concerned. Indeed, as Chapter 7 notes, the EU has been a regular and major target of countervailing duty measures and challenges within the WTO.

[168] For example: P Marsden and I Kokkoris, 'The Role of Competition and State Aid Policy in Financial and Monetary Law' (2010) 13 *Journal of International Economic Law* 875.

[169] See: C-D Ehlermann and M Goyette, 'The Interface between EU State Aid Control and the WTO Disciplines on Subsidies' (2006) 4 *European State Aid Quarterly* 695: M. Slotboom, *Do Different Treaty Purposes Matter for Treaty Interpretation? A Comparison of WTO and EC Law* (London, Cameron May, 2005) 97–126.

Of the potential conflicts that are of particular interest to these crisis measures, it is the definition of what constitutes a financial contribution that is of most significance. A financial contribution granted by a government is narrower under Article 107 TFEU than under Article 1.1(a)(1) ASCM. Under the latter agreement, the DSB has ruled in various disputes that even if a government merely instructs a private body to grant a financial contribution, it will be found to be subsidising even, moreover, if there is 'no cost to government'.[170] However, EU jurisprudence has ruled that for a financial contribution to constitute State aid it must directly correspond to specific government expenditures—this is the so-called 'charge on the public account' requirement. This legislative difference was illustrated during the landmark ECJ case *PreussenElektra*.[171] This dispute, as with the WTO *Canada–FIT* dispute discussed in Chapter 2, concerned a government measure that also required private regional electricity suppliers to purchase electricity produced from renewable energy producers in their area of supply at prices fixed above market prices. However, unlike the *Canada–FIT* Panel findings, the ECJ pronounced that the measure conferring an economic advantage did not involve either a direct or indirect transfer of state resources. This reading implies that if, as a crisis measure, an 'independent' financial institution is instructed by a Member State government to grant 'a financial contribution' that benefits certain actors operating in the private sector, it will not—ceteris paribus—be deemed State aid under current EU case law, but it could be challenged as an actionable subsidy under the WTO's ASCM.

The next divergence of relevance here is located in the contending notions of *specificity* versus *selectivity*; or in other words, whether the subsidy targets an enterprise or group of enterprises, industry or group of industries collectively. Under the WTO, the concept of specificity used is based on the principle that if a subsidy is made generally available to an economy it is presumed that there will not be any anti-competitive distortions in the allocation of resources. Consequently, only once a subsidy is deemed to be 'specific' is it assessed as to whether it is 'actionable' under Part III, and as to the application of countervailing duties under Part V. That is, only subsidies that are specific within an economy are subject to the ASCM disciplines.

The ASCM's overall concept of specificity is not prima facie at odds with the textual definition of selectivity under the Article 107(1) TFEU, which concerns

[170] The Panel Report *US–Export Restraints* closed a loophole in subpara (iv) of Art 1.1(a) by avoiding circumvention and preventing a government from acting through an intermediary (a private body) to confer the types of financial contributions found under subparas (i)–(iii), at para 8.53. 8.24. ibid, 689. This finding was confirmed in Panel, *European Communities–Countervailing Measures on Dynamic Random Access Memory Chips from Korea*, WT/DS299/R ('*EC–DRAMs*'). Similar reasoning (and language) is found in Panel Report, *United State–Countervailing Duty Investigation on Dynamic Random Access Memory Semiconductors from Korea*, WT/DS296/R, 21 February 2005 ('*US–DRAMS*'), ¶7.33, and in Panel Report, *Korea–Measures Affecting Trade in Commercial Vessels*, WT/DS273/R, 7 March 2005 ('*Korea–Vessels*'), ¶7.370.

[171] Case C-379/98, *PreussenElektra AG v Schleswag AG*, [2001] ECR I-2099.

favouring certain undertakings or the production of certain goods. However, it differs markedly in its interpretation. This was indicated in the 2002 ECJ case *Spain v The Commission*,[172] which is not unlike the US 'Cash for Clunkers' scheme. This ECJ dispute involved a scheme to facilitate the replacement of commercial vehicles through the use of an interest subsidy for loans to finance eligible new vehicles.[173] The scheme was open to natural persons, SMEs, regional public bodies and bodies providing local public services. Article 88(3) TEU (now Article 108(3) TFEU) requires that Member States inform the Commission of any plans to grant or to alter aid. Member States do not have the right to put such plans into effect if they have not received Commission authorisation. Any aid granted on the basis of a scheme that has not been notified to the Commission is illegal and must be refunded. If the Commission considers that an aid plan is incompatible with the internal market, it initiates infringement proceedings against the Member State concerned. This suspends application of the measures proposed until there is a final decision.

In this case, the Spanish authorities did not notify the Commission because they did not deem this scheme to be State aid. Moreover, once challenged they defended their position with reference to the WTO ASCM's definition of a 'specific subsidy' in Article 2.1(b) because the measure did not favour certain undertakings or the production of certain goods, but rather targeted an indeterminate group of potential beneficiaries.[174] To recall, the ASCM Article 2.1(b) excludes subsidies accorded pursuant to neutral criteria or conditions that do not favour certain enterprises over others, and which are economic in nature and horizontal in application, such as number of employees or size of enterprise. The Commission, however, claimed otherwise—rather, that this measure was selective because, inter alia, it benefited only undertakings that needed commercial vehicles and that SMEs were the only enterprises eligible for aid while the exclusion of large enterprises could not be justified through the 'nature and general scheme of the system'. The ECJ findings supported the Commission's concept of selectivity in interpreting the concept broadly to embrace all measures that are not of general application. The contested measure was therefore deemed to be State aid within the meaning of the Treaty. Furthermore, the ECJ explicitly pronounced that the fact that the contested measure would not be considered a 'specific' subsidy under the WTO ASCM did not reduce the scope of the definition of aid under Article 92(1) of the Treaty (now Article 108(3) TFEU). The ECJ found that the support given to certain undertakings in funding part of those charges was not a consequence of the nature or general scheme of the system of charges in question and must be considered to favour those undertakings.[175]

[172] Judgment of 26 September 2002 in Case C-351/98, *Spain v Commission* [2002] ECR I-8031, ECLI EU C 2002 530.

[173] The 'Plan Renove Industrial'.

[174] *Spain v Commission* (n 172) ¶24–30.

[175] ibid, ¶32.

The third relevant potential conflict between the requirements of the WTO ASCM and the TFEU can be identified in the types of State aid deemed compatible with the internal market requirements. As noted above, there are various types of aid available to the auto industry that do not have to be notified under the GBER block exemptions. Other exemptions are permitted based on Article 107(2) and (3). These provisions condition when the prohibition on aid under Article 107 TFEU does not apply. Article 107(2) is an exhaustive list of aid compatible with the internal market:

- aid having a social character granted to individual consumers, provided it is granted without discrimination related to the origin of the products concerned;
- aid to make good the damage caused by exceptional events, such as natural disasters;
- aid for certain areas of the Federal Republic of Germany affected by the division of Germany.

Article 107(3) TFEU sets out an illustrative list of cases where exemption from the Article 107(1) prohibition is possible, but not automatic. Upon individual examination, based on a body of soft law consisting of guidelines, communications and block exemptions, the Commission may declare the following horizontal or sectoral aid to be compatible with the rules:

- aid to certain underdeveloped regions, including new Member States;
- aid to promote the execution of a major project of European interest or remedy a serious disturbance in the economy of a Member State;
- aid to facilitate the development of certain economic activities or areas, provided it does not adversely affect trading conditions to an extent contrary to the common interest;
- aid to promote culture and heritage conservation (with the same proviso).

When approving these exemptions, the Commission does not need to take into account the distortions to international trade that the measure effects,[176] whereas the WTO rules will. Indeed, as noted, it is significant that a 'crisis measure' implemented with the aim of rescuing or restructuring a failing industry approved under the TFEU Article 107(3)(b) or (c) will nevertheless be deemed an actionable subsidy under the ASCM if it can be shown to cause or threaten to cause adverse trade effects. To repeat, there is no formal exception to this.

In Part III this book will continue this analysis by focusing on the enforcement of these international and regional rules, when violated during an economic crisis.

[176] The Community Guidelines on State Aid for Rescuing and Restructuring Firms in Difficulty ([2004] OJ C244/02) were prolonged until the rules were modernised under the 2012 State Aid Reform initiative. See Commission Communication concerning the prolongation of the application of the Community guidelines on State aid for rescuing and restructuring firms in difficulty of 1 October 2004 ([2012] OJ C296/02).

Part III

Enforcing International Trade Law in a Crisis

6

Challenging Bailouts and Buy National Measures

I. Overview

Part II's assessment of the legality of the crisis measures implemented in the financial and manufacturing economy in the case study countries indicated that the financial sector has been largely unregulated by international or domestic law, and as a result none of the bank bailout's were actionable under the GATS or RTAs. However, in the manufacturing sector, certain crisis measures were actionable under the WTO ASCM. There are two mechanisms within the WTO for disciplining the use of non-compliant subsidies, including those implemented through government procurements: one discipline is the direct limitation on subsidy practices by WTO rules, including the WTO GPA and ASCM, through bringing a claim to the WTO DSB. The other is the imposition of countervailing duties by affected importing countries. This chapter assesses whether and how the non-compliant crisis measures in the case study countries were disciplined using either of these two mechanisms.

Chapter 6 first examines the response of the wider WTO Membership to the stimulus packages implemented in the case study countries. The chapter then looks at the response at the regional level by examining the TFEU in the EU as the only example of an RTA with binding collective rules with an independent enforcement mechanism for regulating subsidies and government procurement. The results of this analysis serve to inform the conclusions of this book on the role and enforcement of the rules governing unnecessary distortions of competition through public bailouts and buy-nationals.

II. WTO Consultations and the Dispute Settlement Body

Before bringing a case, a Member shall exercise its judgment as to whether action under these procedures would be fruitful. The aim of the dispute settlement mechanism is to

> secure a positive solution to a dispute. A solution mutually acceptable to the parties to a dispute and consistent with the covered agreements is clearly to be preferred.[1]

Despite the legal avenue for challenging actionable measures under the ASCM, or less emphatically under Article XXIII:1(b) and (c), this examination of the disputes that took place between 2008 and 2013 indicates that the WTO DSB was not called upon to form a Panel to examine challenges against any of the stimulus measures. Nevertheless, some political statements threatening action were made to the press[2] and it is possible that disputes related to these stimulus measures emerged but were resolved in consultations. It has been said that while the greater legalism of the WTO is significant, experience indicates that the real 'action' is likely to be found in pre-trial negotiations.[3]

In 2000, five years after the establishment of the WTO, it was pointed out that although the transition from GATT to WTO heralded a more rule-orientated approach to jurisprudence, this conclusion should be tempered by the fact that 'fully three-fifths of all disputes end prior to a panel ruling, and most of these without a request for a panel'.[4] The researchers reasoned that because the WTO remains a court without a bailiff,[5] the effectiveness of the regime disproportionately manifests itself in the form of settlements prior to a ruling. Indeed, they went as far as to claim that once a ruling has been issued on a dispute, it is somewhat counter-intuitively actually less likely to end with full or partial satisfaction of the complainant's initial demands. The researchers surmised from this that: '[N]o functioning legal system can wait until then to exert its primary impact.'[6] The data supporting this position suggested that between 1995 and 1999, of the 185 disputes initiated at the WTO, only 80—or approximately 43 per cent—led to establishing a Panel. Table 6.1 at the end of this chapter, indicates that of these, only 62—or 33.5 per cent—resulted in a Panel ruling, and of these just over a fifth resulted in an Appellate Body report. This led to the calculation that in the majority of cases—55 per cent—no panel was ever established.

[1] DSU Art 3.1.

[2] In February 2009, Reuters reported that Brazil may challenge the legality of a 'Buy American' clause in the recently approved US economic stimulus package at the WTO. The Brazilian Foreign Minister Celso Amorim said: 'It's a complex legal analysis, but we're doing it. … [Going to the WTO] is a real option.' See: http://www.reuters.com/article/2009/02/17/us-brazil-us-wto-idUSTRE51F52920090217. Likewise, the following month, the European Commission warned the US government that it may launch a legal challenge at the WTO if the USA's massive economic stimulus package is approved with a 'Buy American' provision. A *European Voice* article reported the Commission as stating that the version of the stimulus package adopted by the US House of Representatives on 29 January may unfairly discriminate against EU businesses, because it stipulates that iron and steel to be used in infrastructure projects contained in the package must be produced in the USA. hwww.europeanvoice.com/article/2009/02/eu-attacks-buy-american-proposal/63818.aspx.

[3] ML Busch and E Reinhardt, ‚Bargaining in the Shadow of the Law: Early Settlement in GATT/WTO Disputes' (2000) 24 *Fordham International Law Journal* 170.

[4] ibid, 158–59.

[5] ibid, 159, quoting GE Rossmiller.

[6] RE Hudec, *Enforcing International Trade Law: The Evolution of the Modern GATT Legal System* (London, Butterworth, 1993) 360.

Table 6.1: Patterns of GATT/WTO dispute escalation

Stage of Escalation	Disputes Initiated			
	1948–1999	1948–1988	1989–1994	1995–1999
Initiated	620	313	122	185
… of which Panel established	276 (44.5%)	137 (43.8%)	59 (48.4%)	80 (43.2%)
… of which Panel ruling issued	233 (37.6%)	120 (38.3%)	51 (41.8%)	62 (33.5%)
… of which Appellate ruling issued	—	—	—	44 (23.8%)

Note: Since adjudication in the first years of GATT relied less on formal panels than on other bodies (e.g., working parties or the entire Council) to issue judgments, the term "panel" above includes those alternative authorities as well. The figures in parentheses reflect the row's percent of the total cases initiated in that period. Cases filed in 2000, as well as 17 earlier WTO disputes whose panels had not yet had a suitable chance to form or issue a ruling as of July 2000, are not included.

Reproduced from ML Busch and E Reinhardt, 'Bargaining in the Shadow of the Law: Early Settlement in GATT/WTO Disputes' (2000) 24 *Fordham International Law Journal* 161.

This conclusion built on earlier studies that had also indicated that the right to a panel did not inspire more early settlement, more escalation, or more resolution through concessions at the panel stage. Moreover, while highly democratic dyads are more likely to achieve concessions, this is only at the consultation stage. Similarly, the threat of a DSB ruling tends to induce early settlement or plea-bargaining, although once an adverse ruling is issued, the defendant is much less likely to concede. The claimant's leverage depends primarily on ignorance of the defendant's intent to comply. Once a ruling is made, that anticipatory effect is moot: either the defendant complies or not. As a result, this frees defendants who do not suffer costs for non-compliance to act according to type. Consequently, the researchers concluded, one can expect defendants to make greater concessions before rulings than after.[7] The data suggests that rather than supporting the argument that the WTO DSU heralded the introduction of a legalistic—as opposed to diplomacy based—dispute resolution system, these percentages actually did not change dramatically over the GATT/WTO timeframes assessed here. Extending Hudec's existing analysis of the outcomes of disputes across the different stages of dispute settlement, Reinhardt and Busch found that over two-thirds of disputes ending prior to a ruling, exhibited full or partial concessions by the defendant. They confirmed prior conclusions that even in the event of an adverse ruling, the

[7] See: ML Busch, 'Democracy, Consultation, and the Paneling of Disputes under GATT' (2000) 44 *Journal of Conflict Resolution* 425; E Reinhardt, 'Adjudication without Enforcement' (2001) 45 *Journal of Conflict Resolution* 174.

WTO framework ensures that the DSB can only deliver a punch that would not hit anyone.[8]

Reinhardt and Busch further submit that early settlement will have a tendency to take place *in the shadow of the law* if that law is weak in enforcement capacity. This detailed examination of the different stages and outcomes of settling disputes from 1948 through to 2000 concluded that the possibility that a Panel might issue an adverse ruling was in itself enough to induce greater concessions through early settlement, even from defendants not inclined to comply in the event of an adverse ruling. In other words, uncertainty about the defendant's preferences still plays a significant role in the bilateral bargaining process.[9] Importantly, these results do not serve to undermine the achievements of dispute settlement in either the GATT or WTO DSB. Rather more pragmatically, these conclusions have significant implications for discussions of reforms of the system; most obviously in terms of the appropriate levels of transparency and privacy maintained during consultations.[10]

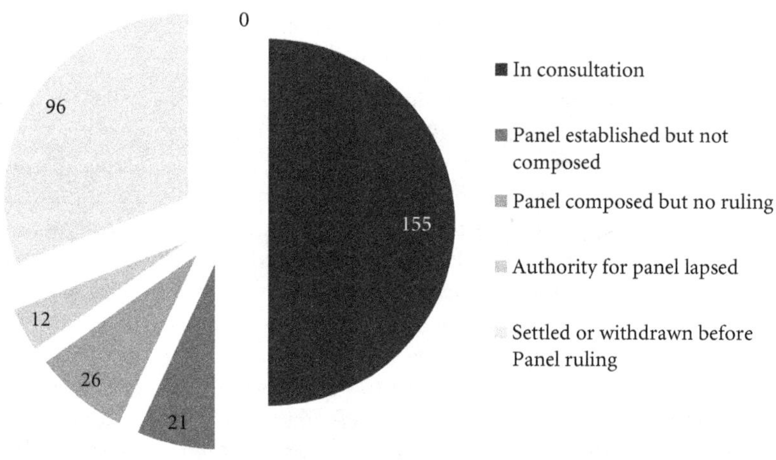

Figure 6.1: Numerical breakdown of disputes that have not resulted in a WTO Panel (Source: http://wto.org/english/tratop_e/dispu_e/dispu_current_status_e.htm. Accessed 22/11/2016)

Later work from 2007 submits, somewhat alarmingly, that most of the empirical research related to the DSB omits from its datasets the near one-third of all WTO-filed disputes that were classified either as 'pending' or 'inactive'. Furthermore, of those disputes that do not result in a panel, the WTO is 'apprised of a settlement

[8] While beyond the scope of this research, see: RE Hudec, '"Transcending the Ostensible." Some Reflections on the Nature of Litigation Between Governments' (1987) 72 *Minnesota Law Review* 211, 219.

[9] For further discussion, see Reinhardt (n 7).

[10] See WJ Davey and Amelia Porges, 'Performance of the System I: Consultations and Deterrence' (1998) 32 *International Law* 695, 703.

in only 25 per cent of these cases'.[11] After following up on these *abandoned* disputes, this empirical analysis concluded that while some disputes were settled via another WTO dispute concerned with similar legal matters, others were simply not pursued. One can speculate that this could be the due various factors, for example, the realisation of the lack of merit of a case, or more problematically, the lack of resources to pursue it. This is confirmed by Davis's 2012 analysis of the role of domestic politics to generate demand for adjudication as an enforcement strategy.[12]

Whatever the causes, this conclusion begs serious questions about the numerical success rate claimed for the WTO's DSB, both at the panel and pre-panel consultation stages. For the purposes of pursuing this argument, data from the WTO database of the status disputes through to October 2013 was collected for analysis.[13] The results set out in Figure 6.1 indicate that of the 467 disputes brought to the WTO DSB within this timeframe since it commenced in 1995, 291—or 62 per cent—have not resulted in a panel ruling. Of these, 93 disputes—or 32 per cent—were successfully settled or withdrawn before a Panel was established. However, an even greater proportion of these 291 disputes, just over half—or 151 disputes—are currently officially listed as still being in consultation.

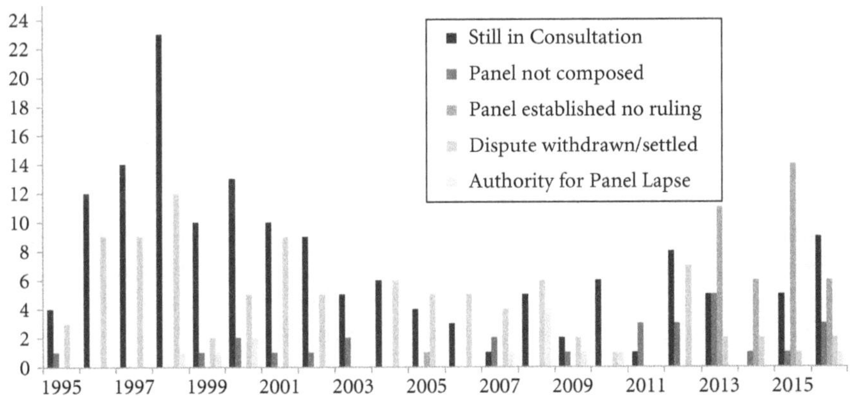

Figure 6.2: WTO disputes currently in consultation or without panel ruling 1995–2013. Source: www.wto.org/english/tratop_e/dispu_e/dispu_current_status_e.htm

[11] KM Reynolds, 'Why Are So Many WTO Disputes Abandoned?', American University, Department of Economics Working Paper no 2007-05, http://w.american.edu/cas/economics/repec/amu/workingpapers/2007-05.pdf (accessed 7 October 2013).

[12] CL Davis, *Why Adjudicate? Enforcing Trade Rules in the WTO* (Princeton, NJ, Princeton University Press, 2012). Davis indicates that the decision to invoke a dispute does not proceed solely on the merits of the case alone. When the harm from cheating and benefits of cooperation are shared broadly across states—as in a systemic fiscal crisis—enforcement represents a public good where each state may seek to free-ride on actions of others rather than 'play the role of policeman.' See R Axelrod and RO Keohane, 'Achieving Cooperation Under Anarchy: Strategies and Institutions' (1985) 38 *World Politics* 235.

[13] http://wto.org/english/tratop_e/dispu_e/dispu_current_status_e.htm (accessed 7 January 2017).

Figure 6.2 presents a chronological assessment of how disputes have fared in the WTO if they did not reach the stage of receiving a formal Panel ruling. The chronology indicates that 94 disputes were settled or terminated by being withdrawn or through a mutually agreed solution. These are numerically clustered towards the early years of the WTO DSB's existence. Of those panels that have been established since 1995, 22 have not yet been composed. Of those Panels that have been composed since 1995, 18 have yet to provide a ruling but these are clustered in the post-2011 period and this is to be expected due to the timeframes necessary for a Panel to establish and issue a report. Nevertheless, in 7 disputes, the authority for a panel has lapsed.

In the period of direct interest to this research, 2008–12, the data suggests that consultations were requested 30 times since the outbreak of the crisis in 2008. Of these, half—or 15 disputes—were settled or withdrawn from the WTO DSB, while 12 panels have been established but not composed. There are 17 panels that have been composed mostly since 2011 that have not yet made rulings. Again, this is explained away by the length of time it takes for a Panel to circulate an interim report, which is normally 6 months from the Panel's composition, or three months if urgent. The Panel's composition takes place after 60 days of consultations and the selection process can take up to 45 days.[14]

However, an examination of the matters addressed in these disputes indicates that none of them appear to be directed at a specific crisis measure enacted within any of the case study countries. (See Boxes 6.1, 6.2, 6.3, and 6.4.) After the USA announced the 'Buy America' initiative, several governments reacted negatively; the WTO GPA committee discussed the legality of this measure and section 1605 ultimately included a provision confirming the continued applicability of the USA's international obligations under the WTO GPA and NAFTA. However, there were no challenges from non-GPA WTO Members as to the prohibited local content requirement of the Buy America Act under the ASCM. Furthermore, Canada negotiated an Agreement on Government Procurement bilaterally with the US, rather than using the already available and arguably more obvious forum of the WTO GPA to build upon their scheduled commitments.

Box 6.1: Ongoing consultations from pre-2008 involving the United States as respondent (controlled for disputes that do not relate to goods or services, ie agricultural products, TRIPs)

DS118	United States—**Harbour Maintenance Tax** (Complainant: European Communities)	Consultations requested: 6 February 1998 Current status: in consultations
DS186	United States—**Section 337** of the Tariff Act of 1930 and Amendments thereto (Complainant: European Communities)	Consultations requested: 12 January 2000 Current status: in consultations

[14] See www.wto.org/english/tratop_e/dispu_e/disp_settlement_cbt_e/c6s1p1_e.htm.

DS200	United States—**Section 306** of the Trade Act 1974 and Amendments thereto (Complainant: European Communities)	Consultations requested: 5 June 2000 Current status: in consultations
DS218	United States—Countervailing Duties on Certain **Carbon Steel Products** from Brazil (Complainant: Brazil)	Consultations requested: 21 December 2000 Current status: in consultations
DS225	United States—Anti-Dumping Duties on Seamless **Pipe** from Italy (Complainant: European Communities)	Consultations requested: 5 February 2001 Current status: in consultations
DS239	United States—Anti-Dumping Duties on **Silicon Metal** from Brazil (Complainant: Brazil)	Consultations requested: 18 September 2001 Current status: in consultations
DS262	United States—Sunset Reviews of Anti-Dumping and Countervailing Duties on **Certain Steel Products** from France and Germany (Complainant: European Communities)	Consultations requested: 25 July 2002 Current status: in consultations
DS274	United States—Definitive Safeguard Measures on Imports of **Certain Steel Products** (Complainant: Chinese Taipei)	Consultations requested: 1 November 2002 Current status: in consultations
DS319	United States—**Section 776** of the Tariff Act of 1930 (Complainant: European Communities)	Consultations requested: 5 November 2004 Current status: in consultations
DS325	United States—Anti-Dumping Determinations regarding **Stainless Steel** from Mexico (Complainant: Mexico)	Consultations requested: 5 January 2005 Current status: in consultations
DS346	United States—Anti-Dumping Administrative Review on **Oil Country Tubular Goods** from Argentina (Complainant: Argentina)	Consultations requested: 20 June 2006 Current status: in consultations
DS368	United States—Preliminary Anti-Dumping and Countervailing Duty Determinations on Coated Free Sheet **Paper** from China (Complainant: China)	Consultations requested: 14 September 2007 Current status: in consultations

DS424	United States—Anti-Dumping Measures on Imports of **Stainless Steel Sheet** and Strip in Coils from Italy (Complainant: EU)	Consultations requested: 1 April 2011 Current status: in consultations
DS464	United States—Anti-dumping and Countervailing Measures on **large residential washers** from Korea (Complainant: Korea, Republic of)	Consultations requested: 29 August 2013 Current status: in consultations

Box 6.2: Ongoing Consultations from pre-2008 involving Brazil as respondent (controlled for disputes that do not relate to goods or services, ie agricultural products, TRIPs)

DS229	Brazil—Anti-Dumping Duties on Jute Bags from India (Complainant: India)	Consultations requested: 9 April 2001 Current status: in consultations
DS197	Brazil—Measures on Minimum Import Prices (Complainant: United States)	Consultations requested: 30 May 2000 Current status: in consultations
DS183	Brazil—Measures on Import Licensing and Minimum Import Prices (Complainant: European Communities)	Consultations requested: 14 October 1999 Current status: in consultations
DS116	Brazil—Measures Affecting Payment Terms for Imports (Complainant: European Communities)	Consultations requested: 8 January 1998 Current status: in consultations
DS81	Brazil—Measures Affecting Trade and Investment in the **Automotive Sector** (Complainant: European Communities)	Consultations requested: 7 May 1997 Current status: in consultations
DS65	Brazil—Certain Measures Affecting Trade and Investment in the **Automotive Sector** (Complainant: United States)	Consultations requested: 10 January 1997 Current status: in consultations
DS52	Brazil—Certain Measures Affecting Trade and Investment in the **Automotive Sector** (Complainant: United States)	Consultations requested: 9 August 1996 Current status: in consultations
DS51	Brazil—Certain **Automotive** Investment Measures (Complainant: Japan)	Consultations requested: 30 July 1996 Current status: in consultations

Box 6.3: Ongoing Consultations from pre-2008 involving EU or Member States as respondent (controlled for disputes that do not relate to goods or services, ie agricultural products, TRIPs)

DS459	EU—Certain Measures on the Importation and Marketing of **Biodiesel** and Measures Supporting the Biodiesel Industry (Complainant: Argentina)	Consultations requested: 15 May 2013 Current status: in consultations
DS385	European Communities—Expiry Reviews of Anti-dumping and Countervailing Duties Imposed on Imports of PET from India (Complainant: India)	Consultations requested: 4 December 2008 Current status: in consultations
DS307	European Communities—Aid for Commercial Vessels (Complainant: Korea, Republic of)	Consultations requested: 13 February 2004 Current status: in consultations
DS242	European Communities—Generalized System of Preferences (Complainant: Thailand)	Consultations requested: 7 December 2001 Current status: in consultations
DS172	European Communities—Measures Relating to the Development of a Flight Management System (Complainant: United States)	Consultations requested: 21 May 1999 Current status: in consultations
DS131	France—Certain Income Tax Measures Constituting Subsidies (Complainant: United States)	Consultations requested: 5 May 1998 Current status: in consultations
DS130	Ireland—Certain Income Tax Measures Constituting Subsidies (Complainant: United States)	Consultations requested: 5 May 1998 Current status: in consultations
DS129	Greece—Certain Income Tax Measures Constituting Subsidies (Complainant: United States)	Consultations requested: 5 May 1998 Current status: in consultations
DS128	Netherlands—Certain Income Tax Measures Constituting Subsidies (Complainant: United States)	Consultations requested: 5 May 1998 Current status: in consultations
DS127	Belgium—Certain Income Tax Measures Constituting Subsidies (Complainant: United States)	Consultations requested: 5 May 1998 Current status: in consultations

Box 6.4: Ongoing Consultations from pre-2008 involving India as respondent (controlled for disputes that do not relate to goods or services, ie agricultural products, TRIPs)

DS120/2	India—Measures Affecting Export Of Certain Commodities	Consultations requested: 11 March 1998 Current status: in consultations
DS149	India—Import Restrictions	Consultations requested: 28 October 1998 Current status: in consultations
DS150	India—Measures Affecting Customs Duties	Consultations requested: 30 October 1998 Current status: in consultations
DS279	India—Import Restrictions Maintained Under the Export and Import Policy 2002–2007	Consultations requested: 23 December 2002 Current status: in consultations
DS304	India—Anti-Dumping Measures on Imports of Certain Products from the European Communities	Consultations requested: 8 December 2003 Current status: in consultations
DS318	India—Anti-Dumping Measures on Certain Products from the Separate Customs Territory of Taiwan, Penghu, Kinmen and Matsu	Consultations requested: 28 October 2004 Current status: in consultations
DS380	India—Certain Taxes and Other Measures on Imported Wines and Spirits	Consultations requested: 22 September 2008 Current status: in consultations

Boxes 6.1, 6.2, 6.3, and 6.4 list those disputes that both involve the case study countries as respondents and have also been in long-term consultation without resolution. The picture that emerges indicates that formally there are still disputes in ongoing consultations involving each of the case study countries as respondent, which are concerned with those manufacturing sectors that were also heavily protected by the individual respondents during the 2008–12 crisis. Box 6.1 indicates that the USA has several disputes that remain officially unresolved in the WTO DSB as regards steel products in the areas of safeguards, anti-dumping and countervailing duties. As noted, steel was explicitly targeted for protection through the US government's buy-national measures during the

recent crisis. In the case of Brazil, Box 6.2 indicates that half of the officially unresolved consultations pertain to the automotive industry dating back to 1996 and 1997, and furthermore involve the USA, the EU and Japan. Again, the Brazilian auto industry was the primary recipient for crisis protection during 2008–12 but no challenges were brought. As for the EU, Box 6.3 indicates that several EU Member States, including Ireland, have been in consultations with the USA since 1998 over specific income tax measures that the USA claimed constitute subsidies. Subsidies were the favoured bailout measure of EU Member States during the crisis, but, once again, none were targeted for challenge within the WTO DSB. Box 6.4 highlights that a range of India trade measures that have been challenged, targeting both imports and exports, as well as anti-dumping measures. This mirrors the widely scattered measures the Indian government sought to implement to stimulate the domestic economy during the crisis.

It can be reasonably postulated that if a previous dispute in a given sector has not been successfully resolved through WTO consultations in the earlier disputes, a WTO Member will not expend further resources trying to resolve a dispute on a similar matter with the same non-compliant Member through the WTO DSB if it arises again. In other words, the available data suggests that during the crisis years the WTO DSB did not provide a forum for resolving challenges to non-compliant crisis measures, either in consultations or through a establishing a Panel. Indeed, this examination suggests that the DSB has long been unable to resolve disputes on similar matters or products among these case study governments. The following section therefore examines whether these measures were instead resolved through remedies.

III. WTO Trade Remedies 2008–13

One of the 'safety valves' of the GATT/WTO dispute settlement system is the ability of Members, under certain circumstances, to use trade remedy laws to lessen the adverse impact of various trade practices on domestic industries, producers and workers. Such remedies are deemed consistent with international obligations provided that they conform to the trade remedy provisions agreed to as part of the Uruguay Round and other trade agreements. The relevant remedies for a bailout or buy national measure would be countervailing duties (CVD). These are designed to give relief to domestic industries that have been or are threatened with the adverse impact of imported goods subsidised by a foreign government or public entity and sold at lower prices than similar goods produced in the domestic market. The relief provided is an additional import duty placed on the subsidised imports.

Given the increased use of subsidies in the form of bailouts and buy-national policies as economic stimulus measures from 2008 through 2012, it might be expected that some governments would impose CVD measures against some of the actionable government subsidies provided by the case study countries. Indeed, Figure 6.3 indicates that there was a spike in the number of initiations and impositions of CVDs during 2008–12, with 2010 being the peak with 19 CVDs imposed, which is more than at any time since 2000.[15] Figure 6.4 further indicates that there was a rise in CVD measures initiated and imposed in the base metals and auto industry sector during the 2008–12 crisis years. However, this increase was not of the magnitude of a decade earlier. This is even the pattern in the case of the base metals sector, where the maximum CVDs imposed in any single year was 7 in 2010, compared with the high of 13 CVDs imposed in 1999. In the case of the vehicle sector, the most CVDs initiated in any single year of the recent crisis amounted to one in both 2012 and 2013, which was unprecedented.

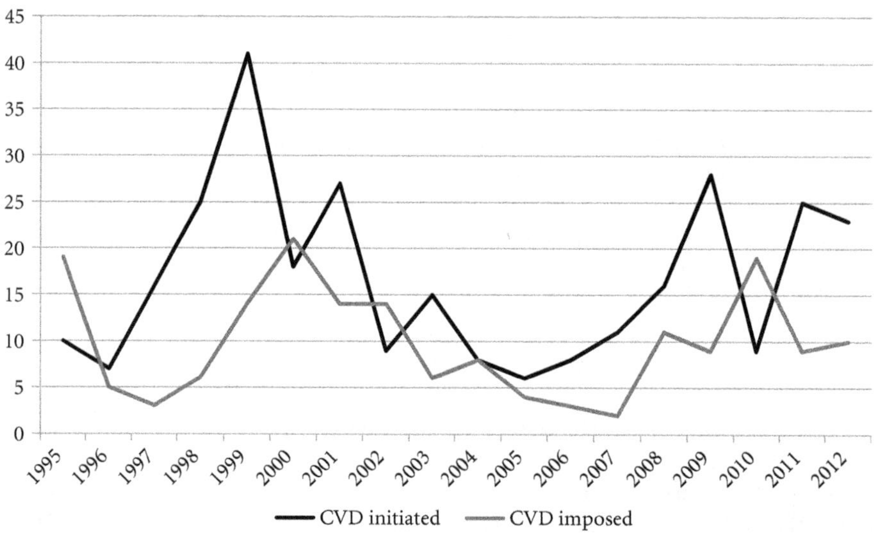

Figure 6.3: A chronology of CVD initiated and imposed between 1995 and 2012 in absolute numbers

[15] This was also a recession period in the US during early 2000.

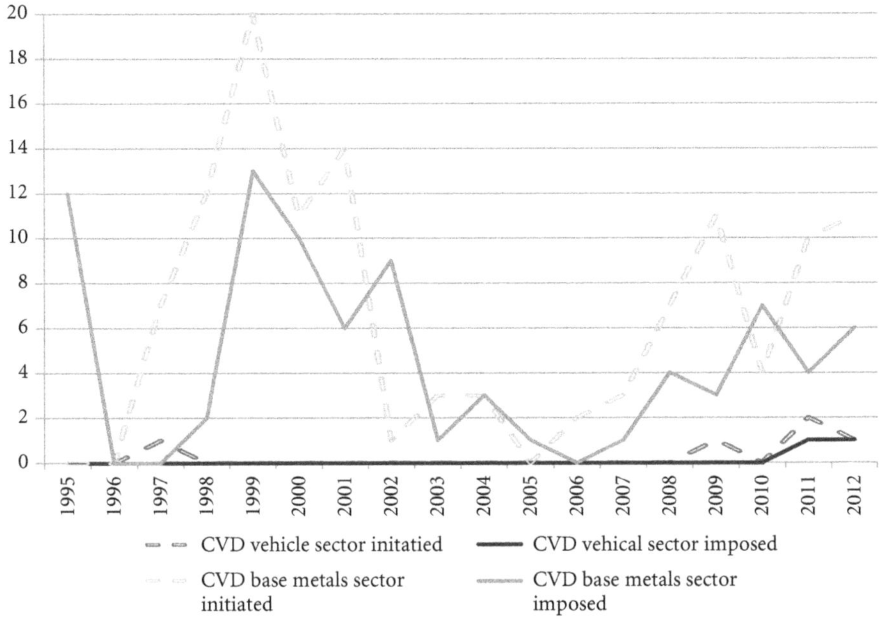

Figure 6.4: CVDs initiated and imposed in vehicle and base metals sector

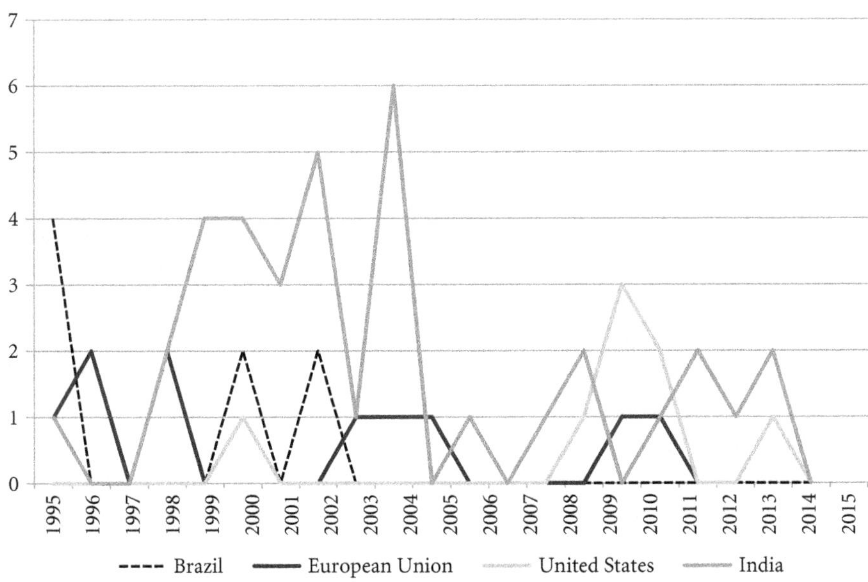

Figure 6.5: All CVD measures imposed on case study countries, 1995–2012

If we examine more specifically those CVDs imposed on this research's case studies in Figure 6.5, it is of note that of those CVDs imposed in the non-agricultural sector, only two are related to the sectors targeted for protection under government stimulus packages, both imposed by China on the USA, both on the vehicle and steel sectors, see Table 6.2.[16] The EU and Brazilian manufacturing sector subsidies were not remedied by any WTO Member, while the US subsidies were only countervailed by one Member, leaving the non-compliant measures intact. To recall, India did not implement large targeted bailouts or buy-national measures during the 2008–12, rather a diverse fiscal stimulus strategy was directed across the economy. While India has historically been a frequent target for CVDs—73 since 1995—the most frequent target being base metals (30 CVDs), the crisis years 2008–12 did not cause a significant increase in CVDs imposed (Table 6.3).

Table 6.2: CVDs imposed on case study countries since 2003

Member imposing	Partner affected	Initiation	In force	Withdrawn	Product description
Australia	United States	22 Jun 2010	19 Apr 2011		Biodiesel
China	United States	01 Jun 2009	10 Apr 2010		Grain Oriented Flat-rolled Electrical Steel
China	United States	06 Nov 2009	15 Dec 2011		Saloon cars and cross-country cars
Peru	United States	26 Aug 2009	22 Aug 2010		Pure biodiesel (B100) and blends containing more than 50 per cent biodiesel (B50)
EU	Brazil	19 Feb 2004	18 Nov 2004	03 Mar 2011	PET film (polyethylene terephthalate)

[16] Saloon cars and cross-country cars; and grain-orientated flat-rolled electrical steel. See Box 6.2.

Table 6.3: Chronology of CVDs imposed 1995–2016—focus on India. (Source: WTO Subsidies and Countervailing Duties Database, available at www.wto.org/english/tratop_e/scm_e/scm_e.htm, accessed 29 January 2017.)

Countervailing Initiations: By Exporter 01/01/1995—30/06/2016

Exporter	1995	1996	1997	1998	1999	2000	2001	2002	2003	2004	2005	2006	2007	2008	2009	2010	2011	2012	2013	2014	2015	2016	Total
Argentina						3	1					1	1		1			1		1			9
Australia					1																		1
Austria								1															1
Belgium				1																			1
Brazil			1	1	1	1	2					1									2	1	10
Canada		1	1	1			2	2		1											1		9
Chile			1		1		1																3
China										3		2	8	11	13	6	9	10	14	14	9	13	112
Colombia									1														1
Czech Republic					1																		1
Denmark				1																			1
Ecuador																			1				1
European Union	3	1	1	1	1			1	2						1	1		1	1				14

(continued)

Table 6.3: *(Continued)*

Exporter	1995	1996	1997	1998	1999	2000	2001	2002	2003	2004	2005	2006	2007	2008	2009	2010	2011	2012	2013	2014	2015	2016	Total
Former Yugoslav Republic of Macedonia					1																		1
France				2	2		2					1											7
Germany			1				2																3
Greece			1						1														2
Hungary							1																1
India	1		3	6	5	7	8	2	8	1	1	1	1	2	1	1	5	2	6	4	6	2	73
Indonesia				1	5	1	2				1	1			1		2	2	2	1	1	1	21
Iran, Islamic Republic of															1								1
Israel						1																	1
Italy	3	2	1	3	1		1	1	1												1		14
Korea, Republic of				5	4	1	1	2		1	1	1			1		1	1	1	4	3	1	28
Malaysia					2						1			1	1				1	2			8
Mexico																				1			1
Netherlands							1													1			2
Norway		1																					1

(continued)

Table 6.3: ***(Continued)***

Exporter	1995	1996	1997	1998	1999	2000	2001	2002	2003	2004	2005	2006	2007	2008	2009	2010	2011	2012	2013	2014	2015	2016	Total
Oman																	2	1		2	1		6
Pakistan						1									1			1		1	1		5
Peru			1																				1
Philippines					1															1			2
Poland					1				1														2
Russian Federation																				1	2		3
Saudi Arabia				1													1						2
Singapore					1																		1
South Africa		2	1	1	1	1													1				7
Spain			1	1					1														3
Sri Lanka																						1	1
Taipei, Chinese			1		5					1									1	1	1		10
Thailand	1				5	1				1	1				1		2		1	1			14
Trinidad and Tobago			1				1													1			3
Turkey	1						1												2	5	3		12

(continued)

Table 6.3: ***(Continued)***

Exporter	1995	1996	1997	1998	1999	2000	2001	2002	2003	2004	2005	2006	2007	2008	2009	2010	2011	2012	2013	2014	2015	2016	Total
Ukraine																				2			2
United Arab Emirates															1		1	1					3
United Kingdom							1																1
United States	1				1	1					1		1	2	4	1	1	2				1	16
Venezuela, Bolivarian Republic of			1		1																		2
Viet Nam															1		1	1	2	2			7
Total	10	7	16	25	41	18	27	9	15	8	6	8	11	16	28	9	25	23	33	45	31	20	431

Note: All actions notified to the WTO that are taken at the level of a customs union (European Union, Eurasian Economic Union, Southern African Customs Union, Gulf Cooperation Council) are counted one time each.

IV. Regional Regulatory Responses to the Crisis

Of the RTAs assessed here, to recall, the TFEU is the only RTA to provide somewhat integrated binding collective rules to regulate both subsidies/State aid, and procurement practices among its Member States. As such, it provides the most instructive counterpoint with the WTO Agreements currently available. Moreover, the pioneering nature of this economic framework offers an inspiring model for promoting trade liberalisation, as well as peace through trade. The development of the TFEU is of heuristic value in offering lessons and options about working with rather than against the tensions between open, non-discriminatory trade and strongly held national values and objectives among multiple sovereign governments.

The following section therefore assesses the operation of the TFEU competition and procurement rules constraining discriminatory state behaviour during the crisis.

A. The TFEU and the European Commission

A part of the European Economic Recovery Plan adopted in January 2009 involved the Commission's early approval of a Temporary Framework[17] to provide Member States with additional possibilities to address the effects of the credit squeeze on the real economy and to maintain continuity in companies' access to finance.[18] The European institutions moved fast to control the Member States in their resort to domestic solutions to the financial crisis. Chapter 5 noted that during the first phase of the crisis, from roughly summer 2007 until October 2008, the Commission still applied the R & R Guidelines.[19] Indeed, when the crisis first unravelled, the Commission was only involved on an informal basis during the failing bank takeover discussions in September 2008. However, it was soon understood by the Commission that the conditions set out in the R & R Guidelines were too rigid and procedures too slow to allow for an immediate and adequately coordinated response to a crisis of this magnitude. Thus, the Commission's initial

[17] Temporary Community framework for State aid measures to support access to finance in the current financial and economic crisis ([2009] OJ C83, 1); as further amended by [2009] OJ C261, 2, and [2009] OJ C303, 6. See Appendix 1, measure 2.

[18] With the exception of the possibility to grant limited amounts of up to €500,000 as compatible aid and aid in the form of guarantees, Chapter 5 also noted that the uptake of the Temporary Framework was limited. This €500,000 aid is not included in the statistics as de minimis aid is considered not to be aid according to the definition of Art 107(1) TFEU.

[19] In the rescue of Northern Rock, see: European Commission, MEMO/08/202 02/04/2008. For Sachsen Landesbank, see: Commission Press Release, 'State Aid: Commission Approves Restructuring of Sachsen LB', IP/08/849 (4 June 2008). See also: Commission Communication, Community Guidelines on State Aid for Rescuing and Restructuring Firms in Difficulty, 1 October 2004, [2004] OJ C244, 2, ¶9. See Appendix 2.

informal role was shortly followed by its move to put into place a legal framework that would be able to structure the different rescue measures for the banking sector, which Member States were on the verge of implementing. During the second phase of the financial crisis, post October 2008, the Commission sought recourse to the more permissive Article 107(3)(b) EC. As discussed in Chapter 5, this provision contains possible grounds for approving aid to remedy a serious disturbance in the economy of a Member State.

The pre-emptive strike taken by the Commission in approving the Temporary Framework was significant. Chapter 5 noted, with regard to the UK, that it was becoming apparent that EU Member States were being tempted to introduce their own new rules relating to financial regulation without coordinating with each other, as experienced in the WTO. Acknowledging the tension between domestic crisis management and maintaining a level playing-field within the internal market, the Commission adapted the EU State aid rules to provide enough flexibility to allow Member States to rescue failing institutions promptly but without terminally undermining the State aid rules. Unlike the WTO DG and the WTO Secretariat, the European Commission gave the appearance, if not the substance, of managing the Member States' protectionist instincts through the use of notices, guidelines, frameworks and other soft law policy instruments, including its Crisis Communications and the Temporary Framework, steering the Member States towards desirable behaviours and away from the more regionally destructive and counterproductive ones.[20]

What is significant here is that these Crisis Communications were not legally binding on the Member States themselves. Nevertheless, this leadership initiative was apparently welcomed; EU Member States and other regulatory bodies chose to observe these guidelines and work with the unresolved ambiguities in the language of Article 107.[21] As noted, interpretative ambiguities relate to the extent to which State aid control can be applied to both indirect and direct state intervention in the economy as well as the specific economic and political criteria for deciding what aids are deemed incompatible. The Union's interest is not unequivocal, nor is the full extent of the European Commission's mandate in the economy. Yet despite this, these Communications formed the basis of the temporary framework.

Moreover, although these EU-level Crisis Communications could be characterised as soft legal instruments as regards the Member States, they were nonetheless deemed binding upon the Commission itself. The European courts have acknowledged the normative status of soft law instruments as regards State aid as well as how their effects are recognised. Several 'champion' instruments feature frequently in the case law, namely the guidelines on fines and the leniency notice in competition law, the State aid instruments on aid to be granted to enterprises in

[20] TJ Doleys, 'Managing State Aid in Times of Crisis: The Role of the European Commission', ECPR Fifth Pan-European Conference on EU Politics, Porto, Portugal, 2010.

[21] S Warnecke, 'The European Community and National Subsidy Policies' in S Warnecke (ed), *International Trade and Industrial Policies* (London, Macmillan, 1978) 145.

difficulty, regional aid, de minimis aid, and aid to be granted to SMEs. All of these soft law instruments regulate highly litigated areas, and are taken into account by the European courts when this serves the enforcement of hard, general principles of law. These policy guidelines provided a means to indirectly shape the 'meaning' of treaty rules.[22]

In each Communication, the Commission sought to identify the types of government assistance it would regard as acceptable and on what terms. Each Communication was premised upon the previous one; all of them were founded on the law and jurisprudence of the Guidelines for the Rescue and Restructuring of Firms in Difficulty.[23] In other words, in what can be seen as a display of leadership and strategy, the Commission employed these guidelines to set out its mandate and promulgate its intention to use its delegated treaty authority to steer Member States' crisis measures. The Commission thus leveraged the compliance pull of hard law on itself to encourage government conformity to its normative policy preferences. The Commission was, to an extent, able to reconcile its role as guardian and administrator of State aid rules with the recognition that there was a limit to what it could do given the political environment. The Commission sought to articulate fixed principles whilst simultaneously becoming more flexible in its approach to substantive rules, and more relaxed with procedural requirements: it was, as such, a 'pragmatic way' to handle the situation.[24]

It is axiomatic that the significant differences in the frameworks governing the European Commission and the WTO Secretariat legally constrained their respective responses to the crisis in different ways. First, unlike the WTO notification system, Article 108 TFEU already required EU Member States to notify all planned State aid measures to the Commission and to obtain the Commission's approval *prior* to implementation.[25] Within the WTO however, Article 25.1 ASCM requires that all Members submit a new and full notification of all specific subsidies provided by any level of government in any sector every three years, with updating notifications due in the intervening years.[26] Members that consider that they provide no specific subsidies should also notify this.

Crucially, Article 25.7 clearly states that the notification of a measure does not prejudge the measure's legal status under GATT 1994 and the ASCM Agreement, its effects under the ASCM Agreement, or the nature of the measure itself. That is, notification is primarily a transparency exercise. Nevertheless, only a few WTO Members regularly notify subsidies. This prevents the full potential benefits of

[22] O Stefan, *Soft Law in Court. Competition Law, State Aid and the Court of Justice of the EU* (Alphen aan den Rijn, Kluwer Law, 2012).

[23] Doleys (n 20).

[24] M Hall, 'Competition Law and the Credit Crunch: Do the Usual State Aid Rules Still Apply?' *PLC Magazine*, 22 January 2009, 2.

[25] Except for those measures that the Commission has exempted from notification.

[26] Certain benefits under the ASCM can only be obtained through notification by a Member. For example, a developing country Member that desires that certain subsidies directly linked to a privatisation programme be non-actionable multilaterally under Art 27.13 ASCM must notify the subsidy to the ASCM Committee.

the ASCM rules emerging and has led to proposals for penalising partial or non-notifications. In 2002, the EU proposed, to the WTO, the devising of a mechanism through which the quality and scope of notifications could be scrutinised and if failings were found or suspected a review procedure could be generated through an expedited WTO dispute settlement procedure similar to the one envisaged for spurious initiations or by referring the matter to an empowered Permanent Group of Experts.[27] However, as yet, this proposal has not been taken up.

Under the TFEU, notifications and complaints are examined in two phases. The first phase consists of a preliminary investigation to determine if the notified measure constitutes State aid, and if so, if it is compatible State aid according to the requirements of Article 4.2 to 4.4 of the Procedural Regulation. If the Commission, after a preliminary investigation, finds that doubts are raised as to the compatibility with the internal market, it must open a formal investigation procedure. Throughout, the notifying Member State has the possibility to modify the measure to make it compatible. This is not to imply that the Commission's procedures are infallible. For the record, it has been noted that the Commission does not systematically try to detect non-notified aid measures.[28]

Nevertheless, the Commission takes account of the complexity of the concept of State aid and that the broad interpretation put forward by the CJEU can make it difficult for Member States to interpret whether a particular measure constitutes State aid.[29] Unlike the new neutral WTO monitoring reports published regularly during the crisis, the Commission provided a more powerful normative dynamic by publishing a State aid Scoreboard assessing the impacts of State aid and State aid control. In the first quarter of the year, the Commission sends a spread-sheet to the Member States to be completed with the figures of the actual State aid expenditure for each of the listed measures granted during the previous year. The data received from the Member States are of varying quality and the Scoreboard team spends a lot of time checking the data and adding missing amounts. Problems have been reported in obtaining data from regional and local public authorities. For example, many Member States are late in providing the data but only one infringement procedure has been launched for not respecting the deadline.[30] While the system is not perfect, it does try to maintain a rule of thumb for State aid control in the Member States.

Further, in contrast to the imposed passivity of the WTO Secretariat, not only can the Commission declare that a specific measure does not constitute permitted aid or decide whether to approve of a specific measure but also it can unilaterally decide to launch an ex officio investigation into certain alleged State aid measures. Under Article 4.5 of the Procedural Regulation, all decisions must be adopted

[27] See EC submission in DDA negotiations: Agreement on Subsidies and Countervailing Measures. Ref. 492/02, Rev3.

[28] See 'Do the Commission's Procedures Ensure Effective Management of State Aid Control? The Audit of Special Report No 15/2011', ¶25.

[29] According to the Audit of Special Report, ibid, about 5% of the notifications are made for reasons of legal certainty only.

[30] This was set by the Implementing Regulation no 794/2004. See the Audit of Special Report, ibid.

within two months following the receipt of a complete notification. The notification will be considered as complete if, within two months from its receipt, or from the receipt of any additional information requested, the Commission does not request any further information. If the Commission asks for further information, a new two-month period starts when the Member State submits the information requested. Finally, as noted in Chapter 3, given the collective nature of the TFEU provisions, the standing requirement for making a complaint to the Commission under the TFEU reaches far beyond that of the Member State governments. Competitors or other interested parties who believe that a certain measure constitutes State aid have a legal right to complain to the Commission.

Figure 7.1 somewhat surprisingly indicates that the number of notifications actually fell from an all-time high in 2006 progressively until 2011, when they began to rise again. Nevertheless, the Commission still handled notifications much faster during the crisis; while in 2007–08, it took six or more months to make a decision for 40 per cent of the notifications,[31] by 2009 DG Competition had also created a Financial Crisis Task Force and more than doubled the number of case handlers dealing with aid to the financial sector alone.[32]

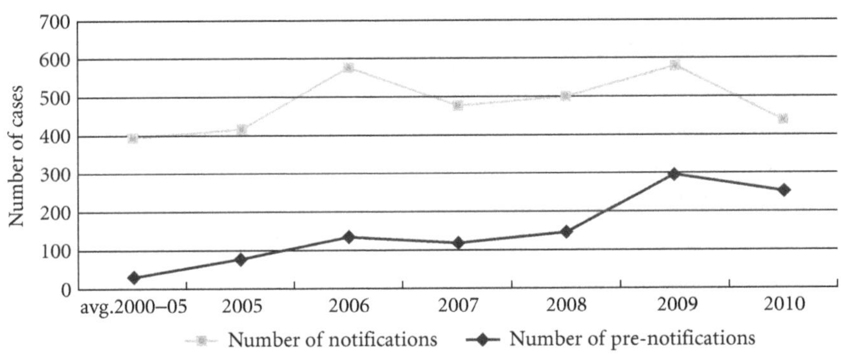

Figure 7.1: The trend in the number of notifications and pre-notifications

Source: European Commission.

Special Report No 15/2011—Do the Commission's procedures ensure effective management of State aid control?

Of further significance here is that towards the tail end of 2012, the European Commission undertook stocktaking of its monitoring and enforcement experience and proposed to modernise State aid to further promote the sound use

[31] Source: European Commission State Aid Statistics: State as of November 2013. Available at: http://ec.europa.eu/competition/state_aid/statistics/statistics_en.html.

[32] Urgent crisis cases were handled much faster than non-crisis cases by relying on less formal correspondence with the Member States and more informal exchange of information by phone calls and e-mails. Many Member States also accepted to receive correspondence and decisions in English (language waiver) in order to speed up the procedure and beneficiaries were involved more closely in the procedure. Several cases were solved within days. ibid.

of public resources and to limit distortions to competition within the internal market. This proposal involves substantive changes to the notion of permissible aid as well as procedural changes in the Commission's ex ante scrutiny of cases.[33] In effect, the Commission was able openly to reflect and acknowledge inadequacies in the current monitoring system and the need to explore new initiatives to work around the delays, inconsistencies and partial information received when Member States are the providers of such information. One possible solution floated is by obtaining timely, reliable, factually correct and complete information directly from the market using market information tools (MIT). An initiative to conduct investigations into particular sectors of the economy and into particular aid instruments was also proposed.

In sum, this assessment suggests that the Commission was both empowered and self-confident enough to respond creatively to the exceptional systemic nature of the crisis. This can be contrasted with the relative conservatism displayed by the WTO DG and the reactive nature of some WTO Members. The Commission took a previously narrow legal interpretation of Article 107(3)(b) and used it as the basis for approving most of the rescue aid measures for financial institutions. Whether or not such an interpretation would be accepted by the General Court is unknown for the nature of this crisis was unprecedented and no challenge was brought. This highlights that the initiative shown by the Commission was underpinned by the solidarity measures created under this agreement, and the (qualified) solidarity shown by the EU Member States to the values of the EU, despite the pressures of the crisis.

Chapter 7 now addresses the implications of this research in terms of the theoretical and operational possibilities for enabling the WTO to respond more conclusively and collectively to unprecedented and systemic events such as global financial crises.

[33] The Commission decided to publish a Notice on the Notion of Aid which summarised the law and dealt, in particular, with certain difficult conceptual matters, such as the interaction between taxation and State aid, the application of the market investor principle and issues such as effect on trade. C Quigley QC, 'Review of the Temporary State Aid Rules Adopted in the Context of the Financial and Economic Crisis' [2012] April *Journal of European Competition Law & Practice*.

7

From the Wealth to the Stealth of Nations

> To give the monopoly of the home market to the produce of domestic industry, in any particular art or manufacture, is in some measure to direct private people in what manner they ought to employ their capitals, and must, in almost all cases, be either a useless or a hurtful regulation. If the produce of domestic can be brought there as cheap as that of foreign industry, the regulation is evidently useless. If it cannot, it must generally be hurtful. It is the maxim of every prudent master of a family never to attempt to make at home what it will cost him more to make than to buy.[1]

I. Overview

In assessing the nature and operation of the international rules to prevent anti-competitive state measures in public procurement and open markets during the recent economic crisis, this book examined the evidence to support the proposition that these provisions, primarily located within the WTO, were largely successful in curbing the knee-jerk protectionist instincts of governments wishing to implement discriminatory policies to protect domestic producer interests. It has been opined that the trade-restrictive measures implemented in the 2008–12 crisis were generally compliant with states' obligations under the WTO's multilaterally negotiated trading system, which provides an organised procedure for resolving disputes.[2] Furthermore, that as a result of this achievement 'the WTO has become stronger and more legitimate and indeed [a] more important international organisation'.[3]

[1] A. Smith, *An Inquiry into the Nature and Causes of The Wealth of Nations*. See ch II 'On Restraints upon the Importation from Foreign Countries of such Goods as can be produced at Home', available at: www.marxists.org/reference/archive/smith-adam/works/wealth-of-nations/book04/ch02.htm (accessed 30 January 2017).

[2] B Ruddy, 'The Critical Success of the WTO: Trade Policies of the Current Economic Crisis' (2010) 13 *Journal of International Economic Law* 476.

[3] R Howse, 'Global Crises and International Economic Law', British Institute for International and Comparative Law (BIICL) Conference, London, 19 October 2012, 1.

The results of this research indicate otherwise, however. Rather it has been found that competitive markets generate a collective action problem: when a foreign trade barrier is non-discriminatory, its removal equally benefits all exporters so that no individual firm has the incentive to mobilise for its removal. This is particularly the case when the opportunity costs for lobbying and enforcement strategies may take years to achieve results.[4] Further, precedent represents a double-edged sword as victory may come back to haunt the government as a precedent against its own policies on related issues, present or in the future.[5] This books therefore concludes that the international rules regulating governments' use of anti-competitive government procurement or subsidy measures are not only incomplete but also not yet equal to the task of coordinating, preventing or removing the unilateral use of these laws in a systemic economic crisis. This final chapter consequently examines the risks involved in non-compliance, and what could be done to improve the ability of the WTO to respond to another crisis, and in so doing, ensure greater compliance with the rules.

With the qualified exception of the TFEU, regional trading agreements are also unable to provide an integrated or coordinated framework for regulating government distortions in open and public markets. These trade agreements are typically lopsided in favour of procurement regulation with explicit exemptions for subsidies in procurement markets, or conversely explicit exemptions for procurement with State aid control. The TFEU provides a partially integrated model for the regulation of public distortions under Article 107. However, a procurement that respects the requirements of the Commission's procurement directives are prima facie deemed to be free from State aid; this prevents an ex ante evaluation of the potentially distorting nature of a particular procurement. State aid control also has gaps in coverage, such as those subsidies that are not directly a charge on the public account. Furthermore, the R&D&I rules include a matching clause that allows for a unilateral subsidy to be imposed that is equal to a detected subsidy for a similar initiative abroad. This simply puts a global downward pressure on subsidy control.

Within the WTO, the financial sector covered by the GATS framework lacks a comprehensive subsidy control, while as regards the manufacturing sector the burden of this regulation falls onto the ASCM. This is problematic for the regulation of crisis measures due to the fast and temporary nature of these policies. It is difficult to collect sufficient evidence of the adverse effects of discriminatory crisis measures, coupled with the lengthy time it takes to bring a challenge through the WTO DSB to remove or remedy the effects of the non-compliant measure. Furthermore, given the lack of case law interpreting the applicability of the

[4] C Davis and Y Shirato, 'Firms, Governments, and WTO Adjudication: Japan's Selection of WTO Disputes' (2007) 59 *World Politics* 274.

[5] Busch, cited by C Davis, *Why Adjudicate? Enforcing Trade Rules in the WTO* (Princeton, NJ, Princeton University Press, 2012).

Article XX exceptions to the ASCM, it is unclear whether a government would be able potentially to defend the use of a non-compliant crisis measure exception during a severe economic crisis, should it be challenged.

In the domain of international government procurement rules, the research undertaken here similarly indicates that, again, with the exception of the TFEU, regional procurement laws are also largely excluded from state-to-state dispute settlement mechanism unless the parties to the RTA are also WTO GPA parties. However, even within the plurilateral but binding WTO GPA, the scope and coverage is partial and enforcement levels are non-transparent at the sub-state level. Furthermore, there are permitted exceptions to these obligations. These, most notably for this research, include those measures necessary to protect public morals and public order.

These results point to systemic institutional deficiencies within the WTO, suggesting that as an organisation it is not sufficiently developed. The WTO framework for regulating international trade would benefit from the mandate of coordinating and conditioning domestic responses to a systemic economic crisis. This chapter consequently sums up what could be done to strengthen the appropriate enforcement of these international and regional rules to prevent government measures that distort competition in public and private markets in the event of another systemic crisis. The foregoing research indicates that the debate about reforming the DSU[6] needs to be reopened in light of the experience of how these rules operated during the recent crisis. The results of this examination suggest that given the bilateral enforcement infrastructure in the WTO, coupled with the primarily bilateral nature of the provisions, compliance will not readily occur during a crisis if the rational self-interest of individual Members is to ignore other Members' non-compliant crisis measures out of fear that a similar challenge will be made to their equally actionable crisis measures.

This book's assessment also indicated that further deliberation, interpretative guidance and detailed proposals for reform are necessary to prevent erosion of the legitimacy and relevance of the WTO. For in addition to a stalled negotiating round, the non-use of the 'jewel in the crown' of the WTO dispute settlement system to challenge both prohibited and actionable measures during turbulent economic times points to an even more ossified mandate. It is liable to create

[6] See, for example, Davey's assessment of the WTO DSU reform proposals put forward by the Suzuki Group: WT/MIN(99)/8 & Corr 1. This included suggestions to establish a clear sequence between DSU Arts 21.5 and 22 so that in the event of a dispute over the WTO's consistency of an implementation measure, the matter would go first to a compliance proceeding and then, only if a violation were found, would suspension of concessions be authorised. Davey further suggested revising Art 22 DSU to allow a request for suspension of concessions to be made following completion of the compliance proceeding, at which time the DSB would be required to authorise suspension unless there was a consensus not to do so. This proposal provided for a significant expansion of third-party rights and strengthened a number of provisions in favour of developing countries. WJ Davey, 'Reforming WTO Dispute Settlement', University of Illinois, Public Law & Legal Theory Research Paper no 04-01 (29 January 2004).

more sectoral no-go areas for sensitive areas, most notably in the auto industry and steel, to add to oil, shipping and textiles. This negative conclusion was confirmed in November 2014 when Brazil rejected the first-time request[7] by the EU for a panel to study the dispute over taxation and charges applied by Brazil to, among others, the automobile sector.[8] The Secretariat is starved of a significant research budget or mandate as guardian of the agreements and is largely confined to administering committee meetings where the self-interest of the Members controls the agenda. Meanwhile, bilateral and regional trade agreements are negotiating a wider area of trade and trade-related issues and increasingly between the largest trading nations. This sidelines multilateralism, as well as the WTO as a relevant negotiating forum.

Bilateral and regional agreements may strengthen and consolidate their position as alternative 'conflicting power centres' offering parties the opportunity to conclude flexible and more relevant agreements within a reasonably foreseeable timescale, where the WTO has begun to fall short. When seen within this light, the US section 301[9] can be viewed as a 'necessary evil' both in relation to the lack of commitment to the GATT negotiations and to the lack of a credible system of enforcement, where retaliation in addition to peer pressure was sometimes necessary. This 'conflicting power centre' was subsequently and strategically considerably restrained with the introduction of compulsory and obligatory jurisdiction in the WTO DSB.[10]

The analysis of this concluding chapter begins by assessing the case for the collective enforcement of WTO rules during times of crisis, before analysing the potential for creating a more activist WTO Secretariat to overcome the inevitable prisoner's dilemma that occurs when multiple Members erect similar non-compliant trade measures.

[7] See: www.wto.org/english/news_e/news14_e/dsb_18nov14_e.htm.

[8] Meeting of the DSB, 18 November 2014. In response to the EU's claim that these tax advantages resulted in a higher tax burden on imported goods and created incentives to source locally in Brazil and thus were discriminatory and aimed at import substitution, in addition to the tax exemption schemes for Brazilian companies meeting certain export targets, contrary to the prohibition on export-contingent subsidies, Brazil said that its measures were consistent with its multilateral obligations.

[9] To recall: s 301 of the US Trade Act of 1974 (Pub L 93–618, 19 USC § 2411) authorises the US President to take all appropriate action, including retaliation, to obtain the removal of any act, policy or practice of a foreign government that violates an international trade agreement or is unjustified, unreasonable or discriminatory, and that burdens or restricts US commerce. S 301 cases can be self-initiated by the United States Trade Representative (USTR) or as the result of a petition filed by a firm or industry group. Nevertheless, if the USTR initiates a Section 301 investigation, it must seek to negotiate a settlement with the foreign country in the form of compensation or elimination of the trade barrier. For cases involving trade agreements, the USTR is required to request formal dispute proceedings as provided by the trade agreements.

[10] R Guilherme and S Medrado, 'Renegotiating Remedies in the WTO: A Multilateral Approach' (2004) 22 *Wisconsin International Law Journal* 323.

II. Increasing Compliance During Crises: The Case for Collective Enforcement

Compliance with a binding obligation is often viewed as one of the most important benchmarks from which to assess the effectiveness of a law. Unfortunately, this book's research found a failure on the part of the WTO regime to elicit compliance with its obligations governing Members' use of subsidies and government procurement during the recent economic crisis through good-faith performance.[11] Much analysis has been undertaken in the areas of compliance[12] and enforcement. Some of this addresses, for example, the role of arbitrators in determining a reasonable period of time; contract theory; reputational costs; imposing remedies collectively; the multilateral enforcement of DSB findings; and early determination of injuries once nullification and impairment have been established. This section focuses more narrowly on whether there is a case for supporting the collective enforcement of WTO obligations during crisis periods to prevent tit-for-tat protectionist impulses and increase levels of compliance. In keeping with the subject of this book, it questions whether these selected provisions could and should be collectively enforced during a systemic economic crisis. It therefore moves the discussion of these provisions from description to prescription.

The case for collective enforcement action in the WTO is based on the assumption that in the event of non-compliance, some of these rules will have a multilateral effect but bilateral remedies may not be effective enough to make a scofflaw state respect its obligations. As Chapter 4 discussed, remedies for breaches under international law have traditionally been characterised as more bilateral than collective in nature.[13] Under this classification, only those states directly suffering injuries from an illegal act can claim damages.[14] Thus, the classification of WTO obligations as fundamentally bilateral has important consequences in restricting which countries have standing to challenge a breach, for limits on the right of countries to retaliate, and for the non-entrenched status for the WTO Agreement vis-à-vis other treaties.[15]

[11] VCLT Art 26: *pacta sunt servanda*.

[12] This research maintains the distinction between compliance with obligations by individual Members and the procedural issues of enforcement, recognition and execution of decisions of the WTO DSB.

[13] In its Judgment on the merits in the case concerning *Military and Paramilitary In and Against Nicaragua*, the ICJ considered whether the United States had the unilateral right to use force in response to Nicaragua's action against other Central American states. *Military and Paramilitary In and Against Nicaragua* [1986] ICJ Reports 14, ¶106–11. Although the Court ruled that third states could contribute in countermeasures, it ultimately rejected the claim that the United States had a unilateral right against Nicaragua. See ¶146–49 of the ICJ Reports.

[14] See the case of South West Africa (*Ethiopia v South Africa*; *Liberia v South Africa*) (1960–66), where in the applications of South Africa as regards the merits of the case, it was argued that the Court should rule that both Ethiopia and Liberia had no *locus standi* in the case.

[15] *Military and Paramilitary In and Against Nicaragua* [1986] ICJ Reports 14, ¶106–11.

Nevertheless, James Crawford was not alone when he noted in his role as Special Rapporteur that third states should be entitled to act in cases where a breach had a gross and systematic character and was clear and well attested.[16] There is a case for solidarity measures qua collective action in those situations where there is such a strong general interest in compliance that third states should be entitled to take some action to correct the absence of equilibrium that existed in the original relationship. Three situations can be identified where leaving reaction to the injured state alone would be problematic: firstly, when only one state was injured but the violation threatens the stability of all; secondly, when the injured state seeks assistance or is unable to act; and lastly, when there is no injured state but rather people.[17]

This debate has resonance in the academic deliberation on the nature of the WTO's obligations and the case for collective action with reference to the shortcomings of the WTO DSU for developing country Members.[18] For instance, the LDC Group put forward a proposal for the adoption of a multilateral/collective action system of enforcement that aimed to prevent imbalances of trade stopping stronger Members from complying with their obligations when dealing with weaker Members.[19] Despite the radical change to dispute settlement brought about by the WTO, as Chapter 4 argued, the system is still heavily based on bilateralism and it is still only for the complaining Member to apply retaliation in the form of the suspension of concessions or obligations, against the Member concerned, thus restoring the balance of concessions. Even the collective nature of prohibited subsidy rules under the ASCM is accompanied by case law that has been equally bilaterally enforced despite its collective nature.

Collective enforcement of WTO rules would recognise that all WTO Members have a systemic interest in enforcing these rules. Proponents have pointed out that this has already been noted in the *EC—Bananas* dispute when the DSB stated that a challenge to a WTO inconsistent measure was something beneficial for the *collective* membership of the organisation.[20] It has also been argued that a collective action approach in favour of a prevailing developing country could already be taken under Article 21.7, which states that: 'If the matter is one which has been raised by a developing country Member, the DSB shall consider what further action it might take which would be appropriate to the circumstances.' Given that the definition of 'appropriate' does not necessarily mean 'equivalent' or 'limiting' and encompasses both a quantitative and a qualitative dimension,

[16] J Crawford, 'Third Report on State Responsibility', A/CN4/507, Addendum 4, 20, ¶404.

[17] M Koskenniemi, 'Solidarity Measures: State Responsibility as a New International Order' (2001) 72 *British Yearbook of International Law* 337, 343.

[18] BM Hoekman and PC Mavroidis, 'Enforcing WTO Commitments: Dispute Settlement and Developing Countries—Something Happened on the Way to Heaven', CEPR Discussion Paper Draft (26 June 2000).

[19] J Pauwelyn, 'Enforcement and Countermeasures in the WTO: Rules are Rules—Towards a More Collective Approach' (2000) 94 *American Journal of International Law* 621.

[20] Appellate Body Report, WT/DS27/AB/R, ¶136, September 1997.

there would be room to apply creative collective enforcement measures in cases involving developing countries.[21] While such a legal avenue would necessitate the willing involvement of at least one developing country as complainant, this is theoretically possible. Others have argued that a broad interpretation of Article 19.1 of the DSU may also give one the impression that a Panel or Appellate Body has a mandate in some circumstances to permit collective countermeasures.[22]

However, while there may be a normative case and possible existing legal avenues to develop a more collective enforcement mechanism within the WTO system, it nevertheless remains pertinent to consider the relevance of collective enforcement for the purposes of improving global crisis management at the WTO. Effective action to incentivise compliance requires not only the ability of parties to identify defectors but also the capacity to direct retaliation onto defectors. Fundamentally, the parties to an agreement must also have sufficient long-term incentives to punish defectors. Failure to deal with these problems may put cooperation in danger of collapsing.[23]

Yet, if every breach is considered to be an attack on the system, then every violation would be actionable. This would in practice most likely result in a situation where interested and powerful states are transformed into police wardens, but without a legal or moral duty to challenge *all* non-compliant measures. Consequently, in being able to pick and choose among the violations they would wish to enforce, law would become 'indissociable from Great Power policy'.[24] And this reasoning in part explains why the final text of solidarity measures set out under Article 54 of the ILC Articles on State responsibility was reduced to an abstract savings clause:

> Article 54 Measures taken by States other than an injured State
>
> This chapter does not prejudice the right of any State, entitled under article 48, paragraph 1, to invoke the responsibility of another State, to take lawful measures against that State to ensure cessation of the breach and reparation in the interest of the injured State or of the beneficiaries of the obligation breached.

For while Abbot et al argued that lack of precision reduces the strength of a provision, it is also the case that the more precise the rule and the more automatic its application, the less it can take account of the idiosyncrasies of a situation, and the more arbitrary and unjustifiable any decision would appear. In effect, setting out exact criteria for collective action in the WTO may not offer a flexible enough framework to address future crises of unknown character. Yet at the same time,

[21] Pauwelyn (n 19).

[22] H Yenkong Ngangjoh and R Rios-Herran, 'WTO Dispute Settlement System and the Issue of Compliance: Multilateralizing the Enforcement Mechanism' (2004) 1 *Manchester Journal of International Economic Law*.

[23] See most notably R Axelrod and RO Keohane, 'Achieving Cooperation under Anarchy: Strategies and Institutions' (1985) 38 *World Politics* 928.

[24] Koskenniemi (n 17) 344.

providing flexibility through ambiguity offers opportunities for creative misuse, the avoidance of which is what motivated the call for rules in the first place.

> Abstract language does not grasp the specialty of these cases and is open to political abuse. Singling out the relevant properties will point to more exact criteria but will fail as we cannot be sure that future cases will present exactly the same properties that those past cases did. To the contrary, there is every reason to expect they do not.[25]

More problematic, however, is that the research indicates that during the recent crisis the widespread non-compliance with those rules preventing anti-competitive state measures in open and government procurement markets was not primarily due to the ability of players to identify or confront defectors. Indeed, many of these preferential stimulus packages were announced in the media and several monitoring mechanisms were established. Neither was it due to the inability to enforce these rules by focusing retaliation on defectors; for while retaliation is acknowledged to be problematic for some,[26] it is still nevertheless provided for under Article 22 DSU.

These research findings suggest that enforcement was not the greatest problem during the crisis. The greatest obstacle to effective compliance during the crisis was rather the lack of sufficient long-term incentives to bring a case that would punish scofflaw states. The lack of incentive to bring a case due the lack of swift compliance is heightened during a crisis—given that the measure will probably spend at least fifteen months in a state of inconsistency from the first day another Member has requested consultations on the alleged inconsistent measures. The DSU allows a cost-free opportunity to delay compliance for several months.

The challenge in such an environment is to prevent widespread non-compliance translating into long-term judicial inaction among the Members who sideline the rules—trapped in a prisoner's dilemma, they fear they will provoke a similar complaint upon themselves.[27] In other words, the problem during times of crisis is that the incentive system created by bilateral enforcement cannot rise above the mercantilist short-term self-interest of individual parties. It is possible that adopting a collective action system of enforcement changes the incentive structure to increase compliance with international rules during normal times. Under such a system, sanctions could not only be authorised, but also applied in a multilateral manner if the complaining Member so requests. The multilateral approach could also be instrumental in undermining the incentives for nurturing 'conflicting power centres' in the form of RTAs with binding dispute settlement provisions, or a US section 301-type legislation. However, this research finds that such changes to the incentive system under a framework of collective action would still not be

[25] ibid, 350.

[26] See eg WJ Davey, 'Compliance Problems in WTO Dispute Settlement' (2009) 42 *Cornell International Law Journal* article 5, available at: http://scholarship.law.cornell.edu/cilj/vol42/iss1/5.

[27] F Pervez, 'Countersuits and the Politics of Abandoned WTO Trade Disputes' (2016) Political Economy of International Organizations 2016 Annual Meeting Paper. Available at SSRN: https://ssrn.com/abstract=2452620.

immediate enough or strong enough to ensure effective compliance during times of crisis, for it is unlikely another government would want to 'whistle blow' if it, too, is violating its obligations.

In such a situation, there is arguably a need for institutional reform to provide a role for an independent and neutral body to provide greater coordination and steering of the Members towards less trade restrictive measures, which are compliant or explicitly exempted crisis measures. The following section therefore looks at the role of the WTO Director General and Secretariat in ensuring compliance and enforcement of these rules during economic crises.

III. The Institution of the WTO

This section asks whether the institution of the WTO, including the Secretariat and Director General (DG), could play a stronger role in coordinating crisis measures.

A. Role of the WTO Secretariat During Crises

> When you say neutral, we need to ask on what? We are not neutral with regards to liberalization versus protectionism. We do not believe in the introduction of new subsidies for example, or things that are antithetical to the agreements that the Secretariat is supervising here. If you are talking about neutral with regards to the position of countries on the introduction of new issues, eg labor standards, yes. But when it comes to the objectives in our mandate, then I would say we are not neutral.[28]

From the outset, it must be recalled that the WTO is a membership-driven organisation and the Secretariat has not been granted any formal powers. The WTO objective of reducing trade barriers between its Members is intrinsically a bilateral task, undertaken for and between governments. This cannot, therefore, be delegated to unelected international civil servants.[29] Indeed, the Marrakesh Agreement Establishing the WTO provides that the WTO shall continue the practice of decision-making by consensus followed under GATT. The WTO's supreme authority is the biennial Ministerial Conference. The General Council manages day-to-day operations, with Members represented at ambassador level. There are then the Councils for trade in goods, trade in services and trade-related aspects of

[28] The quote is attributed to a 'high-ranking' official within the Secretariat: A Kwa, 'Power Politics in the WTO' [2003] *Focus on the Global South* 46.

[29] At present there is the Doha Development Agenda institutional structure under the leadership of the Trade Negotiations Committee (TNC), which is chaired by the Director-General (ex officio).

intellectual property rights along with the multitude of committees and working groups conducting the daily business of a technical nature.[30]

The aim of the Secretariat is to support the WTO, under the membership-appointed leadership of the DG, with functional, informational and support roles directed towards the needs of the Members.[31] Its limited mandate is set out in Article 27 of the DSU as follows:

> Article 27 Responsibilities of the Secretariat
>
> 1. The Secretariat shall have the responsibility of assisting panels, especially on the legal, historical and procedural aspects of the matters dealt with, and of providing secretarial and technical support.

Additional clarification is offered in the Marrakesh Agreement. This provides that the responsibilities of the DG and of the staff of the Secretariat

> shall be exclusively international in character. In the discharge of their duties, they shall not seek or accept instructions from any government or any other authority external to the WTO. They shall refrain from any action which might adversely reflect on their position as international officers.[32]

Thus, the DG and the staff of the Secretariat represent but do not guard the *collective interest* of the membership. They are tasked with facilitating the objectives of the organisation as defined by the membership as a whole. They are not inherently impassive; nor are they inherently neutral. It should be the primary concern of the Secretariat that Members comply with the rules and that disputes resolved by DSB rulings are well grounded in GATT/WTO jurisprudence. Indeed, it is in this latter area that it has been noted that, for better or worse, the Secretariat is doing more in the area of dispute settlement than that provided for under Article 27 DSU.

Robert Hudec contended that several generations of GATT Secretariat officials played a significant role in strengthening the GATT, most notably in bringing GATT contracting parties to accept the key elements of third-party adjudication of legal claims and the disputes procedures. He argues that while the need for a neutral and objective tribunal had been widely acknowledged from the outset, it had to be equally accepted that political bodies could never achieve the degree of neutrality and objectivity necessary to legitimise an effective legal system. This depiction presents the GATT Secretariat's contribution as an illuminating example of the difference that international civil servants can make in the evolution of international legal institutions.[33] By 1963 GATT had succeeded in developing a

[30] Voting is in principle allowed but not used in practice. Should a referendum be called in order to break a deadlock, the rules stipulate that each Member shall have one vote. Simple majority is the default but some decisions require a qualified majority.

[31] Divisions are headed by a director who reports to one of the four Deputy Directors-General (DDGs) or, in some cases, directly to the Director-General.

[32] Art VI:4 of the Marrakesh Agreement Establishing the World Trade Organization.

[33] RE Hudec, 'The Role of the GATT Secretariat in the Evolution of the WTO Dispute Settlement Procedure', reprinted from J Bhagwati and M Hirsch (eds), *The Uruguay Round and Beyond: Essays in Honour of Arthur Dunkel* (Berlin, Springer-Verlag, 1998) 101–20.

quiet but effective mechanism for adjudicating legal disputes between the parties; and it was the leadership of the GATT Secretariat that is generally credited with having initiated and managed the creation of the Panel procedure.

Notwithstanding this earlier achievement, any judicial activism on the part of the WTO Secretariat in this role is with respect to interpretation and legal reasoning within dispute settlement rather than in promoting ex ante compliance. It is still only for a Member to request a Panel. The Secretariat can neither bring a challenge nor advise a Member to bring a claim—that would be serving the interests of one Member above another, rather than the collective interest of the system itself. This is despite the potential support it can offer under Article 27 particularly to developing country Members. In other words, the Secretariat has no formal independent powers to increase compliance. It is mostly in the area of the substance of the Panel reports that the Secretariat has some influence, although less so on Appellate Body reports. While legal reasoning in settling a dispute may potentially induce such a subsequent change in levels of compliance, this influence would have had no immediate effect on preventing violations of obligations during an economic crisis.

A steering influence from the Secretariat is more likely in the area of the comprehensive peer reviews that each WTO Member must undertake in the Trade Policy Review Mechanism (TPRM).[34] The TPRM establishes voluntary reporting of WTO Members' trade practices and ex officio gathering of information by the TPRB in order to provide WTO Members with more information about the other Members' trade behaviour. This peer review is based on two reports: a factual report prepared by the Secretariat's Trade Policy Review Division and a policy statement by the Member under review. These factual reports are probably the most comprehensive documents available on the trade policies of the individual Member countries and each takes an average of nine months to complete, including several missions to the country under review. Yet even with these mandated reports, the human resources actually made available to the Secretariat permits only 16–18 reviews per year, compared to the 23 reviews that would be required in order to follow the stipulated periodicity. Increasing policy transparency not only highlights non-compliance but reduces and improves the overall ability to deliberate on the effects of trade policies. Undoubtedly, the TPRM is a valuable exercise in producing a comprehensive picture of trade policies and areas in need of attention. Nevertheless, the influence exerted by the Secretariat through the TPRM is limited to soft normative power and the reviews do not take place regularly enough to act as a coordination and management tool for crisis measures. All the reports carry the following disclaimer:

> This is intended to be a purely factual report and is issued under the sole responsibility of the Director-General. It has no legal effect on the rights and obligations of Members, nor does it have any legal implication with respect to the conformity of any measure noted in

[34] The WTO Trade Policy Review Mechanism, para D; para C(v)(b).

> the report with any WTO Agreement or any provision thereof. This report is also without prejudice to Members' negotiating positions in the Doha Round.[35]

That is, trade policy reviews cannot be used to induce compliance, merely to identify it. Furthermore, they cannot be used as the basis of undertaking research into how to resolve complex issues. The WTO Secretariat does not have a strong research dimension, with neither the mandate nor the resources to carry out independent or self-initiated research on a large scale. The few analytical resources that exist are primarily consumed in the process of writing factual reports for the various councils, committees and working groups serviced by the Secretariat.[36]

In the face of its lack of a research mandate, the Secretariat on its own initiative tried to fill the gap creatively through launching an interdisciplinary—economics, law and political science—academic journal, *World Trade Review*, in cooperation with Cambridge University Press. The journal's mission is to publish articles that contribute to the understanding of the issues facing the international trading system through critical analysis and constructive debate. The journal has an independent editorial policy and board to maintain academic credibility. Significantly, WTO Members were not consulted on the launch of the journal and the journal is neither financed by, nor controlled by, the Members of the WTO. This journal could arguably perform a higher-profile advocacy role in the deliberation and dissemination of any necessary reforms to the system, with reference to crisis measures. Clearly such an endeavour is also dependent on securing further independent funding.

B. The Role of the Director General

Is there then a case for the DG as executive manager of the Secretariat and the custodian of the multilateral trading system boldly to take full responsibility for steering Member behaviour? The special role of the DG flows from the fact that he is appointed by, and responsible to, the Members. Yet, despite the normative influence the DG can provide, the position has no formal powers at all because all of the powers emanate from the Members. The DG has a role as a mediator under DSU Article 5.6, but this has only been invoked once. The DG can also be a composer of Panels under Article 8.7, in the event that the parties fail to agree on the panellists. However, again, this is in the area of ex post law enforcement and not everyday compliance.

[35] See fn 1 of the First Monitoring Report: JOB(09)/2, 23 January 2009, 'Report to the Trade Policy Review Body from the Director-General on the Financial and Economic Crisis and Trade-Related Developments'.

[36] Halle and Wolfe note that all of the usual WTO discussions of notifications continued during the crisis, and committees explicitly discussed crisis measures. For example, on many occasions during 2009 the USA faced questions about the Buy America provisions of its stimulus package in the Committee on Government Procurement. M Halle and R Wolfe, 'A New Approach to Transparency and Accountability in the WTO' [2010] Issue Brief *Entwined* 16/09.

The DG has been likened to a general without arms. He cannot order countries to liberalise trade; he cannot interpret the agreements administered by the WTO; he cannot determine the procedures of the WTO; he cannot pronounce on the legality of the trade policies of individual Members; and he cannot call a new round of trade negotiations. Nevertheless, the powers of persuasion, mediation and advocacy can be used to push an initiative that might in time be a useful mechanism in crisis management. One example could be to secure support for the use of market surveillance and research beyond relying on incomplete Member submissions of policy information or a type of subsidy scorecard. Another suggestion is to build support to create an office of Avocat General within the Secretariat, which would prepare, for example, an independent analysis of the legal issues in every dispute settlement proceeding from the viewpoint of overall WTO policy and would present that position to the tribunal. This could serve as an instrument to discuss and clarify what would be considered appropriate crisis measures and, as a relevant example, the relationship of the Article XX public order exceptions to the ASCM during a global crisis.

Needless to say, creating a diplomatic avenue for incremental reform is primarily dependent on the personal charisma and authority of the DG as impartial and respected broker. The office of the DG would perform more decisively if there existed a mandate to take initiatives that could serve to address how to manage compliance in a systemic crisis more effectively. It would also be effective if the DG had an obligation to intervene in a constructive and impartial way when the Members have no individual incentive to move forward on a deadlocked issue. However, whatever the rationale for such initiatives, the domestic political resistance against a more collective enforcement approach will likely force governments, the Secretariat and the DG to proceed in an incremental fashion. This is not impossible, given the GATT regime began as a 'soft law' regime in order to attract the largest possible number of participants. Only later did it develop some procedures to resolve disputes and ambiguity in treaty interpretation. It was during the 1970s that the GATT became a more mature and dynamic regime, capable of incremental expansion of subject matter even while it deepened its commitment to hard law backed by harder enforcement mechanisms.

C. The Coherence Mechanism

One area from which the WTO DG and Secretariat might have derived more strength is the coherence mechanism established under the Marrakesh Agreement, which mandates the WTO to cooperate, as appropriate, with the IMF and the World Bank and its affiliated agencies with a view to achieving greater coherence in global economic policy-making.[37] For 'beyond the direct [bilateral] commercial

[37] As defined by Art III:5 of the WTO Agreement.

benefits this brings to WTO Members, a well-functioning, open, rules-based, trading system makes trade policies more predictable and effective tools for economic management' and therefore of collective interest.[38]

However, this coherence mechanism remains underdeveloped. This could be seen during the crisis when these international organisations produced overlapping and largely competing, not complementary, monitoring reports and analyses. The World Bank, the IMF and the OECD had greater resources for in-house research upon which to base their activities and policy advice, while the WTO Members have remained reluctant to finance such initiatives. The coherence mechanism could have been a potentially strong and effective steering mechanism during the crisis. It was indeed noted that the WTO and the World Bank and the WTO and the IMF negotiated cooperation agreements during 1995–96. More disappointingly, despite ambitious suggestions on both sides as to how their businesses interrelated, in the end the initiatives were basically only procedural and all mention of exchange rates and debt had been expunged:

> The differences in mandate and decision-making structure, the jealousy with which autonomy was defended, the fear of cross-conditionality [Bretton Woods] conditions being used to press WTO commitments and the fear that WTO negotiating positions would be jeopardised by the [Bretton Woods Organisations'] activities combined to make substantive progress impossible. Particularly among developing countries there was concern that if the three organisations 'got their acts together', they would be even more irresistible than before.[39]

The history of the coherence mechanism suggests all would be simple provided that everyone agreed on which path to follow and on the links between policy levers and outcomes. In a membership-driven organization, based on consensus decision-making processes, finding out what everyone agrees to seems an insurmountable task. And this is even without an economic crisis to polarise positions in mercantilist self-interest.

IV. Hodie tibi, cras mihi?[40]

This book therefore concludes that due to both regulatory gaps and insufficient compliance incentives, the WTO did not become the venue for either regulating, resolving or remedying those non-compliant crisis measures, through consultations, Panels or for the most part CVDs. It was therefore unable to generate the global public good of competitive markets. Throughout the crisis, the institutional

[38] M Auboin, 'Fulfilling the Marrakesh Mandate on Coherence: Ten Years of Cooperation between the WTO, IMF and World Bank', WTO Discussion Paper no 13 (2007).

[39] LA Winters, 'Coherence and the WTO' (2007) 23 *Oxford Review of Economic Policy* 61.

[40] Literally translated as: 'Today it's me, tomorrow it will be you.'

response of the WTO was neither formal nor normative.[41] For although the WTO DG[42] took the unprecedented move to establish a Task Force on the Financial Crisis in 2009, to provide a 'radar picture' of governments' policy responses to the crisis, the legal mechanism for providing this information[43] was derived from and confined by the existing TPRM.[44] Unlike in the European Commission, no innovative new legal avenue was sought to provide a stronger leadership response to steer Members towards more coordinated crisis-management measures.

This passivity suggests that there is a more overriding need for the WTO DG and Secretariat to be seen to allow the Members to drive the institution forwards, or indeed backwards, without any explicit guardianship, even in the face of a systemic global crisis with the potential for destructive tit-for-tat protectionism. Paradoxically, this limited, largely soft response to the crisis was both applauded and contested. Bolivia contested the WTO's limited monitoring of the bailouts and stimulus packages on the ground that there was no formal mandate to do so, and moreover, that not all 153 WTO Members had been involved in the process of setting up the mechanism. Further precision on the purpose and length of the activity was demanded, along with the periodicity of reports and meetings, and special rules for developing countries.[45]

Others opined as follows:

> In one of the strongest examples of leadership in the WTO as an institution, Director General Pascal Lamy and Membersof the Secretariat moved swiftly to establish means of monitoring responses to the crisis for protectionism, opening a multilateral conversation aimed at ensuring that the countries in question were aware of the importance of operating within WTO disciplines, and ensuring that there would be early warnings of any protectionist slide.[46]

The results of this research suggest otherwise, however. Beyond the 'soft' peer pressure taking place through greater transparency, data collection and monitoring of Members' trade policies and laws, the formal WTO legal framework regulating

[41] See J Pauwelyn, 'The Formation Process of WTO (Soft) Norms: WTO Reaction to the Financial Crisis and Transparency in WTO Dispute Settlement', Graduate Institute, Geneva, first draft 13 March 2009.

[42] A year into the crisis, at a G-20 meeting in 2009, the G-20 countries responded to a call from the WTO DG Pascal Lamy to create a new transparency mechanism as a collective response to the crisis. The G-20 leaders agreed to 'notify promptly the WTO of any such measures and we call on the WTO, together with other international bodies, within their respective mandates, to monitor and report publicly on our adherence to these undertakings on a quarterly basis'.

[43] See 'Report to the General Council by Director General Lamy in his role as Chairman of the Trade Negotiations Committee', 26 and 27 May 2009, available at www.wto.org/english/.

[44] TPRM para G states that an annual overview of developments in the international trading environment which are having an impact on the multilateral trading system shall be undertaken. The overview is to be assisted by an annual report by the DG, setting out major activities of the WTO and highlighting significant policy issues affecting the trading system.

[45] Cited in Pauwelyn (n 41) 5.

[46] Howse (n 3).

the anti-competitive behaviour of governments during the crisis was either incomplete or largely jettisoned. The empirical analysis submits that when under stress, governments unilaterally and tacitly withdrew the most sensitive sectors of domestic economies out of the ambit of the WTO, as previously happened in the areas of shipping, oil and textiles. The results of this qualitative and quantitative assessment of the role of international rules governing competition in public and private markets suggests that there was an unspoken consensus among the WTO Members to the effect that not only should there be a halt to substantive rule-making, but also those rules previously negotiated could be sidelined and if necessary subject to diplomatic or political, rather than formal legal control. As such, the Members took a move back towards the GATT framework of dispute settlement. This supports the words of Robert Hudec written long before the 2008 crisis:

> [I]t must be recognized that the WTO legal system serves a reluctant government clientele. It is a clientele that has made great strides toward law-respecting behavior in the last forty years, but that still has many reservations about obedience to legal rulings. An agreement adopted with this much reluctance will almost certainly encounter a bias against making its enforcement pressures stronger. To the contrary, one can expect governments to look for ways to cut back on its rigor whenever they can.[47]

V. To the Health or the Stealth of Nations?

> [I]nternational society has the ultimate capacity to enable all societies to promote the ever-increasing well-being of themselves and their members, the ultimate responsibility to prevent societies from doing harm to themselves and to other societies. It is in international society that humanity's capacity to harm itself can achieve its most spectacular effects. And it is in international society that the ever-increasing well-being of the whole human race can, must, and will be promoted.[48]

This book assessed the international and regional regulation seeking to prevent government measures that distort competition in government procurement and open markets, taking the crisis years of 2008–12 as the timeframe for analysis. The findings highlighted inconsistences that need to be addressed by appropriate reforms before the 2008–12 financial crisis recedes from our collective memory, and before another financial collapse takes a further toll on the value and the perceived legitimacy of these international rules.

The first level of the research findings indicated that there are still several gaps in the coverage of the regulation of public restraints of competition in both public

[47] RE Hudec, 'Broadening the Scope of Remedies in WTO Dispute Settlement', originally published in F Weiss and J Wiers (eds), *Improving WTO Dispute Settlement Procedures* (London, Cameron May, 2000) 345–76.

[48] P Allott, *Eunomia: New Order for a New World* (Oxford, Oxford University Press, 1990, reprinted 2001) 180, ¶12.5.

and open markets. This is the case for the framework under the WTO ASCM, fundamentally because of the lack of subsidy control coverage for the trade in services, but also due to the ASCM's inability to distinguish between necessary and unnecessary State aid, unlike the WTO GPA, the GATT and the GATS. Further difficulties in enforcing the ASCM provision during a crisis relate to providing sufficient evidence of the trade effects of a temporary but actionable crisis measure.

To a lesser extent this is also the case under the TFEU framework in the EU: not only are public undertakings seen to be excluded from the coverage of the rules that govern the anti-competitive behaviour of private undertakings in the private sector, but so too are a multitude of categories of State aid. Further contributing to the lack of coherence and symmetry of this regulation, a public procurement that is deemed to be in compliance with the EU procurement Directives are prima facie presumed to be exempt from State aid control. Any wishlist of reforms to the WTO ASCM to address these deficiencies would therefore seek to include (i) extending subsidy control to services; (ii) improving notifications and transparency; (iii) clarifying that similar public interest overrides exist in the form of exceptions under the ASCM as exist under the other covered agreements; (iv) offering interpretative guidance on the use of measures necessary for public morals with respect to crisis measures, given the seeming lack of coherence a Member need display in setting these values. This research also makes a recommendation that there are cogent reasons to re-examine the prevailing exclusion of procurement and subsidies from the scope of Article I:1 MFN obligation in light of measures such as matching clauses and the 'Buy European' proposal.

Within the TFEU, the recommendations revolve primarily around (i) advocating new legal interpretations of the coverage of the TFEU competition and State aid rules to procurements in compliance with the Directives and (ii) re-examining the prevailing exclusion of public undertakings from the scope of those rules regulating the anti-competitive behaviour of private undertakings. Within the other RTAs, an integrated to approach to regulating public restraints of competition in open and government procurement markets is still nascent. The research indicates that building a coherent approach to regulating public restraints of competition would involve balancing the typically asymmetrical design of these two sets of regulation with a view to integrating their approach to regulating and enforcing them under a binding dispute settlement system. This would entail a move from a *form* to an *effects* approach to assessing both sets of regulations.

The second level of analysis indicates that with the exception of the TFEU, these provisions at both the WTO and regional level, where binding, are overwhelmingly bilateral in their nature and in their supporting enforcement infrastructure. That is, these non-compliant bilateral provisions are enforced only if successfully challenged by another 'injured' government. Within the WTO if the potential of the Secretariat is to be realised, an independent monitoring system and enforcement mechanism appear to be necessary to bring a scofflaw WTO Member into compliance in the event that no other Member brings a challenge. Furthermore, the Secretariat needs to be liberated financially and normatively as to the associated research it can undertake and the authoritative interpretations it can issue to defend these agreements, particularly during a systemic global economic crisis. Without increasing the deliberations taking place within the organisation, it is difficult to see how self-reflection can take place with a view to promulgating *modernisation from within.*

As regards the EU, the TFEU reflects the Union's collective values above the traditional mercantilist thrust of the individual Member States commercial activity. This has been actively interpreted into both the provisions and their enforcement qualities. Other RTAs exist possessing direct effect on domestic law, yet they have not been enforced to this extent. The Commission is supported with broad monitoring and enforcement powers to force scofflaw Member States into compliance and defend these collective values. A cautious and more literal approach has been preferred within the WTO. The overriding objective seems to be to defend the rules but to preserve domestic sovereignty and a membership-driven organisation. Moreover, although the Commission was criticised continually during the crisis, it harnessed this criticism positively through its initiative to modernise State aid control, and address some of the problems encountered during the crisis both at the Member State and institutional level. The WTO Secretariat has not been able to undertake a similar stocktaking and reform process due to the limitations of its bilateral nature and general lack of self-confidence.

Recommendations for reform on this level are politically charged. Nevertheless, these include, at a minimum, an increase in the monitoring powers of the Secretariat. Transparency increases compliance and at present the notification systems under both the ASCM and GPA are woefully unable to meet the task of producing a comprehensive understanding of the extent and nature of the Members' measures. Even without independent enforcement powers, the increased transparency from such a strong information collection initiative would usefully serve to increase compliance and enforcement. The salient issues that arise from an effective transparency measure could be deliberated on in committee meetings with a view to producing authoritative interpretations to guide the Members—in this case, towards a more coordinated and managed response to systemic panic and increased protectionist lobbying during a global crisis.

Again, it is self-evident that the different nature and enforcement characteristics of the WTO and TFEU rules have had significant consequences for ability of these two organisations to manage and steer the anti-competitive measures governments were tempted to implement during the 2008–12 economic crisis. That is, there is little wiggle room under the present legal framework for collective enforcement within the WTO. Changes to the WTO enforcement nature along the lines of the TFEU would require a sea-change in the perceptions of the Members. They would have to acknowledge the collective values of multilateral trade and the necessity of the organisation itself in defending these values above their own singular interests. And then they would have to negotiate rules to that effect. This seems attractive but less likely. If substantive changes to the enforcement system were to occur, even if only with regard to systemic global economic crises, this would be a positive development. The third level of research indicated that while remaining subject to criticism for 'blowing in the wind', the European Commission was able to appear to take a more decisive normative role in managing the protectionist instincts of Member States.

The research findings confirmed that the WTO Secretariat and DG were more limited in their mandate and did not seek empowerment through the use of the coherence mechanism, or by working in a complementary way with the Bretton Woods organisations. Consequently, they relied primarily on the peer pressure oriented through the TPRM to communicate passively with the membership and the wider world. In other words, the WTO Secretariat and the DG appeared uncertain in their efforts and consequently their ability to prevent the contagion effects of protectionism because of the overwhelmingly bilateral nature of the provisions and the infrastructure supporting their enforcement. As a result, during the 2008–12 crisis there was non-compliance with the regulation preventing public distortions of competition in procurement and open markets, which was not challenged either by the Secretariat or by other Members.

In short, this is not the description of a mature international organisation entrusted and empowered by its membership to ensure the application of the rules through thick and thin. Rather, it is the depiction of a deliberately undeveloped international structure built on the principles of inter-governmentalism, state sovereignty and an uncertain faith in the performance or legitimacy of collective international trade laws.

This conclusion sadly confirms Hudec's sceptical analysis of the shaky domestic foundations on which international cooperation on trade issues is laid. It pushes these research findings towards the rationalist charge that nations only obey international law to the extent that its serves national self-interest.[49] The political fear of a potential loss of power to international institutions, even in the face of a systemic fiscal crisis, prevented the development of more coordinated, coherent and transparent rules for steering state behaviour through one of the worst contagious recessions in living memory. Domestic governments have yet to accept fully that the principle of non-interference in the domestic affairs of sovereign nations needs to be balanced with international norms to prevent state restrictions of competition from undermining the development of other nations, triggering retaliation and inhibiting a return to economic growth, development and increased social welfare. Such international norms and values have yet to be internalised fully into domestic policy-making. This is an uncomfortable and outmoded reality: in this post-ontological age, we should no longer be defending international laws' existence, but evaluating whether the laws are fair, effective—and enforceable.[50]

[49] See eg L Henkin, *How Nations Behave: Law and Foreign Policy* (New York, Columbia University Press, 1979) 47.

[50] TM Franck, *Fairness in International Law and Institutions* (Oxford, Clarendon Press, 1995).

APPENDICES

Appendix 1: US Trade Measures Notified to the WTO

1. AIG Rescue Package, 16 September 2008

Federal Reserve Actions surrounding AIG rescue package ($85 billion), in exchange for 80 per cent public stake in the firm. AIG restructured under the Economic Stabilization Act 10 November 2008. Additional recapitalization ($37.5 billion)

2. TARP (Troubled Asset Relief Programme), 3 October 2008

Under the Emergency Economic Stabilization Act 2008, allowing the Secretary of the Treasury to purchase, and to make and fund commitments to purchase, troubled assets from any financial institution.[1]

Total amount foreseen: $700 billion ($250 billion upon enactment, another $100 billion if requested by the President, and US$350 billion subject to Congressional approval).

3. Mortgage Lenders Rescue Package, 8 October 2008

Treasury and Federal Housing Finance Agency Actions with respect to Fannie Mae and Freddie Mac (mortgage lenders rescue package).

4. Guarantee Scheme for Troubled Assets, 23 November 2008

Citicorp: guarantee scheme for troubled assets ($306 billion) and capital injection ($20 billion), under the Targeted Investment Programme; complemented by the Asset Guarantee Programme (2 January 2009).

5. The US Auto Industry Financing Programme, 29 December 2008

US Treasury loan to General Motors (GM) $13.4 billion (delivered in three instalments) and to Chrysler $4 billion. The US Treasury is evaluating the restructuring submissions received 17 February 2009, under the terms of the loans to GM and Chrysler.

[1] The Act defines 'financial institution' as including 'any institution, including, but not limited to, any bank, savings association, credit union, security broker or dealer, or insurance company, established and regulated under the laws of the United States or any State, territory, or possession of the United States ... but excluding any central bank of, or institution owned by, a foreign government'.

On 29 December 2008, US Treasury announced that it would purchase $5 billion in senior preferred equity with an 8 per cent dividend from GMAC LLC as part of a broader programme to assist the domestic automotive industry in becoming financially viable. Additionally, on 16 January 2009, the US Treasury agreed to lend up to $1 billion to GM so that GM could participate in a rights offering at GMAC in support of GMAC's reorganisation as a bank holding company. GM drew $884 million under this commitment.

6. The US Auto Industry Financing Programme, April–July 2009

New additional loan to GM Corporation ($2 billion) to provide working capital for the company (prior to its bankruptcy filing). GM filed bankruptcy proceedings on 1 June 2009, and has been offered additional $30.1 billion debtor in possession loan by the US Treasury. The loan is intended to benefit all of GM's continuing operations without regard to geographic location.

The new entity, General Motors Company, emerged from bankruptcy on 10 July 2009 after the completion of the sale of certain GM assets to the 'New GM'. The government converted its loans to 60.8 per cent of the equity in the New GM, loans in the amount of $7.1 billion, and $2.1 billion in preferred stock.

January 2009, US Treasury announced a $1.5 billion five-year loan to a special purpose entity created by Chrysler Financial to finance retail automotive purchases.

7. American Recovery and Reinvestment Act of 2009 (ARRA), 17 February 2009

Providing aid of $787 billion (5.5 per cent GDP).

8. Auto Supplier Support Programme, 19 March 2009

$3.5 billion made available to all critical auto suppliers. The programme provides the same benefits to foreign and local suppliers, through financial protection on receivables from any domestic auto companies.

9. New Generation Electrical Vehicle Development Grant, 5 August 2009

Grant ($2.4 billion) made available for the development of new generation electrical vehicle (48 new advanced battery and electric drive projects), under the American Recovery and Reinvestment Act. Projects not restricted to US entities.

10. Jobs for Main Street Act Effective, 18 March 2010

Jobs for Main Street Act (HR 2847), which includes 'Buy American' provisions.[2]

11. Small Business Jobs Act, effective 27 September 2010

Small Business Jobs Act of 2010 including temporary tax credits and expansion of loan programmes for SMEs.

[2] WT/TPR/OV/W/3.

12. Excise tax credit for ethanol producers, effective until 31 December 2011

Extension of the excise tax credit ($0.45/gallon) for ethanol producers, included in the Tax Relief, Unemployment Insurance Reauthorization, and Job Creation Act 2010.

13. Pilot Loan Programme, 9 May 2012

Global Credit Express Pilot Loan Programme delivering short-term working capital loans to SMEs. Loans may not exceed $500,000 with a fixed-rate financing at a relatively low interest cost fixed at the Commercial Interest Reference rate of 2.6 per cent.

14. Amendments to section 701 of the Tariff Act, 28 June 2012

Amendments to section 701 of the Tariff Act 1930 (19 USC 1671) clarifying that the countervailing duty law can be applied to subsidised goods from non-market economy countries, and that the Department of Commerce can adjust anti-dumping duties applied to goods from non-market economy countries when countervailing duties are applied to the same good.[3]

15. Bank lending cap increase, effective 30 May 2012[4]

Export–import bank lending cap increased from $100 billion to $120 billion for the year 2012, and then to $140 billion in 2014. Section 20 of the Act aims at promoting textile industry financing and determining ways to support: (i) export of textile components or inputs; and (ii) promotion of local jobs that are critical to textile component and input manufacture.

Appendix 2: Brazil's Crisis Measures

Financial Sector

1. Purchase of equity stake in troubled banks to enhance competition and strengthen Brazil's financial system. Authorisation granted to the two largest state-owned banks, Banco do Brasil and Caixa Econômica Federal, to constitute fully owned or controlled subsidiaries as well as to purchase

[3] WTO document WT/TPR/OV/W/6.

[4] To increase confidence in the banks, US regulators conducted stress tests on 19 bank holding companies in April 2009 to ensure that they were sufficiently capitalised given a set of assumptions about losses on various bank assets over the next two years. Following the release of the results in early May, US regulators directed ten of the banks examined to increase their level of capital or to improve the quality by including more common shares. Several banks took advantage of the reduced uncertainty and the increased risk appetite of investors that accompanied the publication of the stress test results to raise equity and issue debt.

participation in financial institutions based in Brazil. (Permanent Delegation of Brazil to the WTO, 22 October 2008.)

2. Additional credit line ($4 billion) for state governments through the National Development Bank (BNDES). (Permanent Delegation of Brazil to the WTO, 17 April 2009.)
3. Liquidity provision to the banking system ($25 billion). Expansion of access to freely convertible currencies. Banco Do Brasil and Caixa Economica Federal (Federal banks) authorised to constitute subsidiaries and acquire participation in financial institutions. (Permanent Delegation of Brazil to the WTO, 4 March 2009.)
4. Additional credit line (R$80 billion ($47.4 billion)) through the National Development Bank (BNDES), allocated to maintain activities already scheduled. The credit line will not generate new commitments. (WTO Document WT/TPR/OV/W/3, 14 June 2010.)
5. Additional credit line ($4 billion) for state governments through the National Development Bank (BNDES). (Permanent Delegation of Brazil to the WTO, 1 February 2010; terminated on 31 December 2009.)

Manufacturing Sector

Auto-Industry

1. Government credits ($1.7 billion) for carmakers; and temporary reduction of the industrial products tax on car sales (until April 2009). (Permanent Delegation of Brazil to the WTO, 7 February 2009.)
2. The Incentive Programme for Technological Innovation and Consolidation of the Productive Chain of Motor Vehicles (INOVAR-AUTO) was created by Provisional Executive Order No 563 and partially regulated by Executive Decree No 7716, both dated 3 April 2012. The Programme aims at supporting technological development, innovation, safety, environmental protection, energy efficiency and quality of cars, trucks, buses and auto parts. The companies qualified may benefit from tax credits (IPI) based on expenses incurred in the country in each calendar quarter. Such expenses must be related to: (i) research; (ii) technological development; (iii) technological innovation; (iv) strategic raw materials; (v) tooling; (vi) collections to the National Fund for Scientific and Technological Development (FNDCT) as provided for in regulations, and (vii) capacity-building of providers. Automobile manufacturers must meet at least three of the following four criteria to be eligible for the new industrial and trade regime: (i) investing a specified share of gross revenue in research and development; (ii) investing a proportion of revenue in engineering; (iii) having some production steps

onshore; and (iv) carrying out energy-efficiency evaluations. (Permanent Delegation of Brazil to the WTO, 15 May 2012, and Decree No 7.716, 3 April 2012.)

3. Regulation of the INOVAR-AUTO regime, providing support to technological development, innovation, safety, environmental protection, energy efficiency and to improve the quality of cars, trucks, buses and auto parts manufactured and traded in Brazil. The regulation establishes the specific conditions under which three categories of eligible companies can benefit from incentives through INOVAR-AUTO: (i) companies that manufacture automotive products in Brazil; (ii) companies that trade automotive products in Brazil; and (iii) companies with investment plans approved by the Ministry of Development, Industry and International Trade. The conditions for admission to the regime include energy-efficiency targets, minimum levels of expenditures in innovation and research and development, and percentage of vehicles included in the certification programme on energy efficiency. (Permanent Delegation of Brazil to the WTO, 17 October 2012 and Decree No 7.819, 2 October 2012.)

Non-Auto

1. Government incentives to specific sectors, ie telecommunications, computers, semiconductors, including extension of tax breaks for certain products, eg stoves, refrigerators, freezers, washing machines, furniture, laminated plastic PET, wallpaper, light fixtures, and chandeliers. (Provisional Executive Order No 563, 3 April 2012, and Permanent Delegation of Brazil to the WTO, 15 May 2012; effective 3 April 2012–30 June 2012.)
2. Announcement of phase 2 of the Growth Acceleration Programme (PAC 2) (estimated investments $520 million for the period 2011–14) encompassing a set of actions and investment goals aimed at creating the necessary conditions for long-term economic growth and social development. (Permanent Delegation of Brazil to the WTO, 2 June 2010.)
3. Complementary measures to Plano Brasil Maior I, including a series of fiscal incentives such as national preference in public procurement to locally produced products in certain sectors, ie textile and footwear (8 November 2011); and motor and machinery, medicines, and pharmaceutical products (3 April 2012) (NCM Chapters 28–30, 35, 42, 61–65, 94, 96), more flexibility on trade financing, incentives for IT industry, and tougher enforcement of trade regulations against unfair trade practices. New support programme through BNDES for preferential loans to foster local production and technological innovation. (WTO document WT/TPR/OV/W/6, 28 June 2012.)

Appendix 3: India's Crisis Measures

(i) across-the-board central excise duty reduction by 4 percentage points;
(ii) additional spending of Rs. 200 billion;
(iii) assistance to certain export industries in the form of interest subsidy on export finance;
(iv) refund of excise duties/central sales tax, and other export incentives;
(v) 2 percentage-point reduction in central excise and service tax.

Appendix 4: European Commission Communications

Financial Sector

1. The Banking Communication issued on 13 October 2008 made the authorisation of state aid in the form of guarantee, capital, asset relief or liquidity support dependent on respect for various essentials. Access to aid was to be non-discriminatory, limited in time, clearly defined and limited in scope. An appropriate contribution was to be provided by the beneficiary. In certain cases behavioural rules, such as a ban on aggressive expansion, and/or follow-up restructuring measures, were to be imposed.

2. This was followed on 5 December 2008 by the Recapitalisation Communication, which provided guidance on the pricing of capital injections made by the state into banks. The pricing of capital was to be reasonable and linked to properly functioning markets so that recapitalisation was to differentiate between banks that were fundamentally sound and those that were distressed. The price of capital injections was to be linked to the risk profile of the beneficiary bank, the type of capital injected by the state (in particular its subordination) and the nature of any safeguards against abuse. Recapitalisation of banks in distress posed a greater risk of distortions of competition, so they were in principle to be required to pay more for state support and be subject to stricter safeguards. Restructuring to restore long-term viability was an essential requirement for distressed banks, a requirement that was extended to all bank beneficiaries of recapitalisation from 1 January 2011. Moreover, in order to keep the duration of state involvement to a minimum, exit mechanisms had to be included to ensure a timely redemption of injected state capital, in particular by providing that remuneration for state capital should increase over time.

3. On 25 February 2009, the Commission adopted the Impaired Assets Communication providing guidance on how relief measures could be applied to remove impaired or toxic assets. Asset relief could take either the form of asset purchase, in which case the state would buy the impaired asset portfolio at a determined price higher than the market price, which constituted the aid, or asset guarantee, whereby the state would take a share of the risk of default or loss relating to the asset. This introduced the (subsequently controversial) notion of the real economic value of assets, being an estimated market value in the longer term contrasting with the present depressed market value in the financial crisis. Asset relief schemes were to be conditional on the following: there must be full disclosure of impaired assets and the costs must be shared between the Member States, shareholders and creditors of the financial institutions; identification of eligible assets and valuation of assets must be made on a coordinated basis; and distressed beneficiary banks must be the subject of restructuring measures so as to ensure a return to normal market conditions.
4. On 22 July 2009, the Commission adopted the Restructuring Communication setting out detailed restructuring conditions for those banks that received large amounts of aid and that had unsustainable business models. Those banks had to demonstrate strategies to achieve long-term viability without state support under adverse economic conditions. The restructuring plan had to include a thorough diagnosis of the bank's problems, including a stress test to demonstrate that a restructured bank would be able to withstand adverse macroeconomic conditions. It was anticipated that in many cases divestments would be essential, either to ensure the viability of core businesses or to compensate for the negative competitive impact of aid on key markets. Banks would be required to contribute to the costs of restructuring as much as possible from their own resources in order to reduce moral hazard and to create appropriate incentives for future behaviour. As with recapitalisation measures, restructuring was required to be accompanied by appropriate measures to ensure that distortion of competition was limited. The Restructuring Communication allows for a number of variations to the requirements applicable under the general rescue and restructuring guidelines. In particular, the restructuring period could last for up to five years, as opposed to the normal period of two years, and the general requirement that the beneficiary meet 50 per cent of the restructuring costs was set aside so that difficulties in accessing private capital could be taken into account. The one-time last-time rule was also temporarily lifted. Because the new rules are sectoral, the Commission was able to specify in greater detail the type of information required to determine whether the proposed restructuring measures were apt to restore a bank's long-term viability. In certain cases, a monitoring trustee was to be appointed, a practice common to merger control but hitherto rarely used in state aid supervision.

Manufacturing Sector Communications

To complement the four Communications on aid to the financial sector, the Commission also adopted a temporary framework for state aid measures to stimulate the so-called real economy, principally so as to deal with difficulties of businesses' access to finance. The main measures set out in the temporary framework were the possibility of Member States to grant a limited amount of aid up to €500,000 per undertaking, subsidised loans and guarantees, more flexible risk capital funding, and trade financing. Member States committed in total some €81 billion, as approved by the Commission, but in fact only about a quarter of that was actually taken up by businesses in the EU, mostly small and medium-sized enterprises (SMEs). Nevertheless the Commission believes that the adoption of these temporary measures by the Member States sent a signal to the markets that they were willing to meet potential demand. However, the Commission acknowledges that it is difficult to assess how effective the temporary framework has been. In particular, the fact that the most popular measure, the grant of up to €500,000 was implemented through schemes that did not require investment or a link to any specific objective meant that it was not possible to assess its impact on long-term recovery.

In December 2011, the Commission prolonged the application of its Communications, with amendments applicable from 1 January 2012 for a second time. In particular, this Second Prolongation Communication supplements the Recapitalisation Communication, by providing more detailed guidance on remuneration for capital instruments that do not bear a fixed return and for fees payable in return for guarantees on bank liabilities, as well as explaining how the Commission will undertake the proportionate assessment of the long-term viability of banks.

4.1 Ireland: Crisis Measures

1. NN48/2008: Guarantee scheme for banks in Ireland, IP/08/1497, 13 October 2008.
2. N9/2009: Recapitalisation of Anglo Irish Bank, IP/09/50, 14 January 2009.
3. N356/2009: Recapitalisation of Anglo Irish Bank, IP/09/1045, 26 June 2009.
4. N61/2009: Change of ownership of Anglo Irish Bank, IP/09/271, 17 February 2009.
5. N149/2009: Recapitalisation of Bank of Ireland, IP/09/483, 26 March 2009.
6. N241/2009: Recapitalisation of Allied Irish Bank, IP/09/744, 12 May 2009.
7. N349/2009: Revised Irish guarantee scheme for financial institutions (Eligible Liabilities Guarantee scheme), IP/09/1787, 20 November 2009.

4.2 UK Crisis Measures

1. NN41/2008: Rescue aid to Bradford and Bingley, IP/08/1437, 1 October 2008.
2. N507/2008: Aid scheme to the banking industry in the UK, IP/08/1496, 13 October 2008.
3. UK Asset-backed Securities Guarantee Scheme, IP/09/613, 21 April 2009.
4. C14/2008: Restructuring package for Northern Rock; Final conditional decision after formal investigation procedure, IP/09/1600, 28 October 2009.
5. N428/2009: Restructuring plan of Lloyds Banking Group, IP/09/1728, 18 November 2009.
6. N422/2009 and N621/2009: Royal Bank of Scotland, impaired asset relief measure and restructuring plan, IP/09/1915, 14 December 2009.
7. N194/2009: Liquidation aid to Bradford & Bingley, IP/10/47, 25 January 2010.
8. NN19/2009: Restructuring of Dunfermline Building Society, IP/10/48, 25 January 2010.
9. SA.34218, UK Credit Easing Schemes, EXME/12/14.03, 14 March 2012.

4.3 Germany: Crisis Measures

1. C9/2008: Restructuring aid to Sachsen LB, IP/08/849, 4 June 2008.
2. C10/2008: Restructuring aid to IKB, IP/08/1557, 21 October 2008.
3. NN44/2008: Rescue aid to Hypo Real Estate 2 October 2008 Holding, IP/08/1453.
4. N512/2008: Aid scheme for financial institutions in Germany (guarantees, recapitalisations & other), IP/08/1589, 27 October 2008N615/2008: Guarantee and recapitalisation for Bayern LB, IP/08/2034 18 December 2008.
5. N655/2008: Guarantee for Nord LB, IP/08/2056, 22 December 2008.
6. N639/2008: Guarantee for IKB, IP/08/2055, 22 December 2008.
7. N17/2009: Guarantee for SdB (Sicherungseinrichtungsgesellschaft deutscher Banken mbH), IP/09/114, 22 January 2009.
8. N244/2009: Commerzbank capital injection, IP/09/711, 7 May 2009.
9. C43/2008: Aid for the restructuring of West LB, IP/09/741, 12 May 2009.
10. N531/2009: Temporary additional aid to West LB, IP/09/1434, 7 October 2009.
11. N264/2009: Recapitalisation of HSH Nordbank, IP/09/854, 29 May 2009.
12. C17/2009: Recapitalisation and asset relief for LBBW (Landesbank Baden Württemberg), IP/09/1058, 30 June 2009.
13. N314/2009: German asset relief scheme, IP/09/1216, 31 July 2009.
14. N400/2009: Additional aid (guarantees) for IKB, IP/09/1235, 17 August 2009.
15. N 456 /2009: Scheme to facilitate the refinancing of export credits, IP/09/1319, 15 September 2009.

16. C17/2009: Landesbank Baden Württemberg 'LBBW'—restructuring plan and impaired assets relief measure, IP/09/1927, 15 December 2009.
17. N694/2009: State guarantees for Hypo Real Estate, IP/09/1985, 21 December 2009.
18. N555/2009: Rescue aid for WestLB, IP/09/1996, 22 December 2009.
19. N161/2010: Recapitalisation of Hypo Real Estate, 19 May 2010.
20. N380/2010: Temporary authorisation of additional State support (guarantees) for Hypo Real Estate and creation of a bad bank structure, IP/10/1172, 24 September 2010.
21. SA.29510: WestLB divestments, 21 December 2010.
22. MC 15/2009: Landesbank Baden Württemberg 'LBBW'—Deka divestment, 14 January 2011.
23. SA.28264 (C15/2009): Restructuring aid for Hypo Real Estate Final decision, IP/11/898, 18 July 2011.
24. SA.33571: Temporary approval of the recapitalisation of NordLB, EXME/11/22.12, 22 December 2011.

BIBLIOGRAPHY

Abbott, KW and Snidal, D, 'Hard and Soft Law in International Governance' (2000) 54 *International Organization*.

Abbott, KW, Keohane, RO, Moravcsik, A, Slaughter, A-M and Snidal, D, 'The Concept of Legalization' (2000) 54 *International Organization*.

Adams, W and Brock, J, 'Antitrust and Efficiency: A Comment' (1987) 62 *New York Law Review* 1116.

Adler, JH, 'Antitrust Barriers to Cooperative Fishery Management' in D Leal (ed), *The Evolution of Property Rights in Fisheries* (2004).

Allott, P, *Eunomia. New Order for a New World* (Oxford and New York, Oxford University Press, 1990).

Andersen, S, 'Policy Handcuffs in the Financial Crisis', Institute of Policy Studies (February 2009).

Anderson, RD and Evenett, S, 'Incorporating Competition Elements in Regional Trade Agreements: Characterization and Empirical Analysis', Working Paper (2006).

Anderson, RD and Holmes, P, 'Competition Policy and the Future of the Multilateral Trading System' (2002) 5(2) *Journal of International Economic Law*.

Anderson, RD and Kovacic, WE, 'Competition Policy and International Trade Liberalization: Essential Complements to Ensure Good Performance in Public Procurement Markets' [2009] *Public Procurement Law Review* no 2, 67.

Anderson, RD and Wager, H, 'Human Rights, Development, and the WTO: The Cases of Intellectual Property and Competition Policy' (2006) 9(3) *Journal of International Economic Law*.

Anderson, RD, Kovacic, WE and Müller, AC, 'Ensuring Integrity and Competition in Public Procurement Markets: A Dual Challenge for Good Governance' in S Arrowsmith and R Anderson (eds) *The WTO Regime on Public Procurement: Recent Developments and Challenges Ahead* (Cambridge, Cambridge University Press, 2011).

Anderson, R et al, *Public Procurement Provisions in Recent Regional Trade Agreements: An Empirical Analysis from the WTO Secretariat* (WTO, Geneva, 2009).

Areeda, PE and Hovenkamp, H, *Antitrust Law: An Analysis of Antitrust Principles and Their Application.* (New York, Aspen, 2011).

Arrowsmith, S, 'Towards a Multilateral Agreement on Transparency in Public Procurement' (1998) 47 *International and Comparative Law Quarterly*.

Arrowsmith, S, *Public Procurement in the WTO* (London, Kluwer Law International, 2003).

Arrowsmith, S, *The Law of Public and Utilities Procurement*, 2nd edn (London, Sweet & Maxwell, 2005).

Arrowsmith, S, 'The Revised Agreement on Government Procurement: Changes to the Procedural Rules and other Transparency Provisions' in S Arrowsmith and R Anderson (eds), *The WTO Regime on Government Procurement: Challenge and Reform* (Cambridge, Cambridge University Press, 2011) ch 10.

Arrowsmith, S and Trybus, M (eds), *Public Procurement: The Continuing Revolution* (London: Kluwer Law International, 2002).

Arrowsmith, S and Anderson, R (eds) *The WTO Regime on Government Procurement: Recent Developments and Challenges Ahead* (Cambridge, Cambridge University Press, 2011).

Arrowsmith, SL, Linarelli, J and Wallace, D, Jr, 'Enforcement and Remedies' in *Regulating Government Procurement* (2000) ch 12.

Aschhoff, B and Sofka, W, 'Innovation on Demand—Can Public Procurement Drive Market Success of Innovations?' (2009) 38(8) *Research Policy.*

Auboin, M, 'Fulfilling the Marrakesh Mandate on Coherence: Ten Years of Cooperation between the WTO, IMF and World Bank', WTO Discussion Paper no 13 (2007).

Axelrod, R and Keohane, RO, 'Achieving Cooperation under Anarchy: Strategies and Institutions' (1985) 38 *World Politics.*

Ayer, AJ, Language, Truth, and Logic, 2nd edn (London, Gollancz, 1946).

Bagwell, K and Staiger, RW, 'An Economic Theory of GATT' (1999) 89 *American Economic Review.*

Bagwell, K and Staiger, RW, *The Economics of the World Trading System* (Cambridge, MA, MIT Press, 2002).

Bagwell, K and Staiger, RW, 'Will International Rules on Subsidies Disrupt the World Trading System?' (2006) 96 *American Economic Review.*

Bagwell, K, Mavroidis, PC and Staiger, RW, 'The Case for Tradable Remedies in WTO Dispute Settlement' in Evenett and Hoekman (eds), *Economic Development and Multilateral Trade Cooperation* (Basingstoke, Palgrave Macillan and The World Bank, 2005).

Bajpai, N, 'Global Financial Crisis, its Impact on India and the Policy Response', Columbia Global Centers. South Asia, Columbia University Working Paper no 5 (July 2011).

Baldwin, R, *The Causes of Regionalism* (Oxford, Basil Blackwell, 1997).

Baldwin, RE, 'Multilateralising Regionalism: Spaghetti Bowls as Building Blocs on the Path to Global Free Trade' (2006) 29 *World Economy.*

Baldwin, RE and Richardson, JD, 'Government Purchasing Policies, Other NTB's, and the International Monetary Crisis', Fourth Pacific Conference on Trade and Development, Ottawa, 1971.

Barfield, C, 'WTO Dispute Settlement System in Need of Change', AEI Briefing Paper (2002).

Barrell, R, Davis, EP, Karim, D and Liadze, I, 'Bank Regulation, Property Prices and Early Warnings System for Banks in OECD Countries', NIESR Discussion Paper no 330 (2010).

Bartels, L, 'Social Issues: Labour, Environment and Human Rights' in Lester and Mercurio (eds), *Bilateral and Regional Trade Agreements: Commentary, Analysis and Case Studies* (Cambridge, Cambridge University Press, 2007).

Bartels, L, 'Applicable Law in WTO Dispute Settlement Proceedings' (2001) 35(3) *Journal of World Trade.*

Baxter, RR, 'International Law in Her Infinite Varieties' (1980) 29 *International and Comparative Law Quarterly.*

Bederman, DJ, 'Constructivism, Positivism and Empiricism in International Law' (2001) 89 *Georgetown Law Journal.*

Beltratti, A and Stulz, R, 'The Credit Crisis around the Globe: Why Did some Banks Perform Better during the Credit Crisis?', Dice Center Working Paper 2010-05, Fisher College of Business (February 2011).

Bensen, CC, 'US Automotive Industry Bailout Programs: Avoiding WTO Potholes on the Road to Economic Recovery', 2009, available at: http://alsb.roundtablelive.org/resources/documents/np%202009%20benson,%20c.pdf.

Bhagwati, J, 'Regionalism and Multilateralism: An Overview' in J de Melo and A Panagariya (eds), *New Dimensions in Regional Integration* (Cambridge, Cambridge University Press, 1994).

Bhagwati, J and Hudec, R (eds), *Fair Trade and Harmonization: Prerequisites for Free Trade?* (Cambridge, MA, MIT Press, 1996).

Bhagwati, J et al (eds), 'The General Theory of Distortions and Welfare', in *Trade, Balance of Payments and Growth: Essays in Honour of CP Kindleberger* (Amsterdam North Holland, 1971).

Bhala, R, 'The Myth about Stare Decisis and International Trade Law (Part One of a Trilogy)' (1999) 14 *American University International Law Review* 845.

Bierzanek, R, 'Some Remarks on "Soft" International Law' (1988) 17 *Polish Yearbook of International Law.*

Birdsall, N and Lawrence, RZ, 'Deep Integration and Trade Agreements: Good for Developing Countries?' in I Kaul, I Grunberg and M Stern (eds), *Global Public Goods: International Cooperation in the 21st Century* (New York and Oxford, Oxford University Press, 1999).

Blank, A and Marceau, G, 'The History of the Public Procurement Negotiations since 1945' in SJ Evenett and B Hoekman (eds), *The WTO and Public Procurement* (Cheltenham, Edward Elgar, 2006).

Bork, RH, *The Antitrust Paradox: A Policy at War with Itself* (New York, Basic Books, 1978).

Bourgeois, JHJ, 'The EEA Rules on Competition: Odd Man Out or Model for Multilateral Rules?' in JHJ Bourgeois, K Dawar and SJ Evenett, *A Comparative Analysis of Selected Provisions in Free Trade Agreements. A Report for the European Commission* (2007).

Brenton, J, Dawar, K and Kuntze, JC, 'Issues and Tensions in Government Procurement of "Green Innovation": A Cross-Country Study', CTEI Working Paper, Graduate Institute, Geneva (2011).

Brou, D and Ruta, M, 'A Commitment Theory of Subsidy Agreements', Staff Working Paper ERSD-2012-15, World Trade Organization, Economic Research and Statistics Division (September 2012).

Brummer, C, 'How International Financial Law Works (and How it Doesn't)' (2011) 99 *Georgetown Law Journal* 257.

Brunel, C and Hufbauer, GC, 'Money for the Auto Industry: Consistent with WTO Rules?', Petersen Institute for International Economics (February 2009).

Brunnermeier, M, 'Deciphering the Liquidity and Credit Crunch 2007–2008' (2009) 23 *Journal of Economic Perspectives.*

Brunnermeier, MK and Pederson, LH, 'Market Liquidity and Funding Liquidity', (10 December 2008) *Review of Financial Studies*, Advance Access.

Brusick, P et al (eds), *Competition Provisions in Regional Trade Agreements: How to Assure Development Gains* (UNCTAD, Geneva, 2005).

Busch, ML, 'Democracy, Consultation, and the Paneling of Disputes under GATT' (2000) 44 *Journal of Conflict Resolution* 425.

Busch, ML and Reinhardt, E, 'Bargaining in the Shadow of the Law: Early Settlement in GATT/WTO Disputes' (2000) 24(1) *Fordham International Law Journal.*

Caprio, G Jr and Klingebiel, D, 'Bank Insolvency: Bad Luck, Bad Policy, or Bad Banking?', *Annual World Bank Conference on Development Economics, 1996* (Washington, DC, The World Bank, 1997).

Chauhan, AK, Director General Competition Commission of India, 'Public Procurement System: Competition Issues', presentation at the Conference of National Productivity Council, Bhubaneswar, 5 February 2013.

Carmody, C, 'WTO Rules as Collective' (2006) 17 *European Journal of International Law.*

Calvani, T, 'What Is the Objective of Antitrust?', in Calvani and Siegfried (eds), *Economic Analysis and Antitrust Law*, 2nd edn (Boston, MA, Little, Brown & Co, 1988).

Carlton, DW and Perloff, JM, *Modern Industrial Organization* (Reading, MA, Addison-Wesley, 2004).

Cass, DZ, *The Constitutionalization of the World Trade Organization: Legitimacy, Democracy, and Community in the International Trading System* (Oxford, Oxford University Press, 2005).

Cecchini, P, 'The European Challenge: The Benefits of a Single Market' in S Arrowsmith, J Linarelli and D Wallace, *Regulating Public Procurement: National and International Perspectives* (London, Kluwer Law International, 2000).

Cimino, C, Hufbauer, GC and Schott, JJ, 'A Proposed Code to Discipline Local Content Requirements', Peterson Institute for International Economics no PB14-6 (February 2014).

Clarke, JL and Evenett, SJ, 'A Multilateral Framework for Competition Policy?' in SJ Evenett et al (eds), *The Singapore Issues and The World Trading System: The Road to Cancun and Beyond.*

Cook, P, 'Competition and its Regulation: Key Issues', Centre on Regulation and Competition Working Paper Series no 2, University of Manchester (October 2001).

Condon, BJ, 'Climate Change and Unresolved Issues in WTO Law' (2009) 12 *Journal of International Economic Law* 895.

Congleton, RD, 'On the Political Economy of the Financial Crisis and Bailout of 2008–2009' (2009) 140 *Public Choice* 300.

Conway, G, *Limits of Legal Reasoning and the European Court of Justice* (Cambridge, Cambridge University Press, 2012).

Corvaglia, MA and Maschner, L, 'The Complementarity of Soft and Hard Law in Public Procurement: Between Harmonization and Resilience' NCCR Working Paper no 2013/10.

Cottier, T, Delimatsis, P and Diebold, NF, 'Article XIV GATS: General Exceptions' in R Wolfrum, P-T Stoll and C Feinäugle (eds), *Max Planck Commentaries on World Trade Law, WTO—Trade in Services* (Leiden and Boston, MA, Martinus Nijhoff, 2008) vol 6, 287–328.

Crawford, J, 'Third Report on State Responsibility', A/CN4/507, *Yearbook of the International Law Commission. Documents of the Fifty-Second Session* (2000).

Damro, C, 'Multilateral Competition Policy and Transatlantic Compromise' (2004) 9(2) *European Foreign Affairs Review*.

Davey, WJ, 'Reforming WTO Dispute Settlement', University of Illinois, Public Law & Legal Theory Research Paper no 04-01 (2004), available at www.dx.doi.org/10.2139/ssrn.495386.

Davey, WJ and Porges, A, 'Performance of the System I: Consultations and Deterrence' (1998) 32 *International Law* 695.

Davis, CL, *Why Adjudicate? Enforcing Trade Rules in the WTO* (Princeton, NJ, Princeton University Press, 2012).

Davis, C and Shirato, Y, 'Firms, Governments, and WTO Adjudication: Japan's Selection of WTO Disputes' (2007) 59 *World Politics* 274.

Dawar, K, 'Establishing Consumers as Equivalent Players in Competition Policy' in P Cook (ed), *Competitive Advantage and Competition Policy in Developing Countries* (Cheltenham, Edward Elgar, 2005).

Dawar, K, 'Disconnection Clauses: An Inevitable Symptom of Regionalism?' (2010) available at: http://www.ssrn.com/link/SIEL-2010-Barcelona-Conference.html.

Dawar, K, 'The Proposed "Buy European" Procurement Regulation: An Analysis', Global Trade Alert 11th Report (2012) www.globaltradealert.org.

Dawar, K, 'The WTO Government Procurement Agreement: The Most-Favoured Nation Principle, the GATS and Regionalism' (2015) 42 *Legal Issues of Economic Integration* 257.

Delimatsis, P, 'Of Bailouts and Rescue Measures: Subsidies in Financial Services', NCCR Working Paper no 2012/24 (April 2012).

Devuyst, Y, 'Toward a Multilateral Competition Policy Regime?' [2000] *Global Governance*, 1 July.

De Paula, LF and Sobreira, R, 'The 2008 Financial Crisis and Banking Regulation in Brazil', UFRGS, artigo aceito para Apresentação no III Encontro da Associação Keynesiana Brasileira de 11 a 13 de Agosto 2010.

Diamond, D and Rajan, R, 'The Credit Crisis: Conjectures and Causes and Remedies' (2009) 99 *American Economic Review* 606.

Doleys, TJ, 'Managing State Aid in Times of Crisis: The Role of the European Commission', ECPR Fifth Pan-European Conference on EU Politics, Porto, Portugal 2010.

Dunoff, JL, 'Linking International Markets and Global Justice' (2009) 107 *Michigan Law Review* 1039.

Dworkin, R, *Law's Empire* (Cambridge, MA, Harvard University Press, 1986).

Edler, J and Georghiou, L, 'Public Procurement and Innovation—Resurrecting the Demand Side' (2007) 36 *Research Policy*.

Ehlermann, C-D, 'State Aid Control in the EU: Success or Failure?' (1994) 18(4) *Fordham International Law Journal*.

Ehlermann, C-D and Goyette, M, 'The Interface between EU State Aid Control and the WTO Disciplines on Subsidies' (2006) 4 *European State Aid Quarterly*.

Eubanks, Eubanks, WW, 'The European Union's Response to the 2007–2009 Financial Crisis', Congressional Service Report, 7-5700 R41367 (2010).

European Commission, 'Competition Policy in the New Trade Order Strengthening International Cooperation and Rules', Report of the Group of Experts (July 1995).

European Commission, DG Internal Market Public Procurement Indicators (2008).

European Commission, 'Proposal for a Regulation of the European Parliament and of the Council on the Access of Third-Country Goods and Services to the Union's Internal Market in Public Procurement and Procedures Supporting Negotiations on Access of Union Goods and Services to the Public Procurement Markets of Third Countries', 2012/060 (COD).

European Commission, 'Green Paper on the Modernisation of EU Public Procurement Policy: Towards a More Efficient European Procurement Market' (2011).

Evans, D, et al, 'Assessing Regional Trade Agreements with Developing Countries: Shallow and Deep Integration, Trade, Productivity, and Economic Performance', University of Sussex, mimeo (2006).

Evenett, SJ, 'Soft Law and International Economic Regulation: The Case of Mergers and Acquisitions', Oxford University, GEP Newsletter (2005).

Evenett, SJ, 'What Can We Really Learn from the Competition Provisions of Regional Trade Agreements?' (2005).

Evenett, SJ, 'What Is the Relationship between Competition Law and Policy and Economic Development?', University of Oxford (2005).

Evenett, SJ, 'Would Enforcing Competition Law Compromise Industry Policy Objectives?', University of Oxford (2005).

Evenett, SJ (ed), 'Broken Promises: A G20 Summit Report by Global Trade Alert' (Global Trade Alert, September 2009), www.globaltradealert.org/gta-analysis/broken-promisesg20-summit-report-global-trade-alert.

Evenett, SJ and Hoekman, BM, 'Public Procurement of Services and Multilateral Disciplines' in P Sauvé and R Stern (eds), *GATS 2000: New Directions in Services Trade Liberalization* (Washington, DC, Brookings Institution Press, 2000) ch 6.

Evenett, SJ and Hoekman, BM (eds), *The WTO and Public Procurement* (Cheltenham, Edward Elgar, 2006).

Evenett, SJ and Hoekman B.M. (eds), *Economic Development and Multilateral Trade Cooperation* (Basingstoke, Palgrave Macmillan and The World Bank, 2006).

SJ, Evenett and J, Whalley, 'The G20 and Green Protectionism: Will We Pay the Price at Copenhagen?', Centre for International Governance Innovation, Policy Brief 14 (April 2009).

Financial Crisis Inquiry Commission, 'The Financial Crisis Inquiry Report: Final Report of the National Commission on the Causes of the Financial and Economic Crisis in the United States' (New York, Public Affairs, 2011) 339.

Finger, JM, 'The WTO's Special Burden on Less Developed Countries' (2000) 19(3) *Cato Journal.*

Fitzmaurice, G, 'The Foundations of the Authority of International Law and the Problem of Enforcement' (1956) 19 *Maryland Law Review.*

Foer, AA, 'American Idealism: Level Playing Fields' 96 (1996) *Business & Society Review* 27.

Foer, AA, 'The Political-Economic Nature of Antitrust' (1983) 27 *St Louis University Law Journal.*

Footer, M, 'International Developments: GATT: Developments in Government Procurement Procedures and Practices' (1993) 6 *Public Procurement Law Review* CS 193–204.

Fox, E, 'Antitrust, Competitiveness, and the World Arena: Efficiencies and Failing Firms in Perspective' (1996) 64 *Antitrust Law Journal* 725.

Fox, EM, 'Towards World Antitrust and Market Access' (1997) 91(1) *American Journal of International Law.*

Franck, TM, *Fairness in International Law and Institutions* (Oxford, Clarendon Press, 1995).

Gal, M, 'Reality Bites (or Bits): The Political Economy of Antitrust Enforcement', in Hawk (ed), *International Antitrust Law and Policy* (Huntington, NY, Juris Publishing, 2001).

Galbraith, JK, *The Great Crash 1929* (Mariner Books, 1954).

Galbraith, JK, *A Short History of Financial Euphoria* (Whittle Books in association with Viking, 1993).

Gamberoni, E and Newfarmer, R, 'Trade Protection: Incipient but Worrisome Trends' in R Baldwin and S Evenett (eds), *The Collapse of Global Trade, Murky Protectionism, and the Crisis* (Centre for Economic Policy Research, 2009).

Gari, G, 'Capital Controls, GATS Disciplines and the Need for a More Coherent Global Economic Governance Structure', copy on file with author.

Georghiou, L, 'Demanding Innovation Lead Markets, Public Procurement and Innovation', NESTA, Provocation 02 (2007).

Geradin, D, 'Competition Law and Regional Economic Integration', World Bank Working Paper no 35 (2004).

Geroski, PA, 'Is Competition Policy Worth It?', Chairman, UK Competition Commission (September 2004).

Giddings, FH, *Principles of Sociology* (London, Macmillan, 1896).

Guzman, AT and Meyer, TL, 'International Soft Law' (2010) 2(1) *Journal of Legal Analysis.*

Graells, AS, 'Competition and the Public Buyer: Towards a More Competition-Oriented Procurement System', Cantoblanco, Madrid (August 2009).

Graells, AS, 'Distortions of Competition Generated by the Public (Power) Buyer: A Perceived Gap in EC Competition Law and Proposals to Bridge It', University of Oxford Centre for Competition Law and Policy, Working Paper, Centre for Competition Law and Policy (L) 23 (2009).

Graells, AS, 'Competition Law against Public Restraints in the Public Procurement Field: Importing Competition Considerations into the EU Public Procurement Directives', Public Procurement: Global Revolution IV—Conference, University of Nottingham, 2010.

Graells, AS, *Public Procurement and the EU Competition Rules* (Oxford, Hart Publishing, 2011).

Graells, AS, 'Public Procurement and State Aid: Reopening the Debate?' (2012) available at: http://ssrn.com/abstract=2037768.

Graells, AS, 'Public Procurement: A 2014 Updated Overview of EU and National Case Law' (2014) available at: http://ssrn.com/abstract=1968371.

Graells, AS and Herrera Anchustegui, I, 'Revisiting the Concept of Undertaking from a Public Procurement Law Perspective—A Discussion on EasyPay and Finance Engineering' (26 November 2015), available at https://ssrn.com/abstract=2695742.

Graham, E and Richardson, JD, *Global Competition Policies: An Agenda* (Washington, DC, Institute for International Economics, 1997).

Gourevitch, P, *Politics in Hard Times: Comparative Responses to International Economic Crises* (Ithaca, NY, Cornell University Press, 1986).

Grazzini, T, 'The Legal Nature of WTO Obligations and the Consequences of their Violation' (2006) 17(4) *European Journal of International Law.*

Guba, EG, *The Paradigm Dialog* (Newbury Park, CA, Sage, 1990).

Guilherme S Medrado, R, 'Renegotiating Remedies in the WTO: A Multilateral Approach' (2004) 22(2) *Wisconsin International Law Journal.*

Guzman, AT and Pauwelyn, J, *International Trade Law* (New York, Wolters Kluwer, 2009).

Cosma, HA and Whish, R, 'Soft Law in the Field of EU Competition Policy' (2003) 14 *European Business Law Review.*

Hall, M, 'Competition Law and the Credit Crunch: Do the Usual State Aid Rules Still Apply?', *PLC Magazine*, 22 January 2009.

Halle, M and Wolfe, R, 'A New Approach to Transparency and Accountability in the WTO', issue brief, *ENTWINED*, 16 September 2010.

Hardstaff, P and Rice, T, 'More Market Access for Less Policy Space—A Bad Deal for Development', joint policy briefing by the World Development Movement and ActionAid (May 2003).

Havighurst, CC, 'A Comment—The Antitrust Challenge to Professionalism' (1981) 41 *Maryland Law Review* 30.

Heise, M, 'The Importance of Being Empirical' (1999) 26 *Pepperdine Law Review*.

Henkin, L, *How Nations Behave: Law and Foreign Policy* (New York, Columbia University Press, 1979).

Herbst, H, 'How Long Can Germany Keep Auto Jobs?', *Bloomberg Businessweek*, 28 September 2009, retrieved from http://www.businessweek.com.

Hoekman, B, 'Competition Policy and Preferential Trade Agreements', Working Paper no 37131, World Bank (2002).

Hoekman, B, 'Proposals for Reforming the WTO World Bank', Policy Research Working Paper 5525 (2011).

Hoekman, B, 'Supply Chains, Mega-Regionals and Multilateralism: A Road Map for the WTO', EUI Working Paper RSCAS 2014/27 (2014).

Hoekman, B and Holmes, P, 'Competition Policy, Developing Countries and the WTO', *The World Economy*, 1999.

Hoekman, B and Mavroidis, P (eds), *Law and Policy in Public Purchasing: The WTO Agreement on Public Procurement* (Ann Arbor, University of Michigan Press, 1997).

Hoekman, BM and Mavroidis, PC, 'Enforcing WTO Commitments: Dispute Settlement and Developing Countries—Something Happened on the Way to Heaven', CEPR discussion paper draft (26 June 2000).

Hoekman, B and Mavroidis, P, 'Economic Development, Competition Policy and the WTO' (2003) 37(1) *Journal of World Trade*.

Hoekman, BM and Saggi, K, 'International Cooperation on Domestic Policies: Lessons from the WTO Competition Policy Debate' in SJ Evenett and BM Hoekman (eds), *Economic Development and Multilateral Trade Cooperation* (Basingstoke, Palgrave Macmillan and The World Bank, 2006).

Holmes, P, 'Trade, Competition and the WTO' in BM Hoekman, A Mattoo and P English (eds), *Development, Trade and the WTO: A Handbook* (Washington, DC, The World Bank, 2002).

Holmes, P, Müller, H, Papadopoulos, A and Sydorak, A, 'A Taxonomy of International Competition Cooperation Provisions', CEPR (2006).

Horlick, GN and Clarke, PA, 'WTO Subsidies Discipline During and After the Crisis' (2010) 13(3) *Journal of International Economic Law*.

Horn, H and Mavroidis, PC, 'Economic and Legal Aspects of the Most-Favored-Nation Clause' (2001) 17 *European Journal of Political Economy*.

Horn, H, Mavroidis, PC and Sapir, A, 'Beyond the WTO? An Anatomy of EU and US Preferential Trade Agreements', 28 May 2009.

Horton, TJ, 'The Coming Extinction of Homo Economicus and the Eclipse of the Chicago School of Antitrust: Applying Evolutionary Biology to Structural and Behavioral Antitrust Analyses' (2011) 42(3) *Loyola University Chicago Law Journal*.

Hovenkamp, H, 'Distributive Justice and the Antitrust Laws' (1982) 51 *George Washington Law Review* 1.

Howe, KR, 'Against the Quantitative–Qualitative Incompatibility Thesis (or Dogmas Die Hard)' (1988) 17 *Educational Researcher*.

Howse, R, 'The Legitimacy of the World Trade Organization' in J-M Coicaud and V Heiskanen (eds), *The Legitimacy of International Organizations* (New York, United Nations University Press, 2001).

Howse, R, 'Legitimacy through "Higher Law"? Why Constitutionalizing the WTO is a Step Too Far', in T Cottier, PC Mavroidis and P Blatter (eds), *The Role of the Judge: Lessons for the WTO* (Bern, The World Trade Forum, 2002) vol 4.

Howse, R, 'Enhancing WTO Legitimacy: Constitutionalization or Global Subsidiarity?' in M Verweij and T Josling (eds), *Deliberately Democratizing Multilateral Organization*, Special Issue of *Governance* (2003).

Howse, R, 'Membership and its Privileges: The WTO, Civil Society, and the *Amicus* Brief Controversy' (2003) 9 *European Law Journal*.

Howse, R, 'Climate Mitigation Subsidies and the WTO Legal Framework: A Policy Analysis', IISD (May 2010).

Howse, R, 'Global Crises and International Economic Law', BIICL Conference, 19 October 2012.

Hudec, RE, '"Transcending the Ostensible." Some Reflections on the Nature of Litigation Between Governments' (1987) 72 *Minnesota Law Review*.

Hudec, RE, *Enforcing International Trade Law: The Evolution of the Modern GATT Legal System* (Salem, NH, Butterworth Legal Publishers, 1993) 360.

Hudec, RE, 'The Role of the GATT Secretariat in the Evolution of the WTO Dispute Settlement Procedure' (reprinted from J Bhagwati and M Hirsch (eds), *The Uruguay Round and Beyond: Essays in Honour of Arthur Dunkel* (Berlin, Springer-Verlag, 1998)).

Hudec, RE, 'Broadening the Scope of Remedies in WTO Dispute Settlement', originally published in F Weiss and J Wiers (eds), *Improving WTO Dispute Settlement Procedures* (London, Cameron May, 2000).

Hufbauer, GC and Schott, JJ, 'Buy American: Bad for Jobs, Worse for Reputation', Policy Brief Number PB09-2, Petersmann Institute (February 2009).

Hufbauer, GC, Shelton Erb, J and Starr, HP, ‚The GATT Codes and the Unconditional Most Favored-Nation Principle' (1980) 12 *Law & Policy in International Business* 59.

Hunja, R, 'Obstacles to Public Procurement Reform in Developing Countries' in S Arrowsmith and M Trybus (eds), *Public Procurement: The Continuing Revolution* (Dordrecht, Kluwer Law International, 2003).

Hunja, R, 'The UNCITRAL Model Law on Procurement of Goods, Construction and Services and its Impact on Procurement Reform' in S Arrowsmith (ed), *Public Procurement: Global Revolution*.

Ikenson, DJ, 'Lasting Implications of the General Motors Bailout', Subcommittee on Regulatory Affairs, Stimulus Oversight and Government Spending Committee on Oversight and Government Reform, United States House of Representatives, 22 June 2011.

International Competition Network, 'Report on Interface between Competition Policy and other Public Policies', prepared by the Turkish Competition Authority, presented at the 9th ICN Annual Conference Istanbul, Turkey.

Institute for International Finance, 'Capital Flows to Emerging Market Economies', 27 January 2009.

IMF Country Report, 'Cyprus: First Review under the Extended Arrangement under the Extended Fund Facility and Request for Modifcation of Performance Criteria', no 13/293 (September 2013).

Janow, ME, 'What Role for Competition Policy in the WTO?' in A Appleton (ed), *The Next Trade Round* (Alphen aan den Rijn, Kluwer, 2003).

Jackson, J, *The Jurisprudence of GATT and the WTO: Insights on Treaty Law and Economic Relations* (Cambridge, Cambridge University Press, 2000).

Jackson, JH, *Sovereignty and the Fundamental Logic of International Law* (Cambridge, Cambridge University Press, 2006).

Jackson, JH, 'The Future Scope of WTO—Issues as Seen in the Sutherland Report' (2006) www.rieti.go.jp/en/events/bbl/06032301.html.

Jenny, F, 'Competition Law and Policy: Achievements and Failures from an Economic Perspective', in Hope (ed), *Competition Policy Analysis* (London, Routledge, 2000).

Jenny, F, 'Dropping Competition Policy from the Trade Agenda after Cancun Would Send Wrong Signal', *Financial Times*, 23 September 2003.

Jenny, F, 'Cartels and Collusions in Developing Countries: Submission by France', presentation to the Fifth UN Review Conference (2005).

Jayasuriya, K, 'Globalization, Law, and the Transformation of Sovereignty: The Emergence of Global Regulatory Governance' (1999) 6 *Indian Journal of Global Legal Studies.*

Jiang, L, 'Developing Multilateral Rules of Government Procurement: The Value of Soft Law' in S Arrowsmith and R Anderson (eds), *The WTO Regime on Government Procurement: Challenge and Reform* (Cambridge, Cambridge University Press, 2011).

Jones, JM, *Tariff Retaliation: Repercussions of the Hawley–Smoot Bill* (Philadelphia, University of Pennsylvania Press, 1934).

Johnson, RB and Onwuegbuzie, AJ, 'Mixed Methods Research: A Research Paradigm Whose Time Has Come' (2004) 33(7) *Educational Researcher.*

Kannan, KP, 'National Policy Responses to the Financial and Economic Crisis: The Case of India', Centre for Development Studies, Trivandrum, ILO Regional Office for Asia and the Pacific, Bangkok (2008). www.ilo.org/wcmsp5/groups/public/---asia/---ro-bangkok/documents/meetingdocument/wcms_101591.pdf.

Kattel, R and Lember, V, Public Procurement as an Industrial Policy Tool: An Option for Developing Countries? (2010) 10(3) *Journal of Public Procurement.*

Kennedy, KC, *Competition Law and the World Trade Organisation: The Limits of Multilateralism* (London: Sweet & Maxwell, 2001).

Keohane, RO, 'Sovereignty, Interdependence, and International Institutions', in LB Miller and MJ Smith (eds), *Ideas and Ideals: Essays in Politics in Honor of Stanley Hoffman* (1993).

Klabbers, J, 'Reflections on Soft International Law in a Privatized World', downloaded from: www.helsinki.fi/eci/Publications/Klabbers/JKSoft_law_and_public.pdf (6 November 2012).

Koskenniemi, M, 'Solidarity Measures: State Responsibility as a New International Order' (2001) 72 *British Yearbook of International Law* 337.

Koskenniemi, M, 'International Law as Therapy: Reading the Health of Nations' (2005) 16(2) *European Journal of International Law.*

Kolasky, W and Dick, A, 'The Merger Guidelines and the Integration of Efficiencies into Antitrust Review of Horizontal Mergers', paper presented at the 20th Anniversary of the 1982 Merger Guidelines: The Contribution of the Merger Guidelines to the Evolution of Antitrust Doctrine (2002).

Kovacic, WE, 'The Future of US Competition Policy', *Antitrust Source*, September 2004.

Krugman, PR, 'Is Free Trade Passé?' (1987) 1(2) *Journal of Economic Perspectives.*

Kuhn, T, *The Structure of Scientific Revolutions*, 2nd edn (Chicago, University of Chicago Press, 1970).

Kwa, A, 'Power Politics in the WTO', *Focus on the Global South* (2003).

Laffont, J-J and Tirole, J, *A Theory of Incentives in Procurement and Regulation* (London, MIT Press, 1994).

Lande, R, 'Wealth Transfers as the Original and Primary of Antitrust: The Efficiency Interpretation Challenged' (1982) 34 *Hastings Law Journal* 65.

Lauterpacht, H, *The Function of Law in the International Community* (Oxford, Clarendon Press, 1933).

Leroux, EH, 'Trade in Financial Services under the World Trade Organization' (2002) 36(3) *Journal of World Trade.*

Levenstein, MC and Suslow, VY, 'What Determines Cartel Success?' (2006) 44(1) *Journal of Economic Literature.*

Linarelli, J, 'The Limited Case for Permitting SME Procurement Preferences in the Agreement on Public procurement' in S Arrowsmith and R Anderson (eds), *The WTO Regime on Public Procurement: Challenge and Reform* (Cambridge, Cambridge University Press, 2011).

Linarelli, J, 'The WTO Agreement on Government Procurement and the UNCITRAL Model Procurement Law: A View from Outside the Region' (2006) 1 *Asian Journal of WTO & International Health Law and Policy.*

Lipimile, GK, 'Competition as a Stimulus for Enterprise Development' in *Competition, Competitiveness and Development: Lessons From Developing Countries* (UNCTAD, 2004).

Lipson, C, 'Why Are Some International Agreements Formal?' (1991) 45 *International Organization* 501.

Liu, LS, 'In Fairness We Trust?—Why Fostering Competition Law and Policy Ain't Easy in Asia', available at: http://ssrn.com/abstract=610822 (19 October 2004).

Lyons, B, 'Competition Policy, Bailouts and the Economic Crisis', CCP Working Paper 09-2004.

Lyons, B, 'Competition Concerns means Lloyds Should Be Required to Float HBOS Following Failure to Divest Branches to the Coop', downloaded from: http://competitionpolicy.wordpress.com/2013/04/25/competition-concerns-mean-lloyds-should-be-required-to-float-hbos-following-failure-to-divest-branches-to-the-co-op/.

Macey, JR, 'The "Demand" for International Regulatory Cooperation: A Public-Choice Perspective' in GA Bermann, M Herden and PL Lindseth (eds), *Transatlantic Regulatory Cooperation Legal Problems and Political Prospects* (Oxford, Oxford University Press, 2000).

Madsen, JB, 'Trade Barriers and the Collapse of the World Trading System during the Great Depression' (2001) 67(4) *Southern Economic Journal*.

Marsden, P, *A Competition Policy for the WTO* (London, Cameron May, 2003).

Marsden, P and Kokkoris, I, 'The Role of Competition and State Aid Policy in Financial and Monetary Law' (2010) 13(3) *Journal of International Economic Law*.

Mathis, JH, *Regional Trade Agreements in the GATT* (The Hague, Asser Press, 2002).

Matsushita, M, 'International Cooperation in the Enforcement of Competition Policy' (2002) 1 *Washington University Global Studies Law Review* 463.

Matsushita, M, 'Basic Principles of the WTO and the Role of Competition Policy' (2004) 3(2) *Washington University Global Studies Law Review*.

Mattoo, A, 'The Public Procurement Agreement: Implications of Economic Theory' (1996) 19 *World Economy* 695.

Maurer, H and Grussenmeyer, P, 'Financial Assistance Measures in the Euro Area from 2008 to 2013: Statistical Framework and Fiscal Impact', European Central Bank Statistics Paper Series no 7 (2015) 9. www.ecb.europa.eu/pub/pdf/scpsps/ecbsp7.en.pdf.

Mavroidis, PC, 'Dispute Settlement Procedures and Mechanisms' (1999) 16 *Arizona Journal of International and Comparative Law*.

Mavroidis, PC, 'Remedies in the WTO Legal System: Between a Rock and a Hard Place' (2000) 11 *European Journal of International Law*.

Mavroidis, PC and Van Siclen, S, 'The Application of the GATT/WTO Dispute Resolution System to Competition Issues' (1997) 31 *Journal of World Trade*.

McCrudden, C, 'Buying Social Justice: Equality and Public Procurement' (2007) 60(1) *Current Legal Problems*.

McCrudden, C, *Buying Social Justice: Equality, Government Procurement, and Legal Change* (Oxford and New York, Oxford University Press, 2007).

Mitchell, AD, 'Good Faith in WTO Dispute Settlement' (2006) 7 *Melbourne Journal of International Law*.

Motta, M, *Competition Policy, Theory and Practice* (Cambridge, Cambridge University Press, 2004).

Mukherjee, S, 'India's Response to Financial Crisis', Economics Discussion 2012, available at: www.economicsdiscussion.net/india/financial-crisis/indias-response-to-financial-crisis/11093.

Munro, C, 'Competition Law and Government Procurement: Two Sides of the Same Coin?' (2006) 6 *Public Procurement Law Review*.

Muris, T, 'The Interface of Competition and Consumer Protection', paper presented at Fordham Corporate Law Institute's 29th Annual Conference on International Antitrust Law and Policy, New York (31 October 2002).

Ngangjoh, YH and Rios-Herran, R, 'WTO Dispute Settlement System and the Issue of Compliance: Multilateralizing the Enforcement Mechanism' (2004) 1(3) *Manchester Journal of International Economic Law*.

O'Keefe, TA, *Latin American and Caribbean Trade Agreements* (Leiden, Martinus Nijhoff, 2009).

Olsen, W, 'Triangulation in Social Research. Qualitative and Quantitative Studies Can Really Be Mixed' in M Holborn Ormskirk (ed), *Developments in Sociology* (Ormskirk, Causeway Press, 2004).

Olson, H, 'Quantitative versus Qualitative Research. The Wrong Question', retrieved from: www.ualberta.ca/dept/slis/cais/olson.htm (June 2014).

Olykke, GS, 'The Legal Basis Which Will (Probably) Never Be Used: Enforcement of State Aid Law in a Public Procurement Context' (2011) 3(1) *European State Aid Law Quarterly*.

Onwuegbuzie, AJ and Teddlie, C, 'A Framework for Analysing Data in Mixed Methods Research' in A Tashakkori and C Teddlie (eds), *Handbook of Mixed Methods in Social and Behavioral Research* (Thousand Oaks, CA, Sage, 2003).

OECD, 'Council Recommendation Concerning Co-operation between Member States on Anticompetitive Practices Affecting International Trade' (1995).

OECD, 'Competition Policy and Efficiency Claims in Horizontal Agreements' (1996), available at: www.oecd.org/dataoecd/1/4/2379526.pdf.

OECD, 'Competition Policy and Environment' (1996), available at: www.oecd.org/dataoecd/34/19/1920007.pdf.

OECD, 'Background Report on the Role of Competition Policy in Regulatory Reform' (2000), available at: www.oecd.org/dataoecd/46/23/32407554.pdf.

OECD, 'Competition Law and Policy Developments in Brazil' (2000) 2(3) *OECD Journal of Competition Law and Policy*.

OECD, *The Size of Public Procurement Markets* (OECD, Paris, 2002).

OECD, 'Competition Law and Policy in Brazil', OECD Policy Brief (2005).

OECD, 'Public Procurement: The Role of Competition Authorities in Promoting Competition', DAF/COMP(2007)34 (2007).

OECD, 'Principles for Enhancing Integrity in Public Procurement' (June 2014), available at: www.oecd.org/gov/ethics/oecdprinciplesforenhancingintegrity inpublicprocurement.htm.

Ortino, F, *Basic Legal Instruments for the Liberalisation of Trade: A Comparative Analysis of EC and WTO Law* (Oxford, Hart Publishing, 2004).

Ostry, JD et al, 'Capital Inflows: The Role of Controls', IMF Staff Position Note 10/04 (February 2010).

Overseas Development Institute, 'Policy Space: Are WTO Rules Preventing Development?', ODI Policy Brief 14 (2007).

Palmeter, D and Mavroidis, PC, 'The WTO Legal System: Sources of Law' (1998) 92 *American Journal of International Law*.

Pauwelyn, J, 'Enforcement and Countermeasures in the WTO: Rules are Rules—Towards a More Collective Approach' (2000) 94 *American Journal of International Law*.

Pauwelyn, J, 'The Nature of WTO Obligations', Jean Monnet Working Paper no 1/02, NYU School of Law, Jean Monnet Centre (2002).

Pauwelyn, J, 'A Typology of Multilateral Treaty Obligations: Are WTO Obligations Bilateral or Collective in Nature?' (2003) 14 *European Journal of International Law*.

Pauwelyn, J, 'The Formation Process of WTO (Soft) Norms: WTO Reaction to the Financial Crisis and Transparency in WTO Dispute Settlement', Graduate Institute, Geneva, first draft (13 March 2009).

Pauwelyn, JP (with A Berman), 'Emergency Action by the WTO Director-General: Global Administrative Law and the WTO's Initial Response to the 2008–09 Financial Crisis' (2009) 6 *International Organizations Law Review* 499.

Pauwelyn, J, Wessel, R and Wouters, J (eds), *Informal International Lawmaking* (Oxford, Oxford University Press, 2012).

Pelkmans, J, 'The Institutional Economics of European Integration' in M Cappelletti, M Seccombe and J Weiler (eds), *Integration Through Law: Europe and the American Federal Experience* (New York, Walter de Gruyter, 1986).

Perreau-Saussine, A, 'The Character of Customary Law: An Introduction' in A Perreau-Saussine and J Murphy (eds), *The Nature of Customary Law: Philosophical, Historical and Legal Perspectives* (Cambridge, Cambridge University Press, 2009).

Pervez, F, 'Countersuits and the Politics of Abandoned WTO Trade Disputes', Political Economy of International Organizations 2016 Annual Meeting Paper. Available at: https://ssrn.com/abstract=2452620.

Petersmann, E-U, 'International Competition Policies: Constitutional Functions of WTO "Linking Principles" for Trade and Competition' (1999–2000) 34 *New England Law Review*.

Pezzutti, D and Teixeira, R, 'The Brazilian Experience of Using Public Procurement Policies to Promote the Development of Micro and Small Enterprises from the Legal Point of View', available at: www.ippa.org/IPPC4/Proceedings/13ProcurementPreferences/Paper13-3.pdf (June 2014).

Pitofsky R, 'Policy Objectives of Competition Law and Enforcement', EUI Conference Proceedings, 2003. Available at: www.eui.eu/RSCAS/Research/Competition/2003/200306COMP-Pitofsky.pdf (June 2014).

Pitofsky, R, 'The Political Content of Antitrust' (1979) 127 *University of Pennsylvania Law Review*, available at: www.eui.eu/RSCAS/Research/Competition/2003/200306COMP-PitofskyAppendix.pdf (June 2014).

Popper, K, *The Logic of Scientific Discovery* (Basic Books, New York, 1959).

Posner, R, *Antitrust Law: An Economic Perspective* (Chicago, University of Chicago Press, 1978).

Qaqaya, H and Lipimile, G (eds), The Effects of Anti-Competitive Business Practices on Developing Countries and their Development Prospects (UNCTAD, Geneva, 2008).

Quigley, C, 'Review of the Temporary State Aid Rules Adopted in the Context of the Financial and Economic Crisis' [2012] *Journal of European Competition Law & Practice*, April.

Rasmussen, H, *On Law and Policy in the European Court of Justice* (Leiden, Martinus Nijhoff, 1986).

Raustiala, K, 'Rethinking the Sovereignty Debate in International Economic Law' (2003) 6 *Journal of International Economic Law*.

Raz, J, *The Authority of Law* (Oxford, Clarendon Press, 1979).

Reich, A, 'The New GATT Agreement on Government Procurement: The Pitfalls of Plurilateralism and Strict Reciprocity' (1997) 31 *Journal of World Trade* 125.

Reinhardt, E, 'Adjudication without Enforcement' (2001) 45(2) *Journal of Conflict Resolution*.

Reinhart, V, 'A Year of Living Dangerously: The Management of the Financial Crisis in 2008' (2011) 25 *Journal of Economic Perspectives* 71.

Reynolds, KM, 'Why Are So Many WTO Disputes Abandoned?', Working Paper 2007-05, American University, Department of Economics. Downloaded from http://w.american.edu/cas/economics/repec/amu/workingpapers/2007-05.pdf (7 October 2013).

Richardson, JD, 'Multilateralizing Conventions' in R. Lawrence (ed), *Brookings Trade Forum* (Washington, DC, Brookings Institution, 1998).

Rickard, SJ and Kono, DY, 'Think Globally, Buy Locally: International Agreements and Government Procurement', on file with author.

Ritholtz, B, *Bailout Nation: How Green and Easy Money Corrupted Wall Street and Shook the World Economy* (Hoboken, NJ, John Wiley, 2010).

Rodik, D, 'Industrial Policy for the Twenty-First Century', Working Paper Series rwp04-047, Harvard University, John F Kennedy School of Government (2004).

Rubini, L, 'Ain't Wastin' Time No More. Subsidies for Renewable Energy, the SCM Agreement, Policy Space and Law Reform' (2012) 15(2) *Journal of International Economic Law*.

Rubini, L, *The Definition of Subsidy and State Aid* (Oxford, Oxford University Press, 2009).

Ruddy, B, 'The Critical Success of the WTO: Trade Policies of the Current Economic Crisis' (2010) 13(2) *Journal of International Economic Law*.

Salerno, O, 'The Global Economic Crisis Sectoral Coverage. Automotive Industry: Trends and Reflections', Working Paper 278, International Labour Office, Geneva (2010).

Schiff, M, Winters, LA and Hoekman, B, *A World Bank Study on Regionalism—Trade Blocs* (1998).

Schiff, M, *Regional Integration and Development* (London, Oxford University Press, 2003).

Schott, J, 'The Automotive Industry' available at: www.dpc.senate.gov/hearings/.../schott-chapter.pdf (June 2014).

Schooner, S, 'Desiderata: Objectives for a System of Government Contract Law' (2002) 11 *Public Procurement Law Review.*

Schooner, S, 'Commercial Purchasing: The Chasm between the United States Government's Evolving Policy and Practice' in S Arrowsmith and M Trybus (eds), *Government Procurement: The Continuing Revolution* (London, Kluwer Law International, 2002) ch 8.

Schwartz, J, '"Justice" and other Non-Economic Goals of Antitrust' (1979) 127 *University of Pennsylvania Law Review.*

Schweitzer, H, 'Competition Law and Public Policy—Reconsidering an Uneasy Relationship: The Example of Art 81' (2007), available at: http://ssrn.com/abstract=1092883.

Seabrooke, L and Tsingou, E, 'Revolving Doors and Linked Ecologies in the World Economy: Policy Locations and the Practice of International Financial Reform', CSGR Working Paper no 260 (June 2009).

Semmelmann, C, *Social Policy Aspects in EC Competition Law* (Law and Society Association, Berlin, 2007.

Shingal, A, 'Services Procurement under the WTO's Agreement on Government Procurement: Whither Market Access?' (2011) *World Trade Review* 10(4).

Sieber, SD, 'The Integration of Fieldwork and Survey Methods' (1973) 73 *American Journal of Sociology.*

Simma, B, *From Bilateralism to Community Interest in International Law* (1994), available at: http://nijhoffonline.nl/book?id=er250_er250_217-384 (June 2014).

Slotboom, M, *Do Different Treaty Purposes Matter for Treaty Interpretation? A Comparison of WTO and EC Law* (London, Cameron May, 2005).

Smith, A, *An Inquiry into the Nature and Causes of the Wealth of Nations* (London, W Strahan and T Cadell, 1776).

Stefan, O, *Soft Law in Court. Competition Law, State Aid and the Court of Justice of the EU* (Alphen aan den Rijn, Kluwer Law, 2012).

Sykes, AO, 'The Economics of WTO Rules on Subsidies and Countervailing Measures', Working Paper no 186, Chicago University, John M Olin Law & Economics (2003).

Tamarisa, NT, 'Exchange and Capital Controls as Barriers to Trade', IMF Working Paper WP/98/81 (1998).

Tanzi, V and Schuknecht, L, *Public Spending in the 20th Century: A Global Perspective* (Cambridge, Cambridge University Press, 2000).

Tarullo, DK, 'Norms and Institutions in Global Competition Policy' (2000) 94(3) *American Journal of International Law.*

Third World Network, 'South Fights for "Policy Space"', UNCTAD XI, São Paulo, 12 June 2004.
Thrasher, RD and Gallagher, KP, '21st Century Trade Agreements: Implications for Long-Run Development Policy', Pardee Papers no 2 (September 2008).
Tinbergen, J, *Centralization and Decentralization in Economic Policy* (Amsterdam, 1954).
Tinbergen, J, *On the Theory of Economic Policy* (Amsterdam, North-Holland, 1952), retrieved from http://hdl.handle.net/1765/15884.
Tosics, N and Gaál, N, 'Government Procurement and State Aid Control—The Issue of Economic Advantage' (2007) 15 *EC Competition Policy Newsletter* 15.
Trachtman J (1999) 'The Domain of WTO Dispute Resolution' (1999) 40(2) *Harvard International Law Journal.*
Trebilcock, MJ, 'International Competition Law and Trade Policy' in GB Doern and S Wilks (eds), *Comparative Competition Policy* (Oxford, Clarendon Press, 1996).
Trebilcock, MJ and Howse, R, *The Regulation of International Trade* (New York, Routledge, 2005).
Trionfetti, F, 'Discriminatory Government Procurement and International Trade' (2000) 23 *World Economy.*
UNCITRAL Model Law on Procurement of Goods, Construction and Services (UNCITRAL, 1994).
UNCTAD, *The Basic Objectives and Main Provisions of Competition Laws and Policies* (UNCTAD, Geneva, 1995).
UNCTAD, 'Closer Multilateral Cooperation on Competition Policy: The Development Dimension', Consolidated Report on issues discussed during the Panama, Tunis, Hong Kong and Odessa Regional Post-Doha Seminars on Competition Policy held between 21 March and 26 April 2002 (15 May 2002).
UNCTAD, 'The Relationship Between Competition, Competitiveness and Development', UNCTAD Doc TD/B/COM.2/CLP30 (23 May 2002).
UNCTAD, 'The Relationship Between Competition and Industrial Policies in Promoting Economic Development', UNCTAD Doc TD/B/C.I/CLP/3 (2009).
UNCTAD, *World Investment Report 2008.*
United Kingdom Department of Trade and Industry Survey, Government Procurement Review, 1994.
United Kingdom Department of Trade and Industry, 'The Benefits from Competition: Some Illustrative UK Cases', DTI Economics Paper no 9. Available at: www.dti.gov.uk/Files/File13299.Pdf.
United Kingdom Office of Fair Trading, *Assessing the Impact of Public Sector Procurement on Competition. Vol 2—Case Studies* (OFT742b) (September 2004).
Vickers, J, 'Economics for Consumer Policy' (2004) 125 *Proceedings of the British Academy.*
Vickers, J, 'The Financial Crisis and Competition Policy: Some Economics' [2008] *Global Competition Policy* 1 (www.ucl.ac.uk/laws/jevons/docs/Vickers_Dec_08.pdf).

Vohra, KK, 'India's Response to the Global Financial Crisis and Current Issues in Deposit Insurance and Credit Guarantee Corporation', DICJ, Kyoto (18 February 2016).

Warnecke, S, 'The European Community and National Subsidy Policies' in S Warnecke (ed), *International Trade and Industrial Policies* (1978).

Weil, P, 'Towards Relative Normativity in International Law?' (1983) 77 *American Journal of International Law*.

Weiler, JHH, 'The State über alles: Demos, Telos and the German Maastricht Decision', in *Festschrift für Ulrich Everling* (Baden-Baden, Nomos, 1995) vol II.

Weiler, JHH, 'Federalism and Constitutionalism. Europe's Sonderweg', downloaded from: https://infoeuropa.eurocid.pt/files/database/000036001-000037000/000036583.pdf (June 2014).

Weiler, JHH, 'The Geology of International Law' (2004) *Zeitschrift für ausländisches öffentliches Recht und Völkerrecht*, 64(3) 547–562.

Weishaar, SE, *Cartels, Competition and Public Procurement* (Cheltenham, Edward Elgar, 2013).

White, LJ, 'The Role of Competition Policy in the Promotion of Economic Growth' New York University Law and Economics Working Paper 132 (2008).

Wilkes, M, 'Feed-in Tariffs for Renewable Energy and WTO Subsidy Rules: An Initial Legal Review', ICSTD Issue Paper no 4 (2011).

Winters, LA, 'Coherence and the WTO' (2007) 23(3) *Oxford Review of Economic Policy*.

Winters, LA, 'Doha and World Poverty Targets', Annual World Bank Conference on Development Economics (2003).

Weber, RH and Grosz, M, 'Governments' Interventions into the Real Economy under WTO Law Revisited: New Tendencies of Governmental Support of the Automobile Industry' (2009) 43(5) *Journal of World Trade*.

Woll, C, *The Power of Inaction: Bank Bailouts in Comparison* (Ithaca, NY, Cornell University Press, 2014).

WTO, Status of Branches as Service Suppliers, Note by the WTO Secretariat, document MTN.GNS/W/176 (23 October 1993).

WTO, Financial Services Background, Note by the Secretariat, S/C/W/312 (February 2010).

WTO, Doc GATS/EL/90/Suppl.3 (26 February 1998).

WTO, Trade Policy Review: United States, Report by the Secretariat, WT/TPR/S/200.

WTO, 'Report to the General Council by Director General Lamy in his Role as Chairman of the Trade Negotiations Committee', 26 and 27 May 2009, available at www.wto.org/english/.

WTO, Trade Policy Review: Brazil 2013, WT/TPR/S/283.

WTO, Secretariat Background Note, 'Cross-Border Supply (Modes 1 & 2)', S/C/W/304 (2009).

WTO, Third Report on the Financial and Economic Crisis and Trade-Related Developments, WTO Doc WT/TPR/OV/W/2 (14 July 2009).

WTO, 'Expanding the Prohibited Red Light Subsidy Category', Draft Text Proposal from the United States to the WTO Negotiating Group on Rules, TN/RL/GEN/146 (5 June 2007).

Yukins, CR and Schooner, SL, 'Incrementalism: Eroding the Impediments to a Global Public Procurement Market' (2007) 38 *Georgetown Journal of International Law*.

INDEX